W9-AVJ-154

Advance Praise for *Pay-Per-Click Search Engine Marketing: An Hour a Day*

Few online marketing channels are so full of promise as search, every marketer's ultimate dream: Right person targeted at the right time! To fulfill this promise and deliver glory you need an expert guide, and that's exactly what David is. In this comprehensive book he'll illuminate, empower, and help you become great. Buy and be awesome!
—AVINASH KAUSHIK, Author of *Web Analytics 2.0* and Analytics Evangelist, Google

David Szetela's brilliant and witty insights into how search marketers can leverage the latest ad channels, formats, and reporting tools from search engines and social media communities shine through in his new book, Pay-Per-Click Search Engine Marketing: An Hour a Day. *In this must-read for anyone who wants to understand paid search, Szetela and Clix Marketing colleague Joe Kerschbaum provide a road map for search marketers to successfully ride the first set of waves for social media advertising.*
—LAURIE SULLIVAN, Editor, MediaPost Search Marketing Daily

Millions of PPC search advertisers are in need of a no-nonsense readable book on the subject. With Pay-Per-Click Search Engine Marketing: An Hour a Day, *David Szetela and Joe Kerschbaum have delivered. With this guide, the authors go beyond Google to help marketers tap the Social Media PPC movement. Do your campaign ROI a favor and pick this book up.*
—KEVIN LEE, CEO, Didit

Every digital marketing agency will tell its clients that search engine optimization and search engine marketing are both in a state of constant change. Pay-Per-Click Search Engine Marketing: An Hour a Day *by my industry colleagues David Szetela and Joe Kerschbaum can serve as a much needed anchor for online marketing professionals who need to keep up with the shifts in search engine advertising.*
—CHRIS BOGGS, SEO Director, Rosetta & SEMPO President

David Szetela is a master-of-the-art and science when it comes to PPC. He could baffle you in a moment with his depth of knowledge. Yet here, he feeds you bite-size chunks of knowledge in a clear and easy to absorb format. Walking you through the complexities of campaign architecture to creative execution, pretty soon you'll be seeing the return on investment you thought only the big advertisers could achieve. And there's more than just AdWords advice. Szetela takes you outside of search engine results into content networks and even Facebook ads. David speaks at major conferences all over the world and has already enlightened thousands of practitioners with his easy going style. Now he's bringing that knowledge directly to your desk. Read and succeed!

—MIKE GREHAN, VP and Global Content Director, Incisive Media

Ecommerce companies from global to regional are all looking for online advertising channels that convert new customers at the best price possible. A good part of increasing your online conversion rates is to understand the best practices for pay-per-click advertising channels across the leading search engines and social media communities. Pay-Per-Click Search Engine Marketing: An Hour a Day by David Szetela, Joe Kerschbaum and the team at Clix Marketing have provided an extremely clear explanation of these best practices—one of the best that I've read to date.

—BARRY SCHWARTZ, CEO, RustyBrick

In 2010, social media communities have become as large as the top search engines in their audience reach. With this important milestone, David Szetela and Joe Kerschbaum have written a book that positions them at the front end of the social media PPC movement.

—DAVE SNYDER, Co-Founder, Search And Social

I have been doing PPC for around 10 years now and David Szetela's book is up there with the best of them. David is a true leader in PPC and this book gives amazing insight into PPC techniques at all levels, but more importantly, it does it with great clarity. It is a must-read and I challenge anybody not to learn an immense amount about PPC from reading it!

—JON MYERS, Head of Search and Associate Director, Mediavest

Paid search represents a substantial opportunity for companies to reach new online customers at the moment they're looking for products and services to purchase. Pay-Per-Click Search Engine Marketing: An Hour a Day takes the guesswork out of successful PPC advertising by providing step-by-step guidelines on planning, implementing, and measuring a successful program.

—LEE ODDEN, CEO, TopRankMarketing.com

David Szetela is one of my best buddies in the pay-per-click advertising industry. He's got a special talent for teaching online advertising marketers best-practices for campaign development, management, and measurement for the every expanding spectrum of paid channels. David's slant is unique, based on timeless marketing fundamentals, and extrapolated brilliantly for today's online landscape. Obviously it's a holy mission from God for Szetela (and his killer team) to share PPC wisdom in the form of this truly new testament, Pay-Per-Click Search Engine Marketing: An Hour a Day.

—MARTY WEINTRAUB, President, aimClear

With Pay-Per-Click Search Engine Marketing: An Hour a Day, *David Szetela and Joe Kerschbaum at Clix Marketing are the first of the PPC advertising gurus to address the fast growing audience in social media communities. More importantly, David carefully lays out the etiquette and context for advertising to Facebook enthusiasts. All small business marketers who are looking to reach new customers via social media should read these guidelines.*

 —JENNIFER EVANS LAYCOCK, Editor, Search Engine Guide

The challenges of PPC advertising can be daunting without the right know-how. Luckily David Szetela, Joe Kerschbaum and the team at Clix Marketing have come up with a valuable guide, Pay-Per-Click Search Engine Marketing: An Hour a Day. *Comprehensive and easy to use, this book can bring even an absolute beginner to an advanced level of proficiency.*

 —RICH STOKES, CEO and Founder of AdGooroo and Author of *Ultimate Guide*
  to Pay-Per-Click Advertising

Paid search is a tricky game and it's important to get things right from the get-go. David's book thoroughly covers core PPC subjects and brings it all together with topics like how to effectively optimize PPC campaigns and extract actionable data from PPC reporting. His industry experience & honed insights will certainly save you your weight in time and money. Pay attention to this book!

 —MONA ELESSEILY, VP of Integrated Marketing Strategy, Page Zero Media

I've known David as a true rock star of the advertising industry since his days at Apple and across several lifetimes of a rapidly evolving industry. As a venture capitalist I always need to ask companies to look at how they can build sustainable revenues for agencies that provide both services as well as expert use of technology platforms. Clix Marketing is pioneering of a pay-per-performance ad agency model is right on the money. And this book will help advertisers understand the efficacy of this model for all parties involved.

 —HEIDI ROIZEN, Corporate director, member of the boards of TiVo and
  Yellow Pages Group

David's skillful handling of the very complex issue of pay-per-click marketing should make any marketer confident in their foray into PPC. Dave takes away the potentially overwhelming fear of PPC and transforms it into a well-handled, systematic approach that will result in a successful campaign. Even more, seasoned markers will be able to pick up many modernized tactics from this book that they can add to their arsenal.

 —MATT BAILEY, President, SiteLogic

You'll find invaluable information that I haven't seen in other PPC advertising books. Topics like persona definition, landing page design, campaign launch checklists and Yahoo and Bing migration complement the solid, comprehensive strategies and tactics in this "PPC Bible." A gem of a book!

—SHELLEY ELLIS, Owner, ShelleyEllisConsulting.com

Search Engine Marketing (SEM) is crucial for any digital strategy; however the path to SEM success can be difficult and confusing. Szetela's new book puts you on the right path to SEM success.

—ERIK QUALMAN, Author of *Socialnomics*

For the first time ever, PPC has been organized and deconstructed in a way that nearly anyone could create and feel confident about their search engine marketing strategy. What used to be a daunting task is now a step-by-step process for success!

—SUSAN BRATTON, CEO, Personal Life Media and Host of DishyMix

This book isn't afraid to tackle the complete PPC puzzle, with sections on copywriting, landing pages and personas. Keep a computer handy as it offers a steady stream of links to tools and resources. Szetela takes us on a perfectly paced tour of PPC advertising never losing sight of the primary goal of the endeavor: to draw qualified prospects to our business and turn them into paying customers.

—BRIAN MASSEY, The Conversion Scientist

"Mr. PPC" David Szetela is back with what is surely the definitive guide to pay-per-click marketing. By breaking down pay-per-click advertising best-practices into easy, bite-sized instructions, he and Joe Kerschbaum are going to make a lot of marketers' lives a whole lot easier, not to mention make them savvy enough to make a lot more money with their ad campaigns. Well done to David and the team at Clix Marketing.

—RYAN SAMMY, Social Media Analyist, Search & Social

If I were learning the PPC ropes today, this is one of the first books I'd read. Clix Marketing's David Szetela and Kerschbaum stand head and shoulders above the rest when it comes to distilling the most vital pieces of information from the often frustrating world of pay-per-click marketing. Pay-Per-Click Search Engine Marketing: An Hour a Day has everything you could ever want in an introductory guide to the topic. It may be the best investment an online marketer could make in 2010.

—KATE MORRIS, SEO Consultant, Distilled Consulting

Every online marketer in the hospitality business needs to read this. The tips in Pay-Per-Click Search Engine Marketing: An Hour a Day are absolutely spot-on. I can see a company's online advertising ROI doubling or tripling after implementing the expert advice in this book.

—BENU AGGARWAL, Founder & President, Milestone Internet Marketing

Most of us in the online marketing industry have been aware for quite some time of Mr. Szetela's position on the bleeding edge of PPC expertise. Now, with the release of Pay-Per-Click Search Engine Marketing: An Hour a Day, marketers can benefit from his extensive knowledge. David Szetela, Joe Kerschbaum and the Clix team have delivered a detailed, nuanced, easy to read guide that may end up being the only PPC SEM book most of us will need to digest and implement for the next year.

—MISSY WARD, Co-Founder, Affiliate Summit

David has built a reputation with PPC trainers as one of the top teachers on the subject of PPC marketing. He has trained thousands of agencies as well as corporate in-house advertising professionals on the topic. Now, with the publication of Pay-Per-Click Search Engine Marketing: An Hour a Day, *a broader audience of search engine marketers can learn David's lessons without breaking the bank.*

—EMILY SPENCE, Business Development, SEOInHouse.com

Pay-per-click advertising has become an increasingly complex marketing tactic to execute successfully. Luckily, David Szetela and Joe Kerschbaum's new book helps novice and intermediate pay-per-click practitioners to implement the best practices of this very important advertising channel. Pay-Per-Click Search Engine Marketing: An Hour a Day answers the prayers of anyone who's ever felt a little disoriented when attempting to market their product online.

—STEWART QUEALY, VP Content Development, Incisive Media

If you want your company to profit from both search and social media advertising campaigns, buy and implement the extremely useful information in this book.

—ANDY BEAL, Co-Author of *Radically Transparent: Monitoring & Managing Reputations Online*

Acquisio is in the business of helping advertising agency professionals manage large scale pay-per-click advertising programs effectively. Pay-Per-Click Search Engine Marketing: An Hour A Day *by the Clix Marketing team David Szetela and Joe Kerschbaum provide lessons and insights that the mainstream advertising industry needs to understand. Here's the opportunity.*

—MARC POIRIER, Co-Founder and CMO, Acquisio

David Szetela's book gives a comprehensive plan for building a competition-beating search marketing strategy. This book is packed with golden nuggets that can improve your PPC results. If you want to build winning campaigns, buy it now!

—CHRIS GOWARD, Co-Founder and CEO, WiderFunnel Marketing Optimization

It is always a pleasure to work with David and know that we are working with the best. David is at the top of his field and we have complete confidence in his services. His work in content marketing is by far the most advanced in the paid search industry. I would recommend David to anybody requiring advanced paid search strategy and outstanding campaign ROI.

 —Fionn Downhill, CEO, Elixir Interactive

David Szetela is the PPC advertising faculty chair at Market Motive for good reason. In David, we have an authority who can clearly articulate the advertising process from the basics to the advanced best practices in online advertising. More importantly, David helps his customers and all readers of this book understand how the methods differ for each PPC advertising channel and how to build successful campaigns for each. It's a must-read for any online advertising professional.

 —Michael Stebbins, Co-Founder, Market Motive

David Szetela and I have been educating thousands of new search marketers via our blogs, newsletters and forums as to how the SEO and SEM world are shifting on a regular basis. After perusing Pay-Per-Click Search Engine Marketing: An Hour a Day, *from David and Joe Kerschbaum at Clix Marketing, it's clear that digging into this book is a great way for search marketers to catch up on all of the latest paid search opportunities, as well as to learn the best practices for each.*

 —Jill Whalen, CEO, High Rankings

David Szetela and Joe Kerschbaum from Clix Marketing provide all of the ingredients for a perfect PPC advertising campaign. As a paid search, web analytics and training professional myself, I often turn to David to compare thinking on the latest PPC developments. His new book Pay-Per-Click Search Engine Marketing: An Hour a Day *showcases his team's key knowledge for any online advertising professional who wisely decides to pick it up.*

 —Frank Watson, CEO, Kangamurra Media

What better way to learn pay-per-click end-to-end than to be walked through the methodologies, tools and techniques by one of the undisputed experts in the space: David Szetela? With this book, David and his crew at Clix Marketing deliver on that promise, but without the expense of hiring them as consultants (though I wouldn't dissuade you from doing that, too, if you have the budget!). Ready to make some money? Then have a seat—this book in hand and your laptop close by—and start reading!

 —Stephan Spencer, Co-Author of *The Art of SEO*, Founder of Netconcepts, and VP of SEO Strategies at Covario

Large-scale pay-per-click advertisers depend upon having two critical pieces in place in order to be successful. First is the technology and second are the people leveraging that technology. At Kenshoo, we address the technology requirements through automated SEM platforms. David Szetela and Joe Kerschbaum with Pay-Per-Click Search Engine Marketing: An Hour a Day, *provide a clear step-by-step best practices guide and reference manual for beginners to experts to sharpen their skills and increase their value in this dynamic and growing space.*

    —GEOFFREY SHENK, Managing Director, Kenshoo

In the complicated and often confusing field of PPC marketing, practitioners need all the guidance they can get. Luckily, David Szetela and Joe Kerschbaum have sent us a manual that's as easy to understand as it is helpful. Everything you're looking for can be found right here in Pay-Per-Click Search Engine Marketing: An Hour a Day. *Buy this book now and gain a true competitive edge.*

    —HEATHER LLOYD-MARTIN, President and CEO, SuccessWorks Search
      Marketing

What a comprehensive book! David Szetela's Pay Per Click Search Engine Marketing: An Hour a Day *is really a dream come true for any beginning PPC marketer. The steps are laid out so neatly—with chapters each meant to represent a month—that really all it will take is a little patience and motivation to reap the rewards from this manual.*

    —JOSH DRELLER, VP of Media Technology and Analytics, Fuor Digital

David reminds readers of the importance of testing ads and he couples this with some fantastic advanced techniques. Not only does this empower his readers to become great search marketers he also gives them the skills necessary to work with an agency, from the client side, holding them to the highest standards.

    —ANDREW GIRDWOOD, Head of Strategy, bigmouthmedia

Practical strategies for making money with pay per click from a master practitioner. Get it before your competitors do!

    —TIM ASH, Author of *Landing Page Optimization* and Chairperson of
      ConversionConference.com

PPC advertising is part art and part science, all seasoned with a generous dose of technology. Rather than make this mix daunting, David Szetela gracefully and clearly ushers his readers through all the permutations of PPC, from its overarching concepts to the down-in-the-weeds tactical stuff. This is an indispensable book for anyone getting started in paid search advertising, and will doubtless teach even some old dogs in the game a new trick or two.

    —REBECCA LIEB, VP, Econsultancy LLC and author of *The Truth About Search
      Engine Marketing*

David is a true leader in the field of SEM. Whether you are going to hear him speak at a conference or reading his book, you know you are getting up-to-the minute information with real life application. I look forward to more great things coming from David, especially with the publication of his second book. This one is not to be missed if you are looking for concrete PPC strategies.

 —BRETT TABKE, Owner, WebmasterWorld Inc

Pay-Per-Click advertising has become increasingly competitive. In order for businesses to compete they need to have a good understanding of the fundamentals and an ability to apply the latest strategies.

David Szetela is well-known in the industry for being able to teach the fundamentals and has always been a leader when it comes to introducing us to advanced PPC and search marketing strategies. If you are looking for a competitive advantage, this book will definitely give you the strategies you are looking for.

 —SEAN GOLLIHER, Founder/Publisher SEMJ.org

David is my go to resource for all things PPC-related. His book is the resource for educating yourself and your employees on running paid advertising campaigns that make money. It's a must-have for any SEM professional's bookshelf.

 —CARRIE HILL, Director of Search Strategies and Client Services, Blizzard
   Internet Marketing, Inc.

PPC expert David Szetela has compiled invaluable insights from his 25+ years experience to both beginners and experienced paid search marketers. This step-by-step guide for developing advanced AdWords expertise is a must for marketers looking to maximize impact and profitability online.

 —ROY MOREJON, President, Interactive Marketing Consultant, B2WE

David's approach to PPC is very impressive as he touches on all aspects and skill level. His unique style gives you the resources you need to drive more profit through paid search marketing

 —JAMIE SMITH, CEO, EngineReady

Finally! A book that cuts through the jargon of online advertising and gives business owners and marketers a clear playbook for creating and managing highly effective PPC campaigns on Google and Facebook. David Szetela's clean writing style connects the new online processes with tried and true traditional advertising concepts. Easy to read; easy to put to use in your own ad campaigns. Now you can improve your bottom line with online advertising.

 —GILLIAN MUESSIG, President, SEOmoz

I wouldn't have thought it was possible to have a single book cover every aspect of PPC campaigns, but David Szetela has done it. This book is destined to become the SEM practitioner's Bible.

>—LANCE LOVEDAY, CEO, Closed Loop Marketing, Author of best-selling book
> *Web Design for ROI*

There are few authorities in the search marketing industry more passionate about PPC than David. Having spent many hours sharing tips and insight at Internet conferences all over the world, I'm delighted he's putting pen to paper and bringing his extensive knowledge to the masses one hour at a time.

>—MEL CARSON, Microsoft Advertising Community & Social Media Manager

The amazing thing about this book is how comprehensive the narrative is. PPC has a ton of moving pieces and a lot of nuance: becoming an expert AdWords and paid search operative means understanding a series of difficult facets related to PPC management and making them work together. This book clearly and thoroughly walks the reader through tactics and strategies around each of these facets, while relentlessly relating everything back to overarching PPC goals. This will be a definite boost to ROI for anyone new to or looking to get more out of paid search.

>—TOM DEMERS, Director of Marketing, WordStream Inc.

It's been enjoyable to watch the rapid and decisive growth of Clix Marketing and the career of David Szetela. It's difficult to think of Pay-Per-Click marketing without thinking of David Szetela and Clix Marketing since the man and company have become ubiquitous with the industry known as search engine marketing. David's book represents a must-read for anyone looking to perfect the game of search marketing...one hour at a time.

>—KRISTOPHER B. JONES, Founder of Pepperjam and author of *Search Engine
> Optimization: Your Visual Blueprint for Effective Internet Marketing*

David has the ability to bring your marketing campaigns to new levels. This new book outlines so much of his insight based on years of testing and trial and error. A must read for the newbie and super resource for those in the know.

>—JEFF SELIG, Director of Analytics, Overdrive Interactive

SEMPO and Econsultancy estimate that companies in North America will spend $16.6 billion on search engine marketing in 2010. To get the best bang for your buck, you'll want to read Pay-Per-Click Search Engine Marketing: An Hour a Day. *Written by David Szetela and Joseph Kerschbaum, this is the complete guide to a winning pay-per-click marketing campaign. The content is so useful I spent a whole Saturday reading it in my pajamas.*

>—GREG JARBOE, author of *YouTube and Video Marketing: An Hour a Day*

Working with small business owners on a daily basis, I know the confusion and frustration they feel in trying to understand how the search engines work. David's book takes the complex concepts of pay-per-click ads and breaks them down into a language everyone can "get." He gives businesses a great step-by-step roadmap for how to get involved in paid search. Even if your company doesn't plan to set up or manage its own campaigns, this is a great book to read just to know what your agency is (or should!) be doing for you.
—DAVID MIHM, President & CEO at GetListed.org, Inc.

David Szetela is one of the true rockstars of the PPC search marketing sector. Clear, concise and creatively illustrated, PPC: An Hour a Day prepares readers to enter and thrive in the rapidly changing world of pay-per-click marketing. If you're advertising in the PPC search marketing environment, this book will both save you money on your overall ad-spend and make you money as your return on investment increases.
—JIM HEDGER, Search Marketing Consultant

David Szetela has produced an awesome step-by-step guide to PPC. This book ranges from the basics to deep insights. Use this book to separate yourself from the pack. Those who do not invest time in their PPC campaigns will never make money at it. Invest your time wisely, and reading through this book, or using it as a reference, is a great way to do that.
—ERIC ENGE, President, Stone Temple Consulting Corporation

This is the definitive how-to book on the art, science, and black magic of Pay-Per-Click (PPC) for marketers, but also for the rest of us. As vendors and advertisers bid on our expectations, knowing how PPC platforms work is critical to our education as active citizens of the social Web. After all, we are the ones saying, "You bet it clicks for me!"
—MARYLENE DELBOURG-DELPHIS, serial entrepreneur

This book is indispensable for beginners and seasoned search marketers alike. You'll be shocked to discover how the most tightly run campaigns are leaving opportunities on the table.
—MONICA WRIGHT, Practice Director of Search Marketing and Internet
    Advertising at MicroArts Creative Agency

This book sets down new rules of PPC SEM as it pertains to the far-reaching and fast evolving tools of Social Media. David is a strategist and thought leader in search marketing, and his book serves as a practical guide for businesses exploring advertising on social channels.
—ANITA PAUL, Founder, Objective Marketer

In typical "David Szetela" style, David brings a no-nonsense approach to the writing of PPC: An Hour a Day. Whether you're a complete novice or an advanced search marketer, David presents step-by-step instruction on how you can be successful with your paid search efforts. Huge value in reading, and implementing, the ideas presented in this book.

—MARK JACKSON, CEO, Vizion Interactive

Paid search advertising is seemingly simple, but full of an amazing number of traps that can cost you money and sales. PPC: An Hour a Day is the missing user manual to creating effective and profitable paid search campaigns. It's a must-read for new PPC advertisers.

—ALEX COHEN, Senior Marketing Manager, ClickEquations

PPC advertising knows no greater champion—and expert—than David Szetela. The great news is that he's taken the time to share his knowledge in a fashion that is digestible, actionable, and beneficial to marketers of every age and discipline. This is the book I wish I would have had when optimizing PPC campaigns!

—JEFFREY ROHRS, Vice President, Marketing, ExactTarget

From the king of paid search himself, this book is exactly what's needed to become proficient in PPC in a short amount of time. A must-read for anyone involved with or interested in PPC SEM.

—JORDAN KASTELER, Co-founder, Search & Social

David's book is a welcome addition to the field of PPC advertising. David places his years of hands-on experience and deep understanding of classical direct marketing at your service in this easy to implement, step-by-step guide to online profits. Your ROI on this book will be astronomical!

—HOWIE JACOBSON, Ph.D., author of Google AdWords For Dummies, askHowie.com

David Szetela does a wonderful job in covering all aspects of creating an effective and efficient pay-per-click program. His book is likely to become a classic in the field.

—AL RIES, Co-author of War in the Boardroom and Positioning: The Battle for your Mind

David Szetela has earned an enviable reputation as a no-nonsense teacher and practitioner of pay-per-click advertising. This book reduces this complex topic into simple, daily practices that bring more customers with superior return on your investment. This book includes advanced techniques and concepts that 90% of your competition has never seen.

—PERRY MARSHALL, Author of The Ultimate Guide to Google AdWords

PPC advertising has revolutionized direct response marketing and filled Google's coffers. Szetela and Kerschbaum have crafted a comprehensive how-to manual that should be on every marketer's bookshelf. Read it to understand the phenomenon that's moving from the search results pages to hot social media properties like Facebook and LinkedIn.

 —JOHN SCULLEY, Venture Partner, Rho Ventures and former CEO,
  Apple Computer and Pepsi

Advertisements on Google, Yahoo, Microsoft and Facebook search results pages are the new "elevator pitches" of the online economy. And surprisingly for many, this new channel doesn't require a PhD in computer science. Szetela's book demystifies the topic and teaches the rudiments in an engaging, step-by-step style that's fully in reach of marketing managers, VPs and CEOs. Business owners large and small need to face the facts: if you aren't tapping into the power of PPC advertising, your competitors are probably eating your lunch.

 —JEFFREY HAYZELETT, Former CMO of Eastman Kodak and Author,
  The Mirror Test

Pay-Per-Click Search Engine Marketing:

An Hour a Day

Kevin,

Thanks so much for your encouragement and support!

—David

Pay-Per-Click Search Engine Marketing:

An Hour a Day

David Szetela

Joseph Kerschbaum

WILEY

Wiley Publishing, Inc.

Senior Acquisitions Editor: WILLEM KNIBBE
Development Editor: KATHRYN DUGGAN
Technical Editor: MATT VAN WAGNER
Production Editor: CHRISTINE O'CONNOR
Copy Editor: SHARON WILKEY
Editorial Manager: PETE GAUGHAN
Production Manager: TIM TATE
Vice President and Executive Group Publisher: RICHARD SWADLEY
Vice President and Publisher: NEIL EDDE
Book Designer: FRANZ BAUMHACKL
Compositor: CHRIS GILLESPIE, HAPPENSTANCE TYPE-O-RAMA
Proofreader: CANDACE ENGLISH
Indexer: ROBERT SWANSON
Project Coordinator, Cover: LYNSEY STANFORD
Cover Designer: RYAN SNEED

Copyright © 2010 by Wiley Publishing, Inc., Indianapolis, Indiana

Published simultaneously in Canada

ISBN: 978-0-470-48867-6

No part of this publication may be reproduced, stored in a retrieval system or transmitted in any form or by any means, electronic, mechanical, photocopying, recording, scanning or otherwise, except as permitted under Sections 107 or 108 of the 1976 United States Copyright Act, without either the prior written permission of the Publisher, or authorization through payment of the appropriate per-copy fee to the Copyright Clearance Center, 222 Rosewood Drive, Danvers, MA 01923, (978) 750-8400, fax (978) 646-8600. Requests to the Publisher for permission should be addressed to the Permissions Department, John Wiley & Sons, Inc., 111 River Street, Hoboken, NJ 07030, (201) 748-6011, fax (201) 748-6008, or online at http://www.wiley.com/go/permissions.

Limit of Liability/Disclaimer of Warranty: The publisher and the author make no representations or warranties with respect to the accuracy or completeness of the contents of this work and specifically disclaim all warranties, including without limitation warranties of fitness for a particular purpose. No warranty may be created or extended by sales or promotional materials. The advice and strategies contained herein may not be suitable for every situation. This work is sold with the understanding that the publisher is not engaged in rendering legal, accounting, or other professional services. If professional assistance is required, the services of a competent professional person should be sought. Neither the publisher nor the author shall be liable for damages arising herefrom. The fact that an organization or Web site is referred to in this work as a citation and/or a potential source of further information does not mean that the author or the publisher endorses the information the organization or Web site may provide or recommendations it may make. Further, readers should be aware that Internet Web sites listed in this work may have changed or disappeared between when this work was written and when it is read.

For general information on our other products and services or to obtain technical support, please contact our Customer Care Department within the U.S. at (877) 762-2974, outside the U.S. at (317) 572-3993 or fax (317) 572-4002.

Wiley also publishes its books in a variety of electronic formats. Some content that appears in print may not be available in electronic books.

Library of Congress Cataloging-in-Publication Data

Szetela, David, 1954-

Pay-per-click search engine marketing : an hour a day / David Szetela, Joseph Kerschbaum. —1st ed.

p. cm.

Summary: "The complete guide to a winning pay-per-click marketing campaign Pay-per-click advertising-the "sponsored results" on search engine results pages-is increasingly being used to drive traffic to websites. Marketing and advertising professionals looking for a hands-on, task-based guide to every stage of creating and managing a winning PPC campaign will get the step-by-step instruction they need in this detailed guide. Using the popular An Hour A Day format, this book helps you avoid the pitfalls and plan, develop, implement, manage, and monitor a PPC campaign that gets results. Successful pay-per-click campaigns are a key component of online marketing. This guide breaks the project down into manageable tasks, valuable for the small-business owner as well as for marketing officers and consultants. Explains core PPC concepts, industry trends, and the mechanics that make a campaign work. Shows how to perform keyword research, structure campaigns, and understand campaign settings and various pricing models. Discusses how to write ads, develop and test landing pages, use ad groups, and leverage Google's content network. Covers launching a campaign, bidding for position, monitoring, gathering results, and interpreting and acting on the data collected. Pay-Per-Click Search Engine Marketing: An Hour a Day provides the tools to make the most of this important marketing method."—Provided by publisher.

ISBN 978-0-470-48867-6 (pbk.)

ISBN 978-0-470-91719-0 (ebk)

ISBN 978-0-470-91721-3 (ebk)

ISBN 978-0-470-91720-6 (ebk)

1. Internet marketing. 2. Internet advertising. 3. Web search engines. I. Kerschbaum, Joseph, 1976- II. Title.

HF5415.1265.S97 2010

658.8'72—dc22

2010018066

TRADEMARKS: Wiley, the Wiley logo, and the Sybex logo are trademarks or registered trademarks of John Wiley & Sons, Inc. and/or its affiliates, in the United States and other countries, and may not be used without written permission. All other trademarks are the property of their respective owners. Wiley Publishing, Inc., is not associated with any product or vendor mentioned in this book.

10 9 8 7 6 5 4 3 2 1

Dear Reader,

Thank you for choosing *Pay-Per-Click Search Engine Marketing: An Hour a Day*. This book is part of a family of premium-quality Sybex books, all of which are written by outstanding authors who combine practical experience with a gift for teaching.

Sybex was founded in 1976. More than 30 years later, we're still committed to producing consistently exceptional books. With each of our titles, we're working hard to set a new standard for the industry. From the paper we print on, to the authors we work with, our goal is to bring you the best books available.

I hope you see all that reflected in these pages. I'd be very interested to hear your comments and get your feedback on how we're doing. Feel free to let me know what you think about this or any other Sybex book by sending me an email at nedde@wiley.com. If you think you've found a technical error in this book, please visit http://sybex.custhelp.com. Customer feedback is critical to our efforts at Sybex.

Best regards,

Neil Edde
Vice President and Publisher
Sybex, an imprint of Wiley

To my parents, Eugene and Marie, who had the good sense to predict that suffering under 12 years of nun-driven English classes would give me a life-long advantage. Mom and Dad: You were right. —David

 # Acknowledgments

I now realize that the blood, sweat, and tears that go into a book like this are 1 part the author's and 10 parts those of the team of editorial professionals, and the colleagues and family of the author. In my case, they deserve more gratitude (and apologies) than I have room or time to write.

So here's the short version: First, endless thanks to my wife, Wils. Your good-natured support and love made my most difficult year my happiest year. I promise you'll hardly recognize the post-book version of me: patient, attentive, relaxed, well rested, and 30 pounds lighter. And to my wonderful children, Michael, Franny, and Aimée: We can now look forward to more-frequent dinners and hikes that feature more stories, laughter, and fine mee-yats.

Next I want to thank my coauthor, Joe Kerschbaum, for stepping into the book project fairly late in the game, and taking on a huge responsibility and workload during his "honeymoon period" as the new client services director at my company, Clix Marketing. The fact that he performed masterfully at both, while compiling and publishing his own (fifth) book of poetry, is astounding and admirable. He and the rest of the Clix team deserve maximum credit for keeping our clients happy and progressively prosperous: my droogie James Thompson, the multitalented Mae Flint, the man-who-never-sleeps John Lee, and the crew of Clix freelancers. I also want to thank their spouses for putting up with the odd hours and occasional fire drills that make our clients feel covered 24/7.

Huge thanks and kudos go to my friends Michael Flores and Matt Van Wagner. Michael contributed many of the pages and case studies you're about to read, and we all benefit from the wealth of his hands-on PPC advertising experience and his unquenchable curiosity to test new strategies and angles. Matt served as technical editor of this book, and deserves full credit for turning our inaccuracies and contorted explanations into readable fact. I feel privileged that the humble Clix Marketing blog is host to one of the few examples of Matt's formidable musical talents—a short impromptu trumpet jam that leaves the listener begging for more.

Matt, Michael, and Joe are part of a circle of friends called the *PPC posse*—folks who love PPC advertising enough to make it the center of conversation in presentation rooms, restaurants, and bars during conferences such as Search Engine Strategies (SES), Search Marketing Expo (SMX), ad:tech, and PubCon, and during "off hours" on Facebook and Twitter. It's an odd but likeable crowd—equal parts geeky Steve Wozniak and savvy David Ogilvy. I've been fortunate to interview most of them on my weekly WebmasterRadio.FM show, *PPC Rockstars*, and have learned PPC tips and tricks from each of them.

Before mentioning them all, I want to draw particular attention to Brad Geddes, who recommended me when the Wiley/Sybex editors were looking for an author for this book. For that, and the amazing insight into our craft that Brad has provided in his writing and in our conversations, I'm very grateful. As I am to the rest of the posse: Tim Ash, Chad Baldwin, Michael Behrens, Robert Brady, Scott Brinker, Laura Callow, Christine Churchill, Alex Cohen, Addie Conner, Tom Cuthbert, Craig Danuloff, Bryan Eisenberg, Mona Elesseily, Shelley Ellis, Adam Goldberg, Andrew Goodman, Jeff Hudson, Mary Huffman, Patricia Hursh, Mark Jackson, Howie Jacobsen, Kristopher Jones, Avinash Kaushik, Jon Kelly, William Leake, Brian Lewis, Jon Lisbin, Glenn Livingston, Misty Locke, Joanna Lord, Heather Lutze, Melissa Mackey, Perry Marshall, Jon Meyer, Kate Morris, Mary O'Brien, Marc Poirier, Erik Qualmann, Alissa Ruehl, Jamie Smith, Dan Soha, Michael Stebbins, Don Steele, Richard Stokes, Wister Walcott, Frank Watson, Marty Weintraub, Tony Wright, James Zolman, and Richard Zwicky.

Though my career is well past the quarter-century mark, I'm a relative newcomer to the online marketing world. I was lucky enough to get a helping hand from my friends at Incisive Media and Third Door Media, who welcomed me onto the speaking circuit and into webinars for the SES and SMX conferences. I've also been grateful for the opportunity to speak at many of the excellent PPC Summit conferences put on by Mary O'Brien and her crew.

Not too long ago, I had the great fortune of being adopted into the WebmasterRadio.FM family ushered in by my friend Jim Hedger, and welcomed by the dynamic duo of owners Daron and Brandy Babin. Together with producer extraordinaire Jorge Hermida, they provided the platform that is my weekly radio show, *PPC Rockstars*. Their "work and play are indistinguishable" attitude demonstrates that it's fun to be professional, and professional to be fun. That's also the attitude of the team at Market Motive, who added me to the roster of online marketing superstars: Avinash Kaushik, Brian Eisenberg, Jennifer Laycock, Matt Bailey, Todd Malicoat, Greg Jarboe, and Jamie O'Donnell. Owners John Marshall and Michael Stebbins, marketing superstars in their own right, embody the ethic that professional excellence and personal enjoyment make a satisfying, effective blend.

And finally, speaking of pros, I want to thank the hardworking, long-suffering Wiley/Sybex team: Willem Knibbe, Kathryn Duggan, Pete Gaughan, Christine O'Connor, Connor O'Brien, and Jenni Housh. I remember telling Willem at the start of the project that I'm frequently late, but I always finish. Umpteen extended deadlines later, I'm hoping that they will all forgive my procrastination and take satisfaction in a book we can all be proud of.

—DAVID

I can't thank my wife, Valerie, enough for her unending support and encouragement. To say we had a lot going on in our lives (personally and professionally) about six months ago would be an understatement—and then I took on this project. However, you inspire and motivate me to reach beyond my own ever-expanding boundaries. Now that this project is complete, we can turn our attention to the other mountains that we want to move.

Thanks to the team at PPC Hero. Writing for that blog afforded me the opportunity to explore and comprehend almost every imaginable PPC topic.

David has done a spectacular job of thanking everyone involved in the writing, editing, and production of this book. So, I won't take up a lot of time here doing so again, and let's face it: David said it better than I could anyway. However, I do want to thank the entire Wiley/Sybex team for bringing me on board, answering my stream of questions, and forgoing a few deadlines. You made me feel at home. By this I mean you welcomed me in the door and put me right to work (just like my grandmother used to do).

On that note, I also want to thank David for asking me to join in the fun of writing this book. Thanks for having the confidence that I was the right person to bring into the fold. You rule.

—JOSEPH

About the Authors

Online advertising expert David Szetela is owner and CEO of Clix Marketing, one of the few agencies that specialize exclusively in pay-per-click (PPC) advertising, creating and optimizing ad campaigns running on Google, Yahoo!, Microsoft, Facebook, LinkedIn, and a variety of other ad platforms. Clix is also one of the few agencies paid according to their performance—as a percentage of profit or a commission per sales lead generated.

David's articles on PPC advertising have been published in *MediaPost*, *Search Engine Watch*, *Search Engine Land*, and *MarketingSherpa*, as well as on his company's blog. He is the principal PPC editor of the paper and online publication *SEMJ.org* and the PPC expert faculty member for the online certification company Market Motive. He is also a frequent speaker at search and advertising–industry events such as SES, SMX, PPC Summit, and ad:tech, and he hosts the weekly radio show *PPC Rockstars*, distributed by WebmasterRadio.FM and iTunes. His book on PPC content network advertising, *Customers Now: Profiting from the New Frontier of Content-Based Internet Advertising*, was published by iUniverse in November 2009.

His 25+-year career working for small magazine publishers as well as Apple Computer and Ziff-Davis Publishing has provided him deep experience in direct-response marketing.

He received a bachelor of science degree in nutritional science and microbiology from the University of Connecticut, and a masters' of science degree in flavor chemistry and computer science from Louisiana State University. Six months before he would have received his PhD in flavor chemistry, he became obsessed with the Apple II and dove headfirst into the personal computer industry.

David enjoys gardening, hiking, travel, and playing guitar. He and his wife, Wils, make their home in a succession of Marriotts, Hiltons, and Super 8 hotels, with occasional stays at their sanctuary in Louisville, Kentucky.

Joseph Kerschbaum is client services director at Clix Marketing. He has been working in the search engine marketing (SEM) industry since 2006. Since then he has been sharpening his expertise in PPC advertising, search engine optimization, conversion optimization, and social media marketing.

His articles on the SEM industry have appeared widely on *PPC Hero*, *SEO Boy*, and other industry blogs and journals. He is a regular contributor to *Website Magazine* and *Search Engine Watch*.

Joseph might be one of the only individuals on the planet who splits his time between PPC management and poetry writing and performance. He has published five books of poetry, one spoken-word album, and one spoken-rock album (you just have to hear it to believe it). Joseph has given readings and performed his work around the country. He is also one-quarter of a performance poetry troupe (or poetry rock band), called the Reservoir Dogwoods.

Joseph lives in Bloomington, Indiana, with his wife, three dogs, and one cat. It's a furry household, but he wouldn't have it any other way.

Contents

Chapter 10 Month 7—Test Ads by Using Advanced Techniques   247

Chapter 11 Month 8—Test and Optimize Landing Pages   285

Foreword

In the last six years (from 2004 through 2009), the only form of media to have seen growth in usage is the Internet. While TV has been flat and radio and newspapers have seen double digit declines, people's Internet usage has increased 117%, according to Forrester Research. And yet when you look at where marketing dollars are being spent, online still trails traditional media by a wide margin. Clearly online advertising is poised for continued growth and remains a great place for businesses to find new customers. Search engines create millions of moments of relevance every day by connecting consumers who are looking for a product or service with the companies that offer those exact products or services. With this book you will learn how to create your own moments of relevance to grow your business.

While a search engine marketing (SEM) account can be created at the click of a few buttons, there are some key decisions that can make all the difference between giving up in frustration and achieving returns on your investment beyond your wildest dreams. With David's decade of expertise in search distilled into the pages of this book, you've got a great guide that explains all the concepts of search marketing. It also provides tips and best practices from David's own experiences that can add to the success of your online advertising campaigns.

I'm a frequent speaker at search marketing conferences worldwide, educating audiences of all experience levels in the art and science of SEM and Google AdWords. With new tools and reports being made available all the time, one of my main challenges is to help advertisers prioritize the myriad opportunities. Time and again I've seen that when advertisers take the time to learn more about how AdWords works, they perform better in the long run and they are better able to use the data AdWords provides to help identify the opportunities and the tools best suited to achieve the results they want.

I've had the pleasure of participating in many panels and search marketing conferences with David. At SES New York in 2010 we did a session together on the relevance of ads, and since this topic is at the heart of answering the question of how to get a better ad position, it always draws a crowd and makes for lively discussions with the audience. David cuts through the myths and the hype—expertly explaining and translating complex topics like Quality Score and advertising on the Google Content Network into understandable best practices and actionable methods for driving results.

One of my favorite things about David is the fact that he combines years of experience from the technology and publishing industries with his expertise in pay-per-click marketing. With the online-advertising industry being so young, it's nice to have an expert with some grey hairs who knows how to use traditional marketing and who also really gets online advertising. He shares Google's vision that advertisements, like organic results, are information and should be relevant and useful. That's what users expect and that's what creates a sustainable ecosystem in which all participants, from users to advertisers to publishers, benefit. This basic belief, along with a methodical approach to using data to inform and support marketing decisions, has made David a trusted source in the industry and someone from whom I know you will learn a lot.

Best of luck with your campaigns and please let me know what you think about our program and how it's working for you when you see me at a conference.

—FREDERICK VALLAEYS, PRODUCT EVANGELIST, GOOGLE ADWORDS

Introduction

My first job after grad school was working for a small magazine, book, and software company. As a programmer, it was my dream job; I was able to play with the innards of Apple II computers for most of the day, and for the rest of the day try my hand at every aspect of magazine publishing.

I found myself drawn to and fascinated by direct-mail marketing, which at that time was the primary way magazines acquired subscribers. I loved the creative aspect of it—the challenge of designing envelopes that begged to be opened, persuasive headlines that lured the reader into the letter copy, and forms designed so simply that they nearly filled themselves out.

I had studied nutritional science and flavor chemistry for nine long years of "higher education," so the latent scientist in me loved the testing and optimization aspects of direct-mail marketing. The typical optimization sequence went like this:

1. Create what we felt was a winning mail package consisting of envelope, offer, and reply form.

2. Do a test mailing to a small percentage of a rented mailing list.

3. Calculate the response rate and project the return on investment (ROI) we could expect from a mailing to the entire list.

4. Mail the control package to the majority of the list, and mail variations of the control to smaller portions of the list. Variations could include big ones such as envelope color and size, as well as smaller ones such as the number and positions of fields on the reply form.

5. Judge the winning package, and start again using the winner as the control.

The average time between step 1 and step 5 was an unimaginably long five to six months. It took that long for enough responses to be mailed back to us; to calculate and analyze the data (using the first spreadsheet software, VisiCalc, on Apple IIs); and to design and print the test and control packages.

Fast-forward to 2003: I had been out of the publishing industry for several years, which could be the reason I failed to pay attention to the ads on search results pages. But when I finally looked into the mechanism behind the ads, my first love came back to me like an arrow from a geeky Cupid's bow. It was like direct mail on steroids! Advertisers could test and refine campaigns in days instead of months. Obtaining great results, in the form of increased customers and profit, required equal parts artistic skill at writing persuasively and scientific discipline to pay close attention to results and make improvements accordingly.

I was hooked.

This was near-perfect advertising. Its many modern attributes included the following:

- A payment model whereby the advertiser pays only for clicks on an ad, each delivering a qualified visitor to the advertiser's site

- An ad-ranking model that rewarded the advertisers who created the most persuasive ads

- A built-in conversion-tracking system that measured the number of site visitors who took the action the site owner desired

- A cornucopia of reporting capabilities that, properly interpreted, made continual optimization a snap

Several years later, I'm still enraptured with PPC advertising, and very happy that I chose to focus on it exclusively. The capabilities that have been put into our hands by the search engines are an order of magnitude more powerful than those we enjoyed seven years ago, including the following:

- The ability to track multiple kinds of website-visitor behavior—for example, purchases, e-mail newsletter sign-ups, and catalog requests

- Targeting to different ad networks—most notably, search engines and websites that accept advertising on their pages

- Targeting users of a variety of devices—such as desktop computers, mobile phones, and iPads—and even subsets of those, like specific phone carriers

- More-detailed reporting that exposes almost every nook and cranny of ad campaign performance

- A growing variety of ad types and channels—including animated and video ads, and even television ads

The yang of this bountiful yin is that this growing set of capabilities comes with a higher degree of complexity. It's tougher today to learn the length and breadth of PPC advertising than it was seven years ago.

Hence this book. We've attempted to help you build the skills needed to run and optimize successful PPC ad campaigns, but to do so in small daily and weekly "learning chunks." Our goal is to help you advance from your present skill level—even if you've never written a single ad—to the point where you can call yourself a PPC ninja!

Who Should Read This Book

You should read this book if you are responsible for creating and optimizing the results from pay-per-click (PPC) ad campaigns. You might be an individual contributor working in the online marketing department of a large retailer or agency. Or you might be an entrepreneur who needs to wear many hats until your business grows enough to afford employees who can specialize.

If you're a manager of any level above individual-contributor PPC campaign managers, you'll benefit from skimming this book to gain an understanding of the skills your employees need to develop. And if you're mainly responsible for a different aspect of online marketing—for example, search engine optimization (SEO)—you'll appreciate the synergies between the skills and objectives of PPC compared to SEO.

What You Will Learn

The core of this book is a day-by-day program for creating, launching, and optimizing your PPC campaign. We have divvied up the days so that tasks can be completed in approximately 1 hour. Depending on your familiarity with PPC, and direct-response advertising in general, it may take you more or less time to complete certain tasks.

The chapters are laid out in a way that introduces you to PPC at a very high, theoretical level so that you understand the nature and origin of this advertising model. From there, you move on to the nuts and bolts of keyword research, ad-text creation, and landing-page optimization.

Here's a quick look at what's in each chapter and the two appendices:

Chapter 1: The Art and Science of PPC Advertising helps you understand the historical context of direct-response advertising and the common scientific advertising principles that apply to successful PPC management.

Chapter 2: How the PPC Machine Works presents an overview of how advertisements appear on search engine results pages (SERPs) and why you want to help the search engines provide the best possible user experience.

Chapter 3: Core PPC Skills and Objectives describes the mission-critical skills that you need to sharpen in order to successfully launch and manage your PPC campaign.

Chapter 4: Month 1—Research Keywords and Establish Campaign Structure provides an action plan for creating a highly targeted keyword list and building a PPC campaign structure that will enable you to maximize your click-through rate (CTR) and conversion rate.

Chapter 5: Month 2—Create Great PPC Ads demonstrates how to write persuasive PPC advertisements that will motivate people to click on your ad and take action on your landing page.

Chapter 6: Month 3—Design Effective Landing Pages gives you real-world advice on how to design landing pages that will inspire your audience to complete your desired conversion action and become a paying customer.

Chapter 7: Month 4—Advertise on the Google Content Network offers clear guidance for generating great results on this complex, and often misunderstood, distribution channel.

Chapter 8: Month 5—Launch Your Campaign explores the importance of bidding on your brand and provides a prelaunch checklist that will help get your PPC campaign off the ground successfully, as well as tips for early course-correction for anything that may not go as planned.

Chapter 9: Month 6—Optimize Your Campaign teaches you how to troubleshoot problems that may arise and how to optimize the performance of your campaign in order to generate even better results.

Chapter 10: Month 7—Test Ads by Using Advanced Techniques describes progressive strategies that can elevate your PPC advertisements beyond the competition and presents advanced techniques for ad split testing.

Chapter 11: Month 8—Test and Optimize Landing Pages demonstrates how to improve your landing page performance by conducting tests using Google Website Optimizer.

Chapter 12: Month 9—Migrate Your Campaign to Microsoft and Yahoo! shows you how to download your campaigns from Google AdWords and upload them into Yahoo! Search Marketing and Microsoft adCenter.

Appendix A: Advanced AdWords Editor walks you through one of the most powerful tools available to PPC managers—AdWords Editor—and gives you advanced insider knowledge on how to use this application to its fullest extent.

Appendix B: Facebook PPC introduces you to Facebook's PPC advertising program, which is one of the fastest growing networks on the Internet.

The Companion Website

Because PPC advertising is an extraordinarily fast-moving field, we have created a website to accompany the book, http://ppc1hour.com, where we will post significant changes to the topics described in the book. The site is set up as a blog, so you can subscribe to receive updates whenever they're posted. Neat!

How to Contact the Authors

We love meeting and communicating with other "PPC geeks," so please do contact us for any reason by e-mailing us at david@clixmarketing.com or joe@clixmarketing.com.

David uses Twitter every day to publish links to the most interesting and accurate articles and blog posts about PPC and online advertising. To receive those tweets, follow David on Twitter at www.twitter.com/Szetela.

You can follow Joe on Twitter as well (even though he's not a power-Twitterer like David!) at www.twitter.com/joekerschbaum.

You can also link to David's resource page, http://Szetela.me, which will give you access to his writing, presentations, speaking engagements, and other PPC resources.

The links to our company blog and our company are www.clixmarketing.com/blog and http://clixmarketing.com, respectively.

Finally, we've created two online discussion groups where people congregate to exchange questions and answers on PPC-related topics. Total membership is over 5,000 people, so you're sure to find many kindred souls! The links are as follows:

LinkedIn PPC Pro People: www.linkedin.com/groups?home=&gid=1217347

Facebook PPC Pro People: www.facebook.com/group.php?gid=5849647189

The Art and Science of PPC Advertising

Although pay-per-click (PPC) advertising is a thoroughly modern endeavor, its foundations in direct-response advertising have been studied and refined for almost a century. In this chapter, you'll start on your journey to expertise by taking a look at the core scientific advertising principles common to all direct-response marketing, explore the basic elements of every successful PPC campaign, and examine some of the interesting uses of PPC and the current state of the market.

Chapter Contents
PPC and Direct Advertising Fundamentals
Components of a Successful PPC Campaign
PPC Campaign Uses
The Science of PPC
The Art of PPC
State of the PPC Industry

PPC and Direct Advertising Fundamentals

Succeeding at PPC advertising depends mainly on one thing: your ability to persuade people to take action by using just a few well-chosen words. That's a much more important success factor than understanding the intricacies of search algorithms or the myriad features of the Google AdWords, Yahoo! Search Marketing, and Microsoft adCenter control consoles.

Writing persuasive ad copy using no more than 145 characters is a big challenge—especially if you're up against significant competition. Your words must not only persuade; they must stand out from a page full of words all shouting for your customer's attention (see Figure 1.1). And after your words have convinced the searcher to click through to your site, it's those persuasive words (augmented by graphics) that convince the visitor to become a customer.

Figure 1.1 The travel industry is one of the toughest PPC fields—look at all these well-crafted ads for Hawaiian vacations!

Playing the PPC game without first taking the time to learn the fundamentals of direct-response advertising is like sitting down at the poker table with scant understanding of the rules, and proceeding to drop dollars into the pot while better-trained players scoop that money out.

But here's some good news: Smart marketers have been studying, testing, and refining direct-response advertising techniques for a *long* time. Unless you already have solid experience in this field, we encourage you to read the book *Scientific Advertising* by Claude Hopkins. Written in 1923 (long before the Internet, television, or widespread commercialization of radio), it's one of the first hands-on manuals that teaches fundamentals based on scientific testing. It includes (almost) everything you need to know about writing, testing, and optimizing direct-response advertising campaigns. You can download this public-domain book by going to http://is.gd/rJSx. You should be able to get through its 52 pages in about an hour, so there's no excuse to avoid reading it—do it now!

Nearly 90 years ago, Hopkins wrote the following:

> *The time has come when advertising has in some hands reached the status of a science. It is based on fixed principles and is reasonably exact. The causes and effects have been analyzed until they are well understood. The correct methods of procedure have been proved and established. We know what is most effective, and we act on basic law.*
>
> *Advertising, once a gamble, has thus become, under able direction, one of the safest business ventures. Certainly no other enterprise with comparable possibilities need involve so little risk.*

This aptly summarizes the core appeal of PPC advertising: Having created ad campaigns based on clearly defined best practices, the advertiser can measure the success of those campaigns soon after launching them. The advertiser can then test campaign variations (such as ad copy and landing page design) and immediately improve or optimize campaign elements to achieve steady increases in revenue and profit, sales leads, or donations.

Hopkins espouses a continual testing philosophy—the notion that an advertising campaign is never perfect and that continual improvement can be achieved through testing and optimization. Successful PPC advertisers embrace and practice this philosophy, so you'll learn techniques for testing throughout this book.

Other key concepts from *Scientific Advertising* include the following:

- The best advertising copywriters think and speak like salespeople—the ad itself is a virtual salesperson.
- The best-written ads acknowledge that people are self-centered and respond best to benefits (how the product or service will make them feel) rather than just features (descriptions of the products or services).

- Always assume that people are busy. Hopkins said that three-quarters of paid content is unread by the buyer of that content. That was in 1923—in today's fast-paced world, that proportion may be as high as 90 percent.

- An ad's headline is the most important part of the ad. It is the magnet that pulls attention away from surrounding distractions and starts the reader on the path toward conversion. (*Conversion* is a word you'll see often in this book; it simply means the action you want the site visitor to take—like a sale, or the download of a white paper.)

- Ad designers should adhere to the axiom "If it's not helping, it's hurting." This is especially true when it comes to graphical elements of an ad or landing page: If the graphic is not helping to steer the reader toward the conversion action, it is probably distracting attention away from the conversion action. Hopkins wrote, "Use [graphics] only when they form a better selling argument than the same amount of space [in text content]."

- Samples sell. Offering a physical product at no cost is often a great way to stimulate repeat customers. Downloadable white papers and trial software often result in excellent sales.

- Most advertisers neglect the basics of good ad design—especially testing and refinement of ad copy. Don't assume that PPC advertisers who attain top rankings for their ads are making money—they may be spending top dollar while remaining surprisingly unprofitable.

Scientific Advertising is a gem from start to finish, but one chapter is particularly relevant to the PPC advertiser. In Chapter 15, "Test Campaigns," Hopkins underscores the fact that no aspect of advertising (including the ads themselves as well as the PPC landing pages) should be constructed based solely on the advertiser's intuition:

> *There are many surprises in advertising. A project you will laugh at may make a great success. A project you are sure of may fall down. All because tastes differ so. None of us know enough people's desires to get an average viewpoint.*

Frequently you will find (especially at the beginning of your ad-writing experiences) that the PPC ad you expect to produce outstanding results will prove a loser compared to a test ad that you intuitively sense would be inferior.

NOTE   Want to equip your company or organization to achieve continually improving advertising results? Read Bryan Eisenberg's *Always Be Testing* for solid advice and tactics to imbue your company with the attitude that testing leads to steady gains in sales volume and profitability.

But there's good news: In the fast-moving world of PPC advertising, testing and refinement of ads and landing pages can take place quickly, in days and weeks rather than the months and years necessary to gauge performance of offline advertising campaigns. Frequently, testing can take place on a small scale and at a low cost, determining winning ad and landing page combinations before rolling out campaigns on a larger scale. Then the advertiser can know with certainty that the larger-scale campaign will be successful and profitable.

In the last chapter of *Scientific Advertising*, Hopkins heralds the new advertising age, in which not a penny of advertising expense is wasted:

> *Yet most national advertising is done without justification. It is merely presumed to pay. A little test might show a way to multiply returns. Such methods, still so prevalent, are not very far from their end. The advertising men who practice them see the writing on the wall. The time is fast coming when men who spend money are going to know what they get. Good business and efficiency will be applied to advertising. Men and methods will be measured by the known returns, and only competent men can survive.*

These words drip with irony, because nearly a century later, many advertisers are still flying blind. They don't know the return on their advertising investment. Many site owners still have not put into place the web analytics devices necessary to know the revenue and profit for each advertising dollar spent. This is bad news for them, but good news for you, because by the end of this book you'll likely have a distinct advantage over your competitors.

Now let's take a look at the core elements of a PPC campaign.

Components of a Successful PPC Campaign

To achieve optimal results, all elements of a PPC campaign must be in good working order, operating together synergistically. Like an automobile engine, all parts must be finely tuned together to ensure that the driver gets from point A to point B, quickly and efficiently. If any one part of the engine is defective or inefficient, the engine may run poorly or not at all.

Likewise, if any one part of a PPC campaign is deficient or ineffective, it can drag down the performance of the whole campaign to unacceptable levels.

The individual elements of a campaign are as follows:

Keywords: In search PPC, these are the words and phrases the advertiser chooses to trigger ad display. In content PPC, keywords describe the kind of website pages where the advertiser wants their ads displayed.

Ads: The words and images used to persuade the reader to take action, such as clicking through to a website.

Bid prices: The price the advertiser is willing to pay for each ad-induced visit to the site.

Landing pages: The website pages respondents see when they click on an ad.

Conversion path: The steps the site visitor must take in order to achieve the objective of the site (for example, a sale, a submitted lead, a newsletter sign-up, or a donation).

Let's explore each of these elements a bit further.

Keywords

In PPC search campaigns, advertisers lists words and phrases that they think prospective customers would use in a search query. The advertiser is essentially saying, "Google, if someone uses this phrase as part of a search query, display my ad." (Note that the word *keyword* can mean a single word or a multiple-word phrase.) Keywords can be very general (such as *Hawaiian vacation*) or very specific (such as *reserve a hotel on Oahu*).

It's important for an advertiser to anticipate the many ways that people express themselves when performing a search. Chapter 4, "Month 1—Research Keywords and Establish Campaign Structure," shows you how to build keyword lists to make sure you're covering all the bases.

Keywords in content campaigns play a much different role than the keywords in search campaigns. They tell Google, "Display my ads on site pages that contain all or most of these words." Figure 1.2 shows how ads appear on a page in Google's content network. You'll learn much more about content campaign keywords in Chapter 7, "Month 4—Advertise on the Content Network."

Ads

As mentioned, writing effective PPC ads is an important cornerstone of a successful PPC ad campaign. The advertiser is challenged to pack a lot of meaning and persuasiveness into no more than 145 characters. An ad needs to deliver the following messages in the short time it takes to read it:

- The advertiser's website is likely the best source for satisfying the visitor's need or desire.
- There are clear benefits associated with clicking through to the advertiser's website.
- Visitors know what's expected of them when they arrive at the website.

Ad copywriting is such an important topic that Chapter 5, "Month 2—Create Great PPC Ads," is devoted exclusively to it.

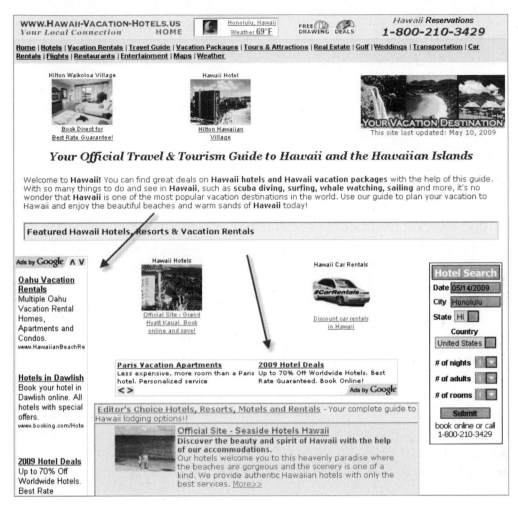

Figure 1.2 Ads appearing on a content network page

Bid Prices

PPC advertising operates under an *auction model*. Advertisers tell the PPC service how much they're willing to pay for a click on an ad and subsequent visit to the advertiser's website. Google takes into consideration how many other advertisers are bidding on the same keywords, and generally speaking, the advertisers willing to pay the most for a click will see their ads displayed closest to the top of the search results page. See Figure 1.3 for an illustration of ad group bid prices.

Ad Group	Status	Max. CPC (USD)	Clicks	Impr.	CTR	Avg. CP...	Avg. CP...	Cost (USD)	Avg. Pos	C...▽	Conv. Rate	C...
Golf Grip	Active	0.32	386	151,696	0.25%	0.22	0.57	86.39	2.4	1	0.26%	86.
Golf Instruction	Active	1.02	954	646,243	0.15%	0.24	0.35	227.48	3.5	1	0.10%	227
Branded	Active	0.32	1	4,626	0.02%	0.24	0.05	0.24	2.8	0	0.00%	0.0(
Chipping	Paused	0.18	0	0	-	-	-	-	-	0	0.00%	0.0(
Equipment	Active	0.32	110	61,375	0.18%	0.23	0.41	25.40	3.8	0	0.00%	0.0(
General Golf	Active	0.32	78	55,046	0.14%	0.21	0.30	16.25	1.6	0	0.00%	0.0(
Golf DVD	Paused	0.18	0	0	-	-	-	-	-	0	0.00%	0.0(
Golf Grip (old)	Paused	0.32	3	1,029	0.29%	0.13	0.39	0.40	5.9	0	0.00%	0.0(
Golf Magazines	Active	0.32	38	45,850	0.08%	0.24	0.20	9.00	5.2	0	0.00%	0.0(
Golf School	Active	0.32	84	43,753	0.19%	0.23	0.45	19.67	3.0	0	0.00%	0.0(
Golf Swing	Paused	0.08	0	0	-	-	-	-	-	0	0.00%	0.0(
Golf Tips	Active	0.32	410	378,397	0.11%	0.19	0.21	78.05	3.7	0	0.00%	0.0(
People	Active	0.32	12	14,280	0.08%	0.21	0.18	2.55	2.9	0	0.00%	0.0(
Pitching	Active	0.32	1,237	1,172,937	0.11%	0.23	0.24	279.40	3.0	0	0.00%	0.0(

Figure 1.3 AdWords Editor screen showing maximum ad group–level bid prices (maximum costs-per-click)

> **NOTE** Strictly speaking, this is not a pure price auction, because the search engines reward good campaign performance with a *quality score* that can cause ads to be displayed in higher positions even though their bids are lower than those of competing advertisers. This is described in detail in Chapter 2, "How the PPC Machine Works."

How much should an advertiser be willing to pay for a click? You'll see detailed guidance for calculating bid prices in Chapter 4. For now, understand that at the beginning of a new PPC ad campaign, this decision usually takes some guesswork, based on the amount competitors are bidding as well as the advertiser's assumption about the number of site visitors who will take the desired action—the conversion. But after a PPC campaign has been underway for a while (anywhere from a few weeks to a few months), the advertiser will know with certainty how much each conversion is costing. Thereafter, they can adjust bids so that the target profitability is consistently achieved.

The object of most PPC campaign optimization efforts (improvement of ad copy, for example) is to drive the average cost per click (CPC) ever lower. That way, profitability will increase steadily over time.

Landing Pages

Many advertisers are surprised to realize that the key element determining whether a site visitor will convert is whether the PPC landing pages are well designed and operating correctly. A PPC *landing page* is simply the page on your site upon which visitors land after clicking on a PPC ad. PPC landing pages can, and often should, look very different from the site's home page and other pages on the advertiser's site. In many cases, advertisers can get much better results when landing pages are customized to match the theme of a particular PPC ad group (the keywords and ad message).

This is often a difficult but crucial concept that's hard for many site owners to grasp. They're accustomed to thinking about their site as analogous to a bricks-and-mortar storefront: one entrance (the home page) through which all customers enter, linked to other pages where site visitors can (hopefully) easily find what they're looking for. Site owners often design their home page to satisfy the needs of casual browsers as well as visitors who are looking for specific items or information.

But with PPC advertising, the site owner has information about the intent of the visitor who has come to the site by clicking on a PPC ad. The site owner knows the search term used, and that the visitor was motivated by the specific messages and benefits mentioned in the ad.

For example, let's say a site sells Hawaiian vacations, and the site visitor has clicked on an ad that promises discounts on the rental of cottages on Oahu. If the PPC visitor arrives on the home page, which necessarily contains a wide variety of links to parts of the site that do *not* pertain to cottages on Oahu, that visitor quite possibly will leave the site without converting.

This is because visitors don't want to take the time and effort to navigate through the site to find pages that pertain to their specific needs. On the other hand, if a site visitor arrives at a page that describes Oahu cottage rentals, that visitor will much more likely conclude that she has come to exactly the right place and will take the desired conversion action. Figure 1.4 shows an example of a good ad and landing page combination.

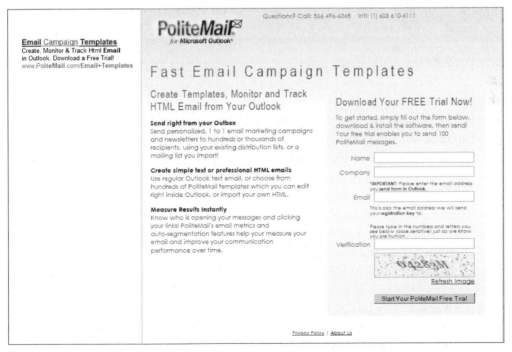

Figure 1.4 This is a great PPC ad (triggered by the keyword *e-mail templates*) with a corresponding landing page. Note that the ad message is featured prominently on the landing page.

Chapter 6, "Month 3—Design Effective Landing Pages," and Chapter 11, "Month 8—Test and Optimize Landing Pages," go into much more detail about landing page design and testing.

Conversion Path

Frequently, the site visitor must traverse more than one page to finalize the conversion action. A typical example is the shopping process on an e-commerce site. Having decided to buy, the visitor must enter shipping information, credit card numbers, and so on.

Every step in the process introduces the possibility that the visitor will become distracted or confused. Site owners are often shocked to find that many visitors, having decided to buy or convert, leave the site in the midst of the conversion process. This is referred to as *abandonment*. The ratio of the number of people who leave the site compared to the number of people who complete the conversion process is known as the *abandonment rate*.

If the conversion process is not designed and optimized correctly, abandonment rates can be as high as 50–80 percent. Obviously, it's in the best interest of the advertiser to continually work to lower this percentage, and Chapter 9, "Month 6—Optimize Your Campaign," shows you how to do this.

PPC Campaign Uses

Although most advertisers will use PPC advertising to garner sales, submitted leads, or donations, others may benefit in ways that are more indirect.

For example, the goal of some ad campaigns is not necessarily to elicit a direct response by the person viewing the ad. Rather, the goal is simply to achieve *branding*—to cause the person viewing the ad to remember the name of a company or the features of a product, which will result in a visit to a bricks-and-mortar storefront. Branding is also an effective way to generate *word-of-mouth marketing*, whereby people viewing the ad tell others about their impression or experience.

PPC advertising excels at eliciting direct responses, but it can also be employed for the purposes of branding, and at a cost lower than traditional offline ad media such as print, TV, and radio. You'll find out how in later chapters.

One important side benefit of PPC advertising is that the advertiser discovers with certainty which words and messages are most effective at persuading customers to buy. Savvy website owners use this information to design other online and offline campaigns.

For example, frequently the best-performing PPC keywords are the ones that should be used when optimizing a website so that search engines rank the site highest in the natural search listing portions of the search results pages. This activity is called *search engine optimization* (often abbreviated *SEO*).

Likewise, savvy PPC advertisers test several advertising messages, and then use the "winning" messages in their other online and offline advertising efforts. For example, an advertiser might find that a particular message (such as "Your children will love their Wii") results in a high return on investment (ROI) in their PPC campaign, and choose to highlight that message in an e-mail campaign.

The Science of PPC

The next chapter covers the mechanics of PPC, but for now it's important to understand that successful direct-response advertising of any kind requires using methods and techniques that are closer to science than to art. Successful PPC advertisers constantly use calculators, spreadsheets, and software tools to plan, construct, measure, and optimize campaigns. If you're not comfortable with the mathematical side of PPC advertising, you may need to find an assistant or colleague who can become proficient in that aspect of the job.

For example, determining the optimal price to pay for each click requires calculations based on the price you're willing to pay for a conversion. Usually this is a simple one-time exercise, but for companies with multiple products or a range of desired conversion actions, the task can get quite complicated.

One of the biggest strengths of PPC advertising is that it's easy to create reports that show exactly what is happening in a PPC campaign at any given time. You can quickly and easily see critical metrics such as the number of ad impressions, the number of clicks, click-through rates (CTRs), the number of sales, the cost of sales, and so on, for any period of time and for any elements of the campaign such as keywords and individual ads. Figure 1.5 shows examples of data types that can be reported.

It's important for you to learn how to interpret this data in order to understand what it means for your business and determine whether your PPC efforts are profitable. The data will also indicate what actions you should take (such as changing bid prices or creating test variations of an ad) in order to optimize campaign performance.

Improving campaign results is dependent on continual testing—displaying two variations of an ad, for example, and then favoring the ad that produces better results. Successful PPC advertisers never stop testing variations in ad copy, banner ad design, landing page design, and content. It's important that you learn and master the methods and tools required to test and to interpret results.

Fortunately, this book covers all of these topics in sufficient detail that you'll be applying the best techniques after just a few weeks of practice.

	A	B	C	D	E	F	G
1	Campaign	Ad Group	Keyword	Quality Score	Impressions	Clicks	Conversions
2	Search - English-speaking	golf advice	golf advice	9	14279	1285	3
3	Search - English-speaking	golf help	golf help	9	77621	1891	8
4	Search - English-speaking	golf advice	golf advice	9	31458	745	3
5	Search - English-speaking	golf advice	golf advice	9	7862	201	1
6	Search - English-speaking	learn golf	learn golf	8	1037905	39421	93
7	Search - English-speaking	golf instructions	golf instructions	8	220332	6093	17
8	Search - English-speaking	golf lessons	golf lessons	8	160741	3679	24
9	Search - English-speaking	golf lessons	golf lessons	8	59311	2062	15
10	Search - English-speaking	golf training	golf training	8	187738	2354	10
11	Search - English-speaking	golf hints	golf hints	8	184155	2321	6
12	Search - English-speaking	golf swing training aid	golf swing training aid	8	73278	1563	5
13	Search - English-speaking	online golf lesson	online golf lesson	8	46238	2127	8
14	Search - English-speaking	simple golf swing	simple golf swing	8	27596	1272	5
15	Search - English-speaking	learn golf	learn golf	8	31747	1239	1
16	Search - English-speaking	golf lessons	golf lessons	8	83690	1044	5
17	Search - English-speaking	learn golf	learn golf	8	29175	781	1
18	Search - English-speaking	golf swing help	golf swing help	8	25027	889	1
19	Search - English-speaking	golf help	golf help	8	9762	653	1
20	Search - English-speaking	golf training	golf training	8	49222	561	3
21	Search - English-speaking	golf stance	golf stance	8	24209	911	1
22	Search - English-speaking	basic golf lessons	basic golf lessons	8	8580	392	1
23	Search - English-speaking	golf instructions	golf instructions	8	16270	379	
24	Search - English-speaking	golf swing help	golf swing help	8	8747	356	

Figure 1.5 Typical PPC data

The Art of PPC

Although PPC advertisers have a big toolkit of scientific tools and techniques to employ, successful PPC advertising requires a mastery of skills that are mainly artistic in nature. Chief among these are the ability to write well and a sense of professional graphic design.

Writing effective, persuasive ads is crucial to the success of a PPC campaign. Often the failure of a campaign can be attributed to poor ad copywriting. Ads may be displayed frequently but fail to elicit a significant proportion of clicks, as evidenced by one of the most important metrics of campaign success: *click-through rate* (usually abbreviated as *CTR*).

Creating nontext ads for display on the PPC content network requires copywriting skills as well as an understanding of how visual images deliver or augment messages and persuade the viewer to take action. In the hands of a skilled professional, an animated banner ad can speak volumes about the advertiser's products, features, benefits, and desired action, taking full advantage of the relatively small space provided by PPC ad units.

Solid copywriting and graphic design skills are also necessary for creating successful PPC landing pages. The PPC advertiser is challenged to create the right combinations of words and graphics that will quickly persuade and steer the site visitor to take the site's desired action. As we stated earlier in this chapter, that action (such as a sale, submitted lead, donation, and so on) is referred to as a *conversion*. The success metric is called the *conversion rate*, which is the number of site visitors who convert divided by the number of PPC visitors to the site. With optimal landing page design, conversion rates of 10–20 percent and higher are common.

Can one person practice and build the scientific and artistic skills necessary to be an expert PPC advertiser? The answer is, "Sometimes." It's certainly rare to find people who are naturally gifted at both. The good news is that the training in this book will equip just about anyone to develop the skills they might lack naturally.

The State of the PPC Industry

Since the inception of PPC advertising in 1998, advertisers have paid Google, Yahoo!, and Microsoft billions of dollars for targeted clicks. Despite the effects of a global recession, almost half of advertisers polled by MarketingSherpa said they intended to increase their PPC spending in 2009. Conversion rates for PPC campaigns have also been climbing steadily—almost half of the respondents in the same study reported that conversion rates have increased over the previous year.

After several experimental efforts in the mid-to-late 1990s, PPC advertising was popularized by the startup company GoTo which was developed at Bill Gross's Idealab in 1998. GoTo had the PPC advertising field to itself until it was renamed Overture in 2001, and expanded as a back-end ad service platform for search engines such as Yahoo! and MSN. Figure 1.6 shows the original GoTo search screen.

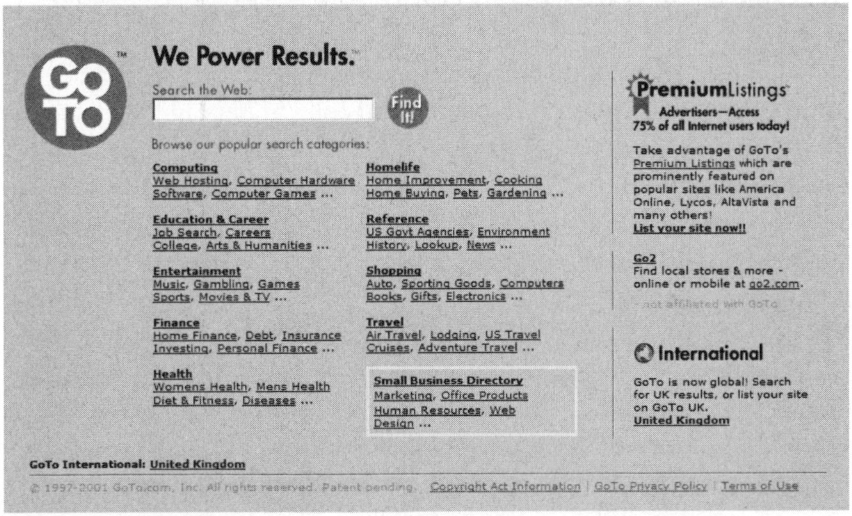

Figure 1.6 GoTo, the earliest popular ad-supported search engine

As Overture became a significant driver of profit for its search engine partners, it continued to grow by acquisition, gobbling up dot-com pioneers such as AltaVista and AlltheWeb. In 2003, Overture was acquired by its biggest customer, Yahoo!.

Google quietly introduced search engine advertising in 1999, but initially advertisers paid on a CPM (cost-per-thousand) impressions basis—not a true PPC model. Google finally introduced PPC search advertising in 2002.

In 2003, Google introduced its AdSense program, whereby site owners could place Google AdWords ads on their site pages and earn a commission from Google whenever someone clicked on an ad. Google also introduced web-based software that simplified the task of creating and managing Google AdWords campaigns. Figure 1.7 shows ads appearing on Google's search results page.

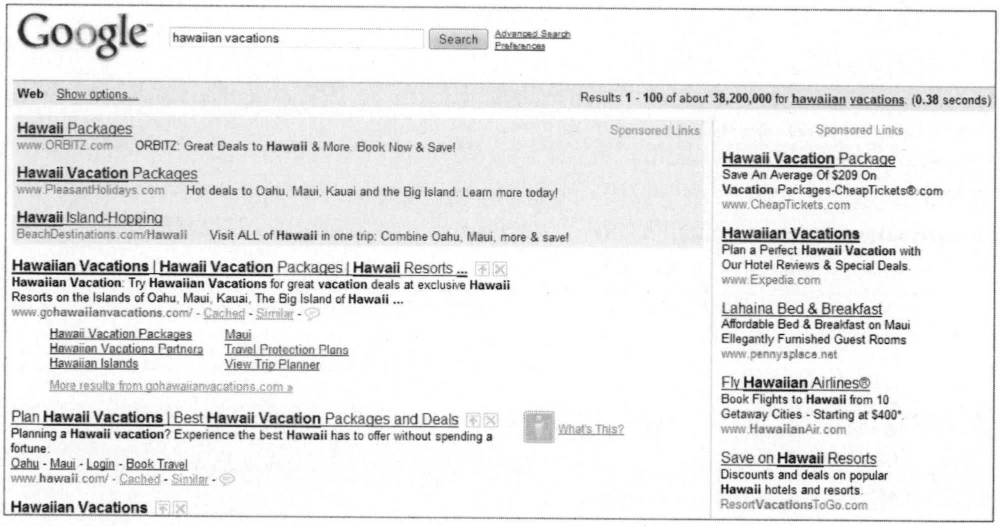

Figure 1.7 Google search results page

Yahoo!, ambivalent about its growth strategy, invested heavily in several directions. Some in the company wanted it to become a media player and compete with the established television networks and movie studios. Others wanted Yahoo! to diversify by creating a growing suite of web-based software services. Many believe Yahoo! neglected its PPC advertising business in the years between 2003 and 2005, allowing Google to pull ahead in market share and functionality. Figure 1.8 shows a Yahoo! search results page.

Microsoft entered the PPC fray late in 2006, and its market share has languished in the single digits. Microsoft has recently decided to focus more attention and resources on PPC and online advertising; this includes a technology-sharing agreement with Yahoo! whereby Microsoft ads will appear on Yahoo! search results pages. In mid 2009 Microsoft introduced a revised version of their Live Search engine, renaming it Bing. Figure 1.9 shows ads appearing on a Bing search results page.

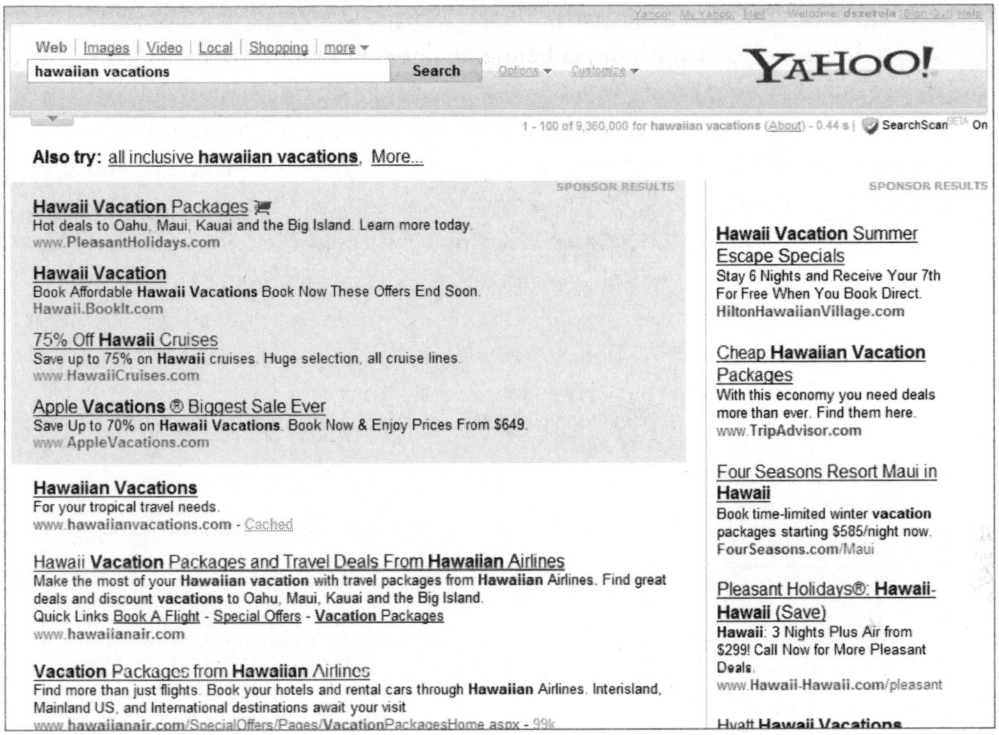

Figure 1.8 Yahoo! search results page

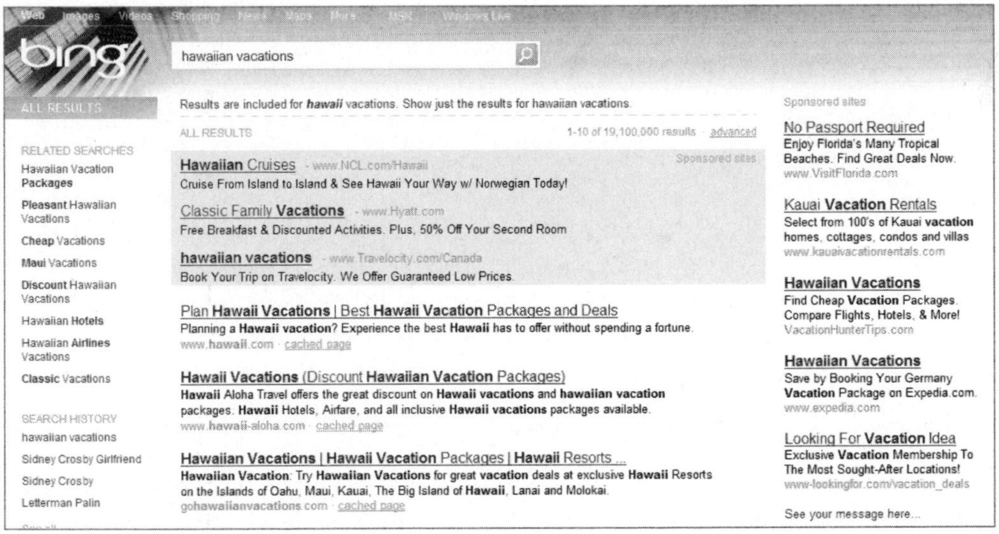

Figure 1.9 Microsoft Bing search results page

Today the "Big Three" players in the PPC industry are Google, Yahoo!, and Microsoft—obviously correlating to the most frequently used search engines. But their share of the market is far from equal. Google earns the biggest chunk of advertising revenue—recent estimates have pegged its share at 85 percent. Yahoo! has a much smaller, but still relevant, share at 9 percent. Microsoft squeaks into third place with a 4–5 percent portion of revenue. The last 1 percent or so is earned by so-called "second-tier" search engines such as LookSmart, Ask, and 7Search.

The year 2009 has been a tough one for businesses worldwide, but advertisers continue to increase PPC advertising spending. In fact, there are indications that many advertisers, drawn by a high ROI and predictable results, are diverting ad dollars away from traditional print, TV, radio, and outdoor advertising to fund additional PPC advertising.

The Interactive Advertising Bureau reported the following in its 2008 Internet Advertising Revenue Report:

> *Despite a difficult U.S. economy, the report indicates that interactive advertising's continued growth—though at a slower pace—confirms marketers' increased confidence in the value in reaching consumers online. Internet advertising revenues in the U.S. remain strong, with Q408 revenues hitting $6.1 billion, and revenues for the year topping $23 billion.*

Spending on PPC advertising seems to be growing faster than spending on other forms of online advertising. *The New York Time*s reported that in 2008, PPC accounted for 57 percent of online advertising, up from 52 percent in 2007.

Most advertisers will be well served by advertising on all of the Big Three search engines. Although Yahoo! and Microsoft deliver much lower click volumes, many advertisers find that conversion rates are better than on Google (due to lower competition, for example), and hence profitability is higher. The combined available clicks from the second-tier search engines is so small that for most advertisers it's not worth the time and effort to use them. That's why this book describes the similarities and differences of creating and managing campaigns just on the Big Three.

How the PPC Machine Works

This book teaches you how to create tightly focused, well-structured pay-per-click (PPC) campaigns. You will learn how to write unique, action-oriented PPC ads. You will also learn how to optimize, refine, and improve the results generated by your campaign. Actually, it's almost impossible to list everything you're going to learn from this book, but we need to start with the fundamentals. In this chapter, we discuss the top-level mechanics of the PPC machine. We cover how PPC advertisements appear on search engine results pages (SERPs), as well as how Sponsored by Google ads appear on various websites throughout the Internet.

Chapter Contents

Think Like a Search Engine

You want to provide the highest-quality product and/or service to your customers. Maintaining a high level of quality keeps your customers happy, increases your retention rates, and turns your clients into evangelists as they tell everyone about their excellent experience with your company. The same goes for the search engines. Their "product" is search results.

Google, Yahoo!, and Bing (and all other search engines) have their own unique algorithms for ranking websites within their index and search results. Going forward, we'll refer to the website listings that are contained within a search engine's index and displayed within the search results as *organic listings*. The search engines go to great lengths to try to provide the best organic results possible—ones that closely match the user's search query. The search engines also display advertisements on the search results page. It's the goal of the engines to display ads whose content is as relevant as possible to the user's search query.

If a search engine consistently serves users with irrelevant, poor-quality results, users will go elsewhere for their querying needs. All of the major search engines (including Google, Yahoo!, and Bing) quite simply want to deliver the best possible user experience to searchers. Each search engine wants to make the information that appears on its search engine results pages (SERPs) as useful, relevant, and informative as possible, no matter what the query. This is why the search engines are *depending on you* to help sustain their success and provide the best user experience possible.

The search engines are depending on you, the advertiser, to keep their profit margins healthy, because the majority of their revenue is generated from advertising. According to a Google Investor Relations Financial Table, in 2008 Google generated more than $21 billion in revenue. Approximately 97 percent of Google's revenue is from advertising, most of which comes from the text and display ads we are covering in this book.

Text ads within search results undergo a thorough approval process before they are even considered for placement. However, the search engines can only approve or disapprove these ads. It is the advertiser's responsibility to target keywords that are relevant to their products, compose PPC ads that are well written and keyword-centric, and once a user clicks on these advertisements, to provide a high-quality post-click experience on their website.

As a result, you want to help the search engine provide the best user experience possible. We're all in this together. Think about it: If people don't trust a certain search engine to provide great results, they'll stop using it. And this means your audience is going to shrink, and your business along with it. However, as long as the search engines continue to enhance their organic listings and advertisers strive to create high-quality advertisements, then everybody wins.

This is where the search engines are coming from. They need to provide a high-quality product, and they need you to help them achieve this goal. And in turn, they will help you achieve your goals. The best part (aside from growing your business and being wildly successful!) is that the search engines reward you for providing high-quality advertisements and a great user experience with better ad positions at more-favorable prices.

Going back to our original analogy, search results are the "product" that search engines provide. You can almost view yourself as having a vendor relationship with the search engines. You provide a critical piece of their revenue puzzle: the advertisements that generate their revenue. They want to keep you happy, and you want to keep them happy.

How and Where Ads Appear on SERPs

You now know that search engines want to provide a great user experience by displaying the most relevant organic and paid listings within their results. But exactly how and where do advertisements appear within the search engines? This is what we're covering in this section.

As we mentioned in the first part of this chapter, a SERP refers to a search engine results page. This is simply the page of results that you receive from a search engine when you conduct a search. First, let's dissect a SERP.

Figure 2.1 is a screen capture of a Google SERP for the search query *gourmet coffee*. Within the image, you can see that we have highlighted the top and right side of the SERP separately from the bottom-left side of the image. The area marked Pay-Per-Click Advertisements (under the Sponsored Links section) contains ads that advertisers are paying to have shown for this particular search query. The section marked Organic Results contains websites that Google has indexed and deemed relevant to this search query.

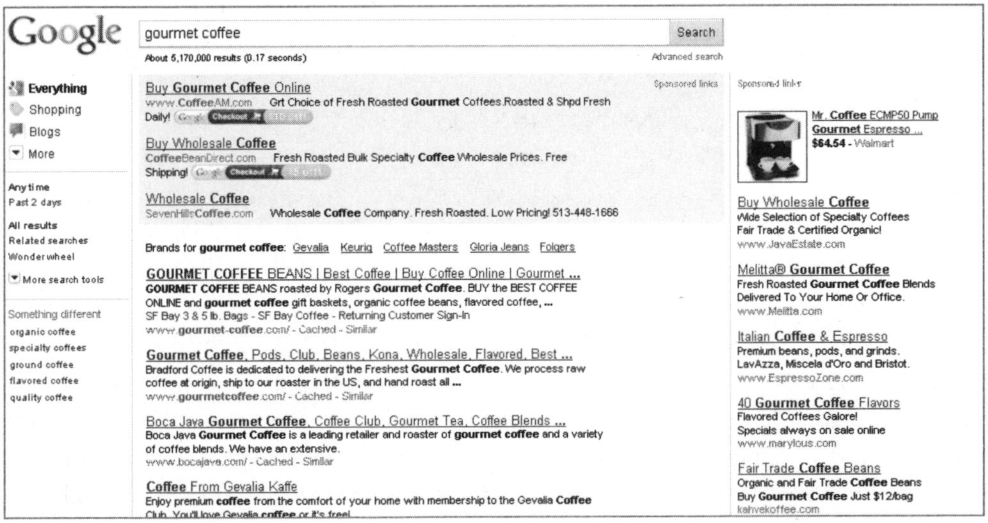

Figure 2.1 On a Google SERP, organic results appear on the bottom left, and the paid results appear on the top and right.

How Advertisements Are Triggered

The following is a quick walk-through of how an advertiser gets an ad displayed for a specific user query (the rest of this book will show you how to do it precisely and optimally):

1. The advertiser opens an account within the Google advertising network called Google AdWords.

2. Within this AdWords account, the advertiser loads a keyword list that is relevant to their products and services, and creates PPC ads to display for these terms.

3. The advertiser sets the price they are willing to pay for each click.

4. When a user enters a query, the search engine reviews all of the ads in its database and then selects and displays the most relevant ads ranked by quality of advertisement and how much the advertiser is willing to pay for that click.

Figure 2.2 is a simple diagram of how ads appear on a SERP.

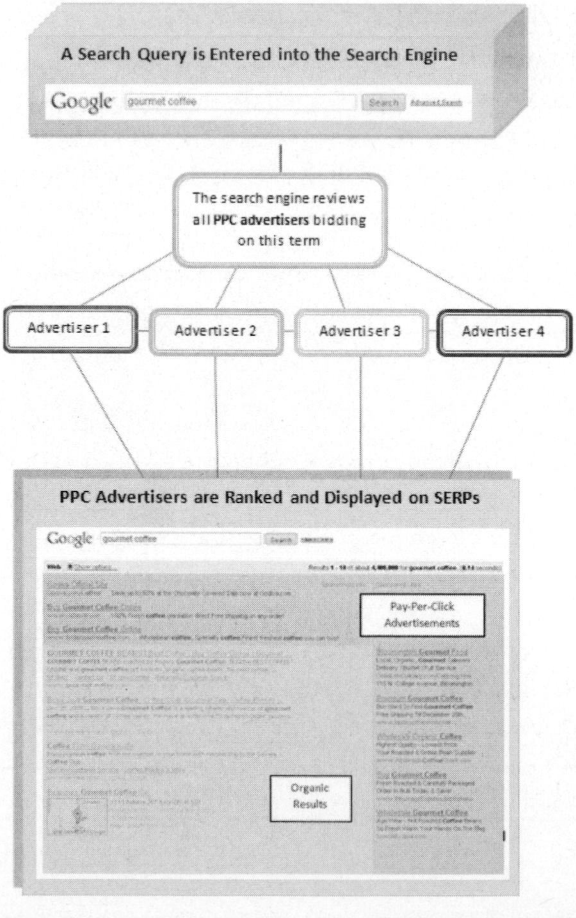

Figure 2.2 Search engines review and rank advertisers for every search query.

Throughout the rest of the book, we're going to show you how to create a great keyword list, upload into AdWords, set smart keyword bids, and write awesome PPC ad copy.

We have covered the mechanics of how a PPC ad appears on a SERP, but with all of the advertisers vying for an individual keyword, how do the search engines determine who gets ranked in the top coveted spots? That's what we cover next!

How Advertisements Are Ranked

The PPC ad-ranking methodology has evolved greatly since the introduction of the paid advertising model. Before we describe how PPC ads are ranked today, let's quickly review the industry evolution:

- In June 1998, the first major sponsored search service—Overture—was launched. A number of other smaller sponsored search services launched around this time, but none of them were as large as Overture.
- Google AdWords was launched in October 2000.
- Yahoo! acquired Overture in 2003.
- Google introduced its Quality Score measurement system in August 2005.
- Until the beginning of 2006, all of the sponsored links on MSN Search were supplied by Yahoo!/Overture. In June 2006, Microsoft severed ties with Yahoo! and created its own ad-serving platform. In 2009, MSN Search evolved into the recently launched Bing search engine.

Of course, numerous other acquisitions and products were launched during this time frame, but these are the major PPC milestones.

Auction Model

Each of the large-scale search engines established an auction model in order to rank advertisements. In this auction system, an advertiser would place a bid on each individual keyword. This bid told the search engine how much each advertiser was willing to pay for a click on each keyword. For example, if an advertiser's bid for the term *gourmet coffee* was $1, this indicated that they were willing to pay up to $1 for a click on this keyword.

Advertisers entered into an auction for each keyword. The advertiser who was willing to pay the most for each click won the auction, and the rest of the bids fell into the descending spots on the page. This method was known as *bid-to-placement*, because you could see all of your competitors' bids for each keyword, and they could see yours. For example, you would have seen a screen that looked like Table 2.1.

▶ **Table 2.1** How Bid-to-Placement Information Was Originally Displayed in a PPC Management Interface

Advertiser	Bid	Rank
Advertiser 1	$1.10	1
Advertiser 2	$0.96	2
Advertiser 3	$0.91	3
Advertiser 4	$0.82	4

Here you could see how much each advertiser was willing to pay in each position. If you wanted to be ranked first, you would adjust your keyword bid to $1.11 or higher. You would then have the number-one ad position—that is, until your competitor bid $1.12. The reasons why this system didn't work are numerous, but here are the major ones:

Bidding wars: In the preceding example, you can see how easy it was to get into a bidding war. It was almost as if you were at Christie's auction house and had a little paddle with a number on it that you kept raising in order to keep an edge over your competition. Maybe you didn't always want the painting that you were bidding on, and you couldn't afford the price you just committed to, but you sure didn't want your competitor to get it either. As a result, advertisers were often playing defense against their competitors (by trying to keep them out of the top spots), while they should have been playing offense by trying to attract qualified traffic to their websites.

This old auction system was seriously flawed, because during these bidding wars it was easy to drive up your competitor's cost per click (CPC). In Table 2.1, you can see that the top advertiser was willing to bid $1.10. This didn't mean that they would pay this amount; it just meant that they were *willing to pay* this amount. In actuality, advertisers paid one cent more than the bid below them. In this example, Advertiser 1 was *willing* to pay $1.10, but they were *actually* going to pay only one cent more than Advertiser 2, which was $0.97 per click.

To drive up a competitor's cost, an advertiser would bid one cent under their closest competitor. In Table 2.1, Advertiser 2 could be fine with being ranked in the second position, but they could raise their bid to $1.09 in order make their competitor pay the *maximum* CPC for that keyword. This happened *all the time*.

Sure, even today there are keywords in almost any sector that remain highly competitive and require aggressive bids in order to rank well. However, with the quality-based ranking method (which we cover in just a few pages), bidding wars are a thing of the past (for the most part).

Poor-quality ads: With the old bid-to-placement method, the quality of an advertiser's PPC ad copy and landing page were not taken into consideration by the search engine. The ad-ranking algorithm focused solely on bid prices. If that advertiser was willing to pay for those clicks, the search was willing to take their money.

Uphill battle for new advertisers: It could be extremely difficult for new advertisers to enter an auction. If a new advertiser wanted their ad to appear for a keyword for which a bidding war was taking place, that advertiser would have to pay these escalated costs in order to get ranked. Also, new advertisers were learning the system, so it was easy to spend a great deal of money without getting good results.

Big budgets vs. little budgets: Not only did new advertisers face an uphill battle in entering an auction; they had a difficult time remaining competitive. Corporations that had very large budgets could set their keyword bids so high that an advertiser with a smaller budget could never compete.

Focus on the wrong PPC tactics: Your keyword bid is just one element of generating an awesome return on investment (ROI) from your PPC campaign. Advertisers need to determine what CPC best garners the ROI, but to achieve the best results, advertisers should be focusing on improving their PPC ad texts, and optimizing their landing pages, contact form, and purchasing process on their website. In the old auction system, optimization wasn't always the core concern.

Search engine companies were hurting themselves with this auction model, which is why they changed it. They were hurting themselves in the sense that advertisers were not helping the search engines provide relevant results and a great user experience.

Also, advertisers were getting burned pretty easily. If you burn someone enough times, they're not going to do business with you anymore. With this bid-to-placement system, users were often being served low-quality advertisements, and advertisers were suffering because their costs could be high and the results would vary.

As you can see, this auction system could be very aggressive. PPC advertising is still driven by an auction system, and the amount an advertiser is willing to pay for each click determines their ad position, but your keyword bid is only part of what helps you achieve good rankings and great results.

Today's PPC auction models take both keyword bid price and ad quality into account. There are minimum bid requirements to make your keywords qualify to enter the auction. There are also minimum quality requirements for your ads and keywords in combination to make them eligible for the auction. If your keywords are completely irrelevant to your ads and your website, they will not be eligible for the auction and won't appear in the SERPs. When your keywords and ads do qualify to participate in the auction, their quality scores and bid prices determine how they will be ranked. Bid price is still very important for achieving the best ad positions, but if you present high-quality ads that receive a positive response from users, you'll be able to rank highly while paying less per click.

Keyword Bids

In the world of PPC today, you can't see your competitor's bids, and they can't see yours. Your keyword bid along with your quality score (which we discuss next) now determines your ad position and how much you will pay per click. Think of it this way: The old system was like a game of tennis, where you were competing directly with your opponent; the current system is more like golf, where the best way to beat your competition is to make your own game better.

For your keyword to be eligible for first-page placement, your bid must meet a minimum requirement. A real-time auction occurs for every search query entered into the search engine. If your bid is too low, your ads will not be considered for that auction. After you've met the minimum bid requirement, the search engine evaluates each advertiser's keyword, ads, and quality score to determine which ads will be displayed and in what order they will appear. The search engine then determines how much each advertiser will pay per click for this particular search query. Remember, this evaluation process occurs for *every query* entered into the search engine.

Even though the auction system has evolved (for the better!) over time, advertisers still pay on a per-click basis. That is why it's still called *pay-per-click* advertising! Your CPC will have a major impact on your ROI. We discuss bidding strategies in Chapter 4, "Month 1: Research Keywords and Establish Campaign Structure."

In the next section, we discuss how ad quality is determined by search engines and how this system affects you. But first, here's a quick side note: In this chapter, we're focusing on CPC bidding and cost. In Google AdWords, there are also cost-per-thousand-impressions (CPM) and cost-per-acquisition (CPA) bidding options. We don't recommend using CPM bidding, because CPC bidding allows you to pay a much lower amount per impression. CPA bidding maximizes conversions and is a very powerful tool that you'll learn about in Chapter 4.

Quality Measurement

When relevant, high-quality advertisements regularly appear within the SERPs, users will learn to trust and value them and be more likely to click on them. When more users trust ads and click on them, the search engines make more money. Because they make money on ads that users trust, search engines continually refine their quality control to offer even better, more-relevant ads that users will trust even more and click even more often. And this cycle goes on and on.

The search engines have full control over what information is displayed in their organic and paid listings. With organic listings, the search engines find and index websites that will be displayed on a SERP. For the PPC side of things, it's up to the advertiser to build a PPC campaign with a foundation of targeted keywords, unique advertisements, and relevant landing pages. Basically, you're bringing your best game to the search engine.

All of the major search engines have implemented quality-based algorithms to evaluate the relevancy of each advertiser's PPC campaign. Each search engine has its own method of evaluating PPC accounts: Yahoo! calls theirs the Quality Index; Google's is called the Google AdWords Quality Score; Microsoft adCenter doesn't have an official name for their quality-based evaluation. Even though these quality-control methods have different names, have varied evaluation methodology, and are reported in different ways, the desired results are essentially the same: to review and score every advertiser's PPC account in order to display the ads with the highest scores (in other words, the highest relevancy).

Going forward, we'll refer to all quality algorithms, regardless of the search engine, as a *quality score*. A quality score affects a number of critical elements of your PPC performance, including the following:

- Whether your ad will show at all
- Where you ad will be ranked on the SERP
- What your minimum first-page bid will be
- Your CPC

As mentioned in the previous section, your quality score and bid will determine your ad rank. Figure 2.3 shows the ad rank formula, as used by Google.

Figure 2.3 The Google ad rank formula

How is a quality score calculated? Most search engines keep their quality-ranking formula a secret so no one can game the system. However, Google has been most forthcoming about the factors that influence their quality score, so we will focus our attention on them (and Google does have the lion's share of search volume). Here is a list of the major elements that influence your Google AdWords Quality Score:

Historical CTR: A click-through occurs when someone sees your ad and clicks through to your landing page. This is the most important element of the Google AdWords Quality Score calculation. Because Google wants to provide high-quality ads, the CTR is a fair indicator of whether users find an ad relevant to a search query.

Account performance history: Google monitors the performance of an entire account over its lifetime. If a certain PPC account consistently has good quality scores for its keywords, this indicates that the account is trustworthy.

Relevance of keywords to the ads in an ad group: We discuss account structure later in the book, but it's safe to say that if your keyword doesn't appear in your PPC ad, Google will not find it relevant. And the users may not either.

Relevance of keywords and the ad to the search query: A great user experience is ensured when there is a logical path from search query to advertisement to landing page. Google awards a higher quality score when the keywords and ad texts within an ad group are closely related to each other.

Historical CTR of the display URLs in an ad group: The display URL is the website address that is displayed in your PPC ad. Google also considers the historical performance of each display URL within a keyword group.

Landing page quality: Google has said that landing pages do not factor into the ad rank formula, but they do contribute to the overall quality score. Improper coding, slow load times, missing privacy policies, and other undetermined factors can lower your quality score.

These are the most important factors of the Google AdWords Quality Score. There are probably other triggers that Google hasn't shared with the world, but this list should be enough to keep your optimization docket full! The other search engines have not been as forthcoming with regard to what factors into their quality initiatives, but if you optimize your Yahoo! and Microsoft adCenter accounts similarly to your Google account, you'll be well on your way to high quality scores across the board.

Quality Score in Action

We've discussed how your quality score can affect your ad rank and CPC, but here is an example of quality score in action.

First, let's say that we have five advertisers all bidding for the same keyword. Take a good look at the following image. You can see each advertiser's quality score and keyword bid.

Ad Rank 1 — Advertiser E / Quality Score: 10 / Keyword Bid: $1.25

Ad Rank 2 — Advertiser D / Quality Score: 7 / Keyword Bid: $1.25

Ad Rank 3 — Advertiser B / Quality Score: 8 / Keyword Bid: $1

Ad Rank 4 — Advertiser C / Quality Score: 4 / Keyword Bid: $1.75

Ad Rank 5 — Advertiser A / Quality Score: 3 / Keyword Bid: $2

You'll notice that the highest-ranked advertiser, Advertiser E, doesn't have the highest keyword bid but does have the highest quality score. This high quality score allows Advertiser E to earn a top spot even without the highest bid. Take a look at Advertiser A, on the bottom. They have the lowest quality score but the highest bid. Simply bidding higher hasn't overcome the negative impact of their low quality score. To achieve a higher ad rank, Advertiser A will need to either raise their bid substantially or write a more relevant ad for their keywords. This is how the ad rank formula works.

Good quality scores will lead to higher rankings, lower CPCs, and a better ROI for your PPC campaign.

How Keyword Match Types Work

Google AdWords allows advertisers to use four keyword match types that determine which Google searches will trigger your ads. When you add keywords to an ad group, it's a good idea to specify the match type for each keyword, rather than accept the default setting. The following sections describe each match type.

Exact Match

When it comes to explaining match types, we can use an analogy of a faucet. By using exact match, you are turning on the faucet just enough to get a small stream of water. With this match type, your ad will be eligible to appear when a user searches for the specific keyword in your ad group—for example, *gourmet coffee*, in this order and without any other terms in the query.

To set a keyword to exact match in your ad group within the Google AdWords web interface, you need to put brackets around it—for example, *[gourmet coffee]*. In AdWords Editor, you can choose the match type for each keyword from the Match Type drop-down menu within the keyword editing screen.

With this matching option set, your ads will appear only for the search query *gourmet coffee*, and nothing else.

Benefits of Using Exact Match Exact match provides the most control over which search queries trigger your ads. If you add *[gourmet coffee]* to your ad group, this is the only search query that will trigger your ad. On average, keywords with this match type have the highest CTR and conversion rate, because they are so tightly focused to only one search query.

Risks of Using Exact Match Using only exact match for your keywords will significantly hinder your campaign's impression volume. The impressions you receive will be highly targeted and relevant, but you may have trouble increasing conversions.

Phrase Match

With this match type, you are opening the faucet more, but it's not wide open. Now you're getting a good stream of search queries. If you enter the phrase-match keyword *gourmet coffee*, your ad will be eligible to appear when a user searches on the term *gourmet coffee*, with the words together in that order. Your ads can also appear for searches that contain other terms as long as they include the exact phrase you've specified (in this example, *gourmet coffee*).

To set a keyword to phrase match in your ad group, you need to put quotation marks around it—for example, *"gourmet coffee."*

When loading the phrase-match keyword *"gourmet coffee"* into your ad group, your ads may also appear for the following search queries:

> *gourmet coffee*
>
> *buy gourmet coffee*
>
> *gourmet coffee reviews*
>
> *gourmet coffee from Austria*
>
> *best gourmet coffee in the world*
>
> *how to brew gourmet coffee*

Benefits of Using Phrase Match Phrase match keywords can expand your reach on Google, but you maintain tighter control than using broad match. With phrase match, you can target the search queries that trigger your ads by including qualifiers with your keywords. For example, let's say you sell running shoes on your website. You may want your ad to appear for search queries related to *running shoes*, so you would add this keyword as phrase match. Your ads will appear when users append words at the beginning or end of your keyword, but the search queries must always contain the words *running shoes*. Your ads won't appear for just the word *running* or just the word *shoes*.

Risks of Using Phrase Match When users can append words to the beginning or end of your keyword, your ads may appear for search queries that are relevant, but the users may have no intention of buying. Users may append phrases such as the ones in the following list to your phrase match keyword *running shoes*:

> *Running shoes reviews*
>
> *Career in running shoes industry*
>
> *Articles about running shoes*
>
> *How to fix running shoes*
>
> *How to clean running shoes*

Sure, these search queries contain your keyword *running shoes*, but the words surrounding them may indicate that the searchers are not ready to make a purchase.

Broad Match

If you don't specify a match type using the preceding methods, Google sets the keyword match type to broad by default. Using the broad match type tells Google to display your ads in response to the widest variety of search queries. Continuing with our faucet analogy, broad match is like turning the faucet on full-blast. If your ad group contains the broad match keyword *gourmet coffee*, your ad will be eligible to appear when a user's search query contains either or both words (*gourmet* and *coffee*) in any order. Your broad match keyword may also be matched to search queries that contain synonyms, plurals, or misspellings, or other search queries that Google deems "relevant."

To set a keyword to broad match, you don't need to do anything to your keyword. Just upload it!

When loading the broad match keyword *gourmet coffee* into your ad group, your ads may also appear for the following search queries:

gourmet

coffee

gourmet coffees

buy gourmet coffee

gourmet Irish coffee

reviews of gourmet coffee

organic coffee shop

gourmet tea

buy gourmet tea

Benefits of Using Broad Match This match type has the greatest potential to expand your reach on Google. Your broad match keywords will be matched to a wide range of search queries. By using Google's Search Query Report, you can learn which queries triggered your ads, and you can add these terms to your campaign. Broad match can aggressively increase your impression volume.

Risks of Using Broad Match The core benefit of broad match is also its core risk. Broad match keywords can be matched to numerous search queries that are not relevant for your product or service. Because it displays your ads on less targeted and frequently irrelevant search queries, your broad match keywords will have lower CTRs and conversion rates.

Negative Match

Negative match keywords are like the water filters you place on your faucet to remove impurities. Negative match keywords filter your ads out from any search result pages when the search query contains one of your negative keywords. By removing your ads from irrelevant search queries, negative match keywords can help you reach the most appropriate audience, reduce your CPC, and increase your ROI. Negative match keywords are especially useful when your account contains lots of broad match keywords.

When you load the broad match keyword *gourmet coffee* into your ad group and add the negative keyword *-reviews*, your ads may appear for the following search queries:

> *gourmet coffees*
>
> *buy gourmet coffee*
>
> *gourmet Irish coffee*

However, your ads will not appear for the following search queries, because you've told Google to remove your ads from search queries that mention *reviews*:

> *gourmet coffee reviews*
>
> *reviews of gourmet coffee*

Benefits of Using Negative Match Negative keywords can improve your performance in two ways. First, by removing your ads from irrelevant search queries, you pay for fewer unproductive clicks. For example, if you find that search queries containing the word *reviews* generally don't turn into sales, you can add this word as a negative match to your ad group, and your ads will no longer show for these searches. Secondly, by preventing your ads from showing on nonrelevant searches, you can reduce the number of ad impressions, which usually has the effect of increasing your CTR. Because CTR is one of the strongest influences on quality score, using negative keywords can really boost your keyword quality score and lead to higher ad positions at lower bid prices.

Risks of Using Negative Match Be careful when adding negative keywords to your ad group, because you may accidently remove your ads from relevant search queries. For example, if you are selling running shoes and you add the negative keyword *-running*, your ads will not appear for any search query that contains the word *running*.

How Ads Appear on the Google Content Network

This chapter has thus far focused exclusively on how and why advertisements appear on the SERPs. Targeting the search network on Google and the other search engines will garner great results. However, this is not your only option for generating traffic via PPC advertising. Another distribution channel within Google AdWords is called the Google *Content Network*.

Many websites earn money by displaying Google AdWords ads. You've probably seen blocks of three or four text ads along with this line of text: *Ads by Google*. Figure 2.4 is an example of these ads as they appear on http://publishingcentral.com.

Figure 2.4 Google ads appearing on a web page via the Google Content Network

Site owners who display such ads are participating in a revenue-sharing program Google calls Google AdSense. The network of sites can display Google AdWords ads and is collectively referred to as the Google Content Network.

When you target the Google Content Network, Google automatically matches your PPC ads to websites with content that is relevant to your keywords. Your ads may appear on popular news sites, blogs, entertainment pages, industry publications, social networking sites, or wherever else your target audience may spend their time on the Internet. Basically, Google matches your keywords and ads to relevant content—which is why it's called the *content network*.

How are your keywords and ads matched to the content on millions of website pages that display Google advertisements? First, Google reviews the page content and determines its theme. Google next reviews your keyword lists and determines their themes. Google then tries to match website content and keyword groups with similar themes. Figure 2.5 gives you a rough idea of how Google may determine the theme for three different keyword groups.

After the Google content-matching algorithm has determined a theme for an ad group, it places the ad group's ads on pages within the content network whose content matches that theme. For example, in Figure 2.6 the page contains content about book publishing and book promotion, and the content of the ads is also about book publishing.

Figure 2.5 How Google determines themes for keyword groups

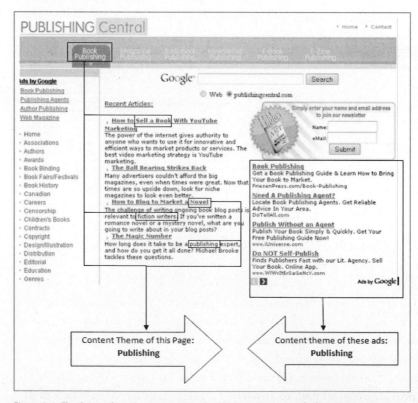

Figure 2.6 The theme of a web page's content should be parallel to the ads that appear on the page.

The intention of a user who is interacting with ads they encounter on websites is extremely different from the intention of a user who is looking at a SERP. When someone types a query into the search engine, that person is actively looking for information, a product, or a service. The user is in the mindset of taking action. Someone who is viewing an article on a web page isn't actively looking for anything—they're already reading the information they want to consume. However, this doesn't mean that the traffic on the content network is any less relevant or valid. You just need to take this into consideration when targeting this distribution network.

You are not restricted to text ads on the Google Content Network. You can also display banner ads. Back in the '90s, banner advertising was all the rage. However, these ad formats started to get a bad reputation because they were poorly targeted and of low quality, and it was difficult to measure their performance. Many advertisers spent a great deal of money without getting reliable results. This is no longer the case. With Google's AdWords system, you have a great deal of control over ad placement in their content network and can reliably measure your results. This book will show you how you can reach new audiences effectively and profitably with banner ads. When creating your PPC strategy, we highly recommend that you include the Google Content Network. According to Google, their content network reaches over 80 percent of unique Internet users around the world. This means that there are billions of ad impressions to be had here. You can greatly increase your click volume by creating a highly targeted content network campaign.

We'll go into more detail on how to create a successful content network strategy later. The purpose of this chapter is to get you familiar with the basics of this distribution network.

After the Click

Everything in this chapter has related to getting the click: how you can get your ads to appear on the SERPs or the content network so searchers and readers can see them and come to your website. It may seem like you have to jump through a lot of hoops to appease the search engines with relevant keywords and ads as well as inspire searchers to actually click on your ads, and all the while you're risking hard dollars to keep an edge over your competitors. But all of that is only the beginning, because a click is nothing more than that: a click (even if it's a click you've paid for!).

Ultimately, it is what you do with visitors *after* the click that makes you money. Think of your PPC campaign as answering a user's question, providing a solution, or completing their thought. The most effective PPC campaigns drive visitors to pages that are very closely aligned with the ads they just clicked. The path from the search query, to the PPC advertisement, to the landing page, to the landing-page conversion action should be a cohesive, fluid movement. Figure 2.7 illustrates how your PPC ad and landing page should provide a logical path to answering a user's question or solving a need.

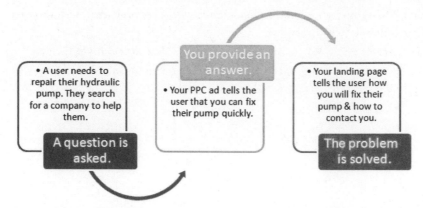

Figure 2.7 The funnel from search query to landing page should be fluid and logical.

If your PPC campaign functions in this way, you'll provide a great user experience by displaying relevant information to queries. And just in case we haven't driven the point home yet: Helping the search engine provide a great user experience will make you more appealing to the search engine and the user. Everyone wins!

This idea of completing a user's thought also applies to the content network. The user may not have been searching for your ad directly but rather may have been viewing content related to your product or service, and you still need to provide the user relevant information. Your landing page should complete the thought process carried over from the content the user was viewing. For example, if someone was reading an article about publishing, and your PPC ad says that they can get published easily with your company, then your landing page should back up this claim and provide a contact form.

Most PPC campaigns we have worked on measure the return on the clicks that we pay for and correlate the cost of the site traffic to some other asset. The simplest such asset is a completed sale. Do we know how much we made from the sale? Almost certainly. Do we know our allowable CPA? Do we know how much we paid for the clicks that brought us this site visitor? Is the value of our now-customer any amount less than the cost of those clicks plus the costs associated with assembling and then delivering a product or service to them? If the answer is yes, we made money! And that's the goal.

Your website doesn't need to be e-commerce–based, where you sell products directly on your website. Other sites focus on their contact form in order to collect leads that can be followed up on by a sales team. Regardless of what your business objectives may be, the point is that you need the user to take a measurable action on your website. And more than that, you want to measure how good you are at it—just like everything else.

In Chapter 6, "Month 3—Design Effective Landing Pages," we go into more detail on how to create a successful post-click strategy. For now, just keep in mind that the success of your PPC campaign hinges on your landing page or website. Getting visitors to your page is only the beginning.

You've learned a lot about how search engines work. Now you can get the strategic foundation of your winning PPC campaign started, which is what you'll do in Chapter 3, "Core PPC Skills and Objectives."

Core PPC Skills and Objectives

Before plunging in to fire up your PPC advertising campaigns, it's worthwhile to strengthen your understanding of key advertising skills and to set some initial objectives for your campaigns. This chapter describes resources that will help you understand the fundamentals of direct-response advertisers, identify the set of target customers and segment them into smaller groups, clarify the stages that a site visitor goes through before becoming a customer, and give you a framework for setting campaign objectives and expectations.

Chapter Contents

Learn Scientific Advertising and Ad Copywriting

Know Thy Customer

What's Your PPC Strategy?

Learn Scientific Advertising and Ad Copywriting

Claude Hopkins' *Scientific Advertising* provides a solid backdrop for understanding the importance of advertising testing and refinement. But it doesn't include detailed, step-by-step instructions for setting up and conducting advertising tests, interpreting the results, and refining advertising efforts accordingly.

Subsequent chapters teach you how to test ad copy, landing pages, and more. You'll give yourself a strong advantage if you take the time to learn more about advertising and/or marketing testing. Here are two excellent resources:

- *Testing, Testing 1, 2, 3: Raise More Money with Direct Mail Tests* by Mal Warwick (Jossey-Bass, 2003)—Systematic testing of copy, envelopes, lists, and so on

- *Always Be Testing: The Complete Guide to Google Website Optimizer* by Bryan Eisenberg and John Quarto-vonTivadar (Sybex, 2008)—*Very* detailed advice and instructions on optimizing websites through testing, including more than 250 specific testing ideas

Want to prepare yourself even better for creating your first PPC campaigns? Read a book or two about promotional writing, oriented toward direct-response advertising. One such resource is the free *Classified Ad Secrets* e-book, which you can download from http://twurl.nl/z5oy4d.

This little gem starts out with a premise that maps very well to PPC advertising: *The ad isn't capable of selling anything.* The purpose of a well-crafted ad is to evoke the following two responses in the reader:

1. The ad seems to relate to a need or desire I have.

2. I should take action to see whether #1 is true or false.

The book's author wisely advises the neophyte advertiser to encourage the ad reader to request information. He describes a method for including a clever call to action in the classified ad: a phone number that's answered by an answering machine that rattles off the benefits of whatever is being sold.

Likewise, the PPC advertiser really just wants the reader to take the next necessary step on the path toward buying or converting: click through to the website. The page that the PPC "clicker" first sees, called the *landing page*, should underscore the benefits of the product or service offered (covered in detail in Chapter 6, "Month 3—Design Effective Landing Pages").

You can skip through the pages describing order forms, mailing lists, and postage considerations (unless you want to appreciate some of the glimpses of "the good old days" of direct-response advertising). But start to pay closer attention when you get to the section titled "How to Write Irresistible Ad Copy." Try not to be offended by the paragraph that reads as follows:

> *Classified ad copy writing is a very exacting craft, not an art in the way that display advertising is. It involves following a few simple guidelines and requires little skill. That's why daily newspapers hire school and college students to take orders—and write—for their classified section over the telephone.*

Although writing good direct-response or PPC advertisements is largely a matter of learning guidelines and best practices, it's a skill that gets better with practice and the accumulation of good data, as discussed in more detail in Chapter 5, "Month 2—Create Great PPC Ads," and Chapter 10, "Month 7—Test Ads Using Advanced Techniques."

Continue to skim *Classified Ad Secrets,* paying extra attention to suggestions for words that attract attention and motivate. You'll also see the AIDA model, which stands for the following:

Attraction

Interest

Desire

Action

This concept will be revisited in Chapters 5 and 6 as part of the ad copywriting and landing page design discussions.

Skim the rest of the book for its wealth of examples, powerful words and phrases, as well as advice on motivating readers. Then you can put the book away for consultation after you read Chapter 5 regarding PPC ad copywriting.

Here are a couple of other good resources that can help you prepare for the lessons and concepts to come:

- *All You Need is a Good Idea!: How to Create Marketing Messages that Actually Get Results* by Jay H. Heyman (Wiley, 2008)—Describes how to create powerful marketing and advertising messages
- *The Adweek Copywriting Handbook: The Ultimate Guide to Writing Powerful Advertising and Marketing Copy from One of America's Top Copywriters* by Joseph Sugarman (Wiley, 2006)—Guidelines and expert advice on what it takes to write copy that will entice, motivate, and move customers to buy

Know Thy Customer

How well do you *really* know your customers? In order to effectively advertise with the goal of bringing in more customers, it's important for your company or organization to collect and record everything you know about your customers—the ones you've been selling to as well as ones you want to target for future sales.

It may surprise you to find that it's difficult to describe a customer set as one homogenous group. That's because most customer sets can (and should) be broken down into smaller subgroups (often referred to as *customer segments*), each with different and distinct characteristics.

The good news is that describing these subgroups will help your company or organization to create marketing and/or advertising messages with laser precision. Understanding customer differences and needs can also help serve existing customers more effectively—and what company couldn't use an increase in customer satisfaction?

In any event, you'll find that the following exercise is the perfect preparation for beginning your PPC campaign by defining personas as described in Chapter 4, "Month 1—Research Keywords and Establish Campaign Structure."

Ask the Right Questions

Step 1 in "Know Thy Customer:" Gather your organization's marketing people into one room—and anyone else who should logically contribute. If your company is small enough, include representatives from the Sales department, and even the president or CEO. If your company is sufficiently marketing-savvy, this should be a short meeting. If it turns out to be a long one, you'll likely emerge from the meeting with a better understanding of the drivers of your company's success—which will have benefits far beyond your PPC advertising campaigns.

Then discuss and answer the following questions:

- Where are your customers located? Are they clustered in particular countries or cities? (You'll need to know this in order to properly use a powerful PPC feature called *geotargeting*.)

- What are the ages and genders of your customers? (The answers for this, as well as the next four questions, will certainly influence the wording you use for ads and landing pages, and equip you to use the demographic-targeting capabilities of some PPC services.)

- What educational level(s) have your customers attained?

- What range(s) of income do your customers earn?

- What are your customers' common occupations? Are they students, employed part-time, employed full-time, or retired?

- Are your customers married, unmarried, or divorced? Are there children in the household?
- What kind of buying behavior do your customers exhibit? Do they regularly conduct research regarding prospective purchases? Do they then buy offline or online? If the latter, how many times do they visit the site before they buy, and over how long a time? (Knowing this will help you decide what search terms potential customers will be using, and hence which keywords you should include in PPC ad groups.)

If your company is in the business-to-business (B2B) space, you should answer the following additional questions:

- What company sizes are you targeting?
- Who is the final decision maker? What is that person's level in the organization?
- How long is the typical sales cycle?
- Will the customers purchase online, or do they require telephone and/or face-to-face contact?

Answers to all of these questions should be understood and shared with anyone who's involved in creating, managing, and optimizing the organization's PPC campaigns. You'll find they will equip you to pick the right keywords, write better ads, design better landing pages, and find the perfect sites for displaying ads to be seen by your target customer segments.

How Do Potential Customers Search?

One critical characteristic of your target customer segments is how they use search engines. Many people, whether they're shopping for a sleeping bag or looking for a small aircraft for their company, will go through several steps known as the *buying cycle*.

Most people take several steps in advance of making a purchase decision, downloading a white paper or trial software, or filling out and submitting a form asking for a salesperson to contact them. These steps can take just a few minutes, an entire day, or in the case of complicated, technical B2B products and services, several weeks or months.

These steps can be broken down into the following three categories:

1. Interest
2. Research
3. Conversion

Figures 3.1 and 3.2 show searches used in the Interest and Conversion phases. Let's look more closely at each step.

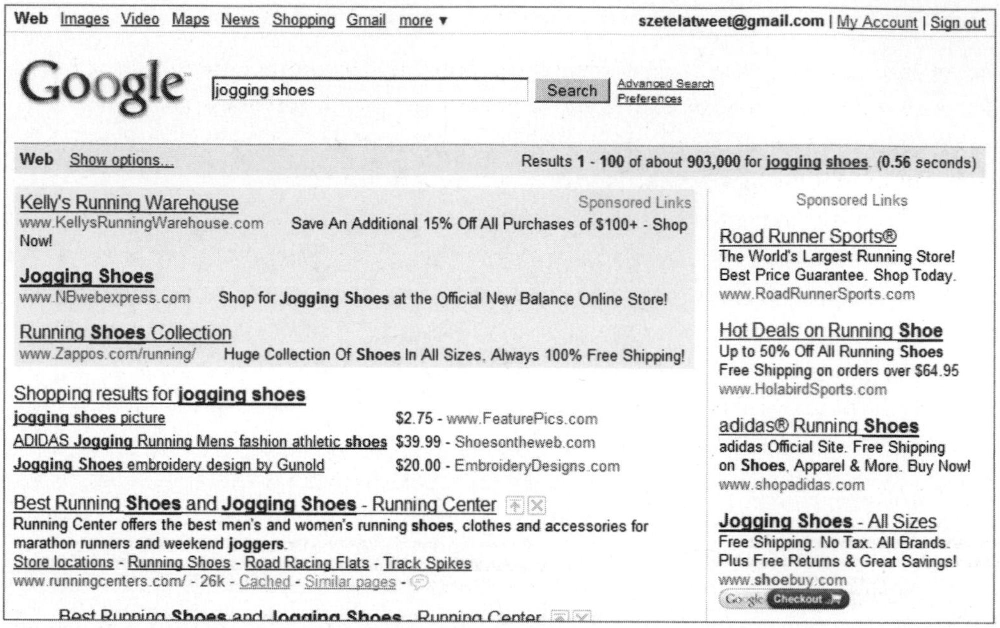

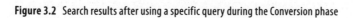

Figure 3.1 Search results after using a broad query during the Interest phase

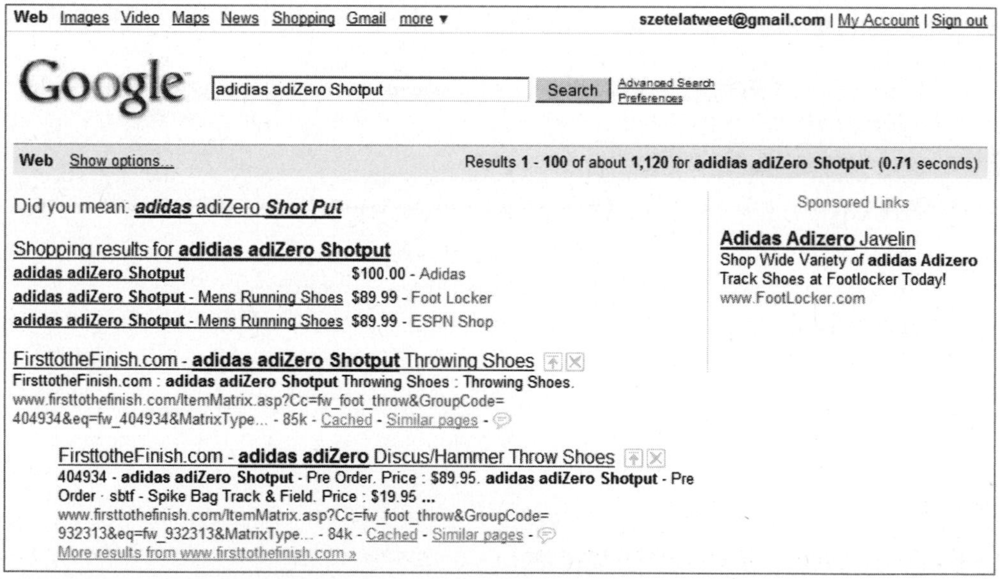

Figure 3.2 Search results after using a specific query during the Conversion phase

Interest

During the Interest phase of the buying cycle, potential customers express a broad need or desire. They may be uncertain about whether their search activity is going to culminate in a purchase or other conversion action. They tend to use generalized search terms, often expressing their needs and/or desires as a question.

Though searchers may visit several sites during this phase, it's unusual for them to take the conversion action at this early stage. Their primary objective is to see whether solutions (products or services) exist that might satisfy their needs and/or desires. They're probably not looking too closely at prices and feature lists quite yet—this is something they'll start to do in earnest when they enter the next phase.

Though site visits don't often culminate in conversions during the Interest phase, these visits are valuable because visitors are mentally registering their impressions of the sites in terms of professionalism, relative pertinence to their needs and/or desires, and so on. Chapter 9, "Month 6—Optimize Your Campaign," points out that such early visits have value because they assist the eventual sale, and hence there is an implicit (and sometimes measurable) return on investment (ROI) related to any costs incurred by the site owner that persuade the visitor to come to the website during this phase.

Table 3.1 lists some products and industries along with search terms that might be used for them during the Interest phase.

▶ **Table 3.1** Search Queries Used during the Interest Phase of the Buying Cycle

Industry	Search Query
Travel	Best hiking vacations
Software	CRM packages for small businesses
Gifts	Ideas for 20th wedding anniversary gift
Financial services	Reduce credit card charges
Industrial storage	Warehouses in Montana
Books	Historical mysteries
Real estate	San Francisco housing prices

Research

Potential customers pass from the Interest to the Research phases after they have made the decision that they intend to take action—to make a purchase or ask for a quote, for example. The search terms they use are more-specific versions of the queries used in the Interest phase.

Although it's somewhat more likely that Research-phase site visitors will convert than those in the Interest phase, many people are still not ready to take action during the Research phase. Though they've decided that they eventually *will* take action, it's important that they narrow their options by comparing prices, feature sets, or vendors.

Table 3.2 lists potential search queries used during the Research phase.

▶ **Table 3.2** Search Queries Used during the Research Phase of the Buying Cycle

Industry	Search Query
Travel	Guided hiking in Glacier Park
Software	Contact management software under $1,000
Gifts	Buy china set online
Financial services	Debt settlement services
Industrial storage	Refrigerated storage in Bozeman
Books	Archeological mysteries
Real estate	Victorians for sale in Russian Hill

Conversion

Not surprisingly, the Conversion phase describes the period during which people decide to take the conversion action. They may have already visited the site that best matches their needs, and they remember the domain name or something specific and distinctive about the site. Or they may still be narrowing the field but deciding among a small number of vendors.

Some typical Conversion phase search queries are listed in Table 3.3.

▶ **Table 3.3** Search Queries Used during the Research Phase of the Buying Cycle

Industry	Search Query
Travel	Glacier Gateway Tours
Software	salesforce
Gifts	Cyber Attic
Financial services	Everest debt
Industrial storage	Diamondstatewarehouse.com
Books	Templar legacy berry
Real estate	Russian Hill values

Such queries would seem to be the most valuable in that they often result in a site visit during which a conversion takes place. Conventional wisdom is for advertisers to pay top price for a click on an ad that is displayed as a result of a Conversion phase search query. Although this logic is sound, it may be less evident that search terms used by people who are closer to the beginning of the buying cycle should be valued highly as well, because without them, many eventual customers would never have become aware of sites that match their needs. Chapter 4 explores this in more detail during its discussion of PPC bidding strategies.

What If There's No Search?

Sometimes a company sells a product for which there is little or no explicit demand. Search volume is very low simply because people don't perceive a need or desire for the product or service. Examples of such products and services include the following:

- Complex, technical solutions or services
- Fundraising by a nonprofit organization (few people search for opportunities to make donations)
- New inventions that solve a problem or fulfill a need, where people are unaware that such a solution exists (for example, those "As Seen on TV" inventions)
- Entertainment (such as books, music, or movies) from little-known or unknown sources

Fortunately, there are ways that such advertisers can still drive traffic to their websites and persuade visitors to convert. First, let's distinguish between two types of advertising: demand fulfillment and demand generation.

Demand fulfillment advertising rightfully assumes that people are actively seeking the product or service being advertised. Search PPC is an obvious example, as are the Yellow Pages (both the paper and online versions). When people consult the latter, they already have a need or desire clearly in mind, and they are merely narrowing the range of possible solutions.

Demand generation advertising assumes no prior need or desire. It's the advertiser's job to interrupt some normal flow—such as a TV show being watched or a magazine being read—with a message that quickly performs the following two functions:

- It interrupts the normal flow, preferably in a sensitive, unobtrusive way.
- It persuades the reader or viewer that there's a benefit to taking an action, such as visiting a storefront, ordering online, and so on.

Referring back to the buying cycle, in demand generation advertising, the target customer is not in any of the phases of the cycle. It's the job of demand generation advertiser to nudge or push the reader or viewer into the cycle, actively engaged and considering the possibility of a purchase or other conversion action.

PPC contextual advertising is ideal for demand generation, as you'll see in Chapter 5.

What's Your PPC Strategy?

There's one more question to answer before you plunge into actually advertising: What do you want to accomplish with your PPC campaigns?

To many, the answer will seem simple: "More-profitable sales!" But at any given time, an organization can have objectives that change in priority, and it's important to acknowledge these when setting performance expectations.

Companies and organizations are usually focused on one of the following business objectives more so than the others:

Sales volume: Growing revenue.

Profitability: Wider profit margins.

Expense control: Limiting or diminishing expenses.

Market share: Capturing a larger portion of the target market. Unless the market is growing quickly, this usually requires increasing sales volume by taking business away from competitors.

If you're a sole proprietor, you can probably state your company's priorities quickly and with conviction. If you're part of a bigger organization, whether you're the owner, CEO, or part of the marketing team, you may be surprised at how many different opinions you get when you ask what the organization's top objectives should be.

It's important to form consensus around the organization's top objectives, because the strategies for your PPC advertising efforts will depend heavily on them.

For example, if the organization's chief objective is to capture more market share, that implies a strategy that closely examines competitor PPC activities, and making sure you are reaching at least the same prospective customers—preferably extending your reach far beyond your competitors'. Chapter 4 will show you how to do this.

If, on the other hand, your organization is focused on profitability, it makes sense to restrict your campaign's scope to advertise just the products that are most profitable, and narrowing your campaign's scope to those customers who are close to the end of the buying cycle.

A similar strategy would be appropriate for organizations that are primarily concerned with cutting costs. They would want to focus more on the "sure bets" rather than devote the advertising budget to more-speculative keywords and sites.

Here's another important decision point for an organization: How quickly does the organization want to pass from the testing phase of the new PPC campaign to the ramp phase? As discussed in more detail in Chapter 4, every new PPC campaign goes through an initial phase during which nearly every aspect of the campaign is being tested: keywords, ad copy, bid prices, landing pages, shopping processes, and so forth. After enough data has accumulated to make the first round of improvements to the campaign, the advertiser can feel more confident that additional advertising dollars spent, along with a steady program of further testing and refinement, will deliver a growing stream of conversions at an acceptable cost—a period we call the *ramp phase*.

Some companies want or need to adopt a very prudent approach. They can't afford to spend advertising dollars without reasonable assurance that there will be an acceptable return on the advertising investment as early as possible.

Other advertisers want to hit the ground running—to immediately start chipping away at competitor market share, for example. They are willing to spend "test money" to accelerate the test phase and get to the ramp phase more quickly.

Now take a minute to record your business objectives. To do this, you can use a Microsoft Word document helpfully provided by the authors of *Search Engine Optimization: An Hour a Day, 2nd Edition* (Sybex, 2008). You can download this worksheet at no charge from http://is.gd/SZVq.

The worksheet has room at the top for you to record your business objectives. If your organization has more than one objective, such as market share and profitability, list both—with the most important one ranked first. The second section is a worksheet that was created to let site owners begin identifying the elements of their site that may require work to help the site rank highly in the search engine listings. Although such work, called search engine optimization (SEO), is not the focus of this book, go ahead and complete the Website Features section of the worksheet. That will help you visualize and enumerate your site's conversion goals in the Conversions column of the worksheet.

Most sites have one primary conversion goal, and one or more secondary goals. For example, the primary goal of an e-commerce site might be to generate revenue through sales. Secondary goals might be to collect subscribers to a newsletter or to have visitors register for a discussion forum.

Likewise, the primary goal of a B2B site might be to collect sales leads via a submitted form, while its secondary goal might be to persuade visitors to download one or more white papers.

You'll see in future chapters that this exercise is crucial in determining the effectiveness of your PPC campaigns. We'll describe how to decide on a value for each conversion type, which may prove surprisingly difficult for nonrevenue objectives. We'll also describe how to set up Google AdWords and Google Analytics conversion tracking so you'll always know the number and value of the conversions being generated by your PPC campaigns.

In an organization of any size, it's critical to prioritize company (and therefore ad campaign) objectives, and set reasonable expectations for how quickly acceptable results can be expected. The extra time you spend sorting these out, and if necessary getting a consensus around objectives and expectations, the clearer your path will be and the easier to choose from among the different strategies presented in the coming chapters.

Month 1—Research Keywords and Establish Campaign Structure

This chapter describes how to structure your keywords into campaigns and ad groups. The account creation method presented in this chapter will help you maximize your click-through rate (CTR) and minimize how much you are charged per click, while hopefully maximizing your volume of profitable impressions, clicks, and actions.

A well-structured campaign is essential for a successful pay-per-click (PPC) initiative. How you structure the contents of your PPC campaign is just as important as the keywords you're targeting and the messaging you highlight in your ads.

Chapter Contents
Week 1: Research keywords
Week 2: Create Your Campaign Structure
Week 3: Adjust Campaign Settings
Week 4: Use Conversion Tracking and set Click Pricing

Week 1: Research Keywords

Keyword research is one of the most important tasks in the discipline of PPC marketing. The search queries that match keywords give you a window into the minds of your prospective customers, and the right combination of words can tell you a lot about a prospect's intent and background. By carefully choosing and organizing your keywords, you can put relevant ads and content in front of the right people at the right time—people who will hopefully become your customers.

Monday: Defining Personas

Assembling a comprehensive keyword list is one of the most important tasks in creating successful PPC campaigns. Your objective is to anticipate every possible way that a prospective customer could search for your product or service.

Your target audience is composed of people with varying backgrounds, living in different geographical regions, who frequently search for the same product in different ways. Knowing this, your target market can be broken down into subgroups whose shared attributes differ from one another. Subgroups can differ in age, location, salary level, and the amount of time the individuals spend doing research before making a buying decision.

We recommend thinking of these subgroups as *personas* or *people types* that encompass a set of common attributes. After you have defined some personas, you can more easily imagine the keywords and ad copy to which each group would respond best.

For example, imagine you are advertising athletic shoes. Your online store sells running shoes, cross-trainers, and high-tops, produced by dozens of different manufacturers under many different brands. You may view your business in a narrow way; for example, you sell running shoes, so that's how your customers will express their need in a search query. But in fact, potential customers will likely use a variety of search terms to express their needs. Here is a list of individuals who may be looking for your athletic shoes:

- An athletic shoe enthusiast who read about the upcoming shoe releases months in advance in glossy magazines received in the mail might search for specific shoes by brand, name, and model with fanatical precision.

- A young woman who wants to add shoes to her outfit might use a search query in which the most important element is *color* (she really, *really* needs a pink pair).

- A young man who is looking for athletic shoes (great!), but uses the search term *sneakers* because that's what they're called in his area of the country.

- A woman who uses the search term *tennis shoes*, even though she is planning to equip her grandchildren for basketball season.

- An overachieving doctor who runs marathons and is also an ideal customer for your website, but he uses search terms that include the word *trainers* or *cross-trainers*.

In this example, it may seem like we're simply talking about synonyms. And of course, synonyms, like misspellings, represent a large chunk of our potential keywords. But the value of defining personas goes far beyond just including in your ad groups many different keywords that all mean the same thing. Each of the scenarios in the preceding list gives you a window into the mind of a person who may be searching for your products in a different way.

Defining personas can help you envision specific attributes of your typical buyers and provide a structure by which you can effectively organize keyword lists, ads, and landing pages (all elements of the PPC advertising process that you will examine in greater detail in later chapters). In this chapter, you'll target the following three personas:

The hard-core runner: This person has been running for years and knows athletic gear very well. Cost for the right product isn't much of a concern. We'll call this runner *Jackie*.

The casual runner: This individual runs at the gym a couple of times per week. Perhaps he runs the occasional 5K. He knows which shoes he likes, but isn't an expert. This person doesn't want to pay a lot but does want a quality product. We'll call this runner *Steve*.

The beginning runner: This individual is just starting to become interested in running. He doesn't know which shoes and athletic gear he needs. This person isn't sure what the typical price is for the right shoe. We'll call this runner *Jesse*.

There certainly could be other personas you could develop by reviewing the website and talking with your sales teams, but for now, you'll focus on just these three personas. Keep them in mind as you expand your keyword list, and you'll revisit these personas on Thursday.

Tuesday: Using Keyword Research Tools

The first step in building your keyword list is to review your marketing materials. This can include your website, brochures, sales letters, and any other documents that you use to describe and sell your products or services. Start your list by choosing words and phrases from these documents that you think prospective customers would use in search queries during their research to find products and services like the ones your company offers.

During the rest of this week, we'll discuss how to add pertinent keywords to this initial list.

There are many keyword research tools available, either as stand-alone software packages or as services accessed online. If you run a search query on Google for the term *ppc keyword tool*, you'll get numerous results. Some of these tools are free, while others must be paid for on either a one-time or a subscription basis. To get you started with your PPC keyword research, we're going to introduce you to our favorite free tools.

Google Keyword Tool

Google provides several useful keyword research tools. The first and most important is the simply named *Google Keyword tool*, which you can find here:

`https://adwords.google.com/select/KeywordToolExternal`

As Figure 4.1 illustrates, Google's Keyword tool gives you two ways to generate lists of keywords; it can scan a website for potential keywords or suggest them based on your seed keyword ideas.

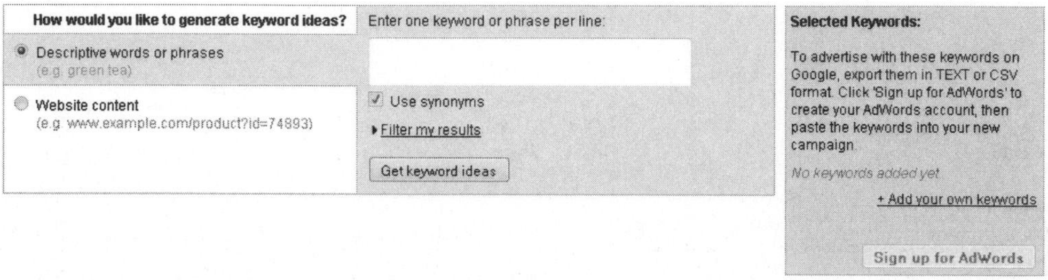

Figure 4.1 Google's Keyword tool is one of the most popular and important keyword research tools.

First, we'll explore the Descriptive Words or Phrases option by using *guitars* as the seed keyword.

Google's tool returned everything from *guitars* (the seed term), to different guitar types such as *electric guitars* and *acoustic guitars*, to a variety of different brands such as *Yamaha guitars* and *Gibson guitars*, to *used guitars*, *guitars for sale*, and about 140 other options. Not only does the Keyword tool provide keyword ideas, but it also shows projected advertiser competition for each suggested keyword, as well as the search volume (how popular a keyword might be), as shown in Figure 4.2.

A second way to use the Google Keyword tool is to enter a web page URL to find keywords related to the content of the page. Figure 4.3 shows the results of a search we conducted for `www.specialteas.com`, a company that sells high-quality, organic teas.

As you can see in the figure, the Keyword tool located root, or seed, keywords, and then expanded on them with more-detailed terms. The root keywords in this example are *loose leaf tea*, *green tea*, and *tea cups*.

We know it may seem significant when Google itself is telling you via its tool what keywords to include based on *your site*, but as with any of the tools, you should not always slavishly follow the suggestions just because Google made them. Because this Keyword tool provides so many results, you need to determine which terms are relevant for your campaign, which terms are likely to be used by people searching for your offerings, and which terms have the highest potential for a great return on investment (ROI).

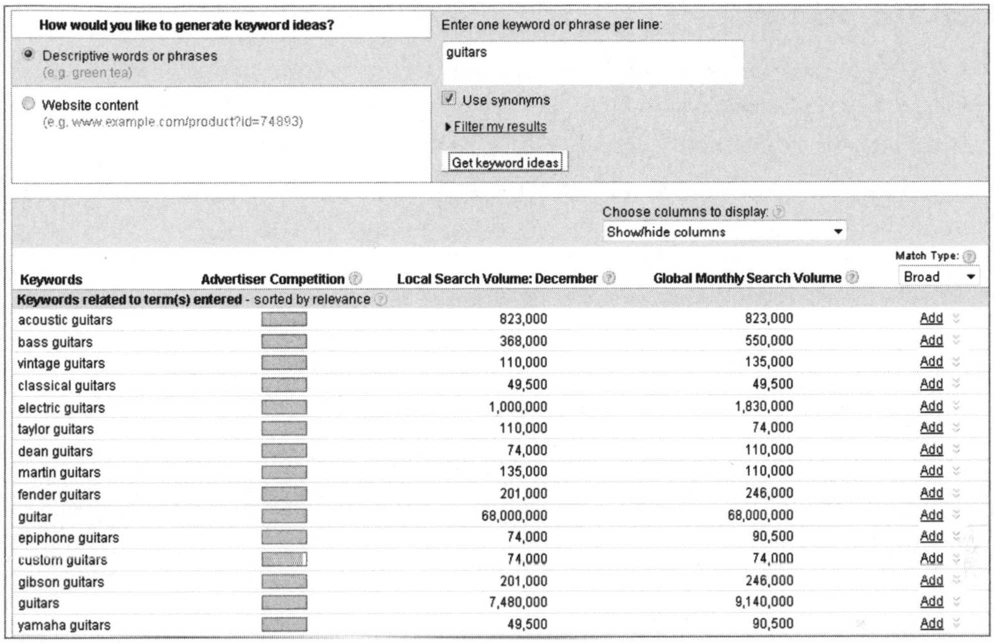

How would you like to generate keyword ideas?

- Descriptive words or phrases (e.g. green tea)
- Website content (e.g. www.example.com/product?id=74893)

Enter one keyword or phrase per line: guitars

Use synonyms

Filter my results

Get keyword ideas

Choose columns to display: Show/hide columns

Match Type: Broad

Keywords	Advertiser Competition	Local Search Volume: December	Global Monthly Search Volume	
Keywords related to term(s) entered - sorted by relevance				
acoustic guitars		823,000	823,000	Add
bass guitars		368,000	550,000	Add
vintage guitars		110,000	135,000	Add
classical guitars		49,500	49,500	Add
electric guitars		1,000,000	1,830,000	Add
taylor guitars		110,000	74,000	Add
dean guitars		74,000	110,000	Add
martin guitars		135,000	110,000	Add
fender guitars		201,000	246,000	Add
guitar		68,000,000	68,000,000	Add
epiphone guitars		74,000	90,500	Add
custom guitars		74,000	74,000	Add
gibson guitars		201,000	246,000	Add
guitars		7,480,000	9,140,000	Add
yamaha guitars		49,500	90,500	Add

Figure 4.2 The Google Keyword tool displays keyword suggestions and indicates projected search volume and competition.

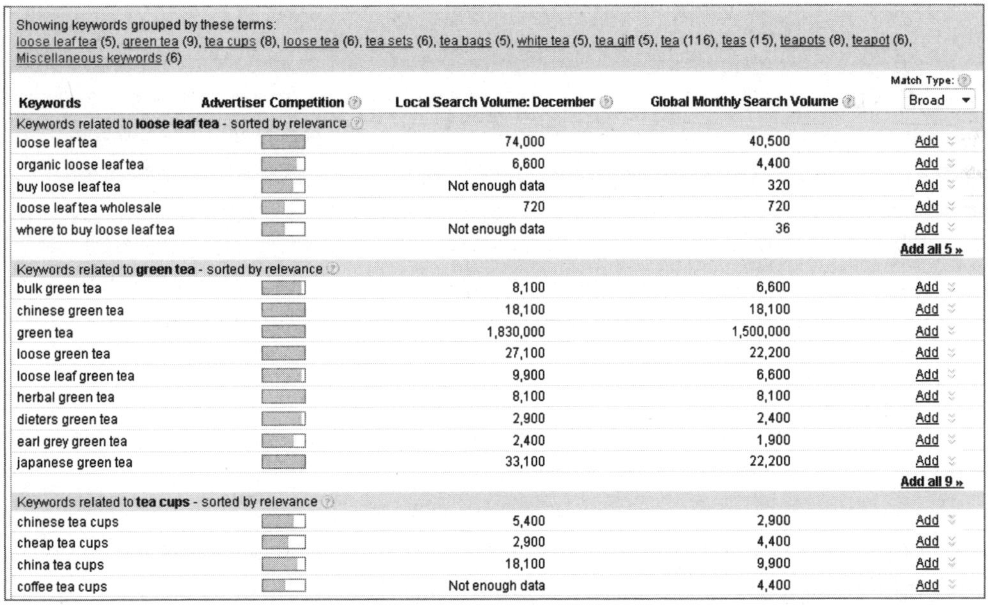

Showing keywords grouped by these terms:
loose leaf tea (5), green tea (9), tea cups (8), loose tea (6), tea sets (6), tea bags (5), white tea (5), tea gift (5), tea (116), teas (15), teapots (8), teapot (6), Miscellaneous keywords (6)

Match Type: Broad

Keywords	Advertiser Competition	Local Search Volume: December	Global Monthly Search Volume	
Keywords related to **loose leaf tea** - sorted by relevance				
loose leaf tea		74,000	40,500	Add
organic loose leaf tea		6,600	4,400	Add
buy loose leaf tea		Not enough data	320	Add
loose leaf tea wholesale		720	720	Add
where to buy loose leaf tea		Not enough data	36	Add
				Add all 5 »
Keywords related to **green tea** - sorted by relevance				
bulk green tea		8,100	6,600	Add
chinese green tea		18,100	18,100	Add
green tea		1,830,000	1,500,000	Add
loose green tea		27,100	22,200	Add
loose leaf green tea		9,900	6,600	Add
herbal green tea		8,100	8,100	Add
dieters green tea		2,900	2,400	Add
earl grey green tea		2,400	1,900	Add
japanese green tea		33,100	22,200	Add
				Add all 9 »
Keywords related to **tea cups** - sorted by relevance				
chinese tea cups		5,400	2,900	Add
cheap tea cups		2,900	4,400	Add
china tea cups		18,100	9,900	Add
coffee tea cups		Not enough data	4,400	Add

Figure 4.3 Using the Google Keyword tool to display keywords based on a tea product website offered numerous keyword suggestions.

Search Engine Autocomplete

Another source for discovering new keywords is the search query autocomplete function available on Google, Yahoo!, and Bing. As illustrated in Figure 4.4 on Google, the autocomplete function guides searchers as they start to type in search queries.

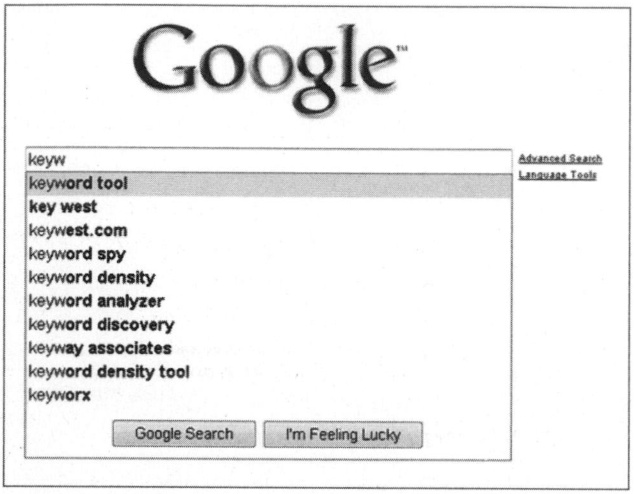

Figure 4.4 The autocomplete function on Google can suggest full queries based on the first word or two that the searcher types.

Let's say we want to find a keyword research tool. As you can see in Figure 4.4, as we started typing the word *keyword*, Google autocompleted the search phrase and displayed a number of options (headlined by their own *keyword tool*). The results are mixed—there are terms relevant to our search query, and there are other terms (such as the Key West–related terms) that aren't. After we finished typing *keyword*, the suggestions were more relevant, as shown in Figure 4.5.

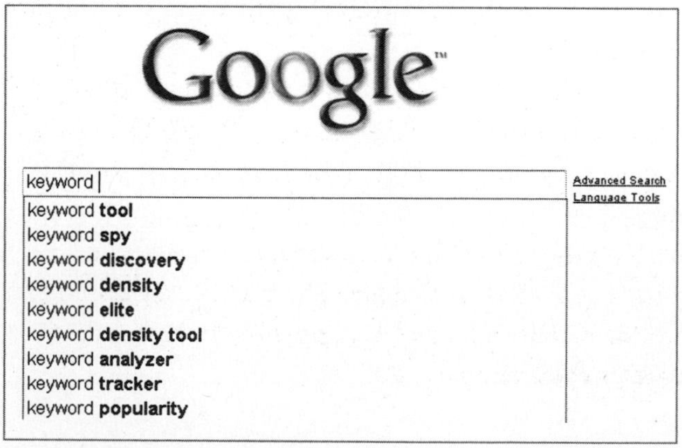

Figure 4.5 As you provide more information to Google, the autocomplete function provides more-detailed search term suggestions.

The autocomplete function often shows terms that aren't at all relevant to your products and services. Hence, the autocomplete function can be a useful source of negative keywords.

The autocomplete suggestions can be influenced by what you have searched for previously. Before using this tool extensively, you should clear your cookies and browsing history.

Google Search-Based Keyword Tool

Another helpful Google-provided tool is the Search-Based Keyword tool (`www.google.com/sktool/#`). This is a great tool that can tell you what search queries have been made on Google that are relevant to your AdWords account and your website. If you are logged in to your Google account, the tool will also suggest keywords that should be relevant to your website but are not currently being used in your AdWords campaigns. To use this tool, just enter your website address, as shown in Figure 4.6.

Website www.specialteas.com
For site list, click here

With words or phrases pots, pans

Tip: Use commas to separate terms or enter one per line.

Find keywords

Figure 4.6 Entering your website URL into the Search-Based Keyword tool

When you enter your website URL, you will be provided with keyword suggestions as well as landing page suggestions for these new terms. To provide results, the Search-Based Keyword tool reviews your current AdWords campaigns and the content of your website against actual Google searches.

Figure 4.7 shows the suggestions that this tool displays for the website `www.specialteas.com`, a company that sells organic, handmade teas. Within the results, you can see keyword and landing page suggestions on the right, and you can sort this information by category on the left.

This tool is very helpful, because the suggestions are actual terms that your potential customers have already searched on using Google. These aren't suggestions that *could* be relevant for your products or services and *may possibly* have search volume; these are search terms that are already being used.

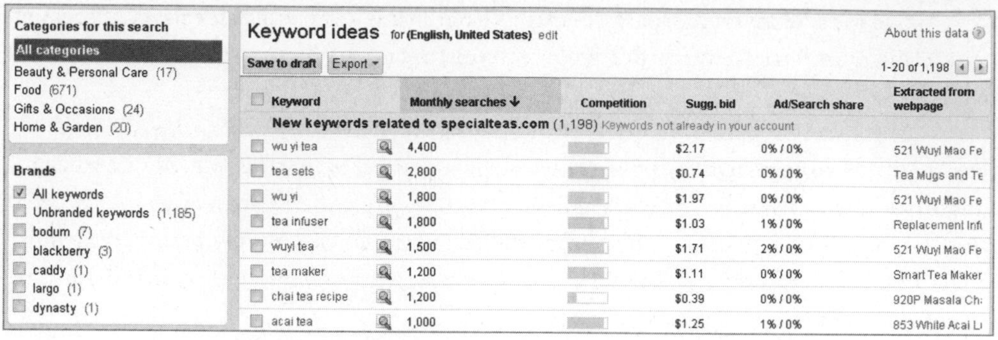

Figure 4.7 The Search-Based Keyword tool provided almost 1,200 keyword and landing page suggestions for the root website.

As we will allude to in the section "Friday: Researching Your Competitors' Keywords," you can research your competitors' websites as well by using this tool. Although Google won't let you *spy* specifically on other advertisers' campaigns and keyword groups, they might just show you 50 or so suggested keywords, complete with suggested bids. And as with the Keyword tool, you will certainly not want to use all the possible keywords that the Search-Based Keyword tool gives you. You will have to review the results, and choose which terms you think will work best for your campaign.

Google Wonder Wheel and Related Searches

Google's Wonder Wheel and Related Searches tools both provide related keyword suggestions, but their results are displayed quite differently. To access either Wonder Wheel or Related Searches, do a search by using Google. Under the Search box and above the first paid listings, there is a Show Options link. If you click that link, a sidebar appears and the link changes to Hide Options, as shown in Figure 4.8.

Figure 4.8 When you click Show Options on Google, you will see a sidebar with the Related Searches and Wonder Wheel tools listed below Standard View.

Google's Wonder Wheel is the most visual of the keyword tools we've discussed so far. Figure 4.9 shows the process of exploring Wonder Wheel to discover new relevant keyword sets.

In Figure 4.9, step 1 shows the original search query, *organic white tea*, and it is surrounded by suggested keyword terms such as *organic acai*, *silver needle white tea*, and *organic green tea*. For this example, we selected *organic oolong tea* (as indicated by the rectangle). In step 2 you can see that the term *organic oolong tea* is surrounded by suggested keyword groups. We selected *organic oolong tea bags*, and in step 3 you can see that we now have suggestions for this term.

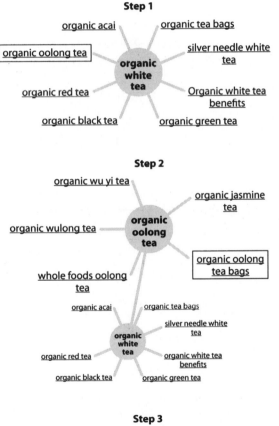

Figure 4.9 The step-by-step process of using Google Wonder Wheel to explore new keyword sets

The Related Searches function works in a similar fashion to the Wonder Wheel. As you conduct search queries on Google, you will be provided with additional relevant search queries. In Figure 4.10, you can see the suggestions provided for the term *organic white tea bags*.

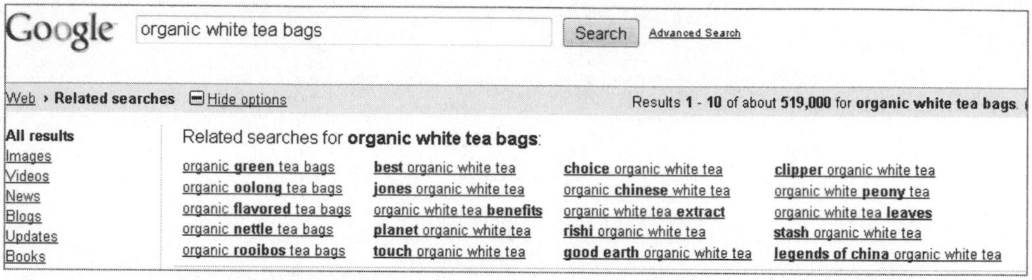

Figure 4.10 The Related Searches function in Google is not as visual as the Wonder Wheel, but it does provide you with a great number of related searches.

You can select any of the suggested keywords in Figure 4.10, and additional terms will be presented. This is another very helpful tool for expanding your keyword list. As with any keyword tool, a large list of keywords may be suggested, but it's up to you to decide which terms are most relevant for your campaign.

SEO Book Keywords

We also like the keyword research tools provided by SEO Book (www.seobook.com). SEO Book is a site ostensibly dedicated to search engine optimization (SEO), but we have found many of their keyword-related tools superb for use in PPC campaigns. You can find these tools at http://tools.seobook.com/keyword-tools.

Of the tools on SEO Book, one of the most uniquely useful is the Misspelling Generator. We use the Misspelling Generator to build the root sections of our permutations and concatenations. For keywords with multiple root words, we often put individual words through the Misspelling Generator to create variations.

SEO Book's Keyword Typo Generator (http://tools.seobook.com/spelling/keywords-typos.cgi) can show you potential keyword misspellings and typographical errors in a few different ways: skipped letters, double letters, reversed letters, skipped spaces, missed keys, and inserted keywords. In Figure 4.11, we selected all of the typo categories, and the tool provided 320 misspelled keywords.

Another tool provided by SEO Book is the Keyword Suggestion tool (http://tools.seobook.com/keyword-tools/seobook). This tool is powered by a service called WordTracker. We like this tool because it centralizes many different tools and functions. In addition to the keywords provided by WordTracker, the SEO Book Keyword Suggestion tool gives daily search estimates for each of the major search engines (Google, Yahoo!, and Bing) and links to additional keyword research and trend information provided by Google and other services.

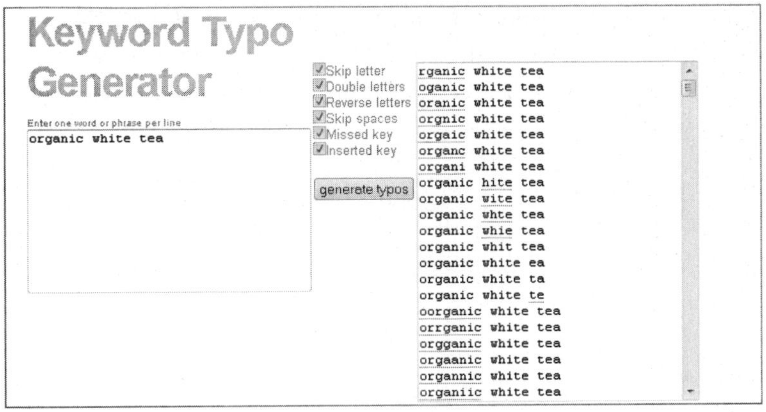

Figure 4.11 SEO Book's Keyword Typo Generator can act as a springboard for keyword generation.

One of those services is Keyword Discovery. The full version of Keyword Discovery is a paid subscription service, but when linked from SEO Book, Keyword Discovery will give you 100 suggestions for the linked-from term.

The Permutator

The Permutator tool by Boxer Software (www.boxersoftware.com/thepermutator.htm) can quickly create keywords containing "all possible combinations of your input keyword lists," as illustrated in Figure 4.12.

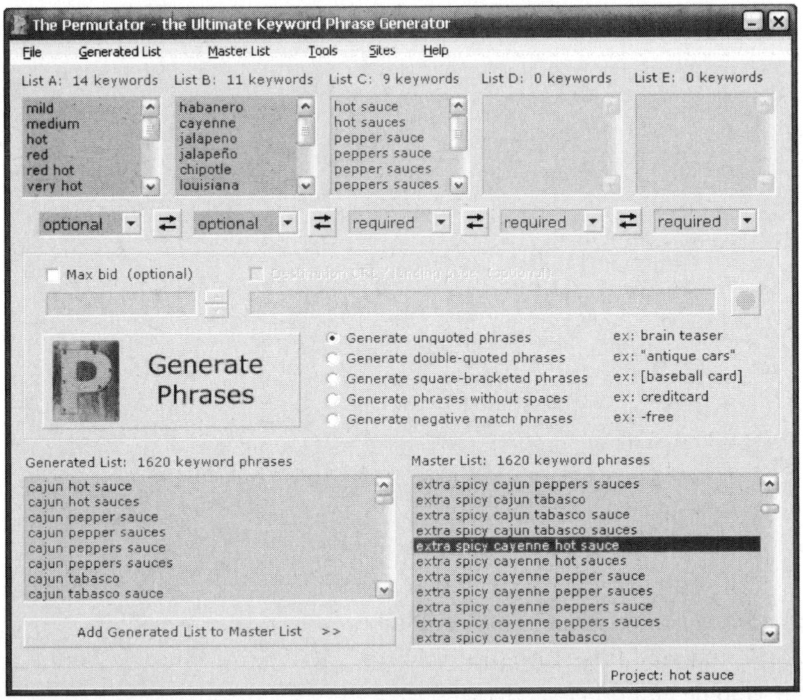

Figure 4.12 The Permutator can help you generate keyword combinations with low advertiser competition.

One advantage of using the keywords created by a tool like The Permutator versus those suggested by Google is that The Permutator is more likely to return keywords (based on your persona, URL variations, or other input elements) that are not being bid on by competitors. Clicks from these keywords will be lower priced because they are likely to be used by few competitors.

Wednesday: Using Your Best Keyword Source—Your Intuition, and Reports

Intuition and reports are two of your best sources for keywords. In fact, they may be *the* two best! *Intuition* gives you the framework for your keywords based on personas, creativity, and drawing from real-world sources of keyword information. *Reports* enable you to maximize your CTRs by serving up exactly the ads to exactly the people who are making very specific queries.

Let's return to the discussion of personas from Monday. These exercises are themselves intuition-based keyword-generation exercises. You try to imagine the words that your personas would use, and you bid on those words. Your work on these personas is a labor of imagination, but in a sense it's limited by what potential customers you can imagine or what kinds of people you know your existing customers to be. You can expand the breadth of your intuition—and your effective keywords—by bringing in more people's intuitions to help you create additional personas, or to imagine more ways those personas would search. This is an exercise that some professional search engine marketers perform with their clients. If you work at an agency with clients, it is something that you can try. If you work in-house at a business, try asking for help from your coworkers, especially those who are *not* marketers.

Present the product or service to your clients and coworkers. Tell them what it does. Now ask them to describe the product—what the product does, what problem the product solves, and what kind of a solution it is to what people—in three or more words. The words they give you don't have to make a lot of grammatical sense. It is probably best if they give you predominantly nouns and adjectives. Why? Because a lot of the time, *this is how people search.*

Your prospects won't always search by using beautifully structured language, anticipated modifiers, and so on. Sometimes they will query *fastest way to lose 10 lbs* and other times *lose weight fast* or perhaps *fast weight loss*. These queries express similar desires: The searcher wants information on how to lose weight *quickly*. Weight-loss advertisers may report queries for *lose weight in a week* or *lose weight in one week*, while numerous keyword tools will suggest they target *rapid weight loss*.

Note that the broad match, two-word keyword *weight loss* will theoretically match to all of these potential queries. Why, then, would you want to expand your keyword lists (at least potentially) to embrace the various phrasings? Here are some reasons:

Ad relevance and differentiation: Weight loss is a perfect example of a niche that has hundreds, if not thousands, of advertisers. All of these competitors are

selling weight-loss solutions, so if you want to speak to the person making one of the weight-loss-related search queries we previously mentioned, you want to speak to the *speed* with which you can guarantee that weight loss. Better yet, you can use that searcher's own language. If you describe losing weight within just one week to someone looking to lose weight in one week, you will typically have a higher CTR than if you were to present a generic weight-loss ad. Similarly, if someone wants to lose specifically 10 pounds, you can speak to that, and address the searcher's specific request. If your competitors are not going the extra distance in their ads, your ads will look that much more uniquely distinctive as well as appropriate.

Decreased costs: When you present more-relevant ads, you will generate higher CTR, and earn higher quality scores. With a higher quality score, your cost per click (CPC) can decrease at the same time your ad position improves.

Customized landing page copy: Just as customizing ad copy can increase CTRs, customizing landing page copy (especially benefit statements) can help increase the chances of conversion (to whatever post-click activity you are going for, such as sales, opt-ins, qualified leads, and so on), sometimes up to 100 percent.

In addition to expanding keywords via your (and your associates') intuitions, you can create more-precise ad groups via ideas from the Search Query Performance report or, alternately, Google Analytics if you have it set up.

One of the most powerful tools available from the AdWords interface is the Search Query Performance report. This report tells you exactly what the prospect *typed in* rather than only what keyword triggered the appearance of one of your ads. Here's how you request one:

1. Navigate to the Reports tab in AdWords and click Create a New Report.

2. Select Search Query Performance as the Report Type, as illustrated in Figure 4.13.

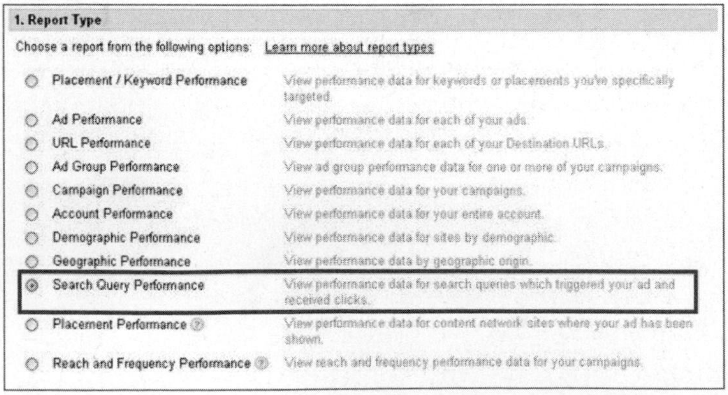

1. Report Type

Choose a report from the following options: Learn more about report types

○ Placement / Keyword Performance   View performance data for keywords or placements you've specifically targeted.

○ Ad Performance   View performance data for each of your ads.

○ URL Performance   View performance data for each of your Destination URLs.

○ Ad Group Performance   View ad group performance data for one or more of your campaigns.

○ Campaign Performance   View performance data for your campaigns.

○ Account Performance   View performance data for your entire account.

○ Demographic Performance   View performance data for sites by demographic.

○ Geographic Performance   View performance data by geographic origin.

◉ Search Query Performance   View performance data for search queries which triggered your ad and received clicks.

○ Placement Performance ⑦   View performance data for content network sites where your ad has been shown.

○ Reach and Frequency Performance ⑦   View reach and frequency performance data for your campaigns.

Figure 4.13 The Search Query Performance report is one of many reporting options.

Because of the nature of broad match and phrase match, your ads may be displaying for search queries that are not currently in your campaign. The Search Query Performance report will give you the actual search query that was matched to your keyword. With this information, you can add new keywords to your campaign, and the best thing is that these new keywords are already being searched on by your target audience.

The Search Query Performance report is also a superb source of negative-match keywords. You might not be able to imagine every variation of a keyword you *don't* want to match to at the beginning of the process, but after you've seen some unprofitable clicks, you will surely know which negative-match keywords to add.

Thursday: Permuting and Concatenating

For this exercise, we recommend that you use a Microsoft Excel document (or a document created by a different spreadsheet software package) to further build your keyword list. We suggest you start with six columns, labeled with two prefixes, two root words (usually product names, and generally both nouns), and two suffixes. By *prefix*, we mean terms that users may append to the beginning of your keyword to search for your product. By *suffix*, we mean terms that users may append to the end of your keywords to search for your product or service.

To get you started on the example, here's the initial keyword list for the Jesse persona (the beginner runner from Monday's lesson):

Prefix 1	Prefix 2	Root 1	Root 2	Suffix 1	Suffix 2
Buy	**Cheap**	Running	Shoe	Store	Online
Compare	**Inexpensive**	Jogging	Shoes	Shop	
	Beginner	Training	Shoe's		
	Beginners		Shoes'		
	Beginner's		Shos		
	Beginners'		Shoos		

Here is the initial keyword for the Steve persona (the casual runner):

Prefix 1	Prefix 2	Root 1	Root 2	Suffix 1	Suffix 2
Buy	**5K**	Running	Shoe	Store	Online
Compare	**Durable**	Jogging	Shoes	Shop	
		Training	Shoe's		
			Shoes'		
			Shos		
			Shoos		

And here is the initial keyword list for the Jackie persona (the hard-core runner):

Prefix 1	Prefix 2	Root 1	Root 2	Suffix 1	Suffix 2
Buy	**Collectable**	Running	Shoe	Store	Online
Compare	**Professional**	Jogging	Shoes	Shop	
	High-end	Training	Shoe's		
	Long-distance		Shoes'		
			Shos		
			Shoos		

Don't worry too much about filling every column, or whether you mix nouns, adjectives, and adverbs. There is no specific "right" way to conduct this exercise. At this point, it's more important that you use your intuition to capture as many words as possible.

Generally, nouns are the most important part of a keyword (you are usually selling the noun), and the prefixes and suffixes (especially ones pertaining to shopping and buying) are crucial to include in your keyword list, because they will match search queries of people who are probably close to making a buying decision.

We'll use Jesse's Excel sheet to walk you through the process of permutation. Take a look at the root words first: *running*, *jogging*, and *training*. Combine these terms with the Prefix 2 column. You can already see how your keyword list is growing. Here is a sample of the keywords you just created:

- *Cheap running shoe*
- *Inexpensive jogging shoe*
- *Beginner's training shoe*
- *Inexpensive running shoes*
- *Beginner's jogging shoes*

Hopefully, you can see how the process of permutation can transform a six-line table into more than 500 keywords. Later in this chapter, you'll learn how to split long keyword lists into small, efficient ad groups.

Friday: Researching Your Competitor's Keywords

Monitoring your competitor's PPC efforts is a good way to keep your edge. By conducting competitive research, you can discover new variations of your core keywords, or completely new ones. There are reasons to take on your competitors head-on for the same keywords, and there are other reasons to make flanking maneuvers in order to avoid direct competition. You can think of competitive research as both a defensive and an offensive tactic.

First, let's cover the defensive aspect of competitive research. There are going to be core keywords that will drive your business. Often there are several competitors who are also bidding on these core keywords. As we said earlier, you want to have bid on many variations of your core keywords, because your target audience is going to be made up of people from varying backgrounds and locations. Your competitors may have thought of terms that you've missed. Adding variations that you discover through competitive research can help *you* maintain a position as the toughest competitor.

Another goal of competitive research is to gain an understanding of your competitors' messaging. What are your competitors saying in their PPC ads? Here's what to look for:

Headline: Does their headline speak more clearly to your target audience? If so, why? If not, why not? Make a list of reasons why their headline is better than yours.

Ad copy: Are your competitors utilizing their limited ad copy more efficiently than you? What benefits and features do they highlight? Make a list of benefits you're not using in your ads.

Call to action: How are your competitors motivating users to click on their PPC ads? Are they offering special deals, free shipping, or free information? Write down reasons why their offers are more compelling than yours.

Some people say the best defense is a good offense. Researching your competitors' keywords will also help you think of new terms that neither you nor they are targeting. During this process, you're looking for holes in your competitors' keyword armor, so to speak. The motivation here isn't to go head-on against your competition; rather, you are looking for terms that all your competitors are missing.

Now that you understand how competitive research is both a defensive and an offensive tactic, how exactly do you find out which keywords your competitors are targeting? You will never know exactly which terms your competitors are bidding on. None of the search engines will provide you with this information, and there is no reputable third-party tool that will provide precise insight into your competitors' PPC keywords.

Competitive analysis shouldn't be the cornerstone of your keyword research. Instead, this process should supplement the construction of your keyword list and make it stronger. There are numerous tools that you could buy to provide good insight into your competitors' PPC activities, but to get you started, we'll describe a few ways that you can do such research on the cheap.

The Ad Preview Tool

By now, you should have a grasp on which keywords are mission critical for your campaign. To gauge the level of competition for each term, you should conduct a search query for each of these. This will give you an idea of how competitive your core terms are, and let you create a list of the competitors with the highest visibility.

To conduct these competitive search queries, you should use the Google Ad Preview tool (`https://adwords.google.com/select/AdTargetingPreviewTool`). By using this tool, you won't generate false impressions for yourself or your competitors (let's play fair!). Another reason to use the tool: Each subsequent search query on Google may cause a different set of ads to be displayed. Google does this because if you don't click any ads during a single search session, it's assumed you are not interested in the set of ads being displayed, and eventually no ads will be displayed for the queries you are making from your computer and your IP address. The Google Ad Preview tool helps you avoid these issues.

When you conduct a search query by using the Google Ad Preview tool, you are not actually conducting a live search on Google; you are getting a preview of what the SERP may look like for that particular keyword. Figure 4.14 shows the results of a search conducted using the term *organic white tea*.

Figure 4.14 The Google Ad Preview tool can give you an idea of how a SERP will appear for your core keywords.

As you can see in the figure, the Ad Preview tool enables you to view ads as if you were searching from a different location. You can select to view ads as they may appear in a different country, state, region, and city, or even a location defined by longitude and latitude coordinates. This way, you can see how search results look in locations other than your own. For example, if you live in Indiana but you want to see what ads are being displayed in California for a certain term, you can do this by using the Ad Preview tool.

Competitors' Website Review

Believe it or not, your competitors may just simply tell you their core keywords. For SEO purposes, companies will utilize a line of code called the *meta keyword tag*, which tells the search engines which keywords are most important to this particular page of their website.

Where do you find this information? When viewing your competitor's website home page, at the top of the browser you should click View and then select Page Source from the drop-down menu that appears. A new window will open that displays the HTML code of this page. The meta keyword tag is usually located at the top of the code, and looks similar to Figure 4.15.

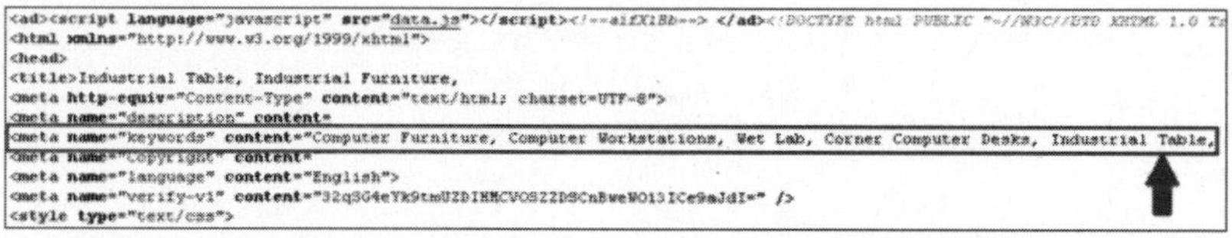

```
<ad><script language="javascript" src="data.js"></script><!--a1fX1Bb--> </ad><!DOCTYPE html PUBLIC "-//W3C//DTD XHTML 1.0 Tr
<html xmlns="http://www.w3.org/1999/xhtml">
<head>
<title>Industrial Table, Industrial Furniture,
<meta http-equiv="Content-Type" content="text/html; charset=UTF-8">
<meta name="description" content=
<meta name="keywords" content="Computer Furniture, Computer Workstations, Wet Lab, Corner Computer Desks, Industrial Table,
<meta name="copyright" content=
<meta name="language" content="English">
<meta name="verify-v1" content="32qSG4eYk9tmUZDIHMCVOSZZDSCnBweWO13ICe9aJdI=" />
<style type="text/css">
```

Figure 4.15 A home page's meta name, meta description, and meta keywords tags

Third-Party Tools

The tools in this section are not free, but their publishers offer free features. They can give you some insight into your competitors' keywords, messaging within their PPC ads, and traffic trends for their websites. Here are some of our favorites:

Compete (`www.compete.com`): As with any of the tools listed in this section, you'll get much more competitive information with the paid version of this software, but the free version will get you started. For example, we entered a competitor's website into Compete and received quite a bit of useful information, as you can see in Figure 4.16 and Figure 4.17.

SpyFu (`www.spyfu.com`): SpyFu offers two methods of competitive research: by keyword and by URL. When searching by keyword, you are provided with quite a bit of information, including projected CPC, clicks per day, and the average number of advertisers. Also, you can see top PPC domains for this term as well as samples of PPC ads. The information provided by SpyFu is helpful, and Figure 4.18 shows just the top of the results page—additional information is provided on the rest of the page.

Figure 4.16 In Compete, you can see traffic trends for your competitors, as well as visits and unique visitors.

Site Description	Referral Analytics ⑦ **pro**		Search Analytics ⑦ **pro**	
Company: SpecialTeas Inc	**Show Destination Sites**			
Location: Stratford, Connecticut United States	Referring Site	Referral Share	Keyword	Search Share
	google.com	32.06%	special teas	3.52%
The SpecialTeas team would	verisign.com	9.10%	teekanne earl gray t...	3.12%
like to welcome you to the world	yahoo.com	7.08%	loose leaf organic h...	3.02%
of fine teas. We are a group of	bing.com	6.61%	organic raspberry le...	2.92%
tea enthusiasts on a mission to	facebook.com	6.29%	teas from around the...	2.73%
help create a new awareness	See all 86 referrals with PRO		See all 85 keywords with PRO	
of fine teas. We invite you to				

Figure 4.17 You can also gain additional insight from Compete, such as site description, top referring websites, and some keyword ideas.

? Stats For:	organic white tea	view cached page >>		
Cost/Click:	$0.45 - $1.22	Advertisers:	16 -7 (-30.43 %)	
Clicks/Day:	0.65 - 0.82	Search Results:	1,770,000 -12,130,000 (-87.27 %)	
Cost/Day:	N/A	Search Volume:	270	

Jul 06 Dec 06 May 07 Oct 07 Mar 08 Aug 08 Jan 09 Jun 09 Nov 09
■ Avg Cost/Click ■ Cost/Click Range

Top PPC Domains for "organic white tea"   ?

Domain	Jul	Aug	Sep	Oct	Nov	Dec
teavana.com						
artoftea.com						
teatulia.com						
theteaspot.com						
mightyleaf.com						
amazon.com						
vitacost.com						
tetleyusa.com						
twoleavesandabud.com						
thefragrantleaf.com						

■ Ad copy changed from previous month
□ Advertiser didn't appear on this keyword

CLICK A COLORED BOX TO SEE THE AD

Watch a Full
Term History Demo
SEE WHAT YOU'RE MISSING

Figure 4.18 SpyFu can indicate how competitive a keyword may be and show the main advertisers bidding on the term.

You can use SpyFu to conduct competitive research by using a specific URL, and get the projected daily AdWords spending range, average ad position, top 10 paid keywords, and other information. You should not, however, take this information as solid fact, but rather as a point of reference. Figure 4.19 shows a sample URL analysis from SpyFu.

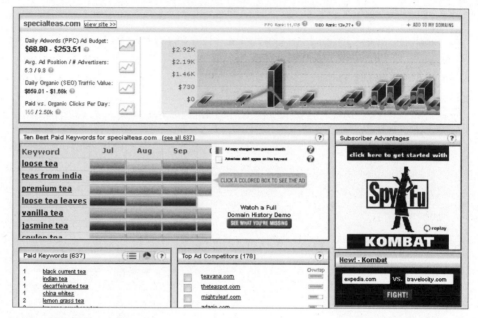

Figure 4.19 A SpyFu URL analysis

KeywordSpy (www.keywordspy.com): If you went ahead and hopped on the Compete and SpyFu bandwagons, you already have quite a bit of information about your competitors. Like the others, KeywordSpy provides speculative stats, top keywords, main competitors, and PPC ad variations. However, it also provides top organic keywords and competitors.

Week 2: Create Your Campaign Structure

Last week, you started the vitally important task of keyword research. This week, we are going to show you how to group those keywords so you can get the best results from them. Some less-experienced PPC marketers think that the *keyword list* is the be-all and end-all of the discipline, but it's not just the keywords in your list that will lead to success—how you structure your keyword groups is just as important.

In Chapter 2, "How the PPC Machine Works," we mentioned that you should assist the search engines by helping them provide a great user experience. A great user experience on a search engine occurs when a user enters a search query and receives relevant, unique, interesting results. High-quality SERPs display both paid and organic listings that appeal to the searcher. Serving the right ads to the right person at the right time requires a tightly themed account structure, which is the challenge you're going to take up this week.

Monday and Tuesday: Planning Your Campaign and Ad Group Structure

Last week, you built an extensive keyword list by using various keyword research tools, reviewing your main competitors, and concatenating your keywords for aggressive expansion. So, what do you do with all of these keywords now? You're going to segregate this keyword list into campaigns and ad groups.

What is a campaign, and what defines an ad group? What is the "right" way of laying out an ad group, and how many keywords should it contain?

> *Campaigns are used to give structure to the products or services you want to advertise. The ads in a given campaign share the same daily budget, language and location targeting, end dates, and syndication options.*
>
> *Within each campaign, you can create one or more ad groups. While a campaign may represent a broad product class, the ad groups within that campaign can be more focused on the specific product you want to advertise.*
>
> —GOOGLE ADWORDS HELP

First, let's discuss how PPC accounts are structured from top to bottom. The universal building blocks of an account are as follows:

- Account
- Campaigns
- Ad groups
- Keywords
- Ads

These are the foundations of a PPC account, but what do they actually look like? Figure 4.20 illustrates the nested tiers of a PPC account.

Campaigns are collections of ad groups. At the campaign level, you can set daily budgets, location targeting, language targeting, and network distribution (Google Search, Search Partners, Content Network, and/or Mobile Devices). These settings apply to all of the ad groups within the campaign. Campaigns should serve as the main theme of a set of ad groups.

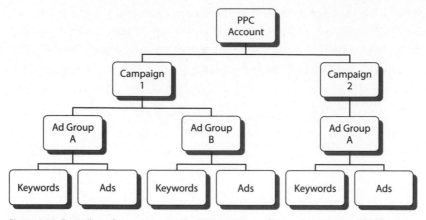

Figure 4.20 Regardless of your strategy or the product or service that you're advertising, the foundation of every PPC account is the same.

Ad groups are collections of keywords and ads. At the ad group level, you can adjust the way you want Google to charge you for clicks: maximum CPC, cost per acquisition (CPA), or cost per thousand impressions (CPM).

Each account is subject to capacity limitations and can contain a maximum of the following:

- 25 campaigns
- 2,000 ad groups per campaign
- 2,000 keywords per ad group
- 50 ads per ad group (any format)
- About 50,000 keywords per account

Ad groups should be variations or subsections of your core campaign theme. This way, all of the ad groups are closely related to the overall theme of the campaign, and all of your ad groups in a single campaign will be closely related to each other.

When plotting your account structure, you should first determine the main themes of your campaigns. Common campaign themes include the following:

Brand keywords: We advise that you create a separate campaign for your branded terms. These keywords are often some of the best performers, and you want to make sure they receive the attention they deserve.

Competitor brand-name keywords: In Chapter 8, "Month 5—Launch Your Campaign," we discuss at greater length bidding on competitor names, but for the sake of this discussion of campaign structure, it's a good idea to create a campaign for these terms.

General high-traffic keywords: These may be the high-volume, low ROI keywords that you need to utilize in order to bolster your sales, but you may need to monitor and manage them closely in order to keep them profitable.

Product-specific keywords: If you offer a wide range of products, you'll want each product to be represented by at least one individual ad group; therefore, you'll want separate campaigns for different product areas or departments.

Seasonal products or service keywords: Products that are affected by seasonality should be organized into their own campaigns or ad groups so that these can be easily paused and resumed according to the season.

This list contains just some examples of common campaign themes used in PPC accounts. Your campaign themes will be defined by your goals. Aside from creating campaigns based on theme, you should think about how the account settings will affect your strategy. Settings that can necessitate separating campaigns within your account include the following:

Different daily budgets: You may want to focus more of your PPC budget toward the keywords that generate the highest ROI.

Different bidding strategies: You may want to implement completely different bidding strategies depending on the contents of your campaign. You may want to utilize CPC bidding in certain campaigns and CPA bidding in others, using Google's Conversion Optimizer.

Different network distribution: You will want to separate your search, content, and mobile campaigns.

Different geo-targeting: You may have different areas of the country that outperform others. You'll want to create separate campaigns to target these high-performing locations.

Different ad scheduling: You may find that different keywords perform better at certain times of the day. At the campaign level, you can determine on which days your ads will appear, and during which times of the day—a technique that's called *dayparting*.

Different site-linking strategy: You can insert additional text links into your PPC ads by using the Ad Sitelinks option. We discuss this advanced PPC ad strategy in Chapter 10, "Month 7—Test Ads by Using Advanced Techniques." This setting is implemented at the campaign level, so you may want to create separate campaigns for various deep-linking strategies.

Even if you determine the most appropriate campaign themes, with the tightest ad groups possible, your account structure is likely to change over time. As your account matures, you will learn what works and what doesn't work, you will find holes in your overall strategy and structure, and your objectives may change, necessitating structural alterations. But don't let this discourage you from starting with a campaign structure that's as perfect as possible!

Creating a Mock Campaign

Let's go ahead and start structuring a mock PPC campaign, just to walk through the process. The account you'll create is for an online shoe retailer. They sell shoes of all kinds, so you'll need to have an account structure that reflects all of the products offered. To keep things simple in this example, you'll focus on setting up only three campaigns—Men's Shoes, Women's Shoes, and Shoe Brands—as illustrated in Figure 4.21.

Figure 4.21 Main themes for the Shoe Seller ad campaign

> *Search Network Ad Groups: An ad group contains one or more ads which target a set of keywords, placements, or both. You set a bid, or price, to be used when your ad is triggered by the keywords or placements in the ad group. This is called a cost per click (CPC) or cost per thousand impressions (CPM) bid. You may also set prices for individual keywords or placements within the ad group.*
>
> —Google AdWords Help

Many advertisers envisage ad groups based on the keywords they contain, but it is more effective to imagine them as thematically linked by the *ads* that they contain. The reason we advocate *tightly grouped* ad groups for searches is that you want the keywords that trigger an ad group's ads to be as closely related to those *ads* as possible. Ideally, when a user sees your PPC ad, that user should say, "This is exactly what I'm looking for!" *That* is what ensures high CTRs for ad and keyword combinations.

Our mantra: *(Almost) every keyword should appear in the ad text.*

Returning to the shoe retailer example, you already determined your high-level campaign themes, and now you're ready to parse them into smaller, individual themes. Usually these themes will fall along product lines, as illustrated in Figure 4.22.

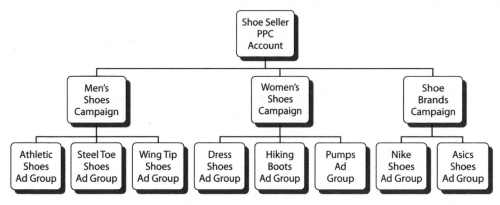

Figure 4.22 Core campaign themes broken down into specific products

Let's dissect a few of these ad groups in order to see the inner workings, starting with the Men's Shoes campaign and the Athletic Shoes ad group. Here is the initial list of keywords:

- *Men's athletic shoes*
- *Athletic shoes for men*
- *Athletic shoes men*
- *Best athletic shoes for men*

Your goal, for each ad group, is to write ads that are unique, benefit driven, and keyword focused. Here are two ads that would perform well in this ad group:

Men's Athletic Shoes

Wide selection of **men's athletic shoes**. Name brands. Free shipping!
www.AwesomeShoeStore.com/**Mens+Athletic**

Best Men's Athletic Shoes

Brands You Want & Great Prices on **Men's Athletic Shoes**. Buy Now!
www.AwesomeShoeStore.com/**Mens+Athletic**

We set in bold the keywords that appear within the ads, because this is how they may appear on the SERPs. You can see the logical connection: If a user searches on a term related to men's athletic shoes, that user will be served one of these ads, which should be highly relevant for the search query.

Another ad group is Dress Shoes, under the Women's Shoes campaign. The keywords in this ad are geared toward women's dress shoes. Here are some examples:

- *Women's dress shoes*
- *Dress shoes for women*
- *Formal dress shoes for women*
- *Buy dress shoes*

Recognizing that you are targeting a female audience searching for dress shoes, you can see that the following ads might perform well in this ad group:

Buy Women's Dress Shoes

Name Brands. Find Your Style for
Work & Weekend. Free Shipping!
www.AwesomeShoeStore.com/**Women+Dress**

Women's Dress Shoes Sale

All Styles of **Women's Dress Shoes**.
Fast shipping. Get 20% Off Now!
www.AwesomeShoeStore.com/**Women+Dress**

The last ad group example we'll walk you through is the Hiking Boots ad group within the Women's Shoes campaign. Here are some of the keywords that would likely appear in this ad group:

- *Women's hiking boots*
- *Hiking boots for women*
- *Best hiking boots for women*
- *Buy women's hiking boots*

Remember that you want your PPC ads to highlight the keywords in each ad group. The ads also should include as many benefits as possible and should have a strong call to action. Here are some ads that might appear in this ad group:

Buy Women's Hiking Boots

Hiking Boots for All Terrains.
Name Brands. 20% off. Buy Now!
www.AwesomeShoeStore.com/**Hiking+Boots**

Buy Women's Hiking Boots

20% Off **Women's Hiking Boots**.
Name Brands. Fast Shipping. Buy Now!
www.AwesomeShoeStore.com/**Hiking+Boots**

Within all of these ad group examples, notice the following:

- The keywords are closely related.
- There are two ads for each ad group in order to test different benefits and phrasing.
- All of the ads highlight the keywords in their respective ad groups.

Employing this methodology will help make your ads as relevant as possible to a user's query, and this high level of relevance will lead to a good CTR, conversion rate, and ROI.

Creating Content Network Ad Groups

Our mantra of making sure your ads are keyword focused can be somewhat confusing when applied to the world of the content network. For one thing, frequently your keywords should not appear in your ad at all (remember, your goal is *distraction* away from page content on the content network, not necessarily relevance *to* the content). Moreover, unlike in a search, ad groups can contain ads that are very different from each other. Within a single ad group, you can include text ads, banner ads, video ads—any of the ad types allowed for the content network. But despite this, we advise creating separate ad groups for each ad type and size. Each ad type and size will exhibit performance characteristics—different CTRs, conversion rates, and costs per conversion.

Creating separate ad groups for each ad type and size will enable you to assign and optimize different bid amounts for each group. This will ensure that you maintain maximum conversion volume while controlling the ROI of each ad group.

Wednesday: Determining the Number and Granularity of Ad Groups

A common question we get when making PPC presentations is, "How many keywords should you include in an ad group?"

There is no single correct numerical answer to this question. Remember our mantra: *(Almost) every keyword should appear in the ad text.* This really means that you should split your keyword lists into as many small subsets as possible. Here again is the example we used in the previous section:

Keywords

- *Women's hiking boots*
- *Hiking boots for women*
- *Best hiking boots for women*
- *Buy women's hiking boots*

Ad

Buy Women's Hiking Boots

Hiking Boots for All Terrains.
Name Brands. 20% off. Buy Now!
www.AwesomeShoeStore.com/**Hiking+Boots**

This ad doesn't include the words *compare* and *online*. But that's OK. The most important thing here is that the ad is displayed when the searcher uses a query related to *women's hiking boots*, and your ad pertains specifically to that kind of shoe. It mentions *hiking boots* twice, and highlights *all terrains* and *name brands*, which could be important benefits to an online shopper. So although you don't have *every* word from the keyword list in the ad, you certainly have included the most important ones.

You should now see that it's OK to create ad groups with thousands of keywords, and other ad groups with only one keyword in each. For example, because you won't typically need to create a separate ad group for each individual misspelling, each of thousands of URL variations can coexist in a single ad group. The limit to the granularity of such ad groups will be the limit of the number of keywords that can be included in a single ad group, which varies from engine to engine, but numbers in the thousands.

Understanding the Benefits of a Well-Structured Account

You've listened to us preach about the importance of a well-structured PPC account. We walked you through the process of setting up campaigns and ad groups that are tightly grouped with small keyword lists and ads that feature most keywords from each ad group. Let's look now at the specific benefits of well-structured accounts:

Faster reporting and analysis: If your keywords are scattered all over your account with little or no rhyme or reason, it's going to be extremely difficult to analyze the account's performance and make improvements. When you run reports for your campaigns, ad groups, keywords, ads, or any other aspect of your account, you need to be able to look at the data and draw conclusions. With poorly structured campaigns and ad groups, reporting will take a lot more time, it will be significantly less reliable, and trending will be difficult to determine.

Efficient account management: After your PPC account is up and running, you want to be able to make changes quickly and efficiently in order to enhance the account's performance. If your account is set up properly, you can make notes and formulate an optimization strategy quickly, and drive straight into your account with confidence that you know exactly what needs to be done and exactly where the strengths and weaknesses lie.

Better PPC ad copy: The more tightly themed your ad groups are, the better targeted your PPC ad copy will be. Yes, the chanting of our mantra continues: Your ad copy should be able to feature almost all of the keywords in your ad group. If you have to use dynamic keyword insertion (DKI), which we'll discuss in Chapter 10 and in Chapter 12, "Month 9—Migrate Your Campaign to Microsoft and Yahoo!," or if you have so many keywords that your ad copy can't feature them, you have some ad-group segmentation to do. Remember, highly relevant, benefit-driven, keyword-focused PPC ads and landing pages are the crux of a successful PPC account. You have to get the account structure right for all of this to occur.

Higher quality scores: Great quality scores hinge on your CTR and the relationship of your PPC ad text to the keywords within your ad group. Your quality score can get a lift when Google can easily determine the theme of your ad group, because all of the keywords are relevant to your ad text and they're relevant to each other. With a higher quality score, you will pay less per click, and your ad position will improve.

Thursday: Getting Acquainted with AdWords Editor

Most of the screenshots and examples that you have seen to this point have been from the Google AdWords web interface. We use the web interface for some tasks, but most PPC experts use AdWords Editor for the majority of their day-to-day tasks.

What is AdWords Editor?

> *AdWords Editor is a free Google application for managing your ad campaigns. Use it to download your account, update your campaigns with powerful editing tools, then upload your changes to AdWords.*
>
> —Google AdWords Help

The web interface is *live*—that is, any changes you make in the web interface typically take effect in real time. You update a bid, and it is updated in your account—ditto for adding or removing keywords and campaigns, reorganizing ad groups, and so on. Although this may seem advantageous, the web interface can be painfully slow at times.

AdWords Editor is a software application that installs on your Macintosh or Windows PC. To use it, you download your entire campaign and its performance data, and can then make campaign changes and judge performance with the speed of a local application. Changes can be made even when you're not connected to the Internet, and uploaded later after you connect.

So, you can work even when Google is performing system maintenance, and leave tasks half done instead of risking a system logout if you wander away from your desk. But by far, the greatest advantage to using AdWords Editor is its time efficiency. Because you can batch and simplify tasks, cut and paste objects as small as a keyword or as large as a campaign, and upload image ads without taking the time to name and rename them each time, AdWords Editor can save you as much as 90 percent of your management time!

One of the many advantages of AdWords Editor is the ability to initiate—but not immediately complete—multiple offline activities. When we set up new ad groups in the AdWords web interface, we have to start with the decision to begin with keywords or placements, take the time to name our ad group, and actually complete an ad before we get to our first keyword. This might not seem like a lot of work (we *do* have to make each of these decisions), but a task such as writing ads can be very tedious when we want to generate dozens of ad groups. In AdWords Editor, we can specify our ad group names ahead of time in a text editor or Excel (named in accordance with our root keywords in all likelihood) and write our ads all at once.

When you are dealing with many ad groups, the ability to bulk-edit similar elements in multiple ad groups can be a tremendous time-saver. For some of our more-complicated content network campaigns, it would take an hour to accomplish a simple task such as editing all the bids in all the ad groups.

AdWords Editor is a wonderful time-saving tool that is next-to-required for PPC advertisers who follow the guidelines set out in this book, particularly because of our large suggested keyword lists with relatively granular ads and ad groups. We've included a detailed guide to using AdWords Editor in Appendix A, "Advanced AdWords Editor."

Friday: Building Out the Campaign

This week, we have been concentrating on the strategic and structural concepts behind building out a campaign. Now comes the time to pull the levers and push the buttons.

As we've mentioned, we always create separate content and search campaigns, but beyond that, how should you subdivide campaigns? As we have mentioned several times, you should start by creating just a few campaigns to achieve the minimum number of conversions (15 per month), and use Google Conversion Optimizer to automate bid management more quickly.

It is, of course, our recommendation that you use AdWords Editor for campaign build-out. AdWords Editor enables you to "walk away" from your work and come back to it without losing work or data. In addition, AdWords Editor makes it easier to modify your campaigns and ad groups on the fly. For example, we often create campaigns with a certain level of granularity, but then consolidate ad groups based on ads as we write them. What seems like a separate ad group at first blush might make sense with its keywords consolidated with another ad group that has similar (especially fewer) words.

We know that you've already learned a lot at this point, but resist the urge to go activate your freshly minted campaigns. The rest of this chapter will help you hone and refine your campaign logistically—setting bids and budgets, tracking sales efforts directly, and so on. Don't worry; you'll be in the marketplace and on the SERPs soon enough!

Week 3: Adjust Campaign Settings

Now that you have the basic architecture of your account determined, it's time to adjust the settings for your campaigns and ad groups. Sometimes campaign settings get overlooked during initial account setup. However, having the right settings can be the golden ticket to better-performing campaigns, and having the wrong settings can be a silent killer of your ROI. Don't let this happen to you! Get your campaign settings correct from the start.

In this section, we focus on account settings within Google AdWords. We cover account settings for Yahoo! and Microsoft adCenter in Chapter 12.

Monday: Setting Budgets and Delivery Methods

Each of the big three PPC platforms enables you to set a daily budget for each campaign. This budget tells the search engine the maximum that you are willing to spend within that campaign each day. By now, you have your campaign structure in place, and if you already know which keywords are most likely to generate a high ROI, you should devote more of your budget to these campaigns.

To adjust campaign settings from within the AdWords web interface while viewing all campaigns or a single campaign, click the Settings tab. When you do this, you'll see a screen similar to Figure 4.23. You can then adjust your budget settings in the Bidding and Budget section, as indicated in the figure.

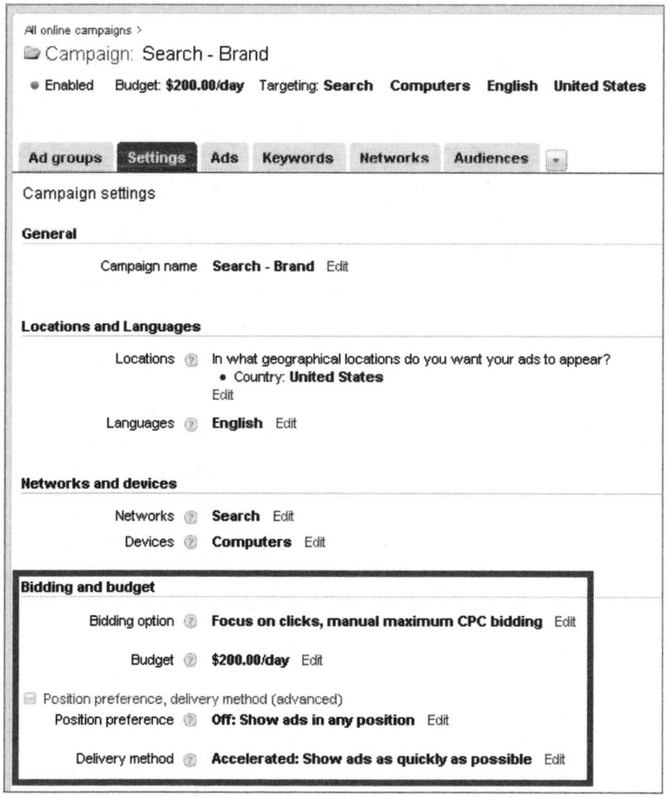

Figure 4.23 Adjust your daily budget in the Bidding and Budget section of your campaign settings.

AdWords will display your ads as often as possible while trying to remain within your daily budget. We say *trying to remain within your daily budget*, because at times your daily click charges will exceed the budget you set. On any given day, as the campaign charges near the daily spending limit for a campaign, AdWords will slow down delivery of your ads. However, sometimes your volume may be such that AdWords doesn't slow down your spending in order to hit your budget exactly.

Another reason your campaign budget may be exceeded on certain days is that AdWords monitors your budget and spending for an entire billing cycle. So, if there are days when you don't hit your budget, AdWords may allow your campaign to overspend slightly in order to hit the budget for the entire billing cycle. On a single day, AdWords may overspend by 20 percent. However, you will never be charged more than the amount allotted for a billing period. For example, if your daily campaign budget is $5, the most you can be charged during a 30-day billing cycle is $150.

Another important setting in the Bidding and Budget section is the Delivery Method setting, shown in Figure 4.24.

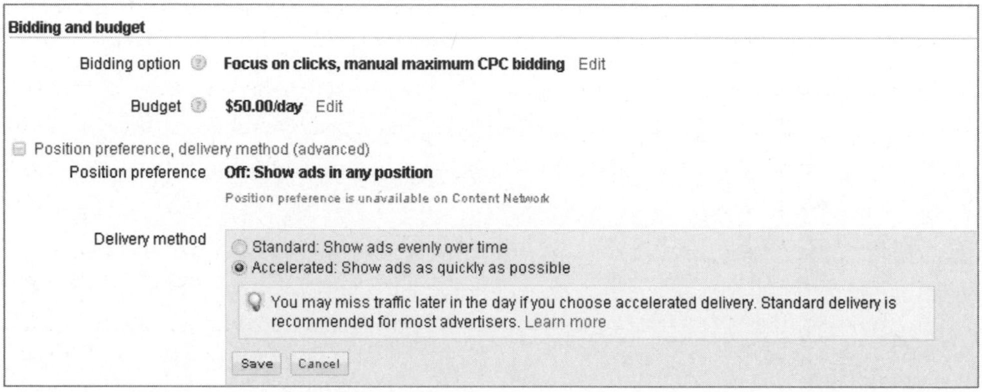

Bidding and budget

Bidding option ⓘ	**Focus on clicks, manual maximum CPC bidding** Edit
Budget ⓘ	**$50.00/day** Edit

⊟ Position preference, delivery method (advanced)

Position preference	**Off: Show ads in any position**
	Position preference is unavailable on Content Network

Delivery method

○ Standard: Show ads evenly over time
⦿ Accelerated: Show ads as quickly as possible

💡 You may miss traffic later in the day if you choose accelerated delivery. Standard delivery is recommended for most advertisers. Learn more

Save   Cancel

Figure 4.24 The Delivery Method setting

There are two options here: Standard and Accelerated. Standard delivery will direct AdWords to spread out your clicks evenly during the course of the day so that your ads are displayed at all times of the day. If click spending reaches the daily limit early in the day, there may be times of the day when your ads aren't displayed. With Accelerated delivery, you are telling AdWords to display your ads as frequently as possible, until your daily budget cap is reached—so whatever time of day the click spending reaches that budget limit, your ads will simply stop running until the beginning of the next day.

If your budgets are set properly, we suggest you utilize Accelerated delivery. Keep in mind that with this delivery option, you need to have a budget in place, even if it's extremely high. This is because something may occur in your campaign that causes a traffic spike, and you may want to have a budget in place to avoid over-spending. Also, we're not fans of Standard delivery because you have no control over when AdWords displays your ads.

When running your first AdWords campaigns, Standard delivery might be a safe way to manage ad delivery so that you don't have any sudden budget-busting surprises. However, if you can afford a high budget, Accelerated delivery will ensure that your ads run as often as possible throughout the day. Choosing Accelerated delivery will give you the opportunity to show your ads as often as possible, but you can still fine-tune when your ads are shown by using Ad Scheduling, which we'll discuss on Friday.

Tuesday and Wednesday: Setting Your Bidding Strategy and Options

There are three main bidding options available for AdWords advertising. They are as follows:

CPC Cost per click (CPC) is the default bidding option for all PPC platforms. In a CPC strategy, the advertiser pays the search engine a certain amount of money each time an ad is clicked. The advertiser pays only when their ad generates a click—unlike a CPM relationship, in which an advertiser has to pay whenever ads are *shown*. CPC is the main strategy used in this book.

CPA Cost per acquisition, or cost per action (CPA), is the default cost structure of affiliate advertising. In a CPA structure, the advertiser pays only when an end user performs a specific conversion action (for example, the user makes a purchase or submits a lead form). CPA is the default bidding option when Google Conversion Optimizer is being used.

CPM CPM stands for cost per thousand (the *M* stands for 1,000). It is the traditional cost structure for radio and other offline media buys. CPM has been the norm when buying display banners from many prominent site publishers and advertising networks. In a CPM relationship, the advertiser pays a certain amount of money for each 1,000 impressions. For example, if an advertiser pays a $3 CPM, they are responsible for $3 if the publisher shows that advertiser's ad 1,000 times, $6 for 2,000 impressions, and $3,000 for 1 million impressions. Of the three most common cost structures (CPM, CPC, and CPA), CPM favors the publisher the most and shifts the majority of the risk to the advertiser. Remember, the advertiser must pay whether or not there is a click, let alone a sale or other action.

Google offers all three of these bid options. Most campaigns are either CPC or CPM. All search campaigns start with the CPC bidding strategy. Advertisers tell Google they are willing to pay a certain amount per click (for CPC bids), and Google can charge any amount of money up to, but not exceeding, the advertiser's maximum CPC. For content campaigns, advertisers can select CPC or CPM bidding. When bidding a CPM campaign, advertisers agree to pay Google a maximum amount per thousand impressions, and Google may charge up to, but not in excess of, that advertiser's maximum CPM bid.

A compelling bidding strategy in AdWords is Conversion Optimizer. Conversion Optimizer is Google's implementation of automated bid management, automatically controlling bid prices at optimal levels to maximize conversions while maintaining conversion costs at target levels. We examine Conversion Optimizer in more detail when we describe optimization strategies and tactics in Chapter 9, "Month 6—Optimize Your Campaign."

To adjust your bidding option, go to your campaign's settings and click the Edit link next to your current bidding option. When you click Edit, you will see the bidding options for clicks, conversions, or impressions, as shown in Figure 4.25. Remember, CPM bidding is available only on the content network.

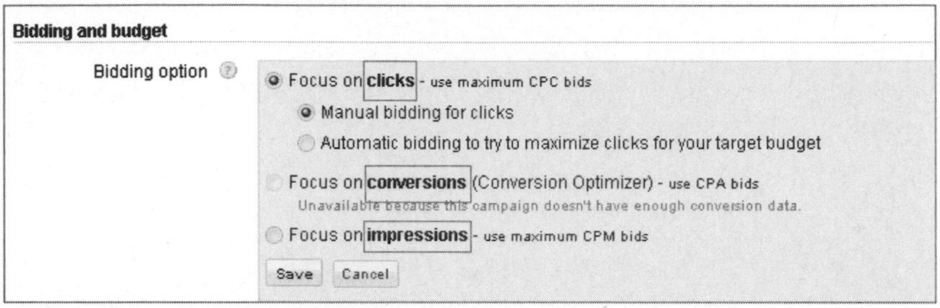

Figure 4.25 Depending on the overall objectives for your campaign, you can bid on clicks, conversions, or impressions.

Thursday: Targeting Networks and Devices

When you create a new campaign, the default setting is to target your ads to the search and content networks. As previously mentioned, we recommend you turn off content in search campaigns and separate the content network into its own campaign.

You can click the Settings tab within each campaign in order to adjust these settings. You can then change the Search and Content distribution settings in the Networks, Devices, and Extensions section, as shown in Figure 4.26.

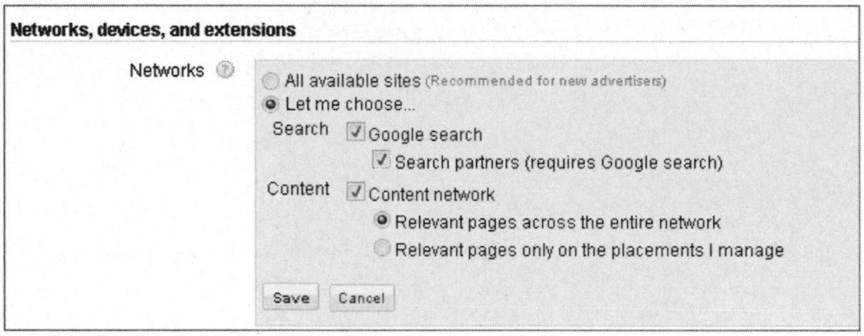

Figure 4.26 Each campaign should be targeted to only one distribution channel: Search or Content.

Search Network

As you can see in Figure 4.26, there are two channels within the Google Search Network:

Google Search: Your ads will appear on Google.

Search Partners: Your ads will appear on sites such as Ask.com. You can opt out of Search Partners, but you can't actually break Search Partners off into its own campaign. Search Partners always requires Google Search to be activated.

Content Network

We discuss the content network at great length in Chapter 7, "Month 4—Advertise on the Google Content Network." For now, here is some basic information about the options for choosing this distribution channel at the campaign level (shown previously in Figure 4.26):

Relevant Pages Across the Entire Network: Your ad may appear on any web page that Google has deemed relevant to your keywords and PPC ads. You will typically buy these ads on a CPC, keyword-targeted basis.

Relevant Pages Only on the Placements I Manage: Google will place ads only on the sites or domains you specify.

Device Platforms

In the Devices section of your campaign settings, you can target computers or iPhones and other smart mobile devices. Similar to separating the search and content networks, we advise that you create separate campaigns when targeting different devices. For example, when you are ready to launch your mobile marketing initiatives, you should create a new campaign and select the iPhones and Other Mobile Devices with Full Internet Browsers option, as illustrated in Figure 4.27.

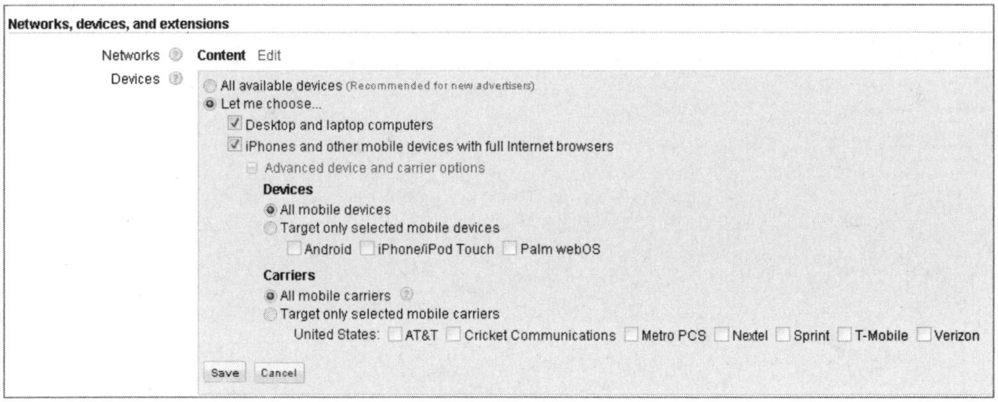

Figure 4.27 You can target the devices on which your PPC ads will appear.

As you can see in the figure, your choices are as follows:

Desktop and Laptop Computers: This is just what it sounds like—your ads will appear on desktop and laptop computers.

iPhones and Other Mobile Devices with Full Internet Browsers: When you launch a new campaign, the default setting will have your ads appearing on all available devices. As you saw in Figure 4.27, creating a mobile marketing campaign has a great number of options. This is why your mobile ads should be run separately from your other ads. Google continually improves the specificity with which you can target mobile ads. You can choose on which mobile device your ads will appear. (As of this writing, there were only three device options: Android, iPhone/iPod Touch, and Palm webOS.) Also, you can choose which mobile carriers you want to target.

Friday: Using Ad Scheduling and Geo-Targeting

On Monday, we discussed delivery options. We mentioned that Accelerated delivery can help generate the maximum exposure for your website, and if optimized properly, this delivery method can really give your PPC campaign a huge boost. Today, we'll discuss two ways to fine-tune your Accelerated delivery in order to show your ads *when* your target audience is mostly likely to take action, as well as how to show your ads *where* they are most relevant.

The two settings we are discussing today are powerful, so adjust them with caution. We don't mean to scare you, but getting your Ad Scheduling and geo-targeting settings right is extremely important. If you don't, your ads may show up at the wrong times and in the wrong locations!

Ad Scheduling

First we'll cover Ad Scheduling. As illustrated in Figure 4.28, you can adjust your Ad Scheduling settings within the Advanced Settings section of your campaign Settings tab.

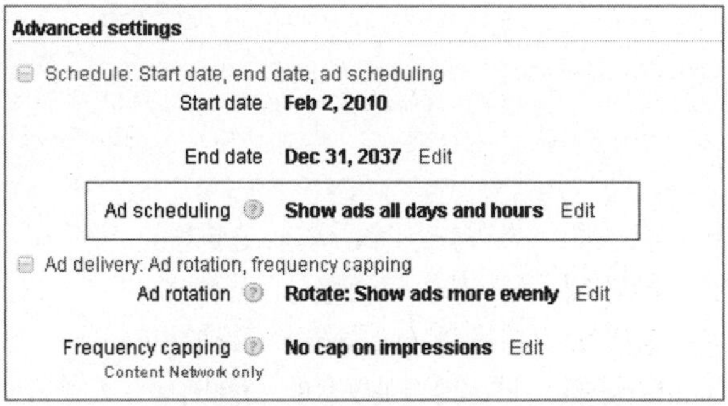

Advanced settings

Schedule: Start date, end date, ad scheduling
Start date **Feb 2, 2010**

End date **Dec 31, 2037** Edit

Ad scheduling **Show ads all days and hours** Edit

Ad delivery: Ad rotation, frequency capping
Ad rotation **Rotate: Show ads more evenly** Edit

Frequency capping **No cap on impressions** Edit
Content Network only

Figure 4.28 Ad Scheduling enables you to automatically increase or decrease bids, or you can stop your ads from running altogether.

Before we get to the "how" of Ad Scheduling, let's first discuss the reasons for using this advanced option. As your PPC account matures and you learn what works and what doesn't, you will discover that during certain times of the day, your target audience is more (or less) likely to convert. You may find that there are entire days that lack in performance. Ad Scheduling can automatically increase your bids during those peak hours when users tend to convert more highly, as well as lower bids when users are less likely to convert. This is why Ad Scheduling is so powerful!

How do you learn at what times users convert best? The AdWords web interface provides some great reports, but it doesn't allow you to see hourly conversion data. You can see impressions, clicks, CTR, average CPC, and cost broken down by hour, but you can't see conversions, conversion rate, and CPC at the hourly level. We suggest you dig into your analytics or shopping cart data to learn this information. Because it's free, we suggest you take full advantage of Google Analytics. Within this software program, you can get hourly conversion data for your PPC campaign. You can learn everything you ever wanted to know about Google Analytics by reading *Web Analytics: An Hour a Day* by Avinash Kaushik (Sybex, 2007). After you have acquired hourly conversion data and you've learned when you should automatically decrease and increase bids, then you're ready to adjust your Ad Scheduling settings.

Let's return to the shoe retailer example for this discussion. Imagine that the retailer has learned that people are less likely to buy shoes between 2 a.m. and 6 a.m., so you've decided to lower all bids by 25 percent during these weak hours. Also, the retailer has discovered that people love to buy shoes between 1 p.m. and 4 p.m., so you're going to increase bids during these times.

When you launched the AdWords campaign for this client, you were targeting all hours of the day with 100 percent of your bids (which is the default setting, and how you should launch your campaign). When you view Campaign Settings and click Edit for Ad Scheduling, a screen like the one shown in Figure 4.29 will pop up in your browser.

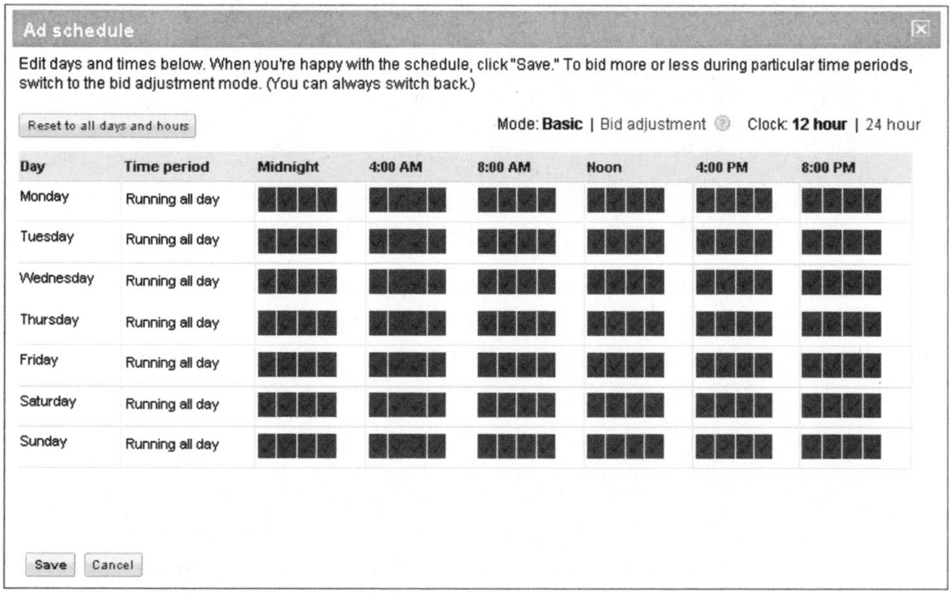

Figure 4.29 When you are targeting all days of the week and all hours of the day, this is how your ad schedule will appear.

Now you're going to adjust your Ad Scheduling settings in order to take advantage of the hourly conversion information that you learned about in Google Analytics. Click Bid Adjustment at the upper right of the Ad Schedule window and adjust your settings as shown in Figure 4.30.

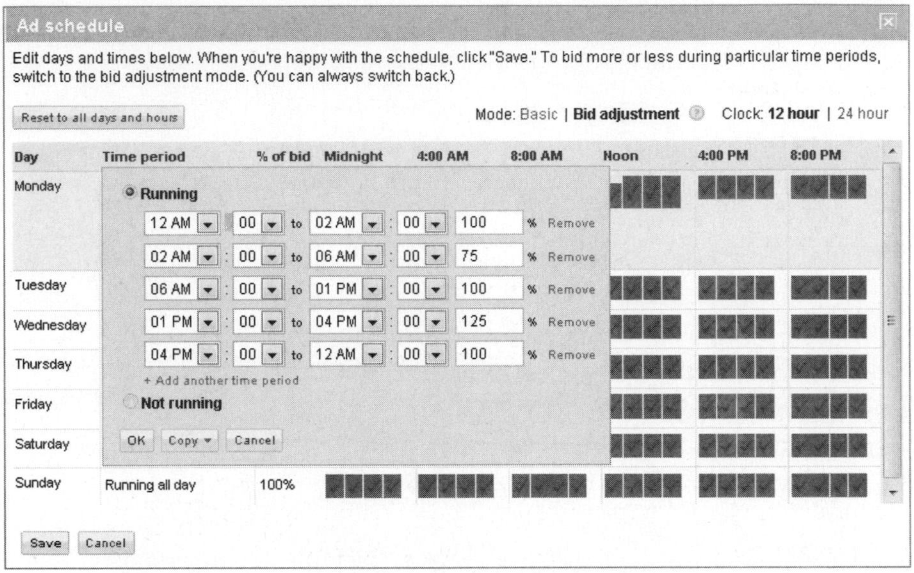

Figure 4.30 Adjusting bid prices to increase the conversion rate and decrease CPC

The adjusted hourly bids are now as follows:

- From 12 a.m. to 2 a.m., your bids are running at 100 percent as usual.
- From 2 a.m. to 6 a.m., your bids will lower 25 percent, and run at 75 percent.
- From 6 a.m. to 1 p.m. your bids will increase back to 100 percent.
- From 1 p.m. to 4 p.m., your bids will increase by 25 percent, to 125 percent.
- From 4 p.m. to 12 a.m., your bids will lower back to 100 percent.

It's *very* important to note that the time zone of your ad scheduling is based on your account settings, *not* the time zone where people see your ad.

Geo-Targeting

Geo-targeting is a powerful functionality that can greatly increase your ROI. Geo-targeting is essential for some businesses. Is there a certain place that you *don't* ship to? If so, you might want to use the Excluded Locations tool. Or if you're an international advertiser, you may want to segregate your creative efforts by language and currency.

Before launching your PPC campaign, you may already know whether you need to target a specific geographic location. This decision might be driven by the fact that you're advertising a brick-and-mortar store that services the local area, or a company that ships to only certain geographic regions.

You can adjust your geo-targeting settings within the Locations, Languages, and Demographics section of your campaign settings, as shown in Figure 4.31.

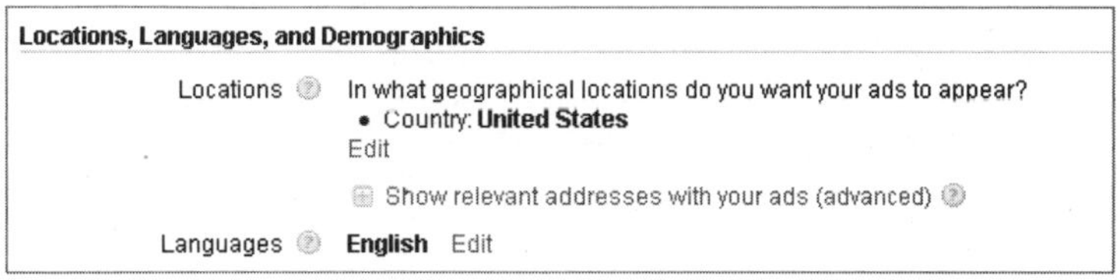

> **Locations, Languages, and Demographics**
>
> Locations ⍰   In what geographical locations do you want your ads to appear?
>   • Country: **United States**
>   Edit
>
>   ⊞ Show relevant addresses with your ads (advanced) ⍰
>
> Languages ⍰   **English**   Edit

Figure 4.31 AdWords geo-targeting

There are a few different ways to target specific areas within AdWords. For this example, you've learned that your shoe retailer sells the most shoes in their hometown of Chicago and in the surrounding Chicagoland area. You are going to adjust your geo-targeting accordingly.

In Figure 4.32, we have selected to target the Chicago metro area. On the left, you can see that we selected Chicago from the menu in AdWords, and this is indicated on the corresponding map.

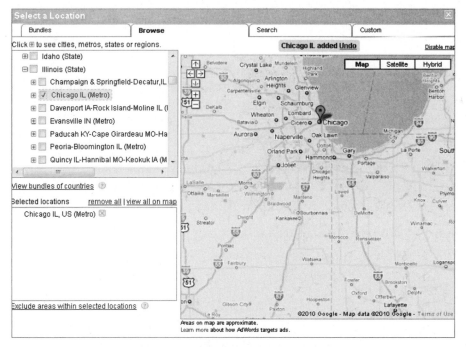

Figure 4.32 Targeting an area by selecting the desired state and city

You can choose to target your ads by entering a physical location and creating a radius around this location. In Figure 4.33, we have entered our address as 444 North Michigan Avenue, and we have chosen to display our ads within a 15-mile radius of this address.

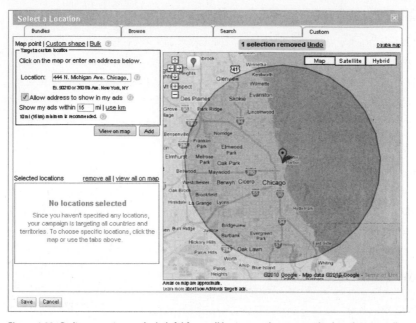

Figure 4.33 Radius targeting can be helpful for small businesses that want to display ads in a small area. You can even target your surrounding neighborhood.

You can also create a custom target area within AdWords. On the Custom tab, you can outline the area on the map where you want your ads to appear. In Figure 4.34, we chose the specific coordinates of where our ad should appear.

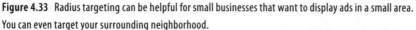

Figure 4.34 If you want to get highly specific about where you ads are displayed, you can draw your own custom targeted area.

Week 4: Use Conversion Tracking and Set Click Pricing

It's called *pay-per-click* advertising, right? But how much *do* you pay for each one of those clicks? How do you know how much to bid?

This week is all about the money. How much are you going to pour into the PPC machine? How are you going to tell how much is coming back out? These are the questions you'll be answering this week.

Monday: Setting Up Conversion Tracking

Google's conversion tracking is one of the most compelling features available on an ad interface loaded with tons of compelling, profit-driving features. PPC is one of the most measurable marketing endeavors, and if you aren't tracking conversions, you are shooting your campaign in the foot and doing your business a great disservice.

Setting up conversion tracking in AdWords is relatively painless. Here's the step-by-step process:

1. Click the Reporting tab within your campaign and select Conversions.

2. On the next screen, click New Conversion.

3. Name the conversion action you will be tracking. For example, if you are tracking leads, you may want to call the conversion **Lead**, or if you're tracking purchases, you may want to call it **Purchase**.

4. Select a tracking purpose from the drop-down menu. The options are as follows:
   - Other
   - Purchase/Sale
   - Signup
   - Lead
   - View of key page

5. Click Save and Continue.

6. Enter the page security level and tracking indicator settings for your website. In Figure 4.35, the page security level is HTTP (the other option is HTTPS). If you are tracking leads that don't have standard revenue, you don't need to enter anything in the Revenue for Your Conversion field. If you don't want a tracking pixel to appear on your confirmation page, select None as the Choose Text Format option.

7. AdWords will provide you with the snippet of code to track this conversion. Insert this code into the confirmation page(s) of your website.

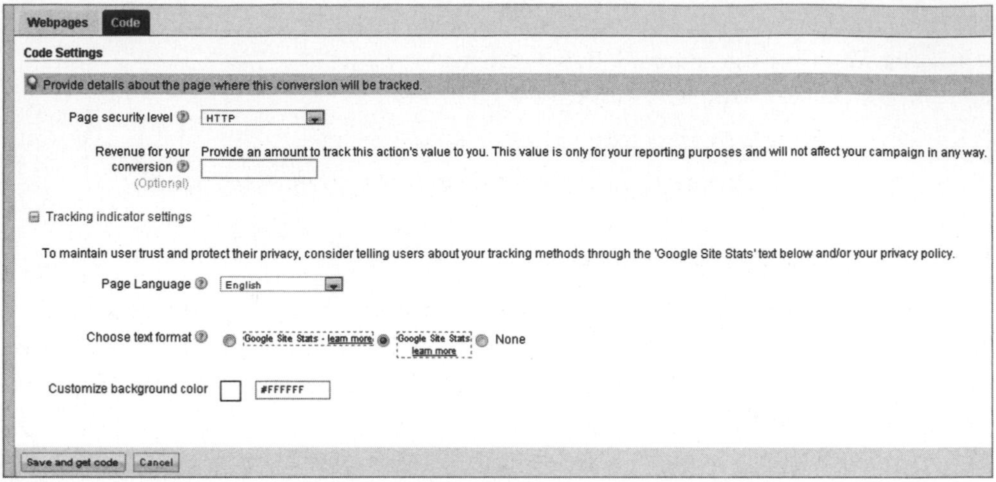

Figure 4.35 Enter your page security level here, and then choose your tracking indicator settings.

Tuesday: Setting Up Google Analytics

Google Analytics is a robust analytics program that can help you gain valuable insight into your PPC performance. You can see where visitors are dropping out of your shopping process; you can see how long they stay on your landing page; and you can learn on which pages visitors convert most highly. The best part is, Google Analytics is free!

When you analyze them properly, you can gain invaluable, numerous insights that are from Google Analytics. We could write an entire book on installing and analyzing web analytics, but luckily we don't have to! As we mentioned last week, a great resource for learning everything you need to know about analytics is *Web Analytics: An Hour a Day*, which shows you how to slice and dice your information so that you become a master of actionable analysis.

For now, here are the basic steps for getting Google Analytics installed on your website and landing pages:

1. Open a Google Analytics account. You can do this by going to www.Google.com/Analytics.

2. After you're in your account, click Add Website Profile.

3. Enter the URL of your website, select your country, and choose a time zone.

4. The next page displays the universal tracking code that needs to be inserted on every page of your website. Copy the code.

5. Insert the snippet of Google Analytics code on every page of your website.

After you complete this process, you should link your Google AdWords account to your Google Analytics account. This way, your PPC traffic is tracked correctly in

Google Analytics, and you can access your Google Analytics account directly through AdWords. To link the accounts, follow these steps:

1. Click the Reporting tab within AdWords.

2. Choose Google Analytics from the drop-down menu.

3. Enter your Google Analytics account ID to link the two accounts.

Wednesday: Testing Conversion Tracking

Testing your conversion tracking is not simply a matter of going to your website and completing a test conversion. You need to click on a PPC ad in order for the PPC tracking cookie to be installed on your computer, and when you convert, a conversion will be registered in AdWords.

Here is the step-by-step process to make sure that your conversion tracking code has been installed correctly:

1. Within any active campaign, create an ad group called **Conversion Test**.

2. Within this ad group, insert one keyword that is nonsensical (for example, *xxxyyyzzz* or *abcd1234*). Use exact match for this keyword.

3. Run a query on Google for this nonsense keyword, and your ad should appear.

4. Click on your ad and complete a test conversion.

    There is a reporting lag within the AdWords interface, so you can't convert and check your account a few minutes later. You should allow at least three hours for processing. If you don't see your conversion then, you may want to give it 5 hours. If after this you don't see your conversion, your conversion tracking code may not be properly installed. However, if a conversion registers, you're finished!

    There are a couple of reasons we want you to make your dummy purchase from a dummy keyword in an irrelevant ad group. One of them is that you will spend less money for the click. One click probably doesn't mean very much in the grand scheme of things, but you're almost certain to spend less money than clicking a "live" keyword. Additionally, *you don't want to pollute your conversion-tracking data.*

Thursday: Determining Your Starting Keyword Bids

How much should you bid on each ad group? Should you start with low bids and go high later, or vice versa? When should you change your bids? What's more important: ad rank, CTR, click volume, or conversion rates? There aren't easy answers for questions like these because, as in all marketing efforts, there are different valid strategies. Which ones are "best" depends on your company's budget, timing, market position, and business objectives.

Determining optimal bidding strategy shouldn't be viewed as a choice between the "right way" and the "wrong way." The best bidding strategy is the one that's most appropriate for your company's situation (in other words, how much can you afford to spend?) and your objectives, including brand awareness, revenue growth, or profitability.

The ultimate objective of most advertising campaigns, including PPC advertising, is to maximize conversions. And one of the main reasons that PPC advertising is so attractive and efficient is because measuring conversions and ROI is easy. In order to serve larger marketing and company goals, it makes sense to continually decrease the average cost per conversion so that your campaigns are increasingly profitable and maximize ROI.

Deciding how much to spend per click at the beginning of a new campaign needn't be pure guesswork. You can "back into" the starting bid price by doing some easy calculations. Although the math is simple, the concepts are powerful. Your ability to calculate and track the following metrics will be largely responsible for the success of your advertising efforts.

Let's start with one of the most important calculations: conversion rate, which is simply the percentage of clicks that result in conversions. For example, if one of your ad groups results in 200 clicks, and 40 of those clicks result in conversions, then the ad group's conversion rate is 20 percent, as shown in the following calculation:

$40 \div 200 = 20\%$

Cost per conversion is easily calculated, too. Simply divide the total spent on clicks by the number of conversions. In the previous example, if each click cost $1.50, the cost per conversion is $(200 \times \$1.50) / 40 = \$7.50$.

Step 1 in this exercise is for you to estimate what you're willing to pay for a sale or sales lead, which is the maximum cost per conversion (also known as cost per action, or CPA). Then you can calculate the maximum click price you can afford (also known as cost per click, or CPC). Before even starting a campaign, you need to determine (or even just estimate) your maximum acceptable cost per conversion. This should be the maximum you're willing to pay for a sale, a lead, or whatever constitutes a conversion for your company.

If you sell only one item, this calculation is easy. If your product price is $35.00, and your gross profit on a sale is $20.00, you might set your maximum cost per conversion to be $10.00 to allow for a net profit of $10.00. This is calculated as follows:

$35 – $15 = $20 gross profit $\div$ 2 = $10 CPA (cost per acquisition)

It gets a little trickier if you sell more than one product, or if your primary objective is to obtain sales leads, and you do not yet have enough data to estimate revenue stream or gross profit. But you need to start somewhere—so use average transaction revenue, or calculate the value of a lead based on your historical ability to convert leads to sales.

Armed with the maximum cost per conversion, you're now on track to calculate the maximum click price (the CPC) you can afford. First, you need to calculate the number of site visitors it will take to obtain one sale or action.

If you have historical data on how well your site visitors convert, this calculation is a snap. The number of visitors you need to receive in order to make one sale is 100 divided by the conversion rate (represented as a whole number rather than a percentage). For example, if your conversion rate is 4 percent, your site gains a sale for every 25 visitors, as shown in the following calculation:

$100 \div 4 = 25$

Second, you need to use the previous two calculations to determine the maximum click price: the maximum conversion price divided by the number of visitors needed for one sale.

Continuing this example, if your maximum cost per conversion is $10, and your conversion rate is 4 percent, your maximum CPC is $10 multiplied by .04, or $0.40 (40 cents). Here's the equation:

max CPC = max cost per conversion × conversion rate

This final calculation of maximum CPC is not simply a dry mathematical exercise—it's crucial to the success of your PPC campaign. If you bid higher than the maximum CPC, you risk losing money. If you bid at or below the calculated maximum CPC, your campaign should remain profitable (assuming sufficient conversions).

What should you do if you don't have historical data that lets you calculate the conversion rate, as in the case of a new product launch? There is no need to bid blindly. Start with your best guess. Be conservative or optimistic, but guess.

Assume these typical results:

- For most PPC campaigns, the minimum conversion rate should be 1 to 1.5 percent.
- Good conversion rates range from 2 to 4 percent.
- 5 percent and above is a very good to excellent conversion rate.
- Anything in the double-digit percentages is extraordinary.

For example, if you're launching a new product and have determined the maximum cost per conversion to be $32, a conservative approach would be to assume a conversion rate of 1 percent. Thus, the starting maximum CPC bid would be $0.48 CPC or:

$32 × .01 = 32 cents per click

Another factor in determining initial click pricing is whether you want to reach maximum profitable conversion volume sooner or later. To help you with that decision, we'll describe two different bidding strategies: aggressive and conservative.

Advertisers who use an *aggressive strategy* start bid prices at a high level—sometimes as much as twice the amount expected to achieve profitability. Then bids are lowered as data accumulates, eventually settling in at CPC levels that ensure profitable conversions. Obviously, this strategy risks burning ad dollars on the way to profitability. However, it enables advertisers to accumulate data quickly and test ads and landing pages in a relatively short period of time.

So the aggressive strategy is appropriate for advertisers who want or need to minimize the time necessary to attain maximum profitable sales volume or market share. It might be used, for example, by a retailer who wants to conduct conversion-optimization testing in time for the holiday buying season.

The *conservative strategy* suits advertisers who are more risk-averse, are working with low ad budgets, or have little experience with PPC advertising. As you might expect, this strategy calls for starting bid prices at a low level, and increasing them gradually over time, as ads and landing pages are tested and CTR and conversion rates improve. Conservative PPC advertisers minimize unprofitable conversions, but the amount of time between starting the campaign and achieving maximum profitable conversions can be much longer than if the aggressive strategy is pursued.

If you want to estimate how much time it will take to "test the waters" and get your ads on the first page of search results, Google provides a data point called First Page Bid Estimate.

How much does Google anticipate it will cost to show your ad on the first page of search results? First Page Bid Estimates can give you an idea of how much it will cost to appear on the first page of Google's SERPs, as shown on the AdWords Editor interface in Figure 4.36.

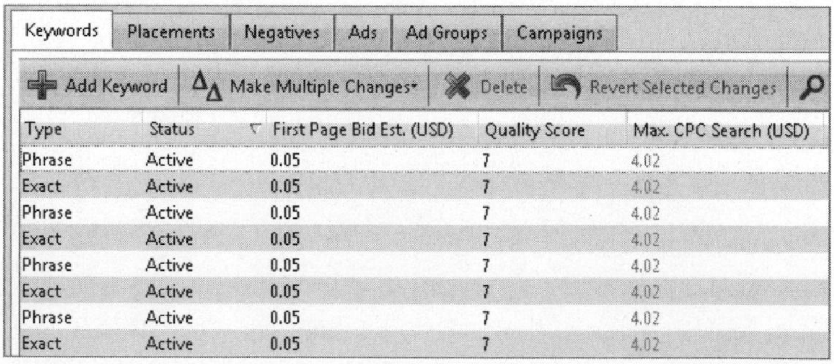

| Keywords | Placements | Negatives | Ads | Ad Groups | Campaigns |

Add Keyword | Make Multiple Changes | Delete | Revert Selected Changes

Type	Status	First Page Bid Est. (USD)	Quality Score	Max. CPC Search (USD)
Phrase	Active	0.05	7	4.02
Exact	Active	0.05	7	4.02
Phrase	Active	0.05	7	4.02
Exact	Active	0.05	7	4.02
Phrase	Active	0.05	7	4.02
Exact	Active	0.05	7	4.02
Phrase	Active	0.05	7	4.02
Exact	Active	0.05	7	4.02

Figure 4.36 First Page Bid Estimates help advertisers determine baseline bids for a conservative bidding strategy.

Friday: Setting Keyword Bids

After you've estimated your initial bids, it's time to actually put those bids in motion!

Here's the basic process for setting bids for your new campaign from the web interface:

1. Create and name a new campaign and ad group.

2. Compose your first ad.

3. Add keywords.

4. Set your keyword bids.

In AdWords Editor, the option to set your maximum bid for a new ad group appears on the very first screens. As illustrated in Figure 4.37, you have the option to set bids—with a variety of specific bid types—before naming campaigns or ad groups, or composing ads.

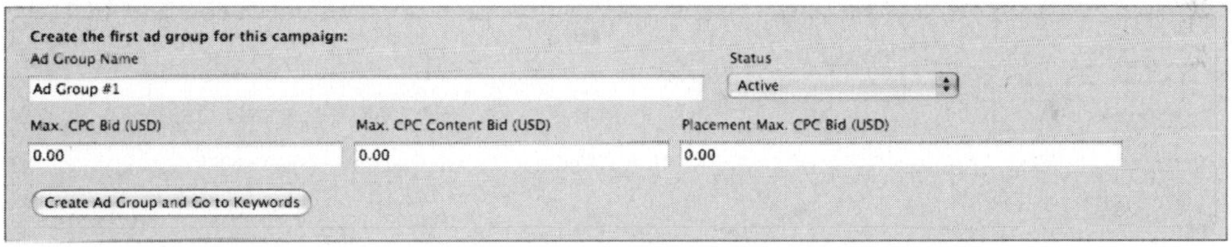

Figure 4.37 This ad group has no name, but three potential bid categories: Max.CPC Bid, Max.CPC Content Bid, and Placement Max.CPC Bid.

Take a breath. You're doing great. Next month, you'll begin what we consider possibly the most rewarding part of PPC marketing: the creative—yet strangely scientific—process of ad copywriting!

Month 2—Create Great PPC Ads

5

Unless you have years of experience writing classified ads, this may be the most important chapter of this book. Designing and writing pay-per-click (PPC) ads is difficult. Squeezing meaning and motivation into a tiny space is a skill that doesn't come naturally to marketers who are accustomed to the relatively expansive space and high bandwidth of advertising media such as print or television.

During this month's exercises, you'll see exactly what words and phrases best motivate people to click on your ad and visit your website. Better yet, you'll learn how to pack tons of persuasive power into a space not much larger than two postage stamps!

Chapter Contents

Week 5: Take Stock of Your Advantages

You may be one of the lucky few PPC advertisers who have the search results page all to yourself. Maybe you sell a product that's absolutely unique (see Figure 5.1).

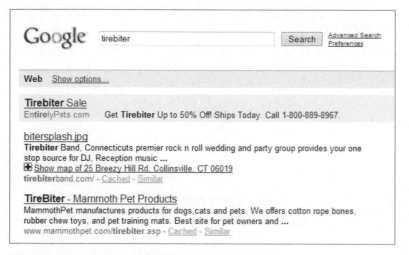

Figure 5.1   A lucky advertiser with no PPC advertising competition

Chances are better, though, that at least a few advertisers are competing head-on with your company—selling similar or even identical products and services. You may even be among the companies whose products or services are similar or identical to those offered by dozens or hundreds of other advertisers (see Figure 5.2).

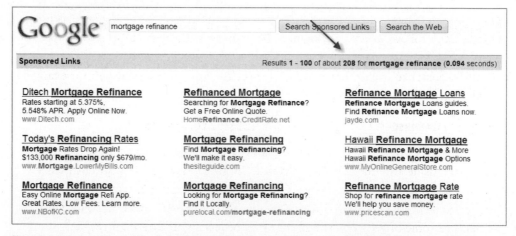

Figure 5.2   Search results page crowded with hundreds of companies bidding on the same keyword: *mortgage refinance*

Even if you face a less-crowded field of competitors, you'll write better PPC ad copy if you take stock of your organization's competitive advantages. You'll be better prepared to highlight those advantages in your ad copy and grab the attention of the searcher away from the crowded field of ads.

So let's begin taking stock of your advantages and articulating them in a persuasive manner.

Monday: Surveying Your Competition

It's a good idea to understand how your competitors are positioning themselves before assessing your own organization's strengths and competitive advantages. By doing so, you'll understand the advantages competitors believe are their most important ones, and gain inspiration for your own organization's list.

Start by simply listing the advantages you know are being touted by your competitors. Here's a list of some of the most common ones:

- Lower price
- Higher quality
- Free and/or fast shipping
- Large selection
- Great customer service
- Prestigious products or brands
- Greater convenience
- Greater security
- Quality or performance guarantee
- Comprehensive feature set

Now use Google to search for common terms that describe your products or services. Look for AdWords ads that are being run by your competitors. Make special note of any advantage messages that are used in their ads. Later you'll use this research to decide whether to use similar messaging (because your prices are lower, for example) or underscore different advantages.

Tuesday and Wednesday: Listing Your Own Advantages and Benefits

Now it's time for you to list your own strengths and competitive advantages. Get input from others inside and outside your organization. In particular, ask your customers what they consider to be your strengths compared to your competitors'. You'll likely be surprised to hear advantages you hadn't previously considered, and that some constituents perceive some of your favorite strengths to be less significant than you do.

We've prepared a worksheet to help you work through the next steps. It's shown in Figure 5.3, and you can download it as a Word document from http://bit.ly/fIEFE.

Advantage and Benefits Worksheet

Advantage	Feature	Benefit

Figure 5.3 The Advantages and Benefits worksheet

You'll be using the worksheet to list not only your organization's strengths and advantages, but also the feature and benefit associated with each strength. Before you plunge into the worksheet, we want to clarify one of the most crucial distinctions in marketing: the difference between a feature and a benefit.

Features are characteristics of your product, service, or organization. *Benefits* are the way people feel after they have taken advantage of a feature.

Table 5.1 shows some examples of features and their corresponding benefits.

One of the most common signs of an amateur advertiser is ad copy that leaves it up to the reader to infer or imagine the benefits of the advertiser's product or service. These advertisers don't realize an important fact: *Frequently, people reading an ad will respond better to a description of a benefit than they will to just a description of a feature.*

▶ **Table 5.1** Features and Benefits

Feature	Benefit
Nonslip surface	I will feel safe and avoid injury.
Free shipping	I will save money that I can spend on something else.
Automatic backup of data	I will feel secure that I won't lose data.
Top quality	I will feel confident that the product won't fail, and I will impress my friends and family.
Large selection	I will save time because I will likely find the perfect match for my needs.
Qualified technicians	I will trust that I have someone to rely on who will solve problems efficiently.

When writing PPC ad copy, picture the majority of your readers as busy people with lots of distractions. They're squeezing some online research in between the dozens of other matters they need to attend to during their stressful day. The space around their computer is cluttered, and whether they're at home or at work, interruptions abound: The phone rings, the baby cries, and so on.

That's why expert advertisers make sure their writing is as explicit as possible. Even the few split seconds necessary to imagine how a feature might deliver a benefit might be too much for the reader to endure. So whenever possible, your ads should not rely exclusively on feature lists—instead, they should specify the *benefits* in clear, simple language.

We'll show you several examples of great PPC ads in the rest of this chapter. And you'll see that the image of the busy reader recurs several times in this book, when we talk about calls to action and landing page design.

Thursday: Creating Causes for Urgency

People love to procrastinate and will go through mental contortions to rationalize why they shouldn't take action immediately. Master ad copywriter Lorrie Morgan-Ferrero has the following to say on the subject:

> *Without a sense of urgency, desire loses its value. Why? Because procrastination is the biggest killer of sales—particularly online, where the chances of a prospect staying on or returning to a website (in order to think about buying), in today's click-happy world, are scarce.*

Red Hot Blog, www.redhotblogging.com

Your ad copy should work to overcome inertia, and whenever possible create a sense that readers will suffer, or fail to benefit, if they don't act right away.

Here's an example:

Buy Gold Now
Gold prices rising faster.
Buy before it hits ceiling!
www.GoldFingers.com

It's easier than you might think to create a sense of urgency. Table 5.2 lists some common examples.

▶ **Table 5.2** Urgency Factors and Messages

Urgency Factor	Sample Message
Limited supply	Only 150 will be sold.
Holiday shipping deadlines	Hurry—orders must be placed by December 19.
Perceived external trends	Mortgage rates might rise soon.
Internal factors	Buy now before our annual price increases.
Peer pressure, prestige	Be the first one in your neighborhood.
Seasonal milestones	Start losing weight before summer.
Limited-time offers	Buy before April 20 and get a free bonus.

As you can see, some of these are very real factors (for example, holiday deadlines), while others (such as the possibility of mortgage rate increases) are implied. In any event, make sure that the message is credible and honest. Online audiences have become particularly wary of hype, and messages that don't seem genuine risk turning off potential customers.

Friday: Collecting Your Resources

Over the past few days, you've collected all the components you need to tell a compelling story in your ads. You've assessed your relative strengths and advantages vis-à-vis your competitors. You've translated every feature into one or more corresponding benefits. You've listed some reasons that people should feel a sense of urgency when they read your ad.

Your exercise today is to do some searches on Google, Yahoo!, and Microsoft Bing to see the ads your competitors are running. Clip and save some representative examples—ones run by your biggest competitors, and others you feel intuitively are better than average.

You'll come back to this list at the end of the month, when you've learned what it takes to be an ad copywriting pro.

Week 6: Write Right

Over the years, we've had the opportunity to take over and improve hundreds of PPC campaigns. Most of them failed in one way or another to follow the ad copywriting guidelines you'll be learning this week; none of them adhered to all the guidelines. Typically the ads looked something like this:

<u>Outdoor Furniture</u>
Tables, chairs, lounges.
Wood and plastic.
www.outdoorfurniture.com

If you think there's room for improvement in this ad, you'll be happy to know you're right—read on. And if you think this ad is just fine—read on very, very carefully.

But first, let's agree on one thing: the objective of your ad. Is it to sell your product? Get a sales lead? Nope. Your ad's objective is mainly this, and only this: *Get the click.*

A resumé won't land you the job, but it will get you to the next step in the process: the interview. A direct-mail envelope's copy won't sell anything, but it will persuade the recipient to take the next step: open the envelope.

Likewise, don't expect your PPC ad to sell anything or to persuade the reader to do anything but take the next step: click to find out more.

It's the job of the PPC landing page to continue the process and lead the "clicker" to the desired conversion action. So the PPC ad and the landing page should work tightly together to guide the visitor smoothly and quickly through the conversion process. This synergy is discussed in greater detail in Chapter 6, "Month 3—Design Effective Landing Pages."

With that in mind, you can start learning and practicing the art of creating great PPC ads.

Monday: The Fundamentals

First, you need to learn the most important techniques for writing successful PPC ads. Then you can spend the rest of the week focusing on the ad's components: the headline, first line, second line, and display URL. This chapter shows you plenty of examples.

One caveat: View these techniques as guidelines that help you write great PPC ads, but keep in mind that your first ads represent a starting point for an ongoing series of tests. Your goal will be to obtain better-than-average click-through and conversion rates from the very start, and then to test variations in ad copy with the goal of continually improving results. Ad testing is covered thoroughly in Chapter 10, "Month 7—Test Ads by Using Advanced Techniques."

Now on to the fundamentals.

Group Keywords Tightly

An ad group's *root keywords* are the ones that represent the core theme of the ad group. For example, the root keywords for an ad group whose theme is *red sneakers* would be, not surprisingly, *red sneakers*. The other keywords in the ad group should include these root keywords, as in these examples:

- Best red sneakers
- Red sneakers online
- Durable red sneakers
- Red basketball sneakers

Ideally, the ad group's root keywords should appear at least once in the ad, preferably in the headline. This helps ensure that the person viewing the ad comes to the all-important conclusion, "This ad exactly matches the intent of my search." Also, keywords included in ads appear in boldface, so they're more eye-catching.

Talk to the Reader

Whenever possible, speak directly to the reader by using words such as *you* and *your*. People respond better when it seems the advertiser is taking a personal interest in them and has what it takes to satisfy the searcher's need or desire.

Here's a "before" example:

Custom-Built Cabinets
Strong materials. Professional
installers. Low prices.
www.wehangem.com

And here's the "after"—a more "you-oriented" version:

Custom-Built Cabinets
Your kitchen, your style, our
cabinets installed by pros.
www.wehangem.com

Tell the Readers What You Want Them to Do

As mentioned earlier, people respond better to ads that tell them explicitly what is hoped or expected of them. Action words and imperative verbs work particularly well, such as the following:

- Get
- Shop
- See
- Find
- Buy

Make It Clear What You're Selling

If your site sells something, make it clear that the ad leads to an e-commerce site—by including price information, for example. This helps ensure that you don't waste money on clicks from people who are only looking for information or samples. For example, a site that sells photos of sports figures can minimize the number of expensive clicks from people who just want to see or print such photos by including a phrase such as *Prices as low as $59!*

The fact is that many people use search engines to research topics, find news, and see pictures and videos. These are generally not the kinds of searches that yield paying customers, so an important goal of your PPC campaigns is to make sure your ads appeal exclusively to people who are seriously interested in converting.

Use Title Case

Often an ad with words in title case (that is, the first letter of each significant word is capitalized) performs better than a version of the same ad with lowercase letters. Here's an example:

> <u>Refinance Your Mortgage</u>
> Apply Now—Lower Rates and a
> Fatter Wallet Every Month!
> YetAnotherMortgageBank.com

Call Readers to Action

Our testing has shown that people will more often take an action if it's explicitly spelled out for them. And try to be more creative than just saying, *Visit our site* or *Click to see.*

Here's an ad with no call to action:

> <u>Get Government Grants</u>
> Many are eligible for money
> from the feds. Up to $15,000.
> www.washingtondough.com

And this time, with an explicit call to action:

> <u>Get Government Grants</u>
> See if you can get up to $15,000.
> Take our 5-minute test!
> www.washingtondough.com

Use Appropriate Punctuation to Emphasize Action

Exclamation points can significantly increase click-through rates (CTRs). And don't omit punctuation marks, because your ads might appear incorrectly under some circumstances. For example, the following ad looks OK when it appears on the side of a search results page:

<u>Get Government Grants</u>
See if You Can Get up to $15,000
Take Our 5-minute Test!
www.WashingtonDough.com

However, the lack of punctuation at the end of the first line will make the ad look odd when it appears at the top of the results page:

<u>Get Government Grants</u>
See if You Can Get up to $15,000 Take Our 5-minute Test! www.WashingtonDough.com

The lack of punctuation may seem like a minor problem, but the properly punctuated version of the ad will very likely result in a higher CTR.

Know that Benefits Sell Better than Features

As you learned last week, your ads should emphasize the benefits of your offering, not just the features. Features describe the product and/or service you're selling, whereas benefits describe the positive emotions your customers will experience.

Here's a feature-oriented ad:

<u>Refinance Your Mortgage</u>
Easy application and low
rates. Lock in yours.
www.yetanothermortgagebank.com

And here's a version that motivates by using benefits:

<u>Refinance Your Mortgage</u>
Apply now—lower rates and a
fatter wallet every month!
www.yetanothermortgagebank.com

If You've Got It, Flaunt It

It really pays to underscore your competitive advantages, especially if you're in a crowded field of competitors. Consider this example:

<u>Hotel Software</u>
Maximize your profits. Top-
rated by experts 2007–2008.
www.hotelsoft.com

Note that any claims of top ratings, best-quality products, and the like must be backed up by evidence that's included on your landing page.

Stand Out

For some industries, such as financial services, medical malpractice, and travel, dozens or even hundreds of companies may be bidding on the same keywords and filling search results pages with very similar-looking ads.

In such situations, it's often better to display ads that are markedly different from the competition. This is borne out by research conducted by MarketingExperiments (www.marketingexperiments.com/ppc-seo-optimization/ppc-ad-copy-tested.html). They found that over-the-top ads performed better than mediocre, straightforward versions, simply because they were more noticeable—like this one for a travel agency:

> ## Have a Bad Trip
> Unless you see our low fares
> and great customer service.
> www.goawaywithus.com

Tuesday: The Headline—The Most Important Characters

The *headline* is the most important determinant of a PPC ad's success. Even ads with poorly written body copy perform better when the headline is well written. This has been borne out by numerous tests, including the previously mentioned MarketingExperiments article.

And what distinguishes well-written headlines from poorly written ones? As mentioned previously, headlines work best when the search term is included. That's because ads with the keyword in the headline say more clearly to the searcher, "We have what you're looking for." And when the words in the headline (or anywhere else in the ad text) are exactly the same as the keywords in the corresponding ad group, the search engines display those words in boldface—calling more attention to the ad and making it more likely that searchers will click on it.

As you learned in Chapter 4, "Month 1—Research Keywords and Establish Campaign Structure," it's best to include a small number of keywords in each ad group. And each keyword in an ad group should consist of the same one, two, or three words, as well as modifying words that might correspond to the way people search.

That takes a lot of manual effort up front, but it pays off because it allows you to include keywords in your ads—especially in the headline.

For example, consider an ad group that contains the following keywords:

- refinance mortgage rates
- mortgage refinancing
- low mortgage rates

If the search term is *refinance my mortgage to get lower rates*, then the ad will be displayed as follows, with important words highlighted:

<u>Refinance Your Mortgage</u>
Apply Now—Lower Rates and a
Fatter Wallet Every Month!
www.yetanothermortgagebank.com

The ad would be much less effective if the keyword list included terms that are less tightly related to the ad copy, such as the following:

- home loans
- loan from bank
- rates on house loans

Table 5.3 lists some keyword-and-headline combinations that illustrate these concepts as well as the ones you learned previously.

▶ **Table 5.3** Keyword and Headline Examples

Ad Group Root Keyword	Headline
Hawaiian vacation	Custom Hawaiian Vacations
CRM software	Powerful CRM Software
Lose weight	Lose Weight—Fast & Easy
Divorce lawyer	Winning Divorce Lawyers
Storage units	Strong, Safe Storage Units
Anniversary gifts	Lovable Anniversary Gifts
Nike Air sneakers	Nike Air Sneakers Sale

If your root keyword is so long that the modifying words won't fit, you can use just your root keyword. However, it's worthwhile to test alternatives, especially in competitive industries. Chapter 10 covers this in greater detail.

Wednesday: Line 1—Features and Benefits

PPC ads work best when you lead off with the features and benefits of the offer in the first line. Frequently this requires more space than just the first line, so it's OK to bleed over into the second line, especially if the call to action at the end of the second line is brief. Table 5.4 provides some examples.

▶ **Table 5.4** Keyword and Line 1 Examples

Ad Group Root Keyword	Line 1
Hawaiian vacation	Relax in Our Hand-Picked Hotels.
CRM software	Never Lose a Customer or a Sale.
Lose weight	Amaze Your Friends w/ Your Sleek New Bod.

Ad Group Root Keyword	Line 1
Divorce lawyer	Get Your Fair Share.
Storage units	Keep Your Valuables Safe & Clean.
Anniversary gifts	She'll Adore You for Another Year.
Nike Air sneakers	Jump Higher and Impress the Hood.

Thursday: Line 2—Urgent Calls to Action

The second line of the PPC ad is where you should give explicit directions to the reader. As mentioned previously, when you tell your readers what you want them to do, they'll more likely take action when they get to your site. Table 5.5 shows examples of second lines that emphasize action and urgency. You'll see that the examples all include an exclamation point at the end of the line—this is intended to connote immediacy, propelling the reader to the desired action.

▶ **Table 5.5** Keyword and Line 2 Examples

Ad Group Root Keyword	Line 2
Hawaiian vacation	Rooms Sell Out Quickly—Book Now!
CRM software	Download the Free Trial Today!
Lose weight	See How 3 Svelte Women Did It!
Divorce lawyer	Request Your Free, Discreet Consultation Today!
Storage units	Reserve Today for a 25% Discount!
Anniversary gifts	See Huge Selection & Low Prices!
Nike Air sneakers	Find Your Size and Style Now!

Friday: The Display URL

Most advertisers are unaware that the display URL of a PPC ad can be fine-tuned to deliver better performance. Only two rules govern the display URL:

- It must contain the root domain name of your site.

- Its syntax must adhere to the rules describing legal URLs.

Note that these rules don't prohibit capitalization, nor do they require that the display URL point to an actual page on the site.

So all of the following are legal display URLs:

- www.BeanCounters.com/Accounting

- ThaiFood.PadThaiHouse.com

- BigBoxStore.com/Free-Parking

Our tests have shown that this technique can yield nice improvements in CTR and can even help increase conversion rates.

Here are the complete ads formed by using the lines from Tables 5.3–5.5, along with display URLs created by using these techniques:

Custom Hawaiian Vacations
Relax in Our Hand-Picked Hotels.
Rooms Sell Out Quickly—Book Now!
GetAwayWithUs.com/Hawaiian_Vacation

Powerful CRM Software
Never Lose a Customer or a Sale.
Download the Free Trial Today!
CRM.CustomerForce.com

Lose Weight—Fast & Easy
Amaze your Friends w/ Your Sleek New
Bod. See How 3 Svelte Women Did It!
FatBeGone.com/Cash-Back-Guarantee

Winning Divorce Lawyers
Get Your Fair Share. Request Your
Free, Discreet Consultation Today!
DewyCheatem.com/Top+Divorce+Lawyers

Strong, Safe Storage Units
Keep Your Valuables Safe & Clean.
Reserve Today for a 25% Discount!
ExtraSpacious.com/Discount_Now

Lovable Anniversary Gifts
She'll Adore You for Another Year.
See Huge Selection & Low Prices!
Anniversary.ForgetHerNot.com

Nike Air Sneakers Sale
Jump Higher and Impress the Hood.
Find Your Size and Style Now!
Pazzos.com/Nike_Air_Styles

Week 7: Explore Industry Examples

This week, you'll look at examples of well-written ads for five kinds of advertisers. You'll apply the techniques described in earlier parts of this chapter, and hopefully gain inspiration for writing ads that will work well in your particular situation.

For each industry example, you'll see the root keyword of the ad group used to trigger the ads.

Monday: The Single-Product Retailer

In the following example, note the implied sense of urgency hinting at the possibility that the $25 discount can be earned today only.

Root keyword: improve golf swing

Improve **Your** Golf Swing
Win More Matches: Hot New DVD Will
Shave Strokes. Save $25 Today!
GolfMore.com/Improve_Swing

In the next example, the headline implies that the advertised software has somehow been rated superior to its competitors. This may seem contrary to the search engines' terms of service that require such claims to be substantiated on the landing page. However, there are many superlatives that the search engines don't prohibit. See if you can find more.

Root keyword: iPhone GPS app

Top iPhone GPS App
Never Get Lost Again: Turn-by-Turn
Directions. Get Free Trial Now!
RazzleSoft.com/iPhone+GPS

Tuesday: The Multiple-Product Retailer

It's often a good idea to include pricing in ads—whether you want to telegraph a lower price than your competitors, or, as in the following example, you want to indicate that bargain-shoppers should *not* click on your ad. Advertisers of top-end products will find this may decrease CTR, but it will keep costs low and profitability high.

Root keyword: high-end necklaces

High-End Necklaces
Feel Like a Princess: See Our
Custom Necklaces—$1,000 and Up.
ZealousGems.com/Necklace

Listing a variety of products as in the following example tells readers that they're likely to find something of interest. And many online buyers are soothed by the promise of a guarantee—that way, they can feel assured they won't lose their money if the product arrives and it's not quite what they expected.

Root keyword: statues for my garden

Charming Garden Statues
Buy Gnomes, Fairies, Saints,
Flamingos. Cash-back Guarantee!
YardGuard.com/Garden+Statues

Wednesday: The B2B Service Provider

In the following example, the advertiser is emphasizing its track record for delivering completed projects within the customer's requested scope and timetable—some of the biggest worries that plague buyers of technical services. And the advertiser is offering proof in the form of testimonials and a downloadable case study. This kind of ad works well when coupled with a landing page that has a simple form enabling the advertiser to collect contact information so the company's salespeople can follow up.

Root keyword: digital imaging service providers

Digital Imaging **Services**
All Projects On Time & On Spec. See
Testimonials & Get Free Case Study.
SuperScanners.com/Digital_Imaging

The following ad includes several emotional triggers. It says to the boss, "I'll be a hero to my employees and visitors if I hire this cleaning service." It also hints that there might be hygienically unsafe problems lurking, and that Office Divas can whisk those problems away. Add the implication that all of this can be obtained at competitive rates, and you have an ad that's nearly irresistible.

Root keyword: office cleaning service

Spotless Cleaning Service
Your Clients & Employees Will Love
Safe, Clean Offices. See Low Rates!
OfficeDivas.com/**Cleaning**_Service

Thursday: The Professional Services Provider

Why do companies hire bookkeepers? To keep them out of trouble! The following ad addresses such fears from the very first line.

Root keyword: bookkeepers

Diligent Bookkeepers
Never Miss a Penny or Pay a Fine.
Request a Free Consultation Today!
Bookkeepers.CountBeans.com

The following ad will stand out from the crowded pack of competing advertisers because it is almost entirely you-oriented. Use Google to search on the root keyword *advertising agencies*, and you'll see what we mean. Ironically, most ads are focused on the agency itself rather than the desired outcome for the prospective client.

Root keyword: advertising agencies

Award-Winning Ad Agency
See How We Can Help You Beat the
Competition and Grow Your Business!
MoBetterClicks.com/Advertising

Friday: The Financial Services Provider

Notice how the following ad telegraphs safety and security, without potentially running afoul of regulators and the search engines' terms of service. Although the ad implies that certificates of deposit are the safest places to tuck the reader's money, it stops short of making any guarantees.

Root keyword: safe investments

<u>The Safest Investment?</u>
No More Shrinking Savings Worries.
CDs May Be Safest. Buy Online!
LittleBank.com/Safe_Investments

Although we don't necessarily endorse artificial scare tactics, the following ad will certainly stand out by implying impending problems unless the reader takes immediate action.

Root keyword: lowest mortgage rates

<u>Get Low Rates Immediately</u>
Mortgage Rates May Be Soaring Soon.
Lock In Your Lowest Rates Now!
Lowest_Rates.MortgagePlaza.com

Week 8: Understand Ads for the Content Network

Chapter 7, "Month 4—Advertise on the Content Network," thoroughly covers the concepts you'll need to be successful at advertising on PPC content networks. You'll see that the rules and techniques for contextual advertising can be very different from those for search advertising.

One of the primary differences is that ads need to work harder to gain the attention of the reader. This is because the readers aren't engaged in the process for searching for information or actively shopping. Instead, they're browsing websites for interesting or pertinent content.

Contextual ads appear adjacent to this content, usually (but not always) on the periphery of the web page—on the left or right side, or at the top or bottom of the page. To some extent, people have become conditioned to ignore such advertising, because they know the ads are tangential to the main attraction: the page's content.

So just as in traditional print advertising (ads appearing in magazines and newspapers), your PPC contextual ads need to distract the reader's attention *away* from the articles and *toward* the ads. To accomplish this, most print advertisers use eye-catching graphics, controversial headlines, and/or outrageous promises.

With PPC search advertising, the reader of the ad is often at or near the *end* of a research-evaluate-buy cycle—sometimes referred to as the *sales funnel*. In other words, the reader has performed several searches and is in the frame of mind to take action immediately—or at least soon.

By contrast, it's safe (and prudent) to assume that most readers of a content ad are at the very *beginning* of that process. They haven't even reached the lip of the sales funnel, so the most important objective of your ad is to grab their attention and push them over the edge.

In that sense, you could say that the goal of search advertising is *demand satisfaction*, whereas the objective of contextual advertising is *demand generation*. People using search engines are often telegraphing their demand in the form of their search, and the advertiser is signaling that they are capable of satisfying that demand.

When a reader sees a contextual ad, there's no preceding demand—so it's the job of the ad to create or incite the demand. This may seem like a drawback, and as you'll see, it's a big challenge that advertisers need to address, but it's also an important opportunity.

There are many products and services for which search volumes are low. That's because demand has not yet built—not enough people know about their existence. Here are some examples:

- Software and technical solutions that solve a problem previously thought difficult or impossible to solve
- New products in niche categories—where the search volume is low, but a significant number of special-interest websites accept contextual advertising
- New art, books, movies, or music—especially ones by not-yet-popular artists
- Nonprofit organizations seeking donations

As you'll see in Chapter 7, contextual advertising campaigns can be an important driver of immediate conversions, as well as an introduction to the advertised site that results in conversions later when people revisit the site. For many advertisers, it's not just an important part of their PPC campaign—it's their main or even sole means of generating demand and driving sales.

Monday and Tuesday: Writing Contextual Text Ads

How do you distract readers away from page content and persuade them to read and click on your ad? As you'll see later in this chapter, static and animated banner ads can more easily grab the reader's attention—when they're properly designed, they stand out discernibly from text-heavy page content.

But not all advertisers have access to the resources needed to create nontext ads. Furthermore, many site owners choose to display only text ads, reasoning that banner ads clutter or compromise the clean design of the site.

Fortunately, there are a number of ways to make text ads jump off the page. Here are some examples:

Scream Think loud. Your ads can, and should, shout their way off the screen. Don't be afraid to be borderline obnoxious—it works for HeadOn (whose ads repeat, loudly: *Apply directly to the forehead!*) and scores of other advertisers. You can afford to be much more disruptive than you are in your search ads for one important reason: *Unlike with search ads, you don't need to worry about including keywords in the ad headline.* Because keywords don't trigger bold words in your content ads, you can use anything you like in your headlines—the more eye-catching, the better. Here's an ad that uses loud and provocative words and images that are designed to be noticed:

> #### Pure Chocolate Lust
> Disgustingly rich chocolates.
> Mouthfuls of decadence!
> www.ChocolateDecadence.com

Bribe Complimentary offers (such as free downloads, free shipping, or trial versions) work well. If you're a B2B advertiser seeking leads, bribe readers with a free white paper. Business-to-consumer (B2C) advertisers can give free samples. Loyalty clubs can give free points. Often, these kinds of "soft offers" will perform better than ads that assume the reader is close to making a decision or purchase. Here's an example:

> #### Free CRM Software
> Keep Customers Happier.
> Download Free Trial Today!
> www.HappyCustomers.com/CRM

Stand Apart Your ads are competing with the web page's content and as many as four other ads within the ad unit, and perhaps several others on the page. Your ad needs to distract attention away from the page content *and* the competing ads—which is no mean feat. Study the competition's ads and make sure yours are different and preferably louder. Consider this example:

> #### The Only Real Citrate
> See the 10 Reasons Our
> Citrates Rate Higher!
> www.TopChemSupply.com/Citrates

Get Imperative Testing has shown that imperatives in headlines and body copy work well to get attention. Words such as *Stop!* and *Wait!* and *Look!* attract the eye as assuredly as if the reader had heard them shouted.

> #### Don't Take Vacation
> Wait! Avoid a Bad Trip.
> Buy Travel Insurance.
> www.TripCoverage.com

Be Malthusian Prey on the reader's most basic emotions. For example, people hate to believe they're missing something important. Tell them what they'll miss or fail to achieve if they don't click on your ad. Or take a cue from the insurance companies and scare 'em. Tell them about the dire consequences they'll experience if they fail to click.

> Is Your Dog Dying?
> You'll never know unless
> you ask these 5 vet questions.
> www.PetPills.com

Good-Better-Best

Hopefully, you're getting the picture: Shy, understated, soft-selling content ads don't work. They quietly beg to be ignored. The good news is that it's not hard to write ads that pop off the page and get results.

Let's wrap up the day by comparing bad and good search ads, and then looking at an example of a good content ad.

Here's an example of a bad search ad—the one you saw at the beginning of this chapter:

> Outdoor Furniture
> Tables, chairs, lounges.
> Wood and plastic.
> www.outdoorfurniture.com

This search ad is typical of many you'll see in the search listings. It simply lists what's being sold, with no mention of competitive advantages or benefits and no calls to action.

Here's a better search ad:

> Outdoor Furniture
> Durable Patio Beauty. See
> Low Prices on Top Brands!
> www.OutdoorFurniture.com/Outdoor

This search ad employs some of the search-ad best practices: capital letters in the body copy and the display URL, benefits (the word *durable*), a call to action, and an extra word in the display URL that corresponds to the search term.

Now let's look at an even better content ad:

> Dazzle the Neighbors
> But Don't Tell Them about Our Low
> Deck Furniture Prices. See Catalog!
> www.FranksFurniture.com

This content ad demonstrates some of the best practices previously described, such as an eye-catching headline that appeals to base emotions.

Wednesday: Writing Static Banner Ads

Remember the adage "A picture is worth a thousand words"? It's true, and that's good news for PPC advertisers. Graphical ads can convey a richness of messages and emotions, and persuade in a shorter period of time than reams of well-written ad copy.

Unique or new product designs can be clearly depicted. Benefits can be telegraphed by using photos of people experiencing the joys of using a product or service. Color, style, and size varieties can be distinguished easily.

Even the design-challenged can create effective, professional-looking static and animated banner ads. Google's Display Ad Builder is available within every advertiser's web interface (see "The Google AdWords Display Ad Builder" sidebar). Yahoo! has a similar tool for its PPC advertisers called Yahoo! My Display Ads.

The Google AdWords Display Ad Builder

In 2008, Google introduced a powerful new feature: the ability to create professional-looking static and animated banner ads, even by advertisers with little or no graphic arts skills. The following illustration shows you where to find Display Ad Builder in your ad group while viewing existing ads.

After clicking Display Ad Builder, the advertiser can select from dozens of static and animated (Flash) ad templates. Some of them are simple and drab, as in the following image.

continues

The Google AdWords Display Ad Builder *(continued)*

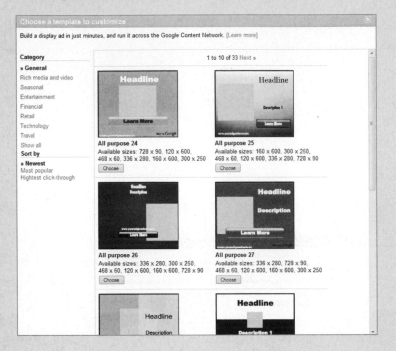

Others are bright and flashy, like the ones in the next image, and designed for use around holidays such as Father's Day or Valentine's Day, or during seasons such as summer and fall.

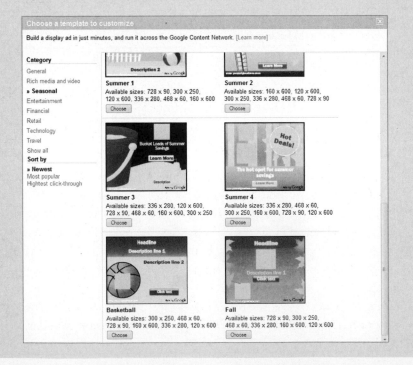

The Google AdWords Display Ad Builder *(continued)*

After choosing a template, the advertiser simply fills in fields with the desired headlines and body copy (and even text in action buttons), uploads graphics such as product shots and logos, and clicks a button. The Builder creates a set of pro-quality banner ads in a variety of popular sizes. The whole process to create a set of ads can take as little as five minutes! The following image shows you the tool in action.

As usual, some techniques can help ensure that your ads are successful. As pointed out earlier, the most important challenge is for the ad to distract the attention of the site visitors away from the main reason they visited the site: the page content. So the ad needs to be eye-catching enough to stand out from the page. This can be a particular challenge for banner ads, given the possibility that website visitors as a whole may have developed "banner fatigue," gliding right over graphic ads on their way to their precious content.

After catching the reader's eye, the real work begins: getting the click. The nontext ad needs to work hard and fast to convince the potential site visitor that there's a strong reason to click on the ad.

So the ad needs to accomplish the following in rapid succession:

Close association: Ensure that the reader understands right away that there is a close connection between the ad copy and the need or desire they intended to express with their search query.

Motivation: Include clear features and benefits that will motivate the reader to conclude clicking on the ad will likely result in the satisfaction of their need or desire.

Prequalification (optional): Make sure the wrong people aren't persuaded to click. You can do this by including a price, for example, so that the reader can't assume clicking on the ad will lead them to a page that offers free information.

Presale (optional): Describe the action you want the reader to take after they've clicked on the ad and arrived at the landing page.

Call to action: For example, *Start Saving Now!*

Guidelines exist for the ad's layout and the location of individual elements. In general (at least in Western civilizations), studies have shown that a site visitor's eye tends to examine the ad starting at the top and then moving down and to the right (see the Eyetrack III article at `http://poynterextra.org/eyetrack2004/main.htm` for more on this topic). This is also true for skyscraper and square ad units. For rectangular ad units, the eye tends to move from the extreme left to the extreme right.

So make sure that ad elements intended to elicit the response "This ad's for me" are located at the top or extreme left of the ad unit. That can be followed by words and images that clearly signal features and benefits that lead the viewer to conclude there's a good reason to click through to the advertiser's site.

Critical to the success of any ad is the call to action. Make that a big, bright, noticeable element (such as a link or a button) that clearly tells the viewer what to do next.

Let's take a look at a sampling of banner ads and see how well they employ these techniques. First up is the ad shown in Figure 5.4 from Tickle, a site that challenges visitors to take tests and quizzes.

Figure 5.4 Tickle banner ad

The ad has one main strength: a clear call to action, in the form of the Click Here button, in the lower right of the ad unit. That's perfect button placement, because as you just learned, that's where the eye usually ends up after tracking down through the ad from the upper left.

The ad is weaker in other respects. First, unless the ad appears on sites specifically related to brain teasers and quizzes, there's only a slim connection between the ad's first main message (IQ Question) and site content (the ad is on a site related to financial services). Second, because the main graphic elements are pictures of insects, the ad is more likely to attract the attention of backyard entomologists than quiz aficionados.

In other words, very little about the ad pops out and grabs the site visitor's attention—it's likely to be ignored by most.

Figure 5.5 shows an even weaker ad. Try to figure out what's being sold.

Figure 5.5 Banner ad selling…olives?

The ad telegraphs a benefit that could be motivating: the $9.99 price. But it's too difficult to figure out what's being sold and why the viewer should buy it. Is it a plate full of olives? Is it two plates (including the mysterious object in the lower left)?

All in all, it's a weak ad with washed-out colors and an important wasted opportunity: On the right side of the banner, where the eye rests after the traverse from left to right, the valuable real estate that should contain a strong call to action instead features a confusing logo that fails to motivate.

Now let's look at some winners. The first, shown in Figure 5.6, is simple and direct.

Figure 5.6 Simple, direct banner ad

The advertiser is a heating-oil buying cooperative. The target audience is thrifty-minded women, who can identify with the ad's central figure: a winter-bundled woman who's surprised at the bagful of money she's saving. The headline is short and sweet, and hits at the emotional level: Stay warm while spending less money on heating oil. And there's a big bold red Click Now button that sits right at the proper spot, at the bottom of the skyscraper. Our only quibble is that the button might help the ad convert better if the text were Join Now, which is the conversion action on the site's landing page.

Our second winner, shown in Figure 5.7, advertises a golf training DVD.

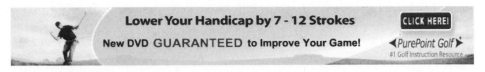

Figure 5.7 Golf DVD ad

The graphic, a male golfer exulting about sinking a difficult putt, is apt to draw the attention of the target audience. Then the headline promises every golfer's dream: shaving strokes off your handicap. The big *GUARANTEED* provides credibility and helps set the stage for a worry-free purchase. The call to action is bold and located in the right position. And the advertiser has swallowed their pride and featured their logo in a relatively subordinate position—just noticeable enough that the site visitor will draw the connection between the brand and the ad.

Next, you'll learn techniques that will help you create the most effective ads there are: animated banner ads.

Thursday: Creating Animated Banner Ads

If a picture is worth a thousand words, an animated picture is worth a million. Movement enables the advertiser to more easily distract the site visitor's attention, and convey complex and emotion-laden messages, much more quickly and easily than can be achieved with a static picture.

Animated banners are more difficult to create and usually more expensive, but the expense is worthwhile. Our own testing has shown well-designed animated banners achieve CTRs that are 50–200 percent better than those achieved by equivalent static banner ads.

The design techniques for animated banners are the same as the ones for static ads: Grab attention, tell a compelling story, and hustle the viewer to the call to action. The difference is that the advertiser has more-effective means to achieve these goals. Lights can flash, words can whirl, and the call to action can grow in size until it dominates the entire ad space.

Let's take a look at some good examples, starting with the one in Figure 5.8, advertising a Colorado Technical University degree program.

Figure 5.8 Effective education ad

The overall design suggests a college diploma at first glance, which should attract the eye of site visitors interested in getting an advanced university degree. The benefit is clear and compelling—what master's degree candidate wouldn't want to look into an opportunity to be finished with the whole thing in less than a year and a half?

The use of animation is subtle. *You Owe it to Yourself* flashes at the bottom left, attracting the eye with a message that's somewhat of a non sequitur, but one that's apt to receive a reaction of, "Yeah, I do!" The flashing text alternates with a flashing button that serves two purposes: It provides the action mechanism and sets up the presale by telling visitors what they should do when they click through to the site.

Let's move on to a quirky favorite: the LowerMyBills.com ad shown in Figure 5.9.

Figure 5.9 Attention-grabbing ad

The animated version of the ad shows a grainy amateur video of two women dancing in an office setting. One of them turns toward the camera and is embarrassed to be caught in such an unbusinesslike act.

The video obviously doesn't relate at all to the selling point of the ad, but because people seem to enjoy witnessing others' embarrassment, it's hard not to get engaged in the video. There's even a replay button, which we suspect is used pretty often.

The *Fed Funds Rate Dropped* . . . message is not particularly strong, but it becomes clear pretty quickly that there's a strong possible benefit. The call to action is easily understood: Select your state and click the Estimate New Payment link, nicely presented as a standard underlined hyperlink.

Friday: Advertising on YouTube

There are several ways to advertise on YouTube, Google's hyper-popular video-hosting site, and only some of them can be controlled with Google's AdWords PPC platform. We'll concentrate on the ones that can be, because advertising on YouTube in featured positions requires a direct contract with YouTube and a commitment of at least $50,000 per month in advertising spending.

But why advertise on YouTube? First, there's the behemoth's massive reach. According to Google, YouTube enjoys the following:

- Hundreds of millions of videos viewed daily
- Hundreds of thousands of videos uploaded daily
- 15 hours of video uploaded every minute

So YouTube is an excellent advertising channel if your product or service can benefit from reaching mass audiences of relatively undifferentiated people.

But it's also possible to target YouTube narrowly. AdWords advertisers can choose to display their ads to relatively tiny, targeted subsets of YouTube site visitors, as well as to visitors to the site who have chosen to embed YouTube videos on their own sites.

Using placement-targeting ad groups (described in Chapter 7), advertisers can easily choose to advertise on specific YouTube pages and even within the videos themselves. Figure 5.10 shows the way advertisers choose the YouTube subsections to target, using the AdWords Placement tool.

In this example, the tool enables advertisers to target not just automobile buffs, but ones who watch videos about particular makes, such as BMW or Mercedes-Benz. Targeting can be even more finely tuned by using Enhanced Ad Groups (described in Chapter 7) that consist of both keywords and sites—telling Google, "Show my ads on pages within these sites that contain these keywords."

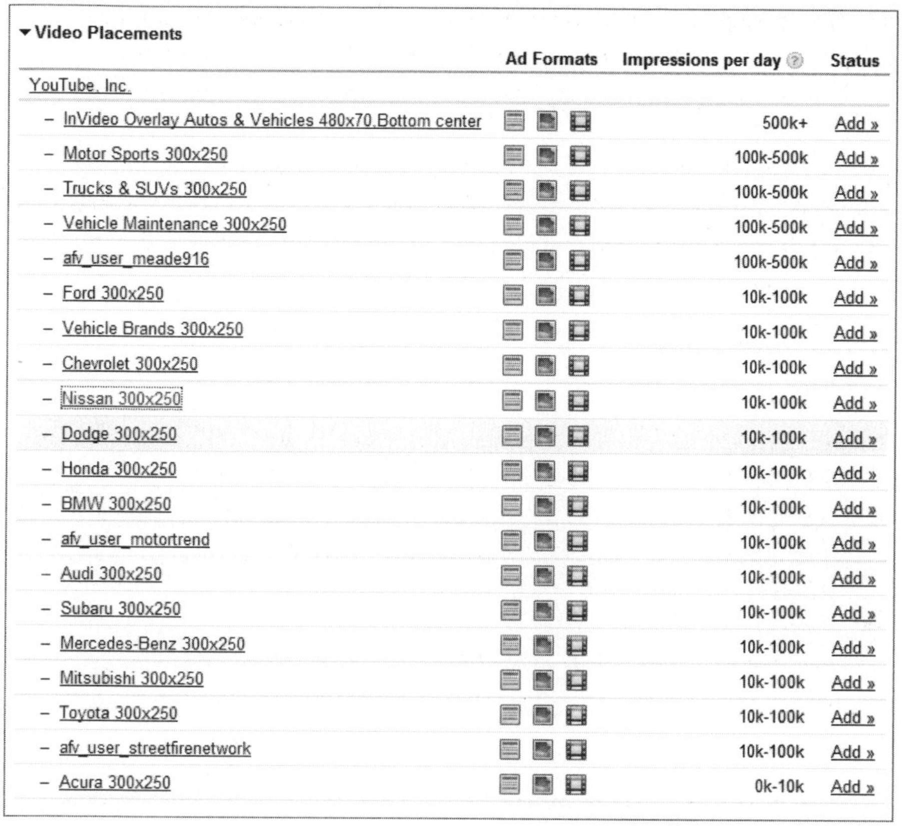

▾ Video Placements

YouTube, Inc.	Ad Formats	Impressions per day	Status
– InVideo Overlay Autos & Vehicles 480x70,Bottom center		500k+	Add »
– Motor Sports 300x250		100k-500k	Add »
– Trucks & SUVs 300x250		100k-500k	Add »
– Vehicle Maintenance 300x250		100k-500k	Add »
– afv_user_meade916		100k-500k	Add »
– Ford 300x250		10k-100k	Add »
– Vehicle Brands 300x250		10k-100k	Add »
– Chevrolet 300x250		10k-100k	Add »
– Nissan 300x250		10k-100k	Add »
– Dodge 300x250		10k-100k	Add »
– Honda 300x250		10k-100k	Add »
– BMW 300x250		10k-100k	Add »
– afv_user_motortrend		10k-100k	Add »
– Audi 300x250		10k-100k	Add »
– Subaru 300x250		10k-100k	Add »
– Mercedes-Benz 300x250		10k-100k	Add »
– Mitsubishi 300x250		10k-100k	Add »
– Toyota 300x250		10k-100k	Add »
– afv_user_streetfirenetwork		10k-100k	Add »
– Acura 300x250		0k-10k	Add »

Figure 5.10 Targeting YouTube auto aficionados with the AdWords Placement tool

When you advertise on YouTube, where will your ads appear? They can appear in any of the following places:

- Your ads can appear within standard text or banner ad units on sites that have chosen to embed YouTube videos. Google calls these *text-heavy publisher content sites.*
- Your text ads may appear embedded within the video itself—within the bottom 20 percent of the overall video-player window. This gets closer attention, because it's hard for the viewer to ignore the ad.
- Specially prepared Flash ads can appear within the same 20 percent of the played video's bottom window. These are called inVideo ads, and must adhere to very stringent requirements related to file size and resolution. These inVideo ads are not strictly self-serve like all other AdWords ads, because the upload and placement of InVideo ads require interaction with and approval of Google account management.

Friday Night: Taking Stock

On Friday of week 5, we asked you to do a quick assessment of your competition, and save copies of the ads of your biggest competitors and others you thought were particularly well written.

Now that you've studied the techniques used by the pros, take a look back at those ads. We hope you can see the huge chinks in your competitors' armor. Most advertisers are amateur ad writers and designers, and they miss one, two, three, or more of the fundamental necessities. Note how many fail to include a single benefit or completely neglect a call to action.

Hopefully by now you're seeing the huge leverage available to you by virtue of your newfound ability to create persuasive, effective advertisements. In the next chapter, you'll apply similar principles to gain a similar advantage. We've helped you maximize the number of people who are persuaded to visit your site; now it's time to help you maximize the number of people who *convert* after they get there.

Month 3—Design Effective Landing Pages

Up to this point, we've been discussing techniques for driving qualified visitors to an advertiser's website. Maximizing the number of visitors at the lowest possible price is important, but it's equally important to maximize the number who take the conversion action. By the end of this chapter, you'll be a pro at driving traffic and converting visitors to customers.

We'll cover techniques for designing PPC landing pages and lead submission forms, and methodologies for testing and optimizing them. So put your sacred cows out to pasture and get ready to unlearn some of the web design practices that may actually be constricting your sales pipeline.

6

Chapter Contents

Week 9: Understand the Differences between Site Pages and Landing Pages

Back in the Stone Age of the Internet, many websites were single pages. HTML editing tools were primitive—many webmasters hand-coded their pages by using just a text editor such as Microsoft Notepad. Hyperlinks were used mainly or exclusively to link to pages off-site.

Soon, the concept of a website as a collection of linked pages was popularized. Early Internet users were called *web surfers*, depicted as nerdy types who spent leisurely hours exploring randomly and without particular intent. Even if they knew exactly what they were looking for, finding it required surfing from site to site, because there were no search engines. Instead there were pages of links to other sites. One such list still exists, lovingly preserved in its pre-1993 state at `http://bit.ly/PbX26`. Figure 6.1 shows it in all its text-only glory.

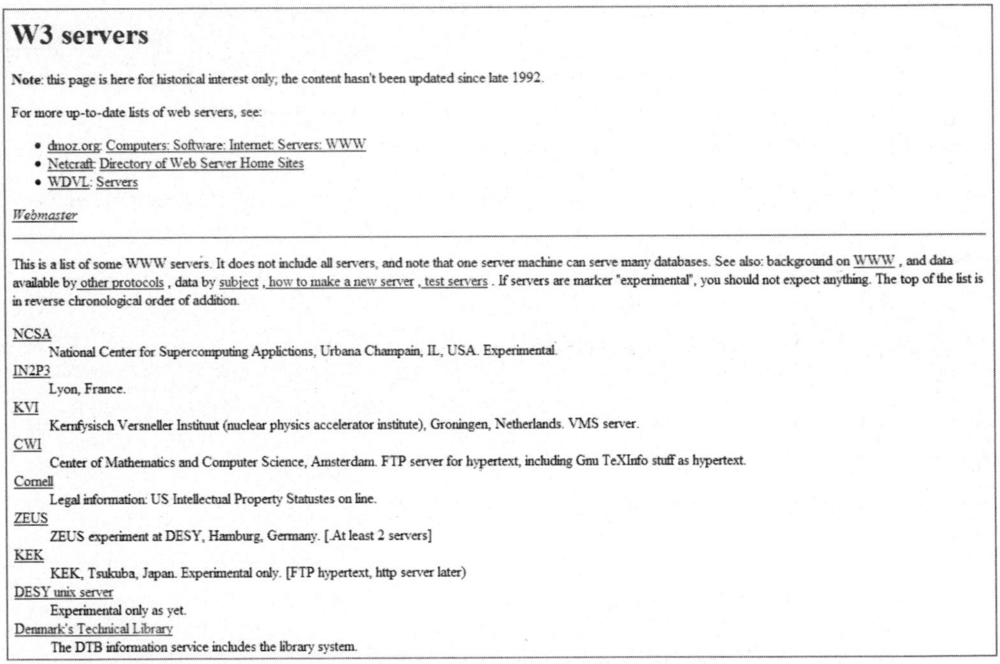

W3 servers

Note: this page is here for historical interest only; the content hasn't been updated since late 1992.

For more up-to-date lists of web servers, see:

- dmoz.org: Computers: Software: Internet: Servers: WWW
- Netcraft: Directory of Web Server Home Sites
- WDVL: Servers

Webmaster

This is a list of some WWW servers. It does not include all servers, and note that one server machine can serve many databases. See also: background on WWW , and data available by other protocols , data by subject , how to make a new server , test servers . If servers are marker "experimental", you should not expect anything. The top of the list is in reverse chronological order of addition.

NCSA
National Center for Supercomputing Applictions, Urbana Champain, IL, USA. Experimental.
IN2P3
Lyon, France.
KVI
Kernfysisch Versneller Instituut (nuclear physics accelerator institute), Groningen, Netherlands. VMS server.
CWI
Center of Mathematics and Computer Science, Amsterdam. FTP server for hypertext, including Gnu TeXInfo stuff as hypertext.
Cornell
Legal information: US Intellectual Property Statustes on line.
ZEUS
ZEUS experiment at DESY, Hamburg, Germany. [At least 2 servers]
KEK
KEK, Tsukuba, Japan. Experimental only. [FTP hypertext, http server later)
DESY unix server
Experimental only as yet.
Denmark's Technical Library
The DTB information service includes the library system.

Figure 6.1 Before there were search engines, there were site lists.

Soon enough, primitive proto-search software tools such as Archie, Jughead, Veronica, and Gopher became available. Although wildly popular and universally embraced, they did little more than find web pages and other files whose filenames were already known.

By the late 1990s, search engines that indexed site pages sparked more widespread use of the Internet for research and shopping. Some *e-commerce* sites such as Amazon.com and eBay benefited from the development of secure transaction encryption and the buying public's increasing comfort with submitting credit card information online.

Shoppers could finally search for and find alternative products and compare prices by typing specific terms—for example, *red dragon mole sauce* or *Nike Women's Shox R4 Sneakers.*

But unfortunately, searching is not always finding. Often, having expressed a specific need or desire, and clicking on a pay-per-click (PPC) ad or a natural search result, visitors are brought to the site's home page and presented with a bewildering assortment of product photos and links. Visitors with ample time, patience, and persistence will, in essence, repeat their search to find the item they specified in their first search. Many, though, will simply return to the search results page and try to find a site that more closely matches their needs.

Before you can design great PPC landing pages, it's important for you to understand one key concept that eludes many site owners: The PPC landing page can, and often should, be designed very differently from the site's home page and other site pages. This week we'll explain why that distinction makes sense and how your conversion rates will benefit when you apply that concept to your landing page design.

Monday and Tuesday: One Store, Many Entrances

Many web designers model sites on the traditional view of a single-entrance bricks-and-mortar shop like the one shown in Figure 6.2. Outside, facing the street, the store's front windows are plastered with signs advertising departments, products, and sales. The store visitors enter through the front door and patiently walk the aisles until they find something—an item they came to the store to buy or something else that caught their eye.

The website equivalent usually consists of many pages, fronted by a single unique home page. The site owner assumes visitors will start at the home page and then use the site's search function or department links to browse the site until they find just the right product to buy.

Figure 6.2 The traditional storefront model used by most site designers

This structure is fine for visitors who arrive at the site after having performed a broad search or via a general link on another site, or by typing in a URL they've seen or heard about from a friend or an offline ad. It's likely this kind of visitor hasn't yet formed a specific need or desire and is content to browse through the site to become familiar with its content, features, and benefits at their leisure.

The one-front-door metaphor is also perfectly appropriate for companies offering no more than two or three products and services; the home page is sufficient for explaining features and benefits, and guiding the visitor to the conversion action. But for site visitors who click on a PPC ad and who are very focused on shopping for a specific item, the experience of landing on the home page can be bewildering and even annoying. Compare it to the experience of a focused shopper walking into a physical store. They know exactly what they want to buy, or at least the general category—for instance, electric drills.

Now imagine that just inside the store entrance, this shopper is met by 20 clerks—each trying to persuade the shopper to come and look at a different product or department. What would you expect that shopper to do?

Most would turn around and walk out of the store. And that's what many focused shoppers do when, having expressed a very specific intent while performing a search land on the home page. They become confused, distracted, or annoyed—and click the Back button to go back to the search results and pick a different site.

The Circular Building Metaphor

Successful PPC advertisers design their sites based on a different metaphor. Think of a circular building with multiple entrances, like the one shown in Figure 6.3. Signs around each entrance describe the products sold just inside the door. The customer who walks through the door sees only the products described by the outside signage. It's easy for customers to find what they're looking for, and they can conduct their transactions quickly and easily.

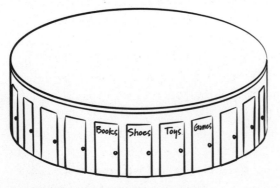

Figure 6.3 Circular building with many entry points

One real-world example of this is Sears stores. Most have multiple entrances, and often those entrances are labeled to indicate which department is just inside the door. The people who enter the hardware department door don't care that Sears also sells baby clothing. They can spend their precious time in the one department that interests them, find what they need, and finish the transaction quickly.

But what if Sears had only one door? Many customers would be frustrated by the necessity to wander around the store trying to find the right department. They'd feel assaulted by the sights and sounds of thousands of products that don't remotely interest them. Some would be distracted from their initial goal, run out of time, and leave before buying anything.

You may be thinking, "Some people love to shop. They're actually attracted by the need and/or opportunity to browse through multiple departments. So the one-door metaphor might be perfect for them."

Absolutely true. But your website can include multiple PPC landing pages that act like the Sears store with multiple entrances—and its home page can satisfy the needs and desires of the casual shoppers as well as the focused ones.

Most PPC landing pages should be designed with the multiple-entrance metaphor in mind. PPC keywords represent the intent and desire of the shopper. PPC ads are analogous to the signs around each of the multiple entrances—describing what's inside the entrance and the benefits the visitor can enjoy. The PPC landing page is like the shopper's experience after stepping inside the door.

Wednesday: The ADHD Site Visitor

The first and most important objective of the PPC landing page is to convince visitors that *they've come to the right place.*

If this crucial first step doesn't happen—immediately—many (and possibly most) visitors will click the Back button and then click on one of your competitor's ads.

Landing page designers should assume that most people visiting the site via PPC suffer from a mild form of attention deficit/hyperactivity disorder (ADHD). They're rushing through their day, bombarded by thousands of distractions, and trying to accomplish a task quickly, which is to buy what your site is offering.

They do a Google search. They click on your ad. They start examining the page at the top-left corner and try to decide whether the page (and by extension, the site) matches their need and/or desire. If it does, they continue scanning the page, and possibly convert. If not, they're gone—possibly forever.

How long does this process take? The answer may surprise you. According to MarketingSherpa (`http://bit.ly/PhACW`), most visitors decide whether to stay on a page within 8 seconds or less. But you can find out yourself: Use your web analytics package to see the bounce rate for your current landing page, and the duration of the visit for those who bounced off the page.

We're betting you'll find that the bounce rate (the total number of visitors viewing one page divided by the total number of visits) is high—over 50 percent—and the time spent on site by the "bouncers" is no more than 30 seconds or so. The bad news is, that's bad. The good news: You're about to learn how to improve this.

Thursday: The Golden Triangle

The first and most important objective of the PPC landing page is to convince the visitor that they've come to the right place. And they frequently draw this conclusion while looking at the landing page's *golden triangle*.

Eye-tracking studies (like the one you can find at http://bit.ly/3xEisy) have shown that people start to examine a landing page by first focusing on the upper-left corner of the page. This is where they begin to form an opinion about whether the page corresponds to the search terms they used.

That's why we call the area shown in Figure 6.4 *golden*: It's the section of the page where the sale or conversion is most frequently won—or lost. If the visitor fails to see something within the first few seconds that corresponds to their search—images, words, or a combination of the two—they likely will leave the page and return to the search results page.

Figure 6.4 The golden triangle

Take some time today to perform some searches and click on ads. Notice how few of the PPC landing pages seem to correspond to the search term you used. Then take heart in the fact that after you've finished reading this chapter, you'll be designing landing pages that grab and hold the visitor's attention right through to the conversion action.

Friday: The Risky Business of Landing Page Links

As mentioned earlier, many site owners mistakenly assume that all of the pages of their site must share common design elements, so they include common elements on every page—most commonly an upper banner, a horizontal row of navigation elements, and a column of deeper navigation links on the left side of the page.

As mentioned, this kind of page structure is perfect for casual shoppers. They can surf the site, following links to departments and products at their leisure. They can use the site's search functionality (if present) to find pages deeper in the site.

The mildly ADHD-afflicted PPC visitor, though, doesn't need to see off-page navigation options. In fact, by including links away from the landing page, the site owner risks the possibility that the focused visitor might become confused or distracted, and fail to take the conversion action they were so close to.

Remember the image of a shopper confronted by 20 shouting salespeople? Now picture the same scene, but preceded by this: The shopper walks into the store, explains clearly to a single salesperson that they're interested in a specific product, and *then* they're accosted by the 20 shouting salespeople, each attempting to convince the shopper to buy a different product.

The most patient, tenacious shopper might press ahead despite the annoying distractions. Most would just turn tail to find another store. That's how a PPC-driven visitor feels when confronted by a landing page full of links.

Just like the focused shopper in a physical store, a PPC-driven visitor signals their intent via the words they use in their search query. Arriving on a landing page that's crowded with links and navigation options that bear no relationship to the item or information they're looking for, they're likely to be distracted at best and annoyed at worst. Either way, they're not likely to persevere through to the conversion.

Now that you've spent a week understanding PPC visitor behavior on poorly designed landing pages, you'll spend the rest of the month learning how to design and create PPC landing pages that focus visitors on converting.

Week 10: Create the Mock-up

This week you'll concentrate on the techniques needed to visualize and lay out the design of the perfect PPC landing page. You might find it useful to dig out a paper and pencil to start sketching ideas over the next few days. Next week you'll learn about turning these ideas into live landing pages.

Monday: Start with the Golden Triangle

As mentioned, the PPC landing page visitor decides within seconds whether the page is related to the desire or need behind their search. During this time, most of their attention is focused in the upper-left corner of the page. So this page real estate is precious and shouldn't be misused. What constitutes misuse? Anything that doesn't reinforce that crucial *I've come to the right place* reaction.

Here are some design elements to avoid:

- Logos and tag lines that occupy most of the golden triangle space
- Graphics and flash animation that don't establish or reinforce the *I've come to the right place* conclusion
- Off-page navigation links
- Search fields
- Customer login fields

So what *should* be included in the golden triangle? Just enough to indicate to the visitor that the page is relevant to the visitor's search.

It's customary to include the company logo in the extreme upper-left of the page. This is especially appropriate if the site's brand is well-known, or if developing a well-known brand is an important objective of the PPC campaign.

But be careful: Many site owners are so in love with their logo that they feature it two to three times larger than it should be. Although that certainly helps reinforce the site owner's brand, in most cases it wastes space that's better used establishing relevance to the visitor's search. So your company logo or name should be large enough for visitors to see it clearly, but not so large that it occupies more than about 30 percent of the golden triangle.

Directly beneath the logo, the visitor should see words or images that relate as closely as possible to the visitor's search query. This could be as simple as the corresponding name of the product or service.

Tuesday: Bullet Points, Not Paragraphs

Having convinced the ADHD site visitor that your page is worthy of more attention, it's time to engage in marketing persuasion. Most site owners include one or more paragraphs that describe the features of the product or service offered. Their tendency is to be as comprehensive as possible, listing every reason anyone would be interested.

For the focused shopper, though, it can be risky to include too much information. Busy people find it difficult to read through paragraphs of dense copy. Frequently, they'll start wading in, become distracted, and either leave the page or leave the room.

Bulleted lists with short statements and sentences are easier to scan and digest by the typical PPC-driven focused shopper. A mix of four to six features and benefits is usually all that's needed to enable the shopper to make a decision and step crisply through the conversion process.

Let's look at an example of how product information can be "bulletized." Here's the paragraph form:

> Make authentic espressos, cappuccinos, lattes, long crema coffees, even hot chocolate and tea, with a push of a button, perfectly every time! Each cup of coffee is made on demand. All you have to do is press a button! Coffee is ground for each cup just before brewing, preserving more aroma than any other brewing system. The coffee can't be fresher! All of the Jura Coffee Centers have an extra large brewing chamber, which holds up to 16 grams of ground coffee…more than any other system on the market. This design allows you to brew up to 16 oz. of coffee at a time.

And here's the same information in a bulleted list:

- Makes one cup at a time from freshly ground coffee

- Biggest capacity—holds 16 grams

- Make espresso, cappuccino, latte, long crema coffee, even hot chocolate and tea, with push-button ease

- Makes the freshest, most aromatic coffee and beverages—guaranteed!

Sometimes a product or service is sufficiently complex that some PPC-driven visitors will want more information than is included in the bulleted list. If you believe or know that to be the case for your target audience, a link or button labeled *Learn More* may do the trick.

That button (or you may prefer to use simple hyperlinked text) can lead to a page that describes your product or service in much more detail. You may include off-page navigation links on that page, because it's quite possible the visitor needs more time and information to make a conversion decision.

Wednesday: The Hero Shot

Should your PPC landing page include a main graphic element (sometimes called the *hero shot*)? The answer is certainly *yes* if it's important for the visitor to see the size, shape, color, workmanship, or other details that are informative and persuasive. Make it a sharp, professional photograph or drawing. If necessary, allow the visitor to click on the image or elsewhere to enlarge the image. But do so in a way that keeps the visitor engaged with the original page—by popping up a new window with the enlarged view, for example.

What if your product or service is intangible or doesn't lend itself to a literal image? Sites advertising software, technical or professional services, and nonprofit organizations often can't feature a product-specific image.

Strong advice: Resist the temptation to feature a stock image that only peripherally relates to your product or service. You've seen examples: the law firm that features an image of blindfolded Lady Justice, or the software vendor that imagines a stylized drawing of mainframes and computer tape will make the page "look good."

Instead, think about using images of people. Depict members of your target market, with facial expressions reflecting the way they feel after enjoying the benefits of your product or service. Site visitors have a positive reaction to images of people feeling the way *they* want to feel. Figure 6.5 shows a poor image for a landing page for a stock-trading service. It risks alienating potential customers who fear the complexity of computer-based stock trading.

Figure 6.5 Complicated hero shot

Figure 6.6 is a better image: a successful young man looking smug after conducting successful stock trades.

Figure 6.6 Simple, clean hero shot

Thursday: Action, Trust, and Privacy

Before pulling it all together with some complete examples tomorrow, let's cover the last details that polish a great PPC landing page.

First, if your sight is warranted or protected by a third-party service providing privacy or security verification, it's a good idea to feature on your landing page the icons or symbols they provide. These images, from companies and agencies such as Thawte, the Better Business Bureau, and McAfee Secure, are widely recognized by Internet users. Often called *trust symbols,* they tell visitors that the site is reputable and trustworthy.

Place such symbols on a part of the page that's visible to the peripheral vision, but make sure they don't impede or obstruct the smooth path the eye travels as it moves from the upper left to the lower right of the page—for example, place them at the top right or bottom left of the page. And it's not absolutely necessary to link the symbols to an off-site page that explains their significance. In fact, doing so might risk losing visitors if they get lost or distracted. If you feel you must include a link from the trust symbols, tag the link with `target="_blank"` so that the click opens up a new page, leaving the PPC landing page open after the visitor leaves the trust site.

Likewise, it's often worthwhile to include *About Us* and *Privacy Policy* links at the bottom of the page—where Internet users are accustomed to finding them. People like to know there's a reputable company behind the site, and the About Us page is an opportunity for you to earn more of the visitor's trust. Some of the search engines require the inclusion of a Privacy Policy link. But again, it's strongly recommended that clicking either link open a new window, so that the original landing page can be easily found.

Let's wrap up our discussion of individual page elements with one last vital link: the button or link that signals the visitor is willing to take the final conversion action. For a lead generation site, this is the *Submit* button that sends the form information to the site owner. On an e-commerce landing page, the link or button might add the featured product to a shopping cart or lead straight to the checkout pages. In the case of a multipage conversion process, the button or link might be labeled *Next Step* and simply lead to the next page.

In any event, make sure the link or button is big and bright. It should be blindingly clear that the visitor needs to click the object in order to take the next step in the conversion process. Don't use light or muted colors for the link or button. And don't worry about the possibility that site visitors will be offended or put off by a big, bold button or link. The risk of that happening is outweighed by the benefit of making the action impossible to miss.

Friday: Sample B2C and B2B Mock-ups

Today we'll put all the pieces together and discuss two sample PPC landing page mock-ups: one for a business-to-consumer (B2C) site, and another for a business-to-business (B2B) site.

The first, shown in Figure 6.7, is for a site that sells golf training products. The landing page is one that a visitor would encounter after searching with a term related to bunker shots—for example, *improve bunker play*.

Starting at the top left of this page, the golden triangle consists of the company's logo, sized large enough to read and recognize, but small enough that it doesn't occupy too much precious real estate. Immediately below that is a big, bold headline that relates precisely to the object of the visitor's search. Hence it's likely that the visitor who has searched using a bunker-related term and who has clicked on an ad that describes the bunker training product will quickly conclude they've come to *exactly* the right place.

Figure 6.7 B2C landing page

The headline is followed by a list of bullet points that highlight the product's features and benefits in a way that's easy to scan and comprehend quickly. The final bullet point telegraphs the risk-free offer, hopefully removing barriers to completing the conversion. For visitors who need more information or time before they make a decision, there's a big *Learn More* button that leads to a more comprehensive description of the product.

The trust symbols at the upper right and the links at the bottom of the page help establish credibility for the site and remove misgivings the visitor might have about buying from an unknown vendor. The hero shot is a standard product photo that makes it clear the customer is buying a media product. Below that is a bright red *Order Now* button—impossible to miss or misinterpret.

Figure 6.8 shows a PPC landing page for a B2B company whose conversion action is the submission of a form. Like on the B2C page, the logo is small but recognizable, and the big headline tells visitors who arrived via a search term such as *e-mail marketing software* that it's worth lingering on the page.

Because software buyers need more information in order to choose, the decision was made not to list the features and benefits as bulleted items. But the strong subheadlines make it easy and fast to scan and grasp the most important selling points.

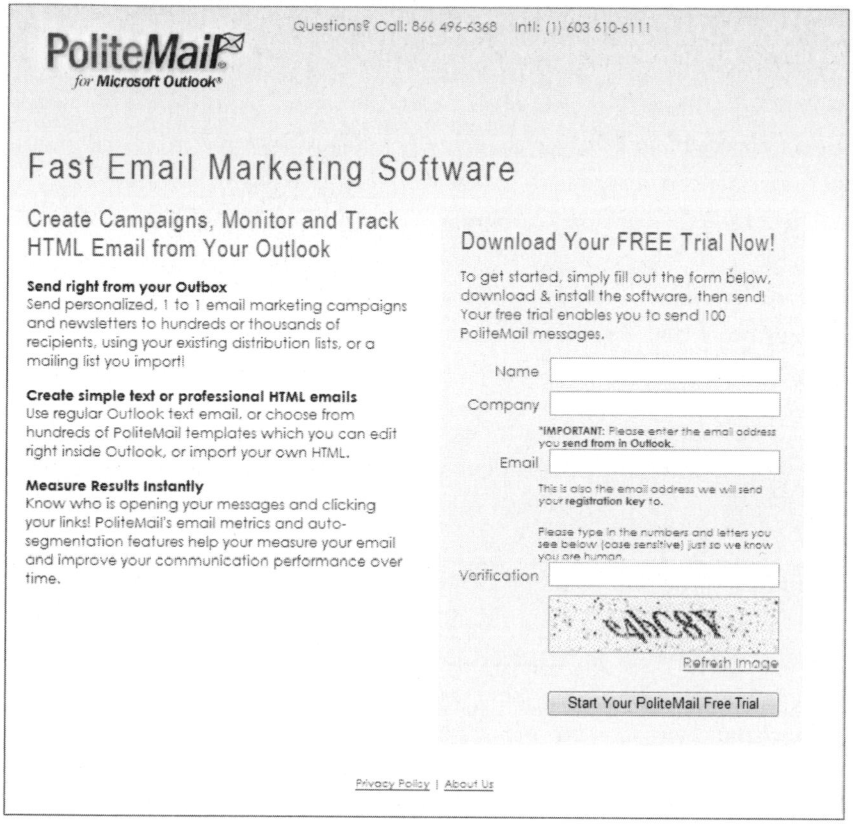

Figure 6.8 B2B landing page

You'll learn more about lead generation forms later in this chapter. The form in Figure 6.8 is short and can be completed quickly. Only the most essential information should be required, because every field of required information decreases response rate.

Notice that the company's phone number is featured at the top of the page. The reason: The company has determined that visitors who prefer to call are more likely to convert than ones who submit their contact information via the form. If this weren't the case, the phone number would be a useless distraction and should be omitted.

Week 11: Lay It All Out

The next setup in PPC landing page development is to render the mock-up as an HTML page. Whether you're creating that page yourself or outsourcing the work to a designer or firm, you're likely to encounter the impulse to "spruce it up." The page might seem too stark to you. If multiple people need to review and approve the design, it's almost inevitable that there will be suggestions for changes in design or content.

Monday: If It's Not Helping, It's Hurting

Just like nature abhors a vacuum, many people see white space as an opportunity—even an obligation—to add design elements. CEOs are especially notorious for this. Their inclination seems to be to shoehorn in every possible reason and incentive to buy.

You can anticipate this reaction by fostering an attitude of *If it's not helping, it's hurting* in your organization. Every addition—whether it's a line of text, a photo, or just a dash of color—should be justified on the basis of whether it's expected to improve the page's effectiveness at meeting the following objectives:

- Convincing visitors that they've arrived at a page matching their desires or needs
- Persuading visitors to move smoothly and quickly to the conversion action

In particular, inclinations to add off-page links should be resisted. Many people are so conditioned to the standard site template with its horizontal and vertical navigation areas that a page without them just seems wrong. Stand firm in your resolve that the only links on the page that take the visitor *away* from the page should be the *Learn More* button or link, and the link from the site logo to the home page.

If you meet with immovable resistance, don't acquiesce completely. Get agreement from the stakeholder to test their suggestion. You'll learn how to do simple testing later in this chapter, and more-complex testing in Chapter 11, "Month 8: Test and Optimize Landing Pages."

Tuesday and Wednesday: Form Design

Designing effective forms is sufficiently important to reaching a site's conversion objectives that several books have been written on the subject. We'll describe simple form design here and show you how to create a form that collects minimal information and can fit entirely on the landing page.

Web forms are wonderful devices that allow the visitor to quickly and easily volunteer information upon which the site owner can act. They're commonly used to collect name, e-mail address, and phone number info that can be used to contact the site visitor.

They're also the most vulnerable spot on the landing page, in that improperly designed forms can result in visitors becoming confused, distracted, or annoyed—and leave the page.

Fortunately, a handful of important techniques can ensure that visitors complete the form submission process quickly and without difficulty. These techniques are described in the following subsections.

People Hate Forms

First and foremost, understand that though marketers love online forms, their ardor is not shared by site visitors. People see a form as a gauntlet they need to run on the way to reaching their objective. They're accustomed to cryptic requests and insulting error messages, and even the possibility that they'll fail to understand the correct way to complete the form, and slink off the page, undeservedly humiliated.

Set Expectations

Tell visitors what you'd like them to do, and how they will benefit after submitting the form information. For example, *Just send us the information below and you'll be minutes away from speeding up your PC's performance.*

Keep Fields to a Minimum

It's important to pare down the number of fields on the form to *only* those that are absolutely necessary. Conversion rates will decrease with every additional field, because every second that ticks by increases the possibility that the visitor will become distracted and leave the page or simply neglect to finish filling the fields.

Painstakingly scrutinize every data point you're collecting. Do you really need the visitor's phone number if follow-up contact is exclusively by e-mail? Is it critical to collect the visitor's job title?

If a data point is simply interesting to know, don't require the visitor to fill in the corresponding field. Mark required fields by the now-standard red asterisk (but be sure to indicate somewhere on the page that items with asterisks are required) and leave the optional fields without an asterisk.

If you're overruled by a zealous marketing department or CEO and forced to collect "nice to know" information, try to get permission to test the form with and without the superfluous fields.

Keep Fields above the Fold

If possible, locate all fields and the action button or link above the fold, i.e., within the portion of the landing page that can be seen without scrolling. Visitors can see that the number of required fields is small and that it will take a minimum amount of time to complete the transactions.

If you must include more fields than can fit above the fold, consider (or test) an alternative that appears to be equally unintimidating. Label the action button *Continue* or *One More Step*. Or use Ajax programming to pop down additional fields on the same page after the action button has been clicked.

Make Submission Easy

Put the action button at the bottom of the form, just below the final field. Don't include a Cancel or Reset button—those are vestiges of a time when programmers wanted to show off their ability to clear field contents without refreshing the page.

Include Privacy Assurances

Internet users are worried about the privacy of their data—especially personal information such as phone numbers and e-mail addresses. Reassure them by featuring at least a disclaimer on the form indicating *We will never misuse or sell your contact information.*

Handle with Care

No matter how simple and straightforward you've designed your form to be, some visitors will enter information incorrectly. Don't be uncharitable and conclude they're clueless—everybody makes mistakes. And the way you alert visitors about mistakes, and help them correct field information, can make or break the conversion. It's so important that we'll devote the entire day tomorrow to the topic.

Thursday: Error Trapping and Handling

No matter how well you've designed your form, you can be certain that some visitors will make mistakes. They'll leave the *.com* off their e-mail address, omit a digit from their phone number, or simply leave a required field blank. They may be well-educated adults—but everyone makes mistakes.

You'll be in the right frame of mind if you imagine yourself as a shop owner who's helping a confused customer. You want to help them and you don't want to offend them. For example, if a customer fails to correctly enter a debit-card PIN at the supermarket's checkout counter, screeching "Error! Invalid PIN entry!" and forcing them to rescan their groceries isn't going to close the sale.

The following subsections describe the most important techniques for handling situations when a visitor makes a form error.

Head Off Problems

Designers have been creating online forms for almost 15 years, so many of the most common errors have been encountered and can be handled by anticipating them. For example, people enter phone numbers is a variety of ways: (800) 366-7772, 1-800-366-7772 and 800.336.7772 are all valid, common phone number strings. There's no reason why your form's error-handling routines shouldn't accept all valid forms. And there's certainly no reason to slow down a visitor eager to convert by forcing them to retype a valid phone number in the only format your form will accept.

Similarly, if your form requests the visitor's state name, don't force them to type it. It's certain some will misspell the name. With a little extra effort on the programming side, you can present the visitor with a drop-down list of state names to choose from.

Locate Labels

Studies have shown that in the case of form fields that mainly ask for familiar information (such as name, phone number, and e-mail address), visitors fill out the forms most quickly and easily when the form labels are located just above the fields, left-justified. When the information requested is less common (for example, a series of free-form questions), response rate is highest when all labels appear to the left of the fields. One such study is described in a Web Form Design video that you can download from http://bit.ly/19oUL9.

Be Especially Polite

Remember the screaming-store-clerk examples? If the visitor makes a spelling mistake or omits a field, don't berate them by displaying a big red error message that shouts "You have made an error! You must go back and correct your error!"

Instead, act like the empathetic salesperson who wants to help the customer complete the transaction. Error messages such as the following are less offensive and demonstrate the site's eagerness to help:

- We need your correct phone number in case it's necessary for us to call you about your order.
- We're afraid the second password doesn't match the first one. Could you please try again?
- The Proposed Budget information helps us tailor a package to your needs. Could you please choose one of the budget amounts from the drop-down menu?

Don't worry about sounding too obsequious—the risk of seeming too soft is not as great as the risk of confusing or alienating the customer.

Pop It Up

To ensure that the visitor notices and acts on the error message, it's safer to display the message in a pop-up window that floats above the form. The only way to proceed is for the visitor to close the error window and return to the form. After the visitor is there, you can highlight the field that needs to be corrected. The previously cited study claims that the best way to do so is to include colored text above *and* below the appropriate field, guiding the visitor to correct the error.

Never Erase Fields

Most regular Internet users have experienced this: They finish filling in a long, complicated form. They confidently click the Submit button, and an error message pops up saying a small mistake has been made. The visitor dispatches the pop-up to fix the mistake—and sees that all of the meticulously filled-in fields are now empty!

As obviously incorrect as this seems, it's still the behavior of forms that are in use by big and small companies. There's no technical excuse for it—it's simply a result of sloppy design or programming.

Test Exhaustively

Think these guidelines don't apply to your form? Are you sure? You can be certain only if you've tested the form completely. Don't rely on a single tester; use several people and ask them to make as many mistakes as they can imagine. The results may surprise you—and may be well worth the effort.

Friday: Spouse Testing before Deployment

The last paragraph yesterday introduced a necessary final step in your PPC landing page creation project: testing. After the page is finished and in final HTML form, don't deploy it until you submit it to the *spouse test*.

That's a euphemism for performing live testing with live people. It's preferable to use friends and family who will be brutally honest with you and who aren't Internet power users. Don't worry if they don't match precisely the profile of your target customer. Their feedback will still be invaluable.

Here are some suggested testing steps:

1. Show the tester the search term and ad that correspond to the landing page. Then show the landing page with everything covered except the golden triangle. Ask whether they would conclude that the page is likely to contain the info they were looking for and the promise of the ad.

2. Uncover the rest of the page and ask the tester to glance at the page and then glance away. Ask them to tell you the most prominent page elements they can remember. Ask whether they think those elements are apt to help convince visitors that they should take the conversion action.

3. Ask the tester to focus on the hero shot and ask whether they feel it makes the conversion seem more attractive, less attractive, or neutral. Or ask them to look at two or more alternate images, and tell you which makes the conversion action more attractive. In any event, don't settle for negative or neutral; if the image doesn't make the conversion action more attractive, find a different one.

4. Have the tester read through the bullet points or paragraphs describing features and benefits. Ask them to point out anything that's unclear or superfluous. Ask whether the order of the bullet points makes sense or whether they should be rearranged.

5. Even if you have thoroughly tested the form, ask the tester to stress-test the form by entering incorrect or out-of-bounds information. You may find new

problems, in which case the extra effort may pay off in future customers who won't drift away from the site.

6. Instruct a different tester to take the conversion option as quickly as possible. Watch for obstacles, confusing instructions, and so on.

Week 12: Design for Testing

Keeping in mind your *Always Be Testing* attitude, it makes sense to assume that the first version of your landing page is decidedly *imperfect*. Although it's tempting to upload and start using the first landing page you've created, you'll save time and money in the long run if you plan for the first few landing page tests—and start running the tests—right away.

Monday: Decide on Test Elements

The number of elements that you should plan on testing in a given period—say, the first six months—depends entirely on the *velocity* of your PPC campaigns: the number of impressions, clicks, and conversions that accumulate per day. For high-velocity campaigns, you can plan on testing many landing page elements. Lower-velocity campaigns will be able to test fewer.

In any event, it makes sense to create a plan that specifies which elements to test and in what order. Naturally, you'll want to start with the elements that are likely to have the greatest impact on the page's conversion rate. Here's a list of the most common elements, in order of most impactful to least impactful:

1. The headline (within the golden triangle)

2. The subheadline

3. The hero shot

4. The action button or link

5. The bullet points

6. The form elements

7. The page's background color

8. The sentence or sentences at the top of the form

9. The absence or presence of the *Learn More* button

10. Just about anything else

By the time you've finished six elements, you'll likely squeeze out 80 percent or so of all the improvement you can expect. If you're in a high-volume, high-margin, or competitive business, it probably makes sense for you to test as many elements as your resources allow.

For the next few days, we'll go through examples that will guide you through the variations you might test.

Tuesday: Headlines, Subheadlines, and Hero Shots

As previously mentioned, the headline is the most influential element on the landing page, because for many visitors, it's *the* impetus for their decision to stay and examine the page further. Said another way, it's the element that's most likely to cause the page to fail, because some (hopefully diminishing) number of people will react to it by leaving the page.

There is an infinite number of headline variations. Some work better than others because they are inherently motivating. Others motivate because of their close relationship to the search term and ad promise.

The best-performing headlines combine the two, glued together with words and phrases that naturally act to move the visitor along to take the next steps in the conversion process.

That said, let's look at a few headline variations. Table 6.1 shows the search terms, ad promises, and associated sample headline variations.

As you can see, you have a lot of latitude to imagine and test very different headlines. And though the search engines have narrow policies regarding the use of superlatives such as *Best* and *#1* in PPC ad copy, there are no such restrictions when it comes to landing page copy. So feel free to trumpet any superlative position you feel is warranted.

You can perform a similar exercise with subheadlines. When the headline and subheadline are very closely related, you can consider them to be one unit and can test them as a pair instead of as separate entities.

▶ **Table 6.1** Testing Headlines

Search Term	Ad Promise	Headlines
Data backup software	For small businesses	Protect Your Business Data. Download the Free Trial Software!
	Free trial download	Concerned about Data Security? #1 Data Backup Solution!
Dozen white roses	Fresh	The Freshest, Most Fragrant White Roses
	Local weekend delivery	Give Fresh, Vibrant White Roses— Even on Sundays!
Reduce my mortgage rates	Lock in before rates rise	Mortgage Rates Are Rising. Lock in the Lowest Rates Now!
	Get four quotes	Get Four Competing Quotes. Reduce Your Mortgage Payments Now!
Baltimore divorce attorneys	Get what you deserve	Get a Free Consultation from Baltimore's Top Divorce Firm!
	Discreet consultation	Don't Lose What You Deserve. Get a Free Divorce Consultation Now!

The hero shot deserves special attention. Table 6.2 lists some illustration variations that can be tested.

▶ **Table 6.2** Hero Shot Tests

Image Type	Test Variations
Human	Age, gender, race
Product	Orientation, background
Drawing	Orientation, color
Abstract image	Orientation, color

Wednesday: Action Buttons, Bullet Points, and Form Elements

It may surprise you to hear that visitors react differently to variations in action buttons. After all, when they've reached that point on the landing page, haven't they already decided whether to take the converting action?

You've already been introduced to the ADHD visitor. For the purposes of landing page design, assume that one of these visitors is distracted several times during a brief visit to your page. (In fact, you might try this while you're spouse testing your page: Purposely distract the tester several times.)

ADHD visitors sometimes need help figuring out how to resume their examination of the landing page. If there's any lag in their ability to find the conversion action button, they may be distracted one more time—and you may lose them. So test variations of your action button, changing the color, the size, the position—and even the words inside.

Especially when it comes to filling out forms, there's another kind of visitor you should know about: the paranoid visitor. They're terrified of identity theft. They suspect that the Web is rife with unscrupulous online vendors who will steal their identity *and* their money, and disappear shortly thereafter. They're the ones who read your landing page's Privacy Policy and About Us pages.

And they pay special attention to the form elements and the action button text. For that reason, it's worthwhile to test both. In particular, test the following:

The presence and absence of fields Test removing even fields that you think are essential (do you really need the e-mail address *and* the phone number?). You may find that conversion rates increase enough to compensate for the information you're not collecting.

Button text Even seemingly insignificant variations can affect response rate. Try low-pressure words such as *Submit* and *Click Here*, as well as alternatives such as *Buy Now*, *Yes!*, and *I Agree*.

Thursday: Testing Never Stops

It may seem counterintuitive that variations in page elements as seemingly insignificant as form field descriptors could affect conversion rates. But in an *Always Be Testing* culture, no rock should remain unturned. And for sites that enjoy a large number of conversions per day, and sites that sell high-priced, high-margin products and services, even a fraction of a percentage point of conversion rate improvement could be *very* worthwhile.

So in addition to the elements in Monday's list, the following are some of the many elements that can be tested:

- The size of the logo
- The presence or absence of a link from the logo to the home page
- The color, font, and point size of any textual elements
- The size and location of the hero image
- The absence or presence of borders around individual elements or the entire page
- If you include a phone number, the area code versus toll-free prefixes such as 800, 888, and 866

The last bullet point may seem so insignificant that it couldn't possibly affect conversion rates. But independent testing by the Engine Ready search agency (`http://bit.ly/IDBth`) has proved it *can* be significant. Remember the big winners in PPC advertising are always testing—everything.

Friday: Simple A/B Testing

Sophisticated tools have been developed to facilitate landing page testing, including Google's Website Optimizer, which is built into Google AdWords. The advantage of such tools is that they enable the designer to test several page elements simultaneously, which can significantly shorten the time required to determine the combination of elements that will result in optimal conversion rates.

The bad news is that Website Optimizer requires installation of JavaScript tags on the landing page, and for many there's a steep learning curve in order to set it up and interpret results. Still, the results are worth the effort, so we cover its use thoroughly in Chapter 11.

Fortunately you can test landing page alternatives with no additional software. Here are the steps:

1. Create two versions of a landing page to be tested—we'll call them A and B—differing only in the element you want to test.
2. Pick one high-velocity ad group—the one that receives the biggest volume of clicks and conversions each day.
3. If you're testing multiple ads in the ad group, pause all but the current winner.

4. Make a copy of the winner, identical except for the destination URLs. For one of the ads, use the destination URL of landing page A; for the other, use the destination URL of landing page B.

5. Make sure the ad group's campaign is set to *Rotate* ads rather than the default *Optimize* (as described in Chapter 4) so that each ad in the ad group is displayed an equal number of times.

Now let the ads run for enough time for the winner to be identifiable. Make sure to base your decision on conversion rate. Ignore any differences in CTR—because the ads are identical, differences will be anomalies based on time, geographic location of the visitor, or other factors.

If you're concerned that the test page might result in lower conversion rates than your control page, simply duplicate the ad with the URL of the control page. For example, if your ad group contains two copies of the ad with the control URL, and one copy of the ad with the test URL, then the test ad will run only 33 percent of the time, reducing the risk. You can add more versions of the control ad if you want to further reduce the frequency of displaying the test ad.

If you want to get actionable results in a shorter period of time, duplicate the test in additional ad groups. You'll need to manually calculate conversion rates for the aggregate data of the ad groups.

After you've determined whether A or B produces better conversion rates, switch to that page for more ads in your campaigns. Start testing the next landing page element on your list. And watch your conversion rates march steadily upward!

Month 4—Advertise on the Google Content Network

Advertising on the Google Content Network enables you to reach a huge number of Internet users. There are literally billions *of ad impressions to be had on the Google Content Network every day, and click traffic typically comes at a deep discount when compared with search costs on a per-click basis.*

But tapping into this huge network requires specific best practices and techniques that are often counterintuitive to pay-per-click (PPC) advertisers who are accustomed to thinking in terms of ads displayed as the result of search engine searches. In this chapter, you are going to concentrate on best practices for building, measuring, and optimizing content network ad campaigns.

Chapter Contents

Week 13: Understand Google Contextual Advertising

Here's how Google describes its software for matching your ads to relevant website pages:

> *The technology that drives AdWords contextual advertising comes from Google's award-winning search and page-ranking technology. Google continually scans the millions of pages from the content network to look for relevant matches with your keywords and other campaign data. When we find a match, your ad becomes eligible to run on that page. Google's extensive web search and linguistic processing technology can decipher the meaning of virtually any content network page to ensure we're showing the most relevant ads. Then, we match ads that are precisely targeted to the content page based on the associated keywords. For example, if someone visits a web page on astronomy he/she would be served Google AdWords ads for telescopes. Contextual advertising benefits web users by linking content with relevant products and services. This is great for Google advertisers like you, because you can now reach more prospective customers on more places on the Web.*

Sounds great, right? You supply the keywords, and Google places your ads on just the pages where your target audience "hangs out," waiting and eager to click on your ad and visit your website. In reality, targeting your ads to the right site pages requires techniques and best practices that aren't obvious to advertisers who are accustomed to targeting ads to search results pages.

This week you are going to learn some of the basics of content network advertising. You will be introduced to the ad units, sizes, and formats that can be displayed on the content network; strategies for placing ads and generating keyword lists; and some of the principles contrasting search campaigns with the content network.

Monday: Ad Types and Sizes

Sites in the Google Content Network can display more ad formats than the Google search results pages. In addition to the standard text ad format as described in Chapter 5, "Month 2—Create Great PPC Ads," content network advertisers can also display a variety of image ads. The formats of these ads range from skyscrapers to leaderboards. You can display static or animated ads, interactive ads, and even click-to-play video ads! This section is an overview of the various image ad formats and sizes, and how you can select and manage them in your campaigns and ad groups.

For the sake of basic illustration and introduction, this section will walk you through some of the image ad formats and sizes. The measurements within the following list refer to pixel size (width × height). Here is a quick rundown of all currently available image ad formats and sizes:

- Banner (468 × 60)
- Leaderboard (728 × 90)
- Square (250 × 250)
- Small square (200 × 200)
- Large rectangle (336 × 280)
- Medium rectangle (300 × 250)
- Skyscraper (120 × 600)
- Wide skyscraper (160 × 600)

Figure 7.1 is an example of a web page that is displaying a wide variety of content ads.

Figure 7.1 This website is displaying Google text ads, medium-rectangle image ads, and small-square image ads.

Here's a quick walk-through of the most common ad-style sizes and what they look like:

Leaderboard: The leaderboard is the most common banner ad type, and the most frequently used nontext ad unit on the content network. As you can see in Figure 7.2, the leaderboard is often at the top of the page, set apart from the rest of the content.

Figure 7.2 The leaderboard ad is familiar to most web users.

Medium rectangle: The medium rectangle is the second most common banner ad size. The 300, as we like to call it, usually costs more than the leaderboard, because it is often clustered more closely with content on the page (see Figure 7.3). These ads are often surrounded on three sides by relevant content.

Figure 7.3 This rectangle ad is on YouTube. In general, the closer an ad appears to the content, the more likely a user is to click.

Wide skyscraper: The wide skyscraper is essentially the vertical equivalent of the leaderboard, as you can see in Figure 7.4. Note that the 160×600 ad size has largely replaced the 120×600 skyscraper ad.

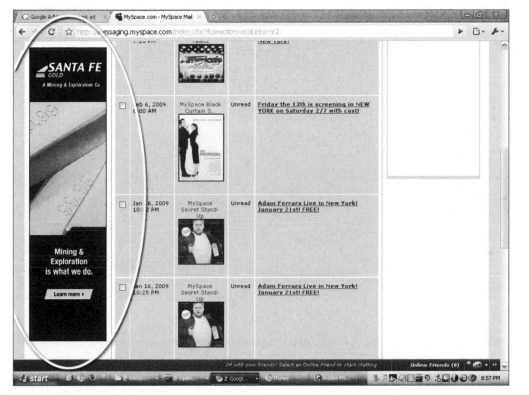

Figure 7.4 The wide skyscraper is one of the most popular ad sizes.

We suggest that you develop the following ad sizes for as many products and services as you can:

- Leaderboard: 728×90
- Medium rectangle: 300×250
- Wide skyscraper: 160×600

Implementing these three ad units *first* will increase your chances of winning auctions, increase your exposure on the content network, and help you launch your campaigns successfully. After you have your ad type and size basics covered, you should start exploring the full range of types and sizes.

How do you know which websites within the Google Content Network display text, image, and video ads? Within the AdWords interface, you can access the Placement tool, which will help you find websites within the content network that you would like to specifically target. This tool can be accessed from several spots in the AdWords web interface, but the easiest is illustrated in Figure 7.5.

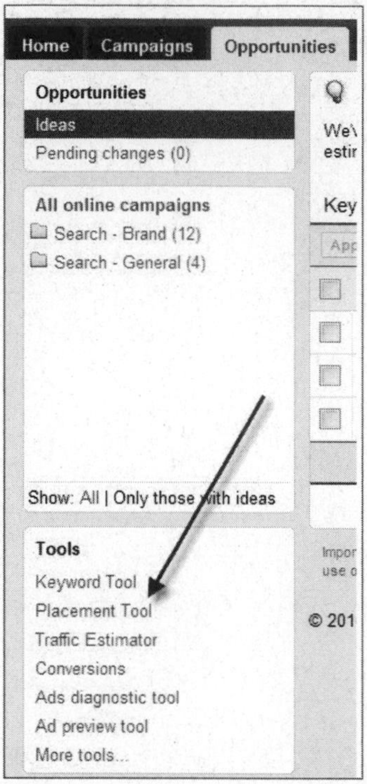

Figure 7.5 Accessing the AdWords Placement tool

Next week, we'll discuss in detail how to use the AdWords Placement tool to build keyword-targeted content ad groups. This week, the focus is on using it to design some awesome image ads.

Tuesday: Ad Formats

In AdWords, you can create content network ads in three formats: text, image, and video. A wide variety of image-ad types can be used, from static .gif or .jpg images to flash banners that include the ability to track mouse behavior and interact with the visitor's mouse.

The AdWords Placement tool tells you which websites accept the different ad types. For example, Figure 7.6 shows the formats that are accepted by FileHippo.com.

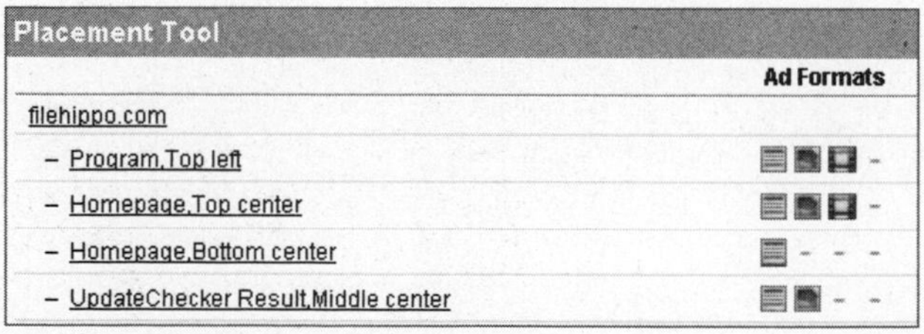

Figure 7.6 Ad formats displayed on FileHippo.com

You can see three icons in the Ad Formats column. The first icon indicates that the website displays text ads, the second icon indicates that the website accepts image ads, and the third icon indicates that the website accepts video ads. To learn which size of each type the website accepts, all you have to do is scroll over the icon, as you can see in Figure 7.7.

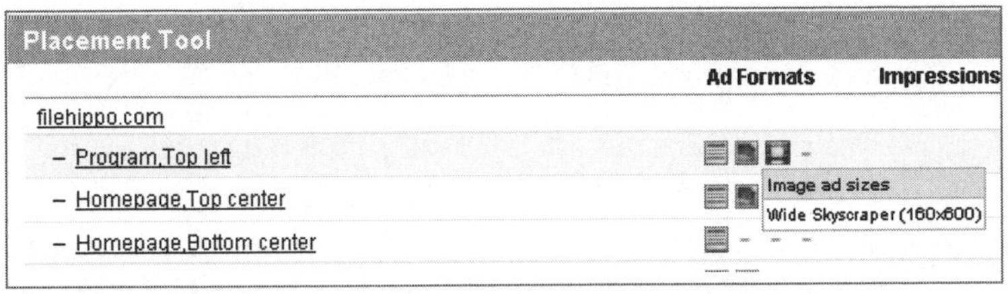

Placement Tool		
	Ad Formats	Impressions
filehippo.com		
– Program,Top left	▦ ▨ ▤	-
– Homepage,Top center	▦ ▨	Image ad sizes
		Wide Skyscraper (160x600)
– Homepage,Bottom center	▦	-

Figure 7.7 Scroll over the ad-type icon to see the sizes each site accepts.

Generally speaking, animated image ads such as Flash (or, in fewer cases these days, animated .gif format) will earn more clicks than static .gif or .jpg images. In our experience, Flash-format image ads have been the most successful ad type because Flash is a fast-loading, yet light and eye-catching format that can help improve the click-through rate (CTR).

Video ads differ from animated image ads in a couple of ways. One of the most compelling is that video ads can play longer pieces of content (up to 2 minutes in length) than Flash ad loops (limited to 15 seconds), and that content can be paired with audio. Additionally, video ads have a *play rate* metric that describes how often they are played.

As illustrated in Figure 7.8, video ads enable users to interact with the ads—to start or stop the ad, and control the volume—*and the advertiser is not charged for these actions!*

Figure 7.8 Notice the special features on this video ad: A) The Play button in the middle of the creative; B) The traditional Play button in the control bar; C) The display URL; and D) the volume control.

Presuming you bid on a cost-per-click (CPC) strategy, you will be charged only when a user actually clicks through to your site (by either clicking the video after it has started playing or clicking the display URL), not when the video is merely played.

Despite the differences (many would say *enhancements*) compared to other ad, media types, video ads compete for essentially the same advertisement real estate as text and image ads on Google Content Network pages.

Wednesday and Thursday: Why Search Ads Don't Work on the Content Network

People react much differently to content network ads than they do to ads they see on the search engine results pages (SERPs). The person seeing your ad on a content network page is not researching possible solutions or comparing prices in advance of making a buying decision. For that reason, ads designed and optimized to perform well when displayed on the SERPs usually don't perform well when displayed on content network pages.

To a person looking at content-network site pages, your advertising is peripheral, or tangential, to the main attraction—which is the nonadvertising content of the page. So like in traditional print advertising, your ads need to distract the reader's attention away from the "articles" and *toward* the ads. In order to be successful, your ads need to seduce people away from what they are doing long enough that they scan, read, and then click on the ad to get to your site. Generally speaking, you need to give them a compelling reason to interrupt their preferred activity and pay attention to yours.

How do print advertisers do that? With eye-catching graphics, headlines that are controversial, and outrageous promises. So how can you design ads that grab the site visitor's attention? Here are some suggestions:

Scream Think loud. Your ads can, and should, shout their way off the screen. Don't be afraid to be borderline obnoxious—it works for HeadOn ("Apply directly to the forehead") and a jillion other advertisers. Seriously, though, you can afford to be much more disruptive in your content network ads than in your search ads for one important reason: Quality score doesn't count. Because keywords don't trigger bold words in content network ads as they do in search ads (as described in Chapter 9, "Month 6— Optmize Your Campaign"), you can use anything you like in your headlines. The more eye-catching, the better. Here's an example:

> Pure Chocolate Lust
>
> Disgustingly rich chocolates.
> Mouthfuls of decadence!
> www.ChocolateDecadence.com

Bribe Remember, the ad reader is at the beginning of—or before—the sales cycle. That reader needs a strong incentive to proceed. Free offers such as free downloads, free shipping, and free trials work well. If you're a business-to-business (B2B) advertiser seeking leads, bribe readers with a free white paper. Business-to-consumer (B2C) advertisers can give free samples. Loyalty clubs can give free points. And so on. Here's an example:

> Free CRM Software
>
> Keep Customers Happier.
> Download Free Trial Today!
> www.HappyCustomers.com/CRM

Stand apart Your ads are competing with the web page's content as well as with the other ads on the page (usually three or four other ads in addition to yours). So your ad needs to distract attention away from the page content and the competing ads—no mean feat. So even more than you do for search ads, study your competition's ads, and make sure yours are different—preferably as loudly as in this example:

> The Only Real Citrate
>
> See the 10 Reasons Our
> Citrates Rate Higher!
> www.TopChemSupply.com/Citrates

Get imperative Our testing has shown that imperatives in headlines and body copy work well to get attention. Words such as *Stop!*, *Wait!*, and *Look!* attract the eye as assuredly as if the reader heard them shouted. Here is an example:

> Don't Take Vacation
>
> Wait! Avoid a Bad Trip.
> Buy Travel Insurance.
> www.TripCoverage.com

Be Emotional Prey on the reader's most basic emotions. For example, people hate to believe they're missing something important. Tell them what they'll miss or fail to achieve if they don't click on your ad. Or take a cue from the insurance companies and scare 'em—tell readers about the dire circumstances they'll experience if they fail to click. Here's an example:

> Is Your Dog Dying?
>
> You'll never know unless
> you ask these 5 vet questions.
> www.PetPills.com

Let's compare bad and good search ads, and then look at an example of a good content network ad.

Example A: Bad Search Ad

The following ad is typical of many you'll see on the SERPs. We consider this to be a bad search ad because it simply lists what's being sold, with no competitive advantages, no benefits, no calls to action—and therefore, it's likely to elicit very few clicks.

> Outdoor Furniture
>
> Tables, chairs, lounges.
> Wood and plastic.
> www.franksfurniture.com

Example B: Better Search Ad

The following example employs some of the best practices for search ads: capital letters in the body copy and the display URL; benefits (the word *durable*); a call to action; and an extra word in the display URL that corresponds to the search term.

> Outdoor Furniture
>
> Durable Patio Beauty. See
> Low Prices on Top Brands!
> www.FranksFurniture.com/Outdoor

Example C: Even-Better Content Network Ad

The following ad demonstrates some of the best practices described previously and an eye-catching headline that appeals to base emotions.

> Dazzle the Neighbors
>
> But Don't Tell Them about Our Low
> Deck Furniture Prices. Buy Now!
> www.FranksFurniture.com/Outdoor

Now that you see how much latitude advertisers have with content network ad copy, here's one more piece of advice: Smart content-network advertisers continually test ad-copy variations. The easiest way to do this is to run A/B split testing—two ads served in rotation (being sure to switch campaign settings from Optimize to Rotate to make sure they run in true rotation).

Because content network advertisers don't need to operate under the same tight constraints as search advertisers (for example, it doesn't matter if keywords aren't included in content network ad text, as you'll see in Chapter 9), advertisers can and should test significantly different ad versions. So right from the beginning of a content network campaign, it makes even more sense to test many ad variations and closely monitor results.

Hopefully you're getting the picture: Shy, understated, soft-selling content network ads don't work. They quietly beg to be ignored. The good news is that it's not hard to write ads that pop off the page and get results.

Friday: Demand Generation vs. Search Satisfaction

If you have a traditional, offline advertising background, you may realize by now that the difference between search-network and content-network advertising is the same as the difference between *demand satisfaction* and *demand generation* advertising.

As the words imply, demand-satisfaction advertisers respond to implied or explicit requests for information about products and services. An offline example of demand, satisfaction advertising is the yellow pages phone book. People use the yellow pages to actively seek products and services that will satisfy their active, immediate needs and desires. Obviously there's a parallel between the offline yellow pages and online search advertising. You could even say that Google is the yellow pages of the 21st century.

Demand-generation advertising is used by companies to find new customers before they are in the buying cycle. This describes most advertising you see—television, radio, print, and outdoor. Demand-generation advertising does its job by interrupting people—whether they're watching their favorite TV show, reading the newspaper, or driving down a billboard-lined street.

Part of your PPC training will be outside the range of this book. Start to pay closer attention to demand-generation advertising you see offline as well as online. Notice which ads seem to be effective at generating interest and demand. Ask yourself whether the ad does the following:

- Attracts your attention
- Quickly captures your interest by conveying a benefit that causes you to look (or listen) more closely
- Convinces you to take the action desired by the advertisers
- Explains clearly how you can take that action quickly and easily

You'll notice a lot of bad, ineffective advertising—but you'll start to notice effective ads from which you can learn valuable lessons. You'll see a billboard that grabs your attention and spurs you to action in the few seconds between noticing it and passing it. You'll hear a radio ad that rises above the drone and prompts your visit to a new restaurant. And you'll hopefully start gaining inspiration for words, concepts, and techniques that will help you design and write demand-generation ads you can display on content network pages.

Week 14: Build Keyword-Targeted Ad Groups

This week, you will learn the basic strategies and implementation techniques to create keyword-targeted content network ad groups, best practices for bidding and campaign organization, and some pro tricks that will give you an edge in targeting sites and maximizing your return on investment (ROI).

AdWords advertisers can and should set a goal to earn 40–50 percent of their campaigns' conversions from content network advertising. Although content advertising CTRs are always lower than what's obtainable via search advertising, conversion rates can be equal, and average CPCs can be lower; therefore, content-network ROI can be equal to or better than search advertising.

Monday and Tuesday: Why Keywords Are Different

The keywords in keyword-targeted content network campaigns function in a fundamentally different way than keywords in search campaigns. The process Google uses to place your ads seems simple and straightforward: Google's ad-matching software examines the words (content) on the content network website's pages, examines its ad inventory (PPC ads and associated keywords), and then displays ads that best match the content of the site pages.

It's a beautiful model: Advertisers get matched with site visitors who are interested in the pertinent ads, site visitors see ads that relate to the interests that drew them to the site, and site owners earn revenue that supports their ability to continue to publish valuable content.

Creating keyword lists for keyword-targeted content network ad groups is simple when you understand this fact: *The keyword list should include words frequently found on pages where you want your ad to appear.*

Targeting Mary

Imagine that you're running PPC campaigns for a company that sells a weight-loss program. In your persona-definition exercise (which you did in Chapter 4, "Month 1—Research Keywords and Establish Campaign Structure"), one of the target segments you define is 30- to 40-year-old married women. Let's now imagine a specific person within that segment, and discuss how to reach her via content network advertising.

Meet Mary, a 37-year-old woman living in a suburb of Cleveland, Ohio. Mary has two children, works part-time (but very hard!), and is married to Joe, a construction worker. She lives in the Midwest and goes to church most Sundays. Mary was considered a local beauty years ago, and still notices men's heads turn when she sometimes visits Joe at the construction site.

What websites do you suppose Mary visits frequently? Here are some possibilities.

Gossip Rags

Mary loves celebrity gossip, so she frequently visits dozens of celebrity news and gossip sites and blogs that are part of the Google Content Network and can display your ads. So the keyword lists that you would use in an ad group targeting these types of sites could be general ones like these:

- celebrity news
- celebs
- movie stars

Or you could target very specific content network pages by using a keyword list with specific celebrity names, like this:

- Pepper Kinsey rehab
- Pepper Kinsey bikini
- Pepper Kinsey cellulite
- Kinsey drunk
- Pepper denies

The ad group for the first keyword list would include the message *Be as slender as a celebrity*, while the ad in the second ad group would deliver the message *Get as slender as Pepper!*

We invented Miss Pepper Kinsey. Please feel free to substitute the naughty, troubled starlet of your choosing.

Television Shows

What kind of television shows and movies does Mary like? Which of her movies might be trending in popularity because they're about to be released on DVD? If Mary is like a lot of Internet movie and TV fans, she might be participating in online discussion forums, reading about new movie releases, or just checking television listings to see when a program comes on.

Television programs are often very persona-specific. For example, most of the people reading content about *Sex and the City* will be women, and most of the people interested in Spike TV's *The Ultimate Fighter* or *Deadliest Warrior* will be men. When you target sites that feature content about these programs, you will be reaching a clearly defined, specific audience.

Hopefully you're getting the picture: To present ads that Mary will likely see and respond to, target sites that match her interests. Other sites that she might frequent are ones with content relating to makeup, fashion, and parenting.

In search ad groups, keywords are intended to match search queries that are usually related to the advertiser's products and services. In contrast, the keywords in a content network ad group should describe the types of pages and sites where you want your ads to appear. So the keyword list for an advertiser's content network campaigns should be very different from the keyword lists for their search campaigns. For example, if a company sells pickled broccoli spears, and uses the word *spears* in its content, network keyword list, the company's ads would likely appear on sites with content that describes Britney Spears ringtones, or worse.

This illustrates one of the reasons content network campaigns garner such poor CTRs. Many ads are displayed on irrelevant sites that get heavy traffic. Ad impressions go sky-high while the number of clicks is proportionately very low.

In our experience, content network advertising is viewed negatively by many search advertisers, who believe that clicks and visitor traffic generated by content network ads are inherently lower-quality than search traffic. However, we believe that this reputation is a result of poorly implemented content network advertising by advertisers with good search-advertising skills, but scant understanding of content network advertising. Using the techniques described in this chapter, your content network campaigns should receive lower CTRs than your search campaigns (for reasons we'll explain later in this chapter), but your conversion rates should be about he same. And the volume of conversions can be significant; it's not unusual for savvy advertisers to receive half of all their conversions via content network advertising.

We'll describe techniques for creating content ad group keyword lists in tomorrow's lesson. But first, here are some overall guidelines:

- Always run content campaigns separately from your search campaigns— don't simply run one campaign that displays ads on the search and content networks, even though that's the default option when you set up a new campaign. Although search engines allow separate content bids in such hybrid campaigns, *don't do it*. Create separate search and content campaigns instead.

- Separate content campaigns into small ad groups. Each group should ideally have 2–10 keywords, but never more than 15.

- Don't bother using different match types, such as Google's phrase and exact match. Match type is ignored by the content-matching algorithms.

- Don't bother with separate bid prices or separate destination URLs for each keyword—these too are ignored, and Google operates based on the ad group's default bid and each ad's destination URL.

- Create ads and keyword lists that, taken together, will match a particular theme or category.

Creating separate search-network and content network campaigns takes a little extra work. To create a separate content network campaign, you'll need to edit the campaign's settings just after creating it. Simply deselect the Google Search check box, and select the Content Network check box. For a keyword-targeted campaign, select the Relevant Pages across the Entire Network option. Figure 7.9 shows the content network campaign settings.

Figure 7.9 Alter your campaign default settings so that your ads appear only on the content network.

Wednesday: Building Your Keyword List

Most advertisers build keyword lists by relying mainly on intuition. We'll describe an alternative method for creating keyword lists for keyword-targeted content network ad groups that's a little more scientific and should give you even more control over where your ads appear.

Let's start with this assumption: If a keyword-targeted ad group's keywords should describe the pages and/or sites where an ad should appear, then the best keyword list is composed of words and/or phrases that appear most frequently on the target sites' pages.

Armed with this realization, we went looking for the ultimate tool for deriving such lists. Ideally, the tool would accept a list of URLs, load every word of content from all pages at the root and in subfolders of that URL, and return a ranked list of one- and two-word keywords.

The tool that comes closest is the cryptically named Textanz, which you can find at www.cro-code.com. A bargain at $22.95, this Windows application takes as input any text file (which can include any web-page file), and displays lists of the most frequently occurring words, as well as lists of frequently occurring phrases containing any number of words you designate.

Assume for this demonstration that you're building keyword-targeted content ad groups for MuscleBound.com, a company that sells bodybuilding equipment. Because the company has a savvy marketing department, its employees understand their customer demographics very well, and through careful surveys have concluded that there's a high interest in bodybuilding among people who enjoy role-playing games (RPGs).

So MuscleBound.com executives have decided that they want their ads displayed on sites frequented by people actively engaged in bodybuilding as well as on sites frequented by people interested in RPGs. Accordingly, they've asked you to create two separate keyword-targeted content ad groups.

To create the keywords list, you can use the Google AdWords Placement tool, a simple Google search, and Textanz software as follows:

1. Use the AdWords Placement tool to find 10 or so sites within the target categories. The list of possible categories includes one specifically related to bodybuilding, as shown in Figure 7.10.

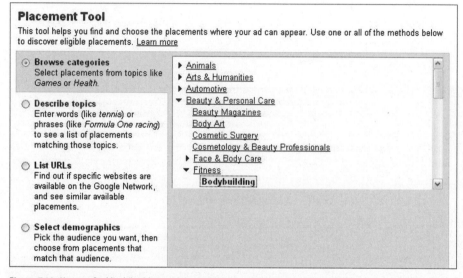

Figure 7.10 You can find bodybuilding and dozens of other topics by browsing categories. This example's path is Beauty & Personal Care > Fitness > Bodybuilding.

2. Load the home pages of the first 10 sites displayed, and do a quick copy-and-paste to copy all of the words on the page to a Notepad document.

3. Do a Google search on the term *Bodybuilding Equipment*, and copy all of the resulting text from the SERP into the Notepad document. (If you have your Google preferences set to show 100 results per page, as we do, this will be a *lot* of text.)

4. Save the Notepad document and then open it in Textanz. Choose Tools > Calculate to produce a list of the most commonly occurring one-word and two-word combinations. Then use your judgment to create a short list of the most frequently occurring words. For example, remove articles and prepositions from the list.

5. You can now use this short list to create your final keyword list. You would also include the negative forms of a few words that appeared frequently—such as *ulcerative* and *colitis*—to make sure the MuscleBound ads don't appear on pages that relate mainly to those terms and aren't relevant to bodybuilding equipment.

Here's the final keyword list for the Bodybuilding ad group that we came up with when we followed these steps:

- *bench press*
- *body building*
- *bodybuilding equipment*
- *exercise equipment*
- *fitness equipment*
- *gym equipment*
- *home gym*
- *home gyms*
- *weight lifting*
- *weight loss*
- *weight training*
- *bodybuilding*
- *equipment*
- *exercise*
- *fitness*
- *gym*
- *gyms*
- *lifting*
- *muscle*
- *training*
- *weights*
- *workout*
- *-colitis*
- *-ulcerative*

The whole exercise took us just a few minutes. We followed the same process to create a keyword list for the ad group targeting RPG sites. Here's the final list for use in the RPG ad group:

- *role playing*
- *roleplaying games*
- *roleplaying game*
- *d&d*
- *rpg games*
- *dungeons & dragons*
- *star wars*
- *video games*
- *games*
- *roleplaying*
- *role-playing*
- *roleplay*
- *game*
- *rpg*
- *-clothing*
- *-costume*
- *-costumes*

In this case, we added negative keywords to prevent ads from appearing on sites related to people just dressing up as RPG characters.

Here's another exercise using a B2B company as an example (we'll shorten the description because most of the steps are similar to the MuscleBound exercise you just conducted). In this exercise, you're creating ad groups for a fictitious company that sells enterprise-level accounting software, BigBeanCounters.com.

The CMO at BigBeans.com has shrewdly deduced that she should create a PPC content campaign to target ads to two kinds of publisher sites. The choice of the first group is obvious: sites that discuss or describe the use of enterprise accounting and financial software. She also decides to target sites that are frequented by financial executives at big companies—especially ones who hire internal accountants. Her logic is that the sites' visitors are CFOs and other financial decision-makers—perfect targets for BigBeans' software.

First, do a Google search on the terms *enterprise accounting software* and *accounting software for big companies*. Then use the Textanz software to list the most frequently occurring one-word and two-word combinations.

Here's the final list of keywords for the Accounting keyword-targeted ad group:

- *accounting*
- *accounting system*
- *accounting systems*
- *bigbeancounters.com*
- *bigbeancounters*
- *bs1 enterprise*
- *enterprise accounting*
- *enterprise financial*
- *enterprise software*
- *enterprise solution*
- *enterprise solutions*
- *erp*
- *erp software*
- *financial management*
- *mas 90*
- *microsoft dynamics*
- *quickbooks enterprise*
- *sage software*
- *-endocrinology*
- *-quicken*
- *-small business*
- *-peachtree software*
- *-microsoft office*

Notice that the list includes a few one-word keywords and many two-word keywords. Always be careful of this fact: The content-matching algorithms work best with unambiguous keywords. Put another way, you risk confusing the algorithms when you use keywords that have several synonyms—more of a danger with one-word keywords than with keywords of two or more words.

So in the preceding example, the keyword *erp* is safe, because it's most commonly used as an acronym for *enterprise resource planning*. Having said this, the term is occasionally associated with a medical term *endocrinology-reproductive physiology*. That's why we included the negative keyword *endocrinology*; in doing so, we're telling the algorithm not to display ads on pages that include the term *erp* and *endocrinology*.

We've also included the names of some of BigBeans' competitors: QuickBooks Enterprise and Microsoft Dynamics, for example. So if a page exists that describes or discusses those products, BigBeans' ads will appear on the same page. And we've included the negative keyword *Peachtree Software*, because that package is used by smaller businesses than our target audience.

Now here's the list for the ad group that targets sites frequented by financial executives who are recruiting accountants:

- *accountant jobs*
- *accounting jobs*
- *accounting staffing*
- *cfo jobs*
- *cfo recruitment*
- *enterprise accounting*
- *enterprise financial*
- *enterprise recruitment*
- *finance*
- *finance jobs*
- *financial jobs*
- *recruiting*

- *recruitment*
- *-army*
- *-navy*
- *-air force*
- *-marines*
- *-marine*
- *-bookkeeper*
- *-bookkeepers*
- *-careerbank*
- *-bookkeeping jobs*
- *-small business finance*

By now, you should be able to figure out why each keyword has been included. The names of American armed forces are there so that the algorithm knows not to place BigBeans' ads on pages whose content deals with, for example, army recruiting. The negative keyword *careerbank* is included because it's a popular job-listing site for lower-level (nonenterprise) jobs.

Here is the sample ad to match the Accounting ad group:

> Don't Miss a Nickel
>
> Big Company Accounting Software
> Saves Time and Money. Free Trial!
> www.BigBeanCounters.com

And here's the ad for the Recruiting ad group:

> Don't Hire an Accountant
>
> Efficient Software Means Fewer
> Employees. Download Our White Paper!
> www.BigBeanCounters.com

Notice that both ads feature *soft offers*—a free trial and a free white paper. This acknowledges that readers of content ads are not yet in the buying cycle, so the objective is to ease them into the sales funnel by providing an easy way to get more information. The white-paper offer is somewhat softer than the free trial, in light of the fact that hiring managers are even further from the sales funnel than people who view ads on sites describing accounting software.

Thursday: Demographic Bidding

Demographic bidding is an advanced feature that enables you to specifically target your audience on the Google Content Network based on age and gender. It's a powerful feature that works only when you are targeting specific sites that track and report their demographic audience profiles to Google. You set up demographic bidding from within a content network campaign's Campaign Settings in the Advanced Settings section by clicking the Demographic Bidding link, and then clicking the Edit link, shown in Figure 7.11.

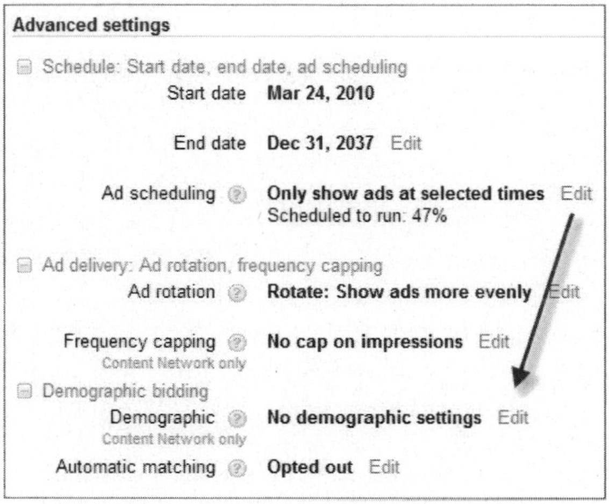

Figure 7.11   The Edit link for the Demographic Bidding setting

Clicking the word *Bid* to the right of one of the demographic segment's Exclude check boxes (see Figure 7.12) enables you to increase your maximum bid prices for that segment by up to 500 percent. That can be useful for targeting a diverse audience while paying extra for a demographic segment within that audience that is more likely to convert than the others. But most advertisers will use demographic bidding to exclude demographic segments by simply clicking the Exclude check box.

We frequently exclude the gender opposite our target persona, and any traffic from people under the age of 18 (because most don't have credit cards). That decision alone can reduce ad spending by 10–15 by helping avoid clicks from people who are outside the target market and therefore unlikely to convert.

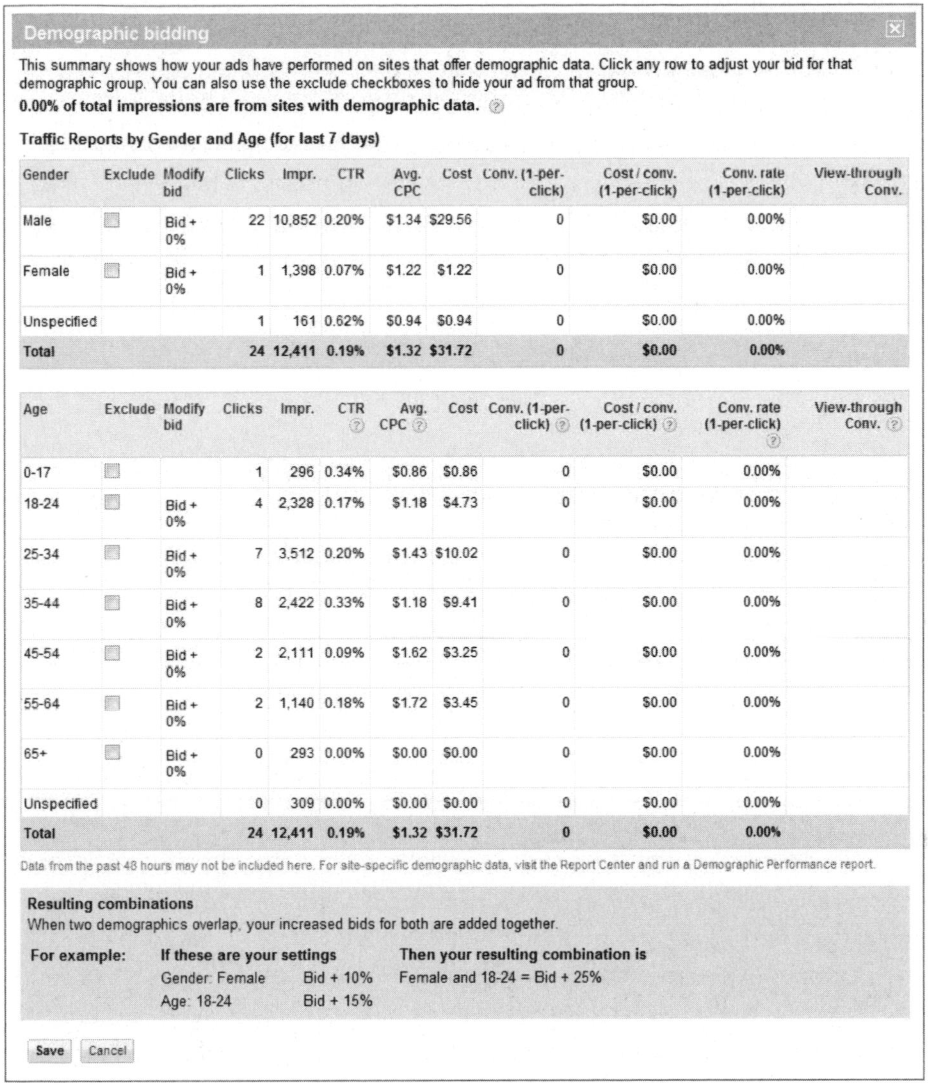

Demographic bidding ⊠

This summary shows how your ads have performed on sites that offer demographic data. Click any row to adjust your bid for that demographic group. You can also use the exclude checkboxes to hide your ad from that group.

0.00% of total impressions are from sites with demographic data. ⓘ

Traffic Reports by Gender and Age (for last 7 days)

Gender	Exclude	Modify bid	Clicks	Impr.	CTR	Avg. CPC	Cost	Conv. (1-per-click)	Cost / conv. (1-per-click)	Conv. rate (1-per-click)	View-through Conv.
Male	☐	Bid + 0%	22	10,852	0.20%	$1.34	$29.56	0	$0.00	0.00%	
Female	☐	Bid + 0%	1	1,398	0.07%	$1.22	$1.22	0	$0.00	0.00%	
Unspecified			1	161	0.62%	$0.94	$0.94	0	$0.00	0.00%	
Total			**24**	**12,411**	**0.19%**	**$1.32**	**$31.72**	**0**	**$0.00**	**0.00%**	

Age	Exclude	Modify bid	Clicks	Impr.	CTR ⓘ	Avg. CPC ⓘ	Cost	Conv. (1-per-click) ⓘ	Cost / conv. (1-per-click) ⓘ	Conv. rate (1-per-click) ⓘ	View-through Conv. ⓘ
0-17	☐		1	296	0.34%	$0.86	$0.86	0	$0.00	0.00%	
18-24	☐	Bid + 0%	4	2,328	0.17%	$1.18	$4.73	0	$0.00	0.00%	
25-34	☐	Bid + 0%	7	3,512	0.20%	$1.43	$10.02	0	$0.00	0.00%	
35-44	☐	Bid + 0%	8	2,422	0.33%	$1.18	$9.41	0	$0.00	0.00%	
45-54	☐	Bid + 0%	2	2,111	0.09%	$1.62	$3.25	0	$0.00	0.00%	
55-64	☐	Bid + 0%	2	1,140	0.18%	$1.72	$3.45	0	$0.00	0.00%	
65+	☐	Bid + 0%	0	293	0.00%	$0.00	$0.00	0	$0.00	0.00%	
Unspecified			0	309	0.00%	$0.00	$0.00	0	$0.00	0.00%	
Total			**24**	**12,411**	**0.19%**	**$1.32**	**$31.72**	**0**	**$0.00**	**0.00%**	

Data from the past 48 hours may not be included here. For site-specific demographic data, visit the Report Center and run a Demographic Performance report.

Resulting combinations
When two demographics overlap, your increased bids for both are added together.

For example:	If these are your settings		Then your resulting combination is
	Gender: Female	Bid + 10%	Female and 18-24 = Bid + 25%
	Age: 18-24	Bid + 15%	

Save   Cancel

Figure 7.12 Demographic Bidding screen

Friday: Ad-Frequency Capping

Some advertisers believe that an ad can lose its effectiveness after being viewed by the same person several times. It certainly seems intuitive that the more times a person visits a website page, sees a particular ad, and neglects to click on it, the less likely they are to ever click on it.

So Google allows the advertiser to *cap* the number of times a particular person views an ad. You access this feature by clicking the Edit link from within a content network campaign's Campaign Settings in the Advanced Settings section, as shown in Figure 7.13.

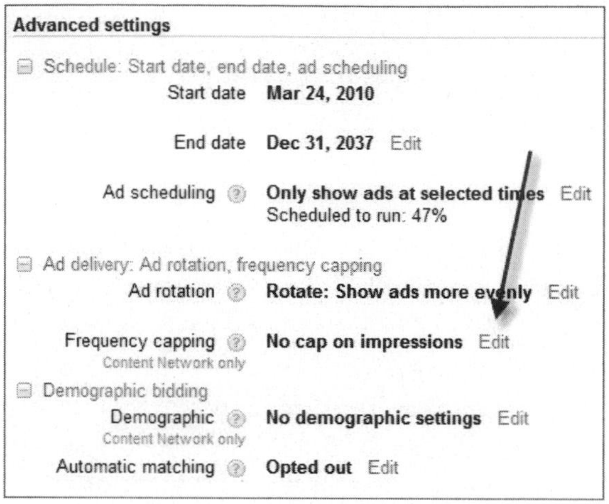

Figure 7.13 The Edit link for the Frequency Capping setting

Doing so reveals the opportunity to customize the feature. You can choose to turn frequency capping on or off, or tell Google to display the ads in the campaign a set number of times per day, per week, or per month, as shown in Figure 7.14. You can also choose to apply that frequency restriction to each ad in the campaign, to all ads in each ad group of the campaign, or to the sum total of all ads in the campaign.

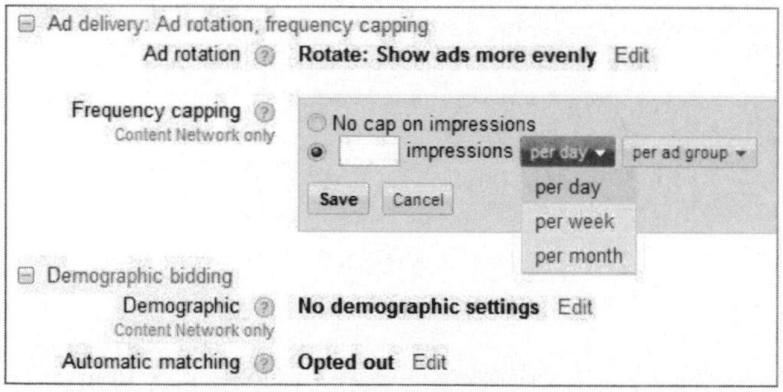

Figure 7.14 Frequency-capping customization options

If you're bidding on a CPM basis, this feature can save significant money because it limits the number of impressions gained by each campaign. Even if you're bidding on a CPC basis, though, you should consider testing this feature if you see that your ads are achieving a low CTR. Implementing frequency capping in this case might lead to better CTR, which in turn could improve your quality score, which could result in lower CPC costs.

Week 15: Build Placement-Targeted Ad Groups

Compared to keyword-targeted campaigns, placement targeting is relatively simple. With placement-targeted campaigns, you tell Google exactly which sites, or sections or pages within sites, should display your ad.

Monday: Placement Targeting

The ability to choose specific sites via placement-targeted campaigns is powerful, but Google does it one better. Advertisers can choose to display their ads on specific pages within a site, or even subsections of pages. For example, advertisers can choose to advertise just on the New York Times website in the business, fashion, health, travel, or sports sections—and many more.

Placement-targeted campaigns offer several advantages over keyword-targeted campaigns. Because a company can target ads to specific sites, it can tailor its ads to appeal specifically to the readers of those sites. For example, an apparel retailer could display ads for travel clothing on travel sites, or even tailor ads to readers of individual sites. So a soap-pad manufacturer could create special ads for the Boston.com sites that say *Beantown Loves Brillo!*

Another big advantage: You can set individual bids for each site. So by running reports that show the CTR and conversion-rate data for each site, an advertiser can fine-tune each site's maximum CPC to achieve acceptable (or hopefully great) ROI for each site.

And yet another advantage: Placement-targeted text ads get stretched and enlarged to fill an entire ad unit—the *expanded text ad*. Google says,

> *An expanded text ad is a text ad that fills an entire ad unit on its own, rather than being grouped with other text ads. Expanded text ads have the same character limits and advertising policies as typical text ads, but are displayed solo and with text enlarged.*

So if a site publisher has specified that a strip of four AdWords ads should appear in a banner at the bottom of a page, placement-targeted text ads will muscle the other ads off the ad unit and be displayed big and bold.

To enable placement targeting, select the Relevant Pages Only on the Placements and Audiences I Manage option (which you can access under the Networks and Devices section after clicking the Edit link next to the word Content), as shown in Figure 7.15.

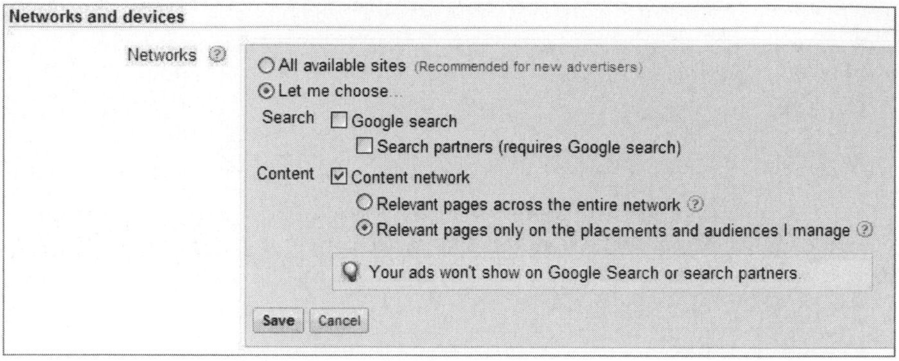

Figure 7.15 Placement targeting is implemented at the campaign level.

Within placement-targeted campaigns, you can assign different per-click bids for each individual site or subdomain. For best optimization, you'll want to take advantage of this. Here's an example: The ad group in Figure 7.16 has a default bid of $1.02 per click, with lower per-click bids of $0.17 or $0.27 on some of the largest weather publishers. In this case, bids of $1.02 produced conversions at acceptable ROI for some sites, but lower bids on the other sites were necessary to produce conversions at acceptable ROI for those.

Placement	Status	Current Bid Max CPC
accuweather.com	Active	$0.17
intellicast.com	Active	$0.27
ktul.com	Active	$1.02
abc3340.com	Active	$1.02
newschannel5.com	Active	$1.02
wunderground.com	Active	$0.17

Figure 7.16 This successful ad group targeted weather-related placements.

Tuesday: Choosing Sites and Placements with the Placement Tool

The AdWords Placement tool is very versatile. You've already seen how you can use it to choose an ad format and create keyword lists. Today you're going to learn about the many ways you can use this tool to determine your ad placements.

First, you can simply click on a category or subcategory name in the left-hand column of the Placement tool (see Figure 7.17). The tool will then display a list of suggested placements under the Placement Ideas heading. There are 594 categories and subcategories.

To add placements to an ad group, select the check boxes next to the placement names and click the Add Placements button. You will then see the dialog box shown in Figure 7.18, which lets you choose the ad group that will receive the placements.

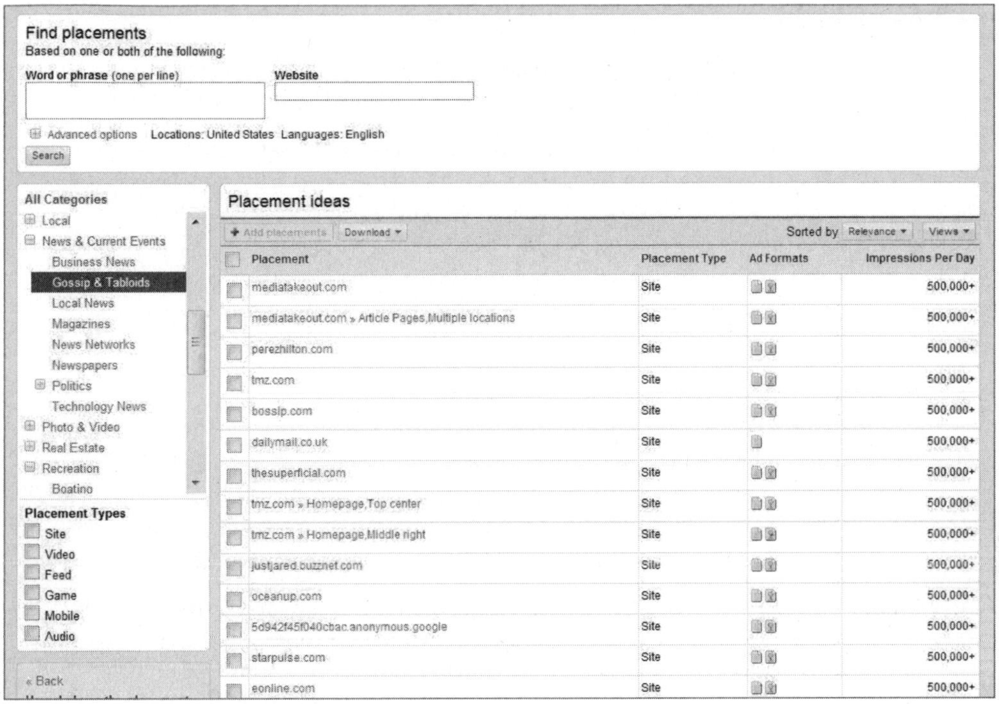

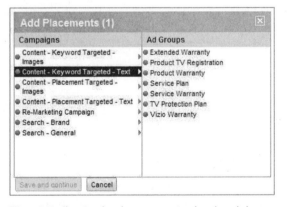

Figure 7.17 The Placement tool

Figure 7.18 Choosing the ad group to receive the selected placements

You can also type a word or phrase in the field labeled as such, and click the Search button. The tool will display a list of placements that match the field contents, like the one shown in Figure 7.19. Note that simple one-word entries seem to work best; the tool may get confused when it tries to work with multiple words and phrases.

Another way to find placements is to type a website URL or domain name into the Website field and click the Search button. The Placement tool will display a list of placements that feature content similar to the URL or domain you entered, like the list shown in Figure 7.20.

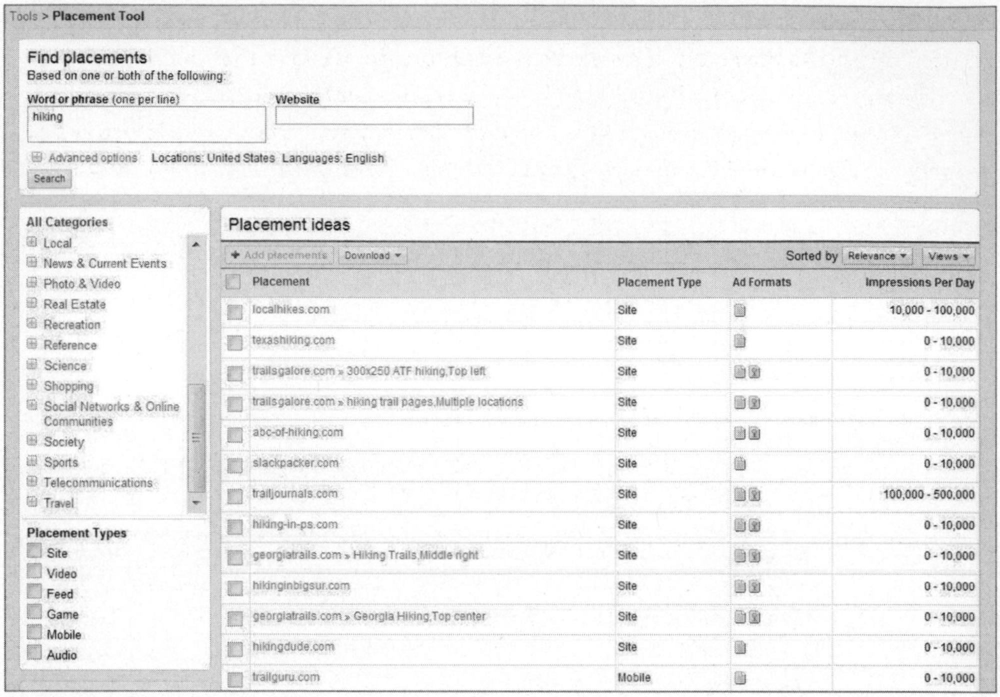

Tools > **Placement Tool**

Find placements
Based on one or both of the following:

Word or phrase (one per line): hiking
Website:

⊞ Advanced options   Locations: United States   Languages: English
Search

All Categories
⊞ Local
⊞ News & Current Events
⊞ Photo & Video
⊞ Real Estate
⊞ Recreation
⊞ Reference
⊞ Science
⊞ Shopping
⊞ Social Networks & Online Communities
⊞ Society
⊞ Sports
⊞ Telecommunications
⊞ Travel

Placement Types
☐ Site
☐ Video
☐ Feed
☐ Game
☐ Mobile
☐ Audio

Placement ideas

✦ Add placements   Download ▾   Sorted by Relevance ▾   Views ▾

Placement	Placement Type	Ad Formats	Impressions Per Day
localhikes.com	Site		10,000 - 100,000
texashiking.com	Site		0 - 10,000
trailsgalore.com » 300x250 ATF hiking,Top left	Site		0 - 10,000
trailsgalore.com » hiking trail pages,Multiple locations	Site		0 - 10,000
abc-of-hiking.com	Site		0 - 10,000
slackpacker.com	Site		0 - 10,000
trailjournals.com	Site		100,000 - 500,000
hiking-in-ps.com	Site		0 - 10,000
georgiatrails.com » Hiking Trails,Middle right	Site		0 - 10,000
hikinginbigsur.com	Site		0 - 10,000
georgiatrails.com » Georgia Hiking,Top center	Site		0 - 10,000
hikingdude.com	Site		0 - 10,000
trailguru.com	Mobile		0 - 10,000

Figure 7.19 Displaying placements based on an entered phrase

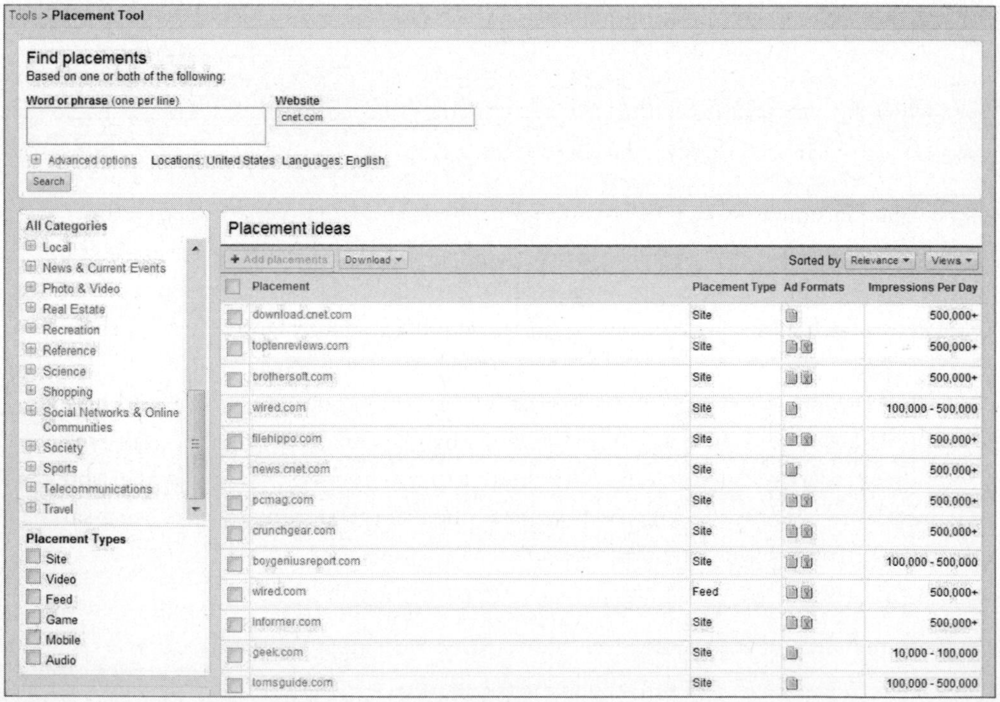

Tools > **Placement Tool**

Find placements
Based on one or both of the following:

Word or phrase (one per line):
Website: cnet.com

⊞ Advanced options   Locations: United States   Languages: English
Search

All Categories
⊞ Local
⊞ News & Current Events
⊞ Photo & Video
⊞ Real Estate
⊞ Recreation
⊞ Reference
⊞ Science
⊞ Shopping
⊞ Social Networks & Online Communities
⊞ Society
⊞ Sports
⊞ Telecommunications
⊞ Travel

Placement Types
☐ Site
☐ Video
☐ Feed
☐ Game
☐ Mobile
☐ Audio

Placement ideas

✦ Add placements   Download ▾   Sorted by Relevance ▾   Views ▾

Placement	Placement Type	Ad Formats	Impressions Per Day
download.cnet.com	Site		500,000+
toptenreviews.com	Site		500,000+
brothersoft.com	Site		500,000+
wired.com	Site		100,000 - 500,000
filehippo.com	Site		500,000+
news.cnet.com	Site		500,000+
pcmag.com	Site		500,000+
crunchgear.com	Site		500,000+
boygeniusreport.com	Site		100,000 - 500,000
wired.com	Feed		500,000+
informer.com	Site		500,000+
geek.com	Site		10,000 - 100,000
tomsguide.com	Site		100,000 - 500,000

Figure 7.20 Displaying placements based on an entered domain or URL

You can also use this feature to find multiple placements within a popular site. Figure 7.21 shows the result of using the domain facebook.com in the Website field. As you can see, there are several individual placements within Facebook that you can separately target—perhaps with ads tailored for each section. Try this on other large properties such as YouTube and WSJ.com (*The Wall Street Journal*).

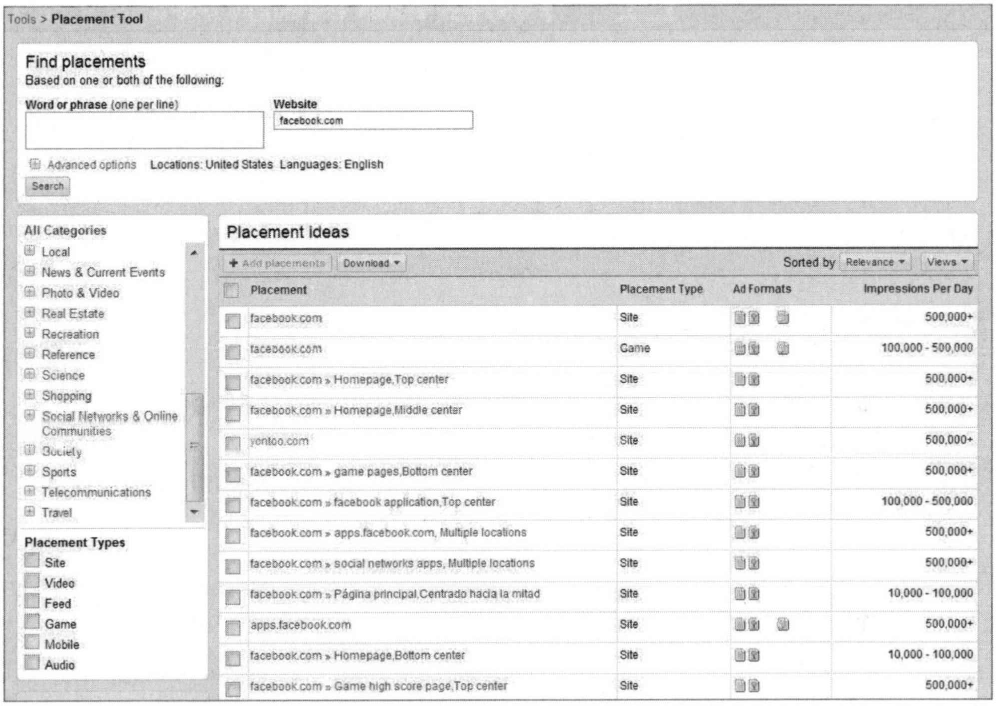

Figure 7.21 Displaying multiple placements within one domain

The Placement tool enables you to filter by many factors and to zero in on smaller subsegments of placements. To reach these filters, click the plus sign next to the Advanced Options link. You can select different locations and languages, as well as other filters such as the gender and age of the placements' average visitors, as shown in Figure 7.22.

As with any automated tools, you will want to use your own intuition and existing knowledge of your market before trusting any placement suggestion. To learn more about a particular placement, simply click on it to reveal more information, as shown in Figure 7.23. Click the link at the bottom of the information window to see a sample website page representing the placement.

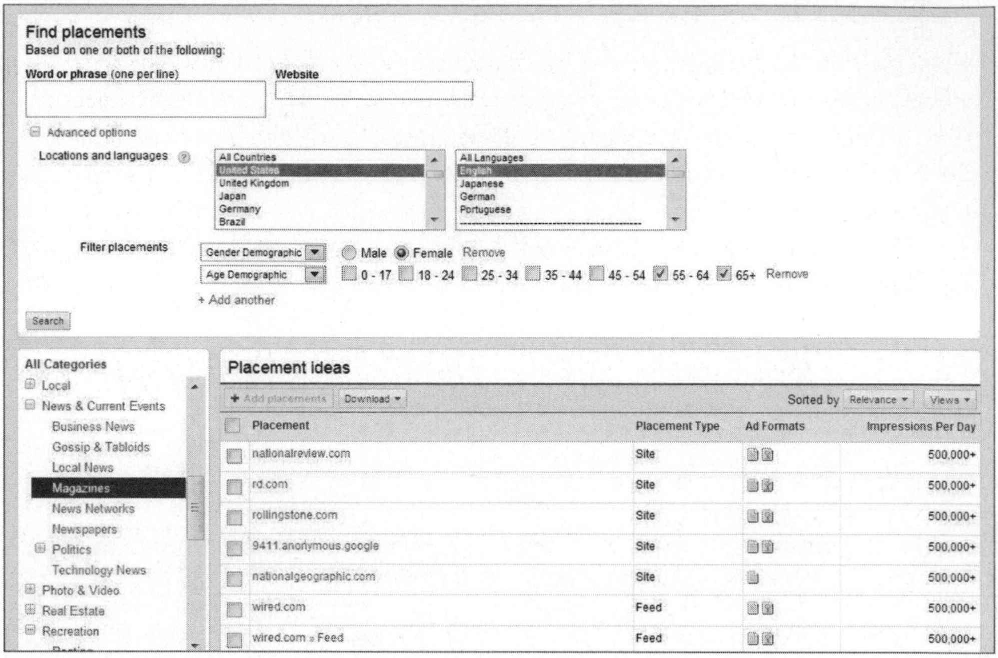

Figure 7.22 Filtering placements based on Advanced Options

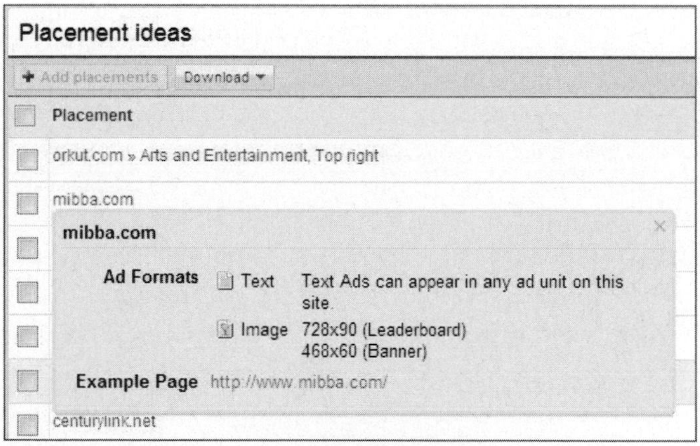

Figure 7.23 Revealing more information about a placement

Wednesday: Other Tools for Choosing Sites for Placements

The Google Content Network is so vast that it's difficult for any single tool (even Google's own Placement tool) to find all of the available placement opportunities. For this reason, we recommend using other tools—some that are Google tools and some that are from other clever companies. Today, you'll get a quick rundown of tools that can help expand your placement-targeted campaigns.

DoubleClick Ad Planner

The DoubleClick Ad Planner (created by Google subsidiary DoubleClick) is a free tool that can help identify websites on the content network that your target audience is likely to visit. Ad Planner is a capable tool with several sort functions that can help you drill down to see targeted websites that are relevant for your product or service. By reflecting on the persona exercise you completed earlier, you should be able to understand and use the audience-filtering capabilities of Ad Planner quickly and easily. Figure 7.24 shows these filtering options.

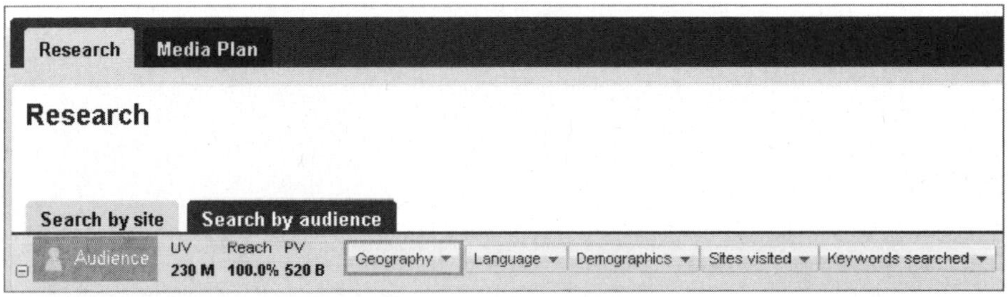

Figure 7.24 In Ad Planner, you can target your audience by geography, language, demographics, sites visited, and keywords searched.

Each filter can help you locate the websites that your audience might frequent. The Geography and Language filters are pretty straightforward, and the Demographics filter can help you zero in on your audience's gender or age. For example, the demographic filtering in Figure 7.25 is revealing sites whose main visitors are females between the ages of 25 and 54 who have a bachelor's degree and make over $50,000 a year.

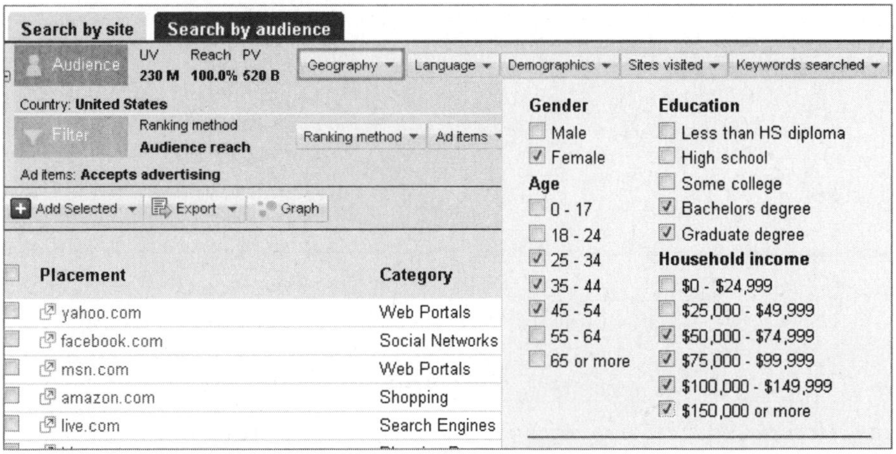

Figure 7.25 Demographic filtering in Ad Planner

You can also find websites within Ad Planner by entering the domain names of other websites with similar content and frequent visitor profiles. The Keywords Searched function works similarly to the Word or Phrase field in the AdWords Placement tool. Just enter one or more keywords that are relevant to the type of site you're searching for, and Ad Planner will suggest a wide range of websites.

As illustrated in Figure 7.26, you can put almost any URL into the Edit Placements and Bids text field, and if the site is a part of the content network, Google will run ads on the site.

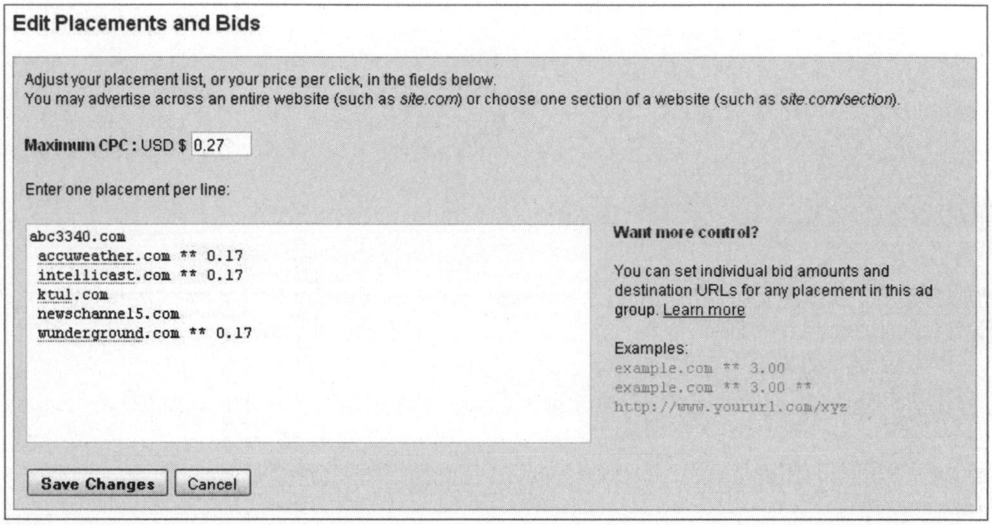

Figure 7.26 Edit Placements and Bids

However, if you're lazy or just thrifty with your time, there's a fast way to identify the sites that can be targeted via placement-targeted campaigns. Using tools such as the ShoeMoney AdSense Crawler and Web Data Extractor, you can find lists of hundreds of sites for your campaigns.

ShoeMoney AdSense Crawler Tool

The AdSense Crawler tool is provided by ShoeMoney Media Group. This tool is not free, but for $9.95, you can test out a trial membership. You can access the ShoeMoney tools at www.shoemoneytools.com. This tool works similarly to the Word or Phrase option in the AdWords Placement tool. Just enter your keywords (there is a limit of 100 keywords) into the search box as shown in Figure 7.27, and AdSense Crawler will provide related websites.

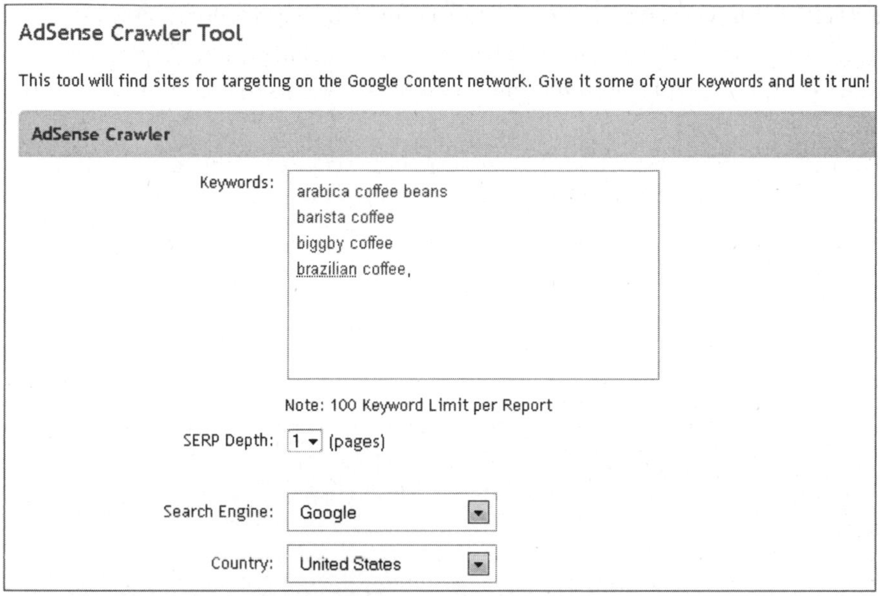

AdSense Crawler Tool

This tool will find sites for targeting on the Google Content network. Give it some of your keywords and let it run!

AdSense Crawler

Keywords:
arabica coffee beans
barista coffee
biggby coffee
brazilian coffee,

Note: 100 Keyword Limit per Report

SERP Depth: 1 ▼ (pages)

Search Engine: Google ▼

Country: United States ▼

Figure 7.27 Enter your keywords into the AdSense Crawler tool, and it will provide a list of sites that are available on the content network.

Web Data Extractor

Web Data Extractor (www.webextractor.com) is a powerful tool for extracting specific kinds of information from web pages. In today's lesson, we will describe how to use Web Data Extractor to find appropriate sites for placement targeting. Here are the basic steps to use the tool's URL-extraction feature:

1. Specify a search term and set a list of search engines.
2. Click the Start button.
3. Look through the resultant text file to identify pertinent site URLs.

We recommend specifying only one search term at a time, because it makes identifying the best sites easier. Web Data Extractor will give you a combination of great sites and irrelevant ones.

Thursday: Bidding Considerations

After you've identified a placement that performs well for you (advertising on it results in clicks and conversions), it's time to optimize the ROI by finding the right bid price for the placement.

Initial Bids and CPM Bidding

CPM bidding is typically used for keyword-targeted campaigns. The same may not be true for placement-targeted campaigns, especially because Google offers an option that will help you estimate the likelihood of an ad appearing on the placements you've targeted, based on the CPM you are willing to bid, as illustrated in Figure 7.28.

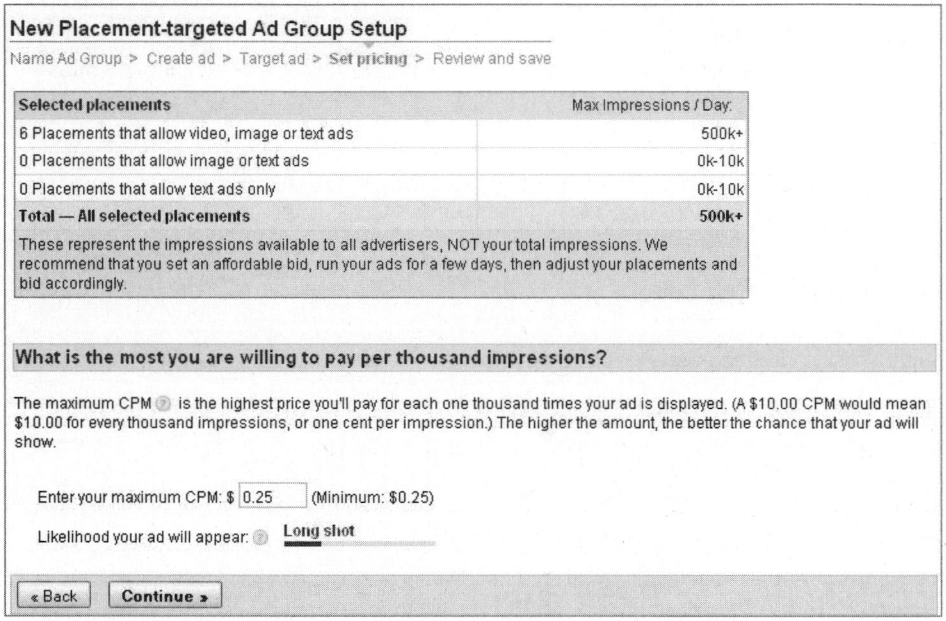

New Placement-targeted Ad Group Setup

Name Ad Group > Create ad > Target ad > Set pricing > Review and save

Selected placements	Max Impressions / Day:
6 Placements that allow video, image or text ads	500k+
0 Placements that allow image or text ads	0k-10k
0 Placements that allow text ads only	0k-10k
Total — All selected placements	**500k+**

These represent the impressions available to all advertisers, NOT your total impressions. We recommend that you set an affordable bid, run your ads for a few days, then adjust your placements and bid accordingly.

What is the most you are willing to pay per thousand impressions?

The maximum CPM ⓘ is the highest price you'll pay for each one thousand times your ad is displayed. (A $10.00 CPM would mean $10.00 for every thousand impressions, or one cent per impression.) The higher the amount, the better the chance that your ad will show.

Enter your maximum CPM: $ 0.25   (Minimum: $0.25)

Likelihood your ad will appear: ⓘ   Long shot

« Back   Continue »

Figure 7.28 Google can estimate the likelihood that your ad will win at auction.

Conversion Optimizer

When you're structuring your campaigns and ad groups, keep in mind that after a campaign has accumulated at least 15 conversions within the previous 30 days, that campaign is eligible to use Conversion Optimizer for automated bid control. Conversion Optimizer works particularly well for placement-targeted campaigns and for keyword-targeted campaigns. In both cases, the bidding algorithms take into consideration conversion behavior of each site across all advertisers, and factors in external variables such as location of the site visitor and conversion likelihood based on the time of the day or the day of the week that the ad is being displayed. This can be a huge benefit for ad groups with many diverse placements, or keyword-targeted ad groups that are directing ads to appear on a wide variety of sites.

A Note on Placement Targeting with Text Ads

Special care must be taken when setting up and optimizing placement-targeted ad groups consisting of text ads. Within any given block of ad space on a website, Google and the website owner want to make as much money as possible. So, Google's ad-display algorithm decides whether displaying one ad or displaying three or four ads in a single ad unit will generate more revenue. In most instances, displaying multiple ads will generate more money.

For a reason that even our Google friends don't seem to know, with placement-targeted text ads, Google enlarges each ad to take up an entire ad block. So, for example, even if the site owner has specified that each ad unit should display four text ads, when a text ad is displayed via a placement-targeted ad group, that ad will be "blown up" to occupy the entire unit. Figure 7.29 is an ad block on a website that would usually display three or four text ads, but as you can see, it's displaying one enlarged text ad. This also means that the advertiser behind such an ad must out-bid all competing advertisers in order for the single ad to show.

Figure 7.29 This ad block would normally display three or four text ads, but as you can see here, it's displaying only one.

This is a significant challenge, and the reason that many advertisers fail to get impressions and clicks for their placement-targeted ad groups consisting of text ads. For example, if the Placement Performance report uncovers a site that performs well when ads appear via a keyword-targeted ad group, and you then add the site to a placement-targeted ad group, you may find that you need to increase bid prices significantly just to gain any impressions and clicks. This is why we suggest that you use only non-text image ads in placement-targeted campaigns.

Friday: Separating Ad Types into Ad Groups

In our keyword-targeted campaigns, we often create multiple ad groups with the *exact same* keyword list, each differentiated by ad type and size. The reason is simple: Each ad type and size will result in different performance. One ad type, say text ads, will result in higher CTRs and conversion rates than another. So it makes sense to set separate bids for each ad type and size—and because content network bids can be managed at only the ad group level, it makes sense to create a separate ad group for each type and size.

Week 16: Launch and Refine Your Content Campaign

It's been a busy three weeks! By now, you've created keyword-targeted campaigns and placement-targeted campaigns. You have built out several tightly-themed keyword lists in order to establish a wide variety of themes for your ad distribution. Also, you have used a few tools to find placements and websites that you want to target. Now it's time to do a final check of your campaigns and launch them! After launch, you'll continue to monitor and optimize your campaigns' performance. In order to achieve success on the content network, you can't just turn on the campaigns and hope for the best. When you activate your account, the real work has just begun.

Monday: Flipping the Switch—Campaign-Management Checklist

Although *flipping the switch* sounds like a single fundamental action, it entails several important tasks. So first off, we are going to run through any and every *i* that needs dotting and *t* that needs crossing from the basic management perspective, just in case. Then we'll reintroduce the Placement Performance report, which will be your most important weapon in refining keyword-targeted campaigns, making them profitable by eliminating inefficient spending, and continually achieving higher and higher CTRs and conversion rates.

Campaign-Management Checklist

Let's run through a short list of things you should cover before launching any new content network campaigns. Some of them might seem basic, but the cost of missing just one or two can be considerable.

Check your budget. Make sure that you are comfortable with your initial budget level based on your risk tolerance. Remember that the budget figure you set is not the average amount you *want* to spend each day; it's the *maximum* you are willing to spend.

Make sure you are comfortable with your CPC bids. Google's guideline is that if you don't know how much to spend for a content-network click, you should set the bid equal to a search bid. There are two schools of thought on this. Based on our observations, we believe that content-network clicks are worth less money than search clicks for similar ad groups. However, there is something to be said for "buying data" by bidding higher at the beginning of a campaign, so that the data accumulates more quickly and optimization decisions can be made sooner.

Make sure search campaigns and content campaigns are separated. It bears repeating that failure to divide these efforts into separate campaigns is one of the worst mistakes you can make. It will be impossible to measure the true effectiveness of ads, and much—maybe even *most*—of your traffic will go to undesirable (or at least imprecisely targeted) pages on the content network.

Campaign-Management Checklist *(continued)*

Make sure ads are set to Rotate. The default in Campaign Settings is Optimize. Optimize shows the highest CTR ads more frequently; Rotate cycles through all the ads in the ad group at an equal clip. Rotate is essential for accurate ad testing.

Enable demographics. Even if you are not specifically targeting social networking sites, enabling demographics in Campaign Settings can be helpful to make sure you don't get clicks from people outside your target audience.

Tuesday: Placement Performance Report

The Placement Performance report is the most important report for optimizing keyword-targeted content campaigns. As illustrated in Figure 7.30, the Placement Performance report shows performance statistics for each domain and URL on which your ads are displayed.

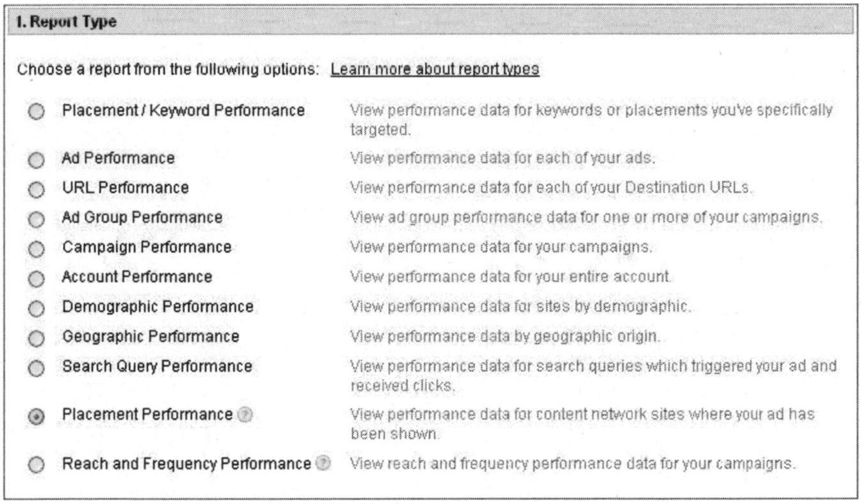

Figure 7.30 The Placement Performance report provides data about sites where your ads have appeared.

If you have Google conversion tracking enabled, the Placement Performance report can show you where all of your conversions are coming from. This is invaluable information for constructing placement-targeted campaigns and enhanced ad groups. Knowing where all the sales come from enables you to modify bids to optimize ROI.

Wednesday: Site and Category Exclusion

Earlier we said that the main reason that advertisers lose money on their content network advertising efforts is that *their ads appear on the wrong websites and pages.* We've explained that the Placement Performance report shows you where your keyword-targeted ads are appearing as well as performance information about each corresponding page and site. Armed with this information, when optimizing you must exclude the "bad" sites from your campaign so that you don't continue to show ads there. As illustrated in Figure 7.31, you can exclude sites as negative placements directly from the Networks tab of the AdWords web interface.

	Clicks	Impr.	CTR ⑦	Avg. CPC ⑦	Cost	Avg. Pos.	Conv. (1-per-click) ⑦	Cost / conv. (1-per-click) ⑦	Conv. rate (1-per-click) ⑦
Search - off	0	0	0.00%	$0.00	$0.00	0	0	$0.00	0.00%
Google search - off	0	0	0.00%	$0.00	$0.00	0	0	$0.00	0.00%
Search partners - off ⑦	0	0	0.00%	$0.00	$0.00	0	0	$0.00	0.00%
Content	10	3,845	0.26%	$0.40	$4.05	1.1	0	$0.00	0.00%
■ Managed placements ⑦hide details	0	0	0.00%	$0.00	$0.00	0	0	$0.00	0.00%
■ Automatic placements ⑦show details	10	3,845	0.26%	$0.40	$4.05	1.1	0	$0.00	0.00%
Total - All networks	10	3,845	0.26%	$0.40	$4.05	1.1	0	$0.00	0.00%

■ **Content: managed placements**   **Hide details**

Placement	Ad group	Status	Clicks	Impr.	CTR ⑦	Avg. CPC ⑦	Cost	Conv. (1-per-click) ⑦	Cost / conv. (1-per-click) ⑦	Conv. rate (1-per-click) ⑦
There are no managed placements in this campaign. You can add managed placements by clicking "+ Add placements " above.										
Total - all managed placements			0	0	0.00%	$0.00	$0.00	0	$0.00	0.00%

⊞ Exclusions

Figure 7.31 Click on the plus sign next to the word "Exclusions" to see and add to the list of excluded placements.

Most of your exclusions will be lists of poorly performing URLs. However, you can also tell Google not to show ads on sites whose content falls into specific categories, such as user-generated content or video-sharing sites. Figure 7.32 shows a set of Topics exclusions that seeks to exclude tragedies or "edgy" content (such as sex). One important caveat: When viewing category performance within the Exclusion tool, set the time period to All Time. This reveals the largest possible time interval and the largest possible data set. You may be surprised that certain categories produce acceptable results, despite your intuition to the contrary.

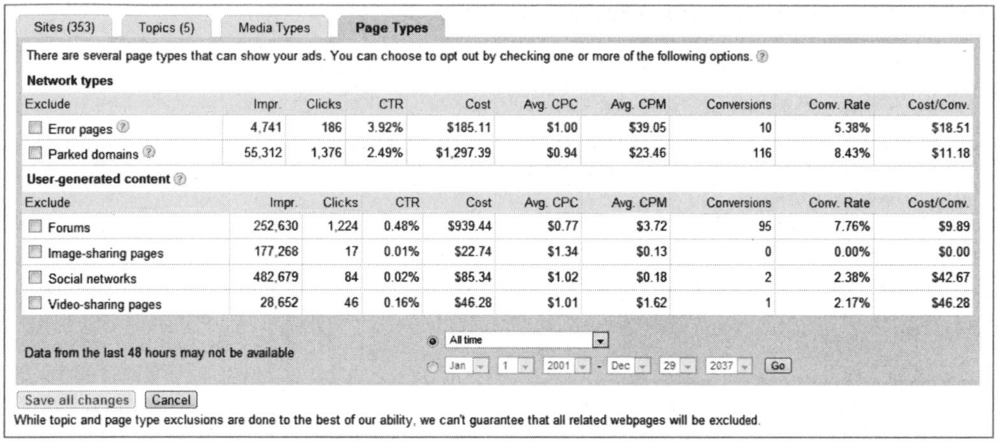

Sites (353) | Topics (5) | Media Types | **Page Types**

There are several page types that can show your ads. You can choose to opt out by checking one or more of the following options.

Network types

Exclude	Impr.	Clicks	CTR	Cost	Avg. CPC	Avg. CPM	Conversions	Conv. Rate	Cost/Conv.
Error pages	4,741	186	3.92%	$185.11	$1.00	$39.05	10	5.38%	$18.51
Parked domains	55,312	1,376	2.49%	$1,297.39	$0.94	$23.46	116	8.43%	$11.18

User-generated content

Exclude	Impr.	Clicks	CTR	Cost	Avg. CPC	Avg. CPM	Conversions	Conv. Rate	Cost/Conv.
Forums	252,630	1,224	0.48%	$939.44	$0.77	$3.72	95	7.76%	$9.89
Image-sharing pages	177,268	17	0.01%	$22.74	$1.34	$0.13	0	0.00%	$0.00
Social networks	482,679	84	0.02%	$85.34	$1.02	$0.18	2	2.38%	$42.67
Video-sharing pages	28,652	46	0.16%	$46.28	$1.01	$1.62	1	2.17%	$46.28

Data from the last 48 hours may not be available

All time

Jan 1 2001 - Dec 29 2037 Go

Save all changes | Cancel

While topic and page type exclusions are done to the best of our ability, we can't guarantee that all related webpages will be excluded.

Figure 7.32 Most of your exclusions will be irrelevant sites your ads have *already* appeared on, but site and category exclusion enables you to remove whole categories and media types.

Thursday: Enhanced Ad Groups

Keywords and placements can be combined in a single ad group, which we call an *enhanced ad group*. This technique enables you to enjoy the precision of a well-executed, keyword-targeted ad group, while directing Google to place ads only on placements you designate. So the keyword-and-placement list tells Google, "Place my ads on the placements listed here, but *only* on those pages that contain these keywords." To create such a "hybrid" ad group, begin by selecting the Relevant Pages Only on the Placements and Audiences I Manage option in your new campaign's settings (as shown previously in Figure 7.15).

A great example is one of the most popular sites on the Internet; almost everybody goes there for entertainment or information because it shows a tremendous array of videos. Just because you have an ad group about bodybuilding that generated sales from ads appearing on YouTube doesn't mean that you should then include YouTube in a placement-targeted ad group. Your success resulted from using *bodybuilding*-related keyword targeting, not YouTube as a whole. Therefore, a sensible strategy is to target YouTube, but include *bodybuilding* keywords in the same ad group, saying to Google, "Show my ads on YouTube pages related to bodybuilding."

By now you should understand that optimizing content campaign performance requires a constant, iterative process of creating placement-targeted or enhanced campaigns, based on best-performing placements that you find by running keyword-targeted campaigns. But there's one more important step: When you add a placement to a placement-targeted ad group, you need to tell Google to stop running ads in reaction to the original keyword-targeted ad group. Otherwise, your keyword-targeted and placement-targeted ad groups will compete with each other, with unpredictable (and probably undesirable) results. You can accomplish this using the Exclusion tool, as shown in Figure 7.33. You can accomplish the same thing by adding negative placements to keyword-targeted ad groups using AdWords Editor.

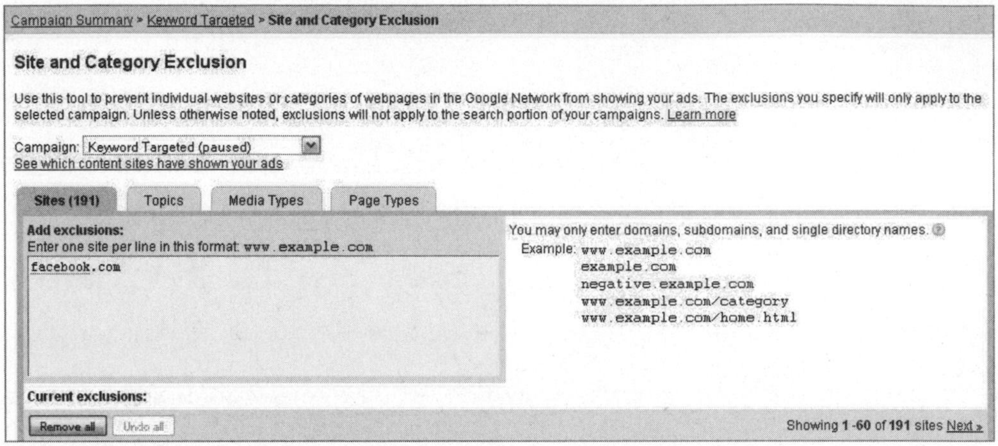

Figure 7.33 In order to effectively target a site at *lower* bids in new hybrid ad groups, you will have to exclude the targeted site from the originals.

Friday: Flipping the Switch (Again) and Judging Performance

Now that your content network campaigns are running, how should you assess their success? Here are some suggestions for monitoring and judging performance:

Check the Placement Performance report: Where did most of your money go? Often when you have an unsuccessful content network campaign, the reason is that one or two bigger—but less well-targeted—sites gobbled up a large portion of your budget. What would your ROI have been but for those sites? Can your reduce bids on—or exclude—those sites and turn campaign performance around?

Assess your ads: How many different ads did you test per size? Did one ad significantly outperform others? Did one ad (or type of ad) bleed money while other ad units performed well? You will want to display more of the performing ads (and model more ads that look and read like those) than the nonperformers.

Check placement bid prices: You will likely have started placement-targeted ad groups with one ad group–level bid price. In other words, you start bidding the same amount for each placement. But as we've noted, performance will vary from placement to placement. So treat the placements in an ad group as you do keywords in a search ad group: Constantly monitor ROI on a placement-by-placement basis, and adjust placement-level bid prices upward or downward as necessary to achieve better and better ROI.

Month 5—Launch Your Campaign

This month you'll learn more about the important topic of bidding on variations of your brand, company, and product names. Then we'll walk you through a checklist of prelaunch campaign settings and make sure you're ready to flip the switch and start running your ads.

After rolling up your sleeves and launching your first campaign, you'll begin the ongoing (some might say never-ending) process of reporting on campaign results and interpreting the data. To that end, we'll introduce you to the concept of optimization—interpreting test results and steadily improving campaign results.

8

Chapter Contents

Week 17: Bid Your Brands

Some pay-per-click (PPC) advertisers operate under a misconception *that they should not be bidding on keywords representing their own brands*, especially when their websites' listings appear prominently in the natural search results. These marketers see bidding on brand-related terms as a waste of budget.

But we believe that including brand-related keywords in your campaigns can be vital to the success of your PPC efforts. Here are reasons this strategy is so effective:

It boosts the CTR for your paid and organic listings: Google tells us that although a brand's paid listing often generates a great click-through rate (CTR) of 20 percent or more, a top organic listing *also* generates a great CTR. For maximum results, a brand appearing on a SERP with top organic and paid listings simultaneously results in a much larger number of clicks. Google says that a brand appearing in both an ad *and* a natural listing can yield a combined CTR of 60 percent!

It gives you the ability to control your message: With PPC advertisements, you get to display and test the exact messaging that will maximize CTRs and conversion rates. With continuous split ad testing, you can improve your response rate by learning what benefits are most important to your target audience. By the nature of PPC, you can act quickly when you discover that certain messages don't work well.

Organic results are nice because they're free. But advertisers are rarely able to specify *exactly* what preclick message they want in front of a prospect. The organic listings are often optimized to gain higher rankings and link acquisition, but the pages that they link to are often not conversion focused, containing weak sales copy and uninspiring calls to action.

If you aren't bidding on your name, a competitor might be: The truth is that if you don't gobble up the ad space that you and your brand so richly deserve, your competitor may occupy it by bidding on your brand terms. The result can be lost profits, because in some cases the searcher will see and click on your competitor's ad before even seeing your organic listing.

Brand searchers are in a buying mood: A person who is conducting a brand-related search is likely to be close to a decision to buy! In this chapter, we show you how to bid on hundreds and ultimately *thousands* of variations of your brand, and every product and service your company provides (at least those that are brand specific). You will be shocked at how even results that are already good can be improved—your CTR will go up and your cost per click (CPC) will go down, while your potential customers get a click closer to *exactly* what they are looking for.

Monday: Your Brand May Be Weaker than You Think

If your PPC campaigns already include brand terms and you're getting good results, it may be tempting to conclude that your brands are particularly strong, or that you're benefitting from offline advertising and PR activities. However, the truth is that the conversions credited to a brand-related keyword are often the end result of an undetermined string of banner ad impressions, or exploratory searches that can even result in more exploratory searches before culminating in the brand-related search that gets credit for the conversion. Certainly brand-related conversions are important, cost-effective, and among all the other positives, make the PPC manager look really good (this is our favorite part, of course). But how do you accurately give credit to the paid actions that precede the brand-related conversion?

The search engine advertising platforms are just starting to provide visibility into this phenomenon, which is sometimes called *multiple exposure attribution*. For example, Yahoo! reports when a conversion was preceded by searches and clicks on ads before the visit that culminated in the conversion—which Yahoo! calls *assists*. Figure 8.1 shows how Yahoo! reports on a combination of assists and actual conversions.

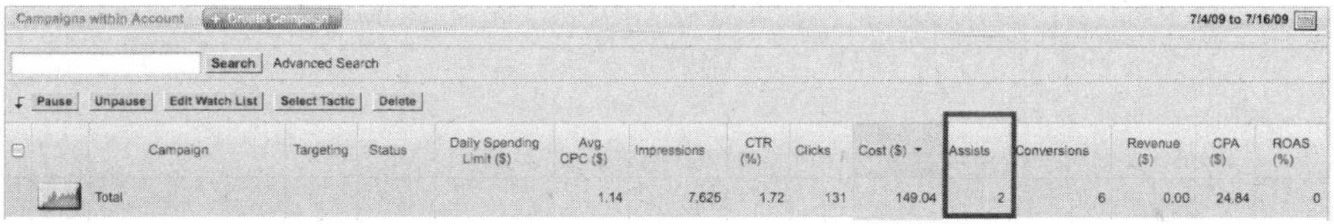

Figure 8.1 Of the six sales recorded by the Yahoo! interface, two were assisted by previous PPC clicks.

Boosting the Performance of Your Brand-Related Keywords

As mentioned, it's important to realize that brand-related keywords may be getting a disproportionate amount of credit for conversions. This is because so many other keywords, as well as every other marketing effort, are doing a lot of heavy lifting for these brand-related keywords. You can think of these brand-related terms as a basketball play. All of your other marketing efforts (and keywords) shoot the ball, but your brand-related terms do an alley-oop and slam-dunk it through the hoop. As illustrated in Figure 8.2, every other marketing channel can give your brand-related terms a big lift.

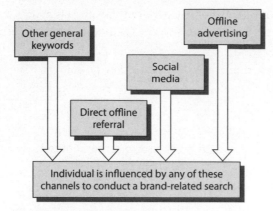

Figure 8.2 A prospect first hears of your brand or product from a variety of channels.

Let's explore the Other General Keywords channel shown in Figure 8.2. Prospective customers usually don't have a specific company in mind when they begin their search for a product or service. They will begin their discovery process with general search queries. Some people will find what they're looking for on the first query. Most will conduct a series of searches that are progressively narrower in scope, as shown in Figure 8.3.

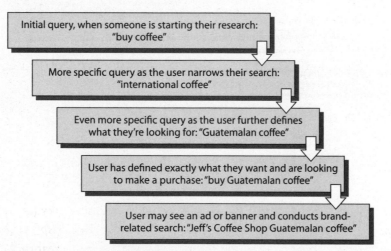

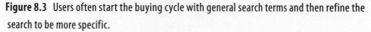

Figure 8.3 Users often start the buying cycle with general search terms and then refine the search to be more specific.

To summarize our advice:

Continue to invest in broad, general keywords: Even when the return on investment (ROI) doesn't appear be very strong on a per-keyword level, these terms may be a valuable source of preliminary clicks or assists, even though you may not be able to measure them directly. If your PPC efforts are resulting in an acceptable average cost per acquisition (CPA), it's likely your brand and non-brand keyword bidding strategy is working correctly, because the brand-related terms should be converting at a much lower CPA than your target average CPA.

Continue to invest in the content network: Content ad campaigns will often drive much greater search volume on your highly profitable brand-term ad groups. As long as the combined effect of your content campaigns and brand search uplift are driving profitable CPA, you have some justification to spend a little more than you normally would on content network ads.

Tuesday: Brand and Domain Name Variations

This section is divided into two parts:

- A general strategy for generating brand-related keywords (which also leads into tomorrow's lesson on URL variations)
- A product-based strategy for brand- and product-related ad groups, keywords, and ads

General Strategy

To practice building keyword lists based on your brand, you'll develop keywords for a fictitious guitar company named Krisp Guitars. Table 8.1 lists some of the root variations you might start with.

▶ **Table 8.1** Baseline Keyword Roots for Krisp Guitars

Root
Krisp
Krisp Guitar
Krisp Guitars

Bidding on the broad-match version of the word *Krisp* alone might be risky (as you'll see when we discuss the "Broad-Match Stomp" next Wednesday), but *Krisp Guitar* and *Krisp Guitars* (the proper name of the client's company) are both great root keywords.

For the purposes of this exercise, consider a user's query on your brand term to be an invitation to close the sale. Therefore, you can craft your marketing messages and point prospects to landing pages to reflect this. Table 8.2 lists the baseline prefixes and suffixes that cleave to that prospect's intent.

► **Table 8.2** Adding Prefixes and Suffixes for Selling Brands

Prefix	Root	Suffix
Buy	Krisp	Online
Order	Krisp Guitar	
	Krisp Guitars	

Pop those columns into Microsoft Excel, and you end up with the following keywords:

- *Krisp guitar*
- *Krisp guitars*
- *Krisp online*
- *Krisp guitar online*
- *Krisp guitars online*
- *Buy krisp*
- *Buy krisp guitar*
- *Buy krisp guitars*
- *Buy krisp online*
- *Buy krisp guitar online*
- *Buy krisp guitars online*
- *Order krisp*
- *Order krisp guitar*
- *Order krisp guitars*
- *Order krisp online*
- *Order krisp guitar online*
- *Order krisp guitars online*

Product-Based Strategy

You can apply the preceding strategy to brands with multiple product lines. Imagine for a moment that you work for a beauty supply company called Enangeline. The new Enangeline online store features lipstick, eyeliner, mineral makeup, and cleansers. Of course, you will bid on "umbrella" brand keywords such as *Enangeline beauty products* and *Enangeline cosmetics*, but you should also develop keyword lists for each product, with roots such as *Enangeline lipstick*, *Enangeline eyeliner*, and so on.

The best results will be obtained by pairing product-specific ad groups with product-specific landing pages, rather than directing clicks to the site's home page or a departmental landing page. For example, if you know that the potential customer is searching for Enangeline lip gloss, you will get the best results—high conversion rates and low costs per conversion—if the corresponding landing page features *only* lip gloss.

Because brand-related keywords are so valuable, it makes sense to bid on many variations—all the different ways a prospective customer might spell and misspell the brand words. As discussed in Chapter 4, "Month 1—Research Keywords and Establish Campaign Structure," the SEO Book website (`www.seobook.com`) can help you aggressively expand your keyword list via the Keyword Typo Generator tool (`http://tools .seobook.com/spelling/keywords-typos.cgi`). Using this tool to generate misspellings of just a few keywords can result in many thousands of variations that could be used as keywords in brand ad groups.

Wednesday: URL Variations

Another technique for capitalizing on the strength of your brand and the use of related search terms at the end of the buying cycle is bidding on keywords that are variations of your site's URL and domain name—like these:

- *http://yourbrand.com*
- *http://www.yourbrand.com*
- *www.yourbrand.com*
- *yourbrand.com*

We recommend this technique for several reasons. First, people often confuse the browser address field with the search engine query field. They type literal URLs into the search field—and frequently misspell the URL. A searcher looking for your site might not find it unless you include the misspelling in your keyword list.

Consider Figure 8.4, which shows a browser setup equipped with the Google toolbar.

Figure 8.4 Some people type web addresses into the search field.

But why bid on literal URLs of your site and its exact domain name? Won't search queries that include those words produce a natural search result at the top of the SERP? The answer is, sometimes yes, sometimes no. Depending on the keywords your competitors are bidding on, the natural listing for your site may appear below competitive ads that do their best to divert the attention of the searcher away from your site.

The most important reason to bid on such terms is this: profitability. Because the people using brand terms in search queries are likely to be close to the end of the buying process, conversion rates for brand keywords are usually the lowest in the ad campaign. That means costs per conversion are usually the lowest of all keywords in the campaign.

We recommend that you bid on a wide variety of URL variations. Table 8.3 shows a relatively simple way to generate such variations, with three columns of prefixes, roots, and suffixes. For the central root section, you can use a base that's similar to what was described in yesterday's "General Strategy" section, complete with misspellings. That said, you should keep the roots relatively simple (because, remember, you are banking on prospects actually trying to type in URLs). You can think up many prefixes and suffixes (especially suffixes if your company does business in other countries) to generate literally millions of variations.

▶ **Table 8.3** Baseline URL Variations

Prefix	Root	Suffix
http://	Yourbrand	.co
http://www.	your brand	.com
www.		[blank]
wwww.		con
www ..		.co.uk
		c.om

After you consider match types, these variations (with only *yourbrand* and *your brand* as roots) will generate dozens of unique keywords. The field marked *[blank]* in the Suffix columns should be simply left empty. After the fields are concatenated, these will result in keywords such as *yourbrand, your brand, www.yourbrand*, and *yourbrand.com*.

Thursday: Competitor Legal and Ethical Issues

We generally recommend that you consider bidding on your competitor's brand terms. This is allowed by all search engines and can be an excellent source of qualified PPC traffic. Having said that, some risk-averse advertisers are wary of bidding on their competitors' brand terms. Although search engines conditionally allow the practice, there is nothing to stop the competitor from threatening or filing legal action in retaliation.

The following subsections briefly describe the specific trademark rules of Microsoft adCenter, Yahoo!, and Google AdWords.

Microsoft adCenter

Microsoft adCenter does not allow you to bid on trademarks *or* use them in ad copy unless you meet the following requirements:

- You are a reseller of the trademarked product or service.

- Your primary purpose is information; that is, you don't sell competing goods.

- The trademark is a dictionary term *being used in the ordinary way*, unrelated to the trademark. For example, adCenter would allow you to bid on *apple* despite its being trademarked in the computer business if, say, you sell fruit.

Yahoo! Sponsored Listings

Yahoo! treats trademarks similarly to Microsoft, though their definition does not specifically include dictionary terms.

Google AdWords

Google does not allow the use of trademarks in ad text that is "competitive, critical, or negative." This precludes you from using a *competitor's* trademark in your ad text, especially with the goal of selling your (presumably competitive) product.

You may be able to run ads that are comparative in nature, rather than critical or competitive, without necessarily including the competitor's name or trademarks. For example, if you are writing ads for Nike and competing against Adidas, your ad might look like the following if you want it to appear when a user search queries *Adidas shoe prices*:

<u>Great Shoes, Great Prices</u>
Nike shoes are rated highest.
Wide selection. Free shipping!
www.OnlineNikeShoeStore.net

In this ad, you are not mentioning your competitor's name. You are just presenting your product as an alternative. You're not being deceptive by displaying your competitor's name in the ad and trying to trick users into clicking on your ad because you've led them to believe that you sell Adidas shoes. You're playing fair, but you're still in the game.

Friday: Competitor-Name Ad Groups

Let's say you have read everything in yesterday's lesson, and you decide that bidding on competitors' names is a good strategy for you. To that end, today's lesson gives you some tips on implementing competitor-name ad groups.

If you decide you are going to advertise against competitors' brands, you should implement URL variations as part of your keyword strategy. These URL variations can serve as the bulk of your keywords, but just as bidding on your own brands' URL variations can uncover areas with high CTR (because there is nothing else for prospects to click, so there's no competition) and low CPCs (again because there is no competition), the same can be true for competitor URL variations.

We recommend creating separate campaigns for your own brand-based keywords, general search keywords, and competitor brand–related keywords.

Week 18: Make Prelaunch Double-Checks

Last week, you learned the basics of how to build campaigns and ad groups. This week, we are going to concentrate on last-minute details and tips—to help you hit the ground running and avoid unnecessary mistakes.

Monday: Budgets and Bid Prices

What should the bidding strategy be for brand and competitor ad groups and keywords? Generally speaking, we allocate the maximum allowable budget and very high CPC bids to brand- and competitor-related ad groups and keywords.

Here's a way to calculate a safe initial bid that should start your campaigns, and then you can optimize your performance after the keyword is launched:

break-even CPC bid = average profit ÷ conversion rate

In the long run, the goal is to make an actual profit, not just break even, but remember that just because you make a $3.50 bid does not mean you will be charged $3.50 per click. However, a high bid is useful for ensuring the maximum number of impressions, clicks, and conversions in the shortest period of time. As long as you're not *losing* money, you should be able to gather the data you need to fine-tune your performance with different CPC (or even CPA) bids.

Now that you have a baseline for bidding on your own brand-related terms, let's turn our attention to competitor keywords. In general, traffic driven by bidding on competitor brand names will be worth only a fraction of the value of traffic driven by your own brand keywords.

As with any recommendations related to bids, setting the optimum bid price will depend on your niche. There are some vertical industries for which average click prices can be more than $100 per click, and others for which 30-cent clicks are no assurance of profitability. Unless you are specifically focused on accelerating sales without strict CPA or ROI targets, we recommend that you start new competitor campaign bid prices at about 80 percent of your break-even CPC bid (average profit ÷ conversion rate).

Tuesday: Campaign Settings

Today's lesson is somewhat of a recap—we have described campaign settings in previous chapters. However, for important search campaigns like the ones we're discussing in this chapter, certain settings require further description.

First, let's cover where you can adjust these settings within a Google AdWords campaign. All of the settings that we describe in this section can be found on the Settings tab within your campaign. When you click this tab, you can adjust the settings for the sections marked in Figure 8.5.

Ad groups	**Settings**	Ads	Keywords	Networks

Campaign settings

General

Campaign name   **R - Smallwares**   Edit

Locations, Languages, and Demographics

Locations ⓘ   In what geographical locations do you want your ads to appear?
  • Country: **United States**
  Edit

  ☐ Show relevant addresses with your ads (advanced) ⓘ

Languages ⓘ   **English**   Edit

☐ Demographic (advanced)

Networks, devices, and extensions

Networks ⓘ   **Search**   Edit
Devices ⓘ   **Computers**   Edit
Ad extensions ⓘ   Use product images and information from my Google Merchant Center account:
  Show additional links to my site within my ad: **None**   Edit

Bidding and budget

Bidding option ⓘ   **Focus on clicks, manual maximum CPC bidding**   Edit

Budget ⓘ   **$400.00/day**   Edit

☐ Position preference, delivery method (advanced)

Advanced settings

☐ Schedule: Start date, end date, ad scheduling
  Start date   **Mar 5, 2007**

  End date   **Dec 31, 2037**   Edit

  Ad scheduling ⓘ   **Only show ads at selected times**   Edit
  Scheduled to run: 100% Bid adjustments: 85-110%

☐ Ad delivery: Ad rotation, frequency capping
  Ad rotation ⓘ   **Rotate: Show ads more evenly**   Edit

  Frequency capping ⓘ   **No cap on impressions**
  Content Network only   Your campaign must be opted in to the Content Network to use this feature.

Figure 8.5 Important campaign settings can be found on the Settings tab.

Here are our recommendations for how you should set up your campaign:

Locations, Languages, and Demographics: Confirm that you have this set to the correct language for your ads and landing pages (in the United States, the default is English). Set this to your desired geographic targets.

Networks, Devices, and Extensions: Make sure you are opted *out* of the content network for all search campaigns. We've said it elsewhere in this book, and we'll say it again: *Your content network and search network campaigns need to be separated.* Unless you have created custom ads for mobile devices, and launched mobile versions of your landing pages and website, we suggest that you target only computers at launch. In other words, deselect the check box related to mobile devices.

Bidding and Budget: New campaigns default to CPC bidding. After you reach the minimum conversion threshold (15 conversions), we recommend switching on Google AdWords Conversion Optimizer.

Advanced Settings: Though we often decrease content campaign bids during off-hours (in the middle of the night or on weekends, for instance), we do not typically use ad scheduling for our brand-focused search network campaigns. Brand-related searches have very high purchase intent, and that intent can frequently happen at any time of the day. Other than specifying whether your campaign is directed to the search network or the content network, Ad Rotation is likely the most important default setting that you should change. The default is Optimize, whereby Google serves ads according to which have higher CTRs. However, for proper ad testing, you *must* change this to Rotate. (We will explore ad testing for branded search campaigns in greater detail on Friday.) We suggest that you use the Accelerated delivery method. This enables your ads to show as much as possible. You can control your spending at the campaign budget level. You can also implement Ad Scheduling to target your ads during certain times of the day.

Although these campaign settings might *seem* basic, you would be shocked at the silly errors even veteran PPC managers make when they get sloppy with checklists. Leaving your ads on Optimize may simply spoil your ad testing, but forgetting to turn off the content network can be *catastrophic* for your ROI!

Wednesday: Keywords—The Broad-Match Stomp

Some advertisers experience runaway spending from broad-match keywords, sadly without any commensurate increase in conversions. The problem is that in its exuberance to pair ads with relevant content, the Google matching algorithms sometimes make very poor matches.

Remember, when you use broad match keywords, Google might pair your ads to queries that *aren't even in your keyword lists*, expanding to plurals, synonyms (or what the algorithm sees as synonyms), or just the *components* of a keyword! Consider the strange case of *Native American Homeopathic Remedies,* a product of what we can only assume are synonyms torn apart and then stapled back together.

Native American Homeopathic Remedies

The keyword was *USA Herbals* (a natural products brand).

The Search Query Performance report revealed, among other strange results, that Google had matched the keyword *USA Herbals* to the search query *Native American Homeopathic Remedies*. Our best guess is that *USA* was "synonymously" extrapolated to *American*, which in turn became *Native American;* ditto on *Herbals* to *Homeopathic*, and then to *Homeopathic Remedies*.

Native American Homeopathic Remedies is just one example of a comically unrelated broad match, and our best example that did not refer, explicitly, to illegal drugs (and there were many). *Herbals* or not, these results were not related to our natural products store any more than *Native American Home Remedies*.

Remember: Use the Search Query Performance report often, especially when your brand-related ad groups are not absolutely kicking butt. It will really help you figure out what might be going wrong. Broad match is often the culprit.

When bidding on brand-related terms, you will typically need to be much less worried about these bad matches than you might be with general terms, especially when the elements of your branded keywords have no synonyms. For example, athletic shoe giant Nike might have nothing whatsoever to worry about (except, perhaps, during those rare cases when a searcher is looking up information related to the Greek goddess of victory), but Nike's competitor New Balance might not be so fortunate.

Bad broad matches occur most frequently when a keyword contains fewer than three words. We already stated in this chapter that we don't typically bid on single-word keywords but we can make exceptions for especially targeted brand-related keywords. This means that we must be most vigilant with two-word keywords.

The solution we suggest is to bid on phrase-match versions of these two-word keywords, but also their equals and opposites. For example, you might replace the broad-match keyword *blue widget* with phrase-match keywords *blue widget* and *widget blue*. This ensures that you will hit most relevant variations to your keywords, but prevent most of the bad spending from overly enthusiastic broad matches.

This strategy comes with some risk, because you may be missing out on some legitimately relevant keyword-to-query matches; but the alternative strategy is continually running search query reports in an endless quest to add negative keywords to offset bad matches. That can be horribly time-consuming, especially compared to the strategy of simply neglecting to bid on one- and two-word broad-match keywords.

Thursday: Verify Ad Destination URLs

Before you actually *flip the switch* to activate your campaigns (next week), you should check all destination URLs of your ads. URL verification is an ongoing process that must follow these guidelines:

- If you are an in-house PPC advertiser, work with your IT team to ensure that your destination URLs work *and* that they will *continue* to work. It's worthwhile to discuss and anticipate changes such as files getting moved, sites switching from one content management system to another, and naming conventions changing, sometimes without addressing backward compatibility.

- If you work for an ad agency or as a consultant, communicate with your clients with the same issues in mind. Agencies are in a more precarious position than in-house PPC experts, because they don't usually work as closely with IT, and might not be "in the loop" when management makes marketing or technology decisions.

- If and when you are forced to change destination URLs in your PPC ads, remember that in the eyes of the search advertising platforms, these ads will be essentially all-new ads. One common mistake is losing historical ad performance data by editing the destination URL of an existing ad. Generally, we make copies of our existing ads, edit them, and then pause the old ones. The practical result is the same (same ad text with a new URL), but the advantage is that when you pause the old ad instead of editing it, you still have easy one-glance access to historical data points (CTR, conversion rate, CPA, and so on).

Friday: Launching Initial Ad Testing

In this section, you'll learn how to launch your initial PPC ad split tests. For now, we'll start off with smaller, easier-to-manage split tests just to get your ad tests up and running. In Chapter 10, "Month 7—Test Ads by Using Advanced Techniques," we'll cover more-advanced strategies for ad split testing.

Ad testing is one of the most important tactics for PPC performance optimization. A search query may match one of your keywords, but that isn't necessarily the initiation of your interaction with the searcher. The engagement with a prospective customer begins when that customer reads your PPC ad. The age-old cliché holds true: You have only one chance to make a great first impression. Continually testing your PPC ads will help improve your CTRs and conversion rates.

Before you launch your first test, make sure you set Ad Delivery to Rotate, as shown in Figure 8.6.

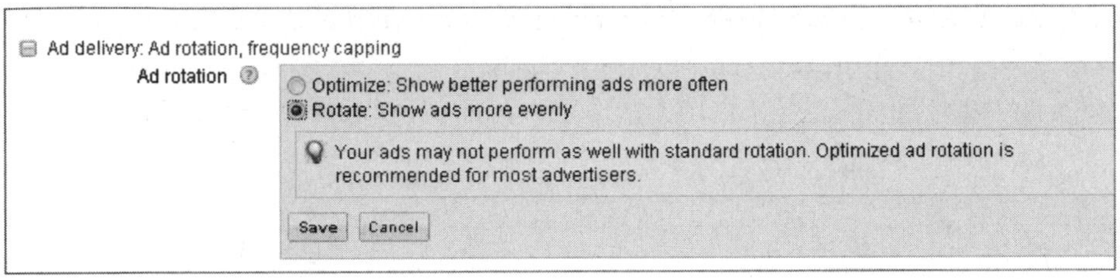

Figure 8.6 If you don't rotate your ads evenly, Google AdWords will choose the ad with the highest CTR.

In Figure 8.6, the two settings you have to choose from are Optimize and Rotate. These are the differences between the two options:

Optimize: As your ads accrue impressions and clicks, AdWords begins to display the ad with the higher CTR more frequently. This means that AdWords monitors your split tests and chooses the winner for you based solely on CTR. Increasing ad CTR is important, but it's more important to compare ads based on their relative conversion rates.

Rotate: This setting enables all of your ads within an ad group to rotate evenly. AdWords does not choose a "winner" and display that ad more frequently. By selecting Rotate, you're giving all of your ads an even chance to compete in the test. There is extra work involved when you rotate ads evenly: It is up to you to monitor, analyze, and optimize your ads. However, this is the most effective way to get the best results if you are measuring your performance through to conversion rates.

Increasing ad CTR is important to drive more traffic to your website and to improve your quality score. However, this is not the only metric for your ad testing. You need to compare the performance of two ads by comparing conversion rate first, and your secondary metric should be CTR. Ideally, your winning ad will have the highest CTR *and* the best conversion rate.

When you launch a new ad group, you should start with at least two ads. Launching with more than two ads will make your tests more complicated, so we suggest keeping it simple to start. The more variables you include in your test, the more difficult it will be to determine statistically valid and actionable results.

After you have two ads running, and they're generating impressions, clicks, and conversions, how do you determine which ad is performing better than the other? You want to make sure that your sample size is large and the variation in performance is distinct in order to make confident decisions. Fortunately, a few tools out there can help you determine the outcome of your split tests. You can use any of the following websites or tools:

- SplitTester (www.splittester.com)
- Teasley Statistical Calculator (www.teasley.net/free_stuff.htm)

- Split Test A/B Calculator (www.splittestcalculator.com)
- PPC Ad Split Testing Tool (www.websharedesign.com/tools/ppc-ad-split-testing-tool)

To give you an idea of how these tools work, let's take a look at Split Test A/B Calculator. In Figure 8.7, we have entered the results of a split that we're running for a client. Both ads have generated a good sample size of more than 300 clicks.

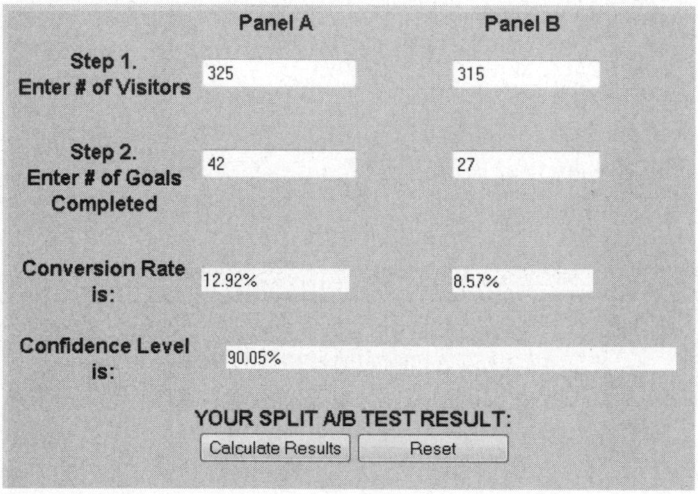

Figure 8.7 Split Test A/B Calculator compares the results of ad split tests.

This Split Test A/B Calculator uses a confidence level of 95 percent to determine whether there is a statistically significant winner in a split test. The confidence level indicates how sure you can be that the results you are seeing represent the actual conversion rate that would be achieved if you were to let the test run for a longer period of time. At that point, you can pause the losing ad.

After you pause the losing ad, you start all over again. First you need to think about why the winning ad performed better than the loser. Is there a clear reason why searchers responded better to the winning ad? Form your opinion, and then try to top your winning ad by writing a better one!

Here are some of the elements you might want to test in a brand-based ad group:

Headlines: Try different eye-catching headlines in your experimental ads (usually we use identical body text and display URLs when testing just the headline).

Body text: Flipping the two lines of body text can be especially effective when each line is a separate sentence or idea. You might be surprised at how much more effective an ad can be simply by putting a benefit statement first and a call to action second, for example. When running this kind of test, we keep all headlines the same and change only the description lines.

Features, benefit statements, and calls to action: Just as you can target different keywords to drive traffic to the same offers, you can use different benefits to sell that same offer to prospective customers. At our best, we try to convey all three of these messages in an effective ad:

- Here's what I have.

- Here's what it will do for you.

- Here's what I want you to do next.

In an ad for a brand-related keyword, you can usually assume that the prospect knows what you have and what it will do for them (especially true when talking about URL variations, which presume navigational intent). For these ads, you can try skipping the first two ideas in favor of an ad that says, "Yes, I have what you want. *This is exactly what you are looking for.* Click here!"

Display URLs: You can sometimes increase CTR by inserting keywords into the display URL.

Landing pages: In the most common tests we run, we display the same ads but toggle between multiple landing pages. Presuming your experimental landing page is relevant (and does not in and of itself trigger increased minimum bids, a drop in quality score, or a relevancy warning), you can ignore differences in CTR when you run this test. The CTR of the ad group should be considered the CTR of all the ads if the ads have the same headlines, body copy, and display URLs (regardless of what the per-ad stats say). Consider only the differences in conversion rate when running this kind of test.

How long you run particular tests will depend on how much traffic you get on your keywords related to your brand. You won't learn much from ad groups that get just a few impressions per day, but you can complete tests quickly in ad groups that accrue several hundred clicks in a single day.

Week 19: Flip the Switch

For seven and a half chapters, we've been preparing you for your first account launch. It's now time to flip the switch and activate your campaigns. Whenever you launch a new PPC campaign, you need to monitor your performance closely at first. Even if you create awesome campaigns with highly relevant keywords and ads that are well targeted, surprises can still pop up after launch.

This week's curriculum includes best practices for early course-correction and some basic benchmarking and tests to help ensure that your fledgling brand-related campaigns, ad groups, and ads are on the right track to driving profitable actions.

Monday and Tuesday: Launching All Your Campaigns at Once?

In the long run, a good PPC account will pay for itself many times over. You should be at least breaking even on every click. Especially on brand-related search ads, the goal is to be making much more money per click than you are spending.

However, it usually takes a fair amount of time and effort to get to the point of a "mature" PPC account. And unfortunately, even with the most logically structured account, something can go wrong. We recommend activating new accounts by launching with your highest-volume ad groups. When you are trying to build initial credibility and an account-level quality score, the high CTRs that your brand-related keywords should generate will be your best asset. A staggered campaign launch will help ensure high CTRs at the beginning.

As illustrated in Figure 8.8, initially launching with your brand-related ad groups may have the smallest amount of search volume, but the traffic will be highly relevant. As you activate other ad groups, your keyword focus will expand. As a result, your volume will increase, but so will your chance for underperforming keywords.

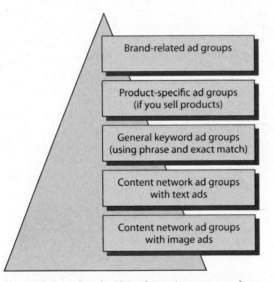

Figure 8.8 As you launch additional campaigns, you expand your reach on the Google Search and Content Networks.

There is no set schedule for the time intervals between campaign launches. After you feel that you have a firm grasp on a campaign's performance, move on to the next campaign. Getting to know a campaign could take only a few days or it could take a little bit longer.

You should take some time right now to determine your launch sequence. This sequence may look similar to Figure 8.8, or it may not. Here are the criteria you can follow to determine the sequence of your campaign activation:

1. Which campaign will help you put the best foot forward? Which campaign will launch with the highest CTRs and highest conversion rates? If you have a strong, recognizable brand, this will be your brand campaign. Launch this campaign first.

2. Which campaign contains keywords that are so relevant for your product or service that when people search on one of these terms, they are almost certainly looking for what you have to offer? These can be product-specific ad groups. Launch this campaign second.

3. Which campaign contains keywords that describe your product or service but are a little more general? Could these terms appeal to searchers early in the buying cycle, or searchers who are conducting research and may not be ready to buy at all? Launch this type of campaign after you have the first two firing on all cylinders.

4. Expand into the content network. It's a great way to expand your volume and generate more sales and revenue. However, exploiting the content network requires a good deal of attention in order to optimize performance. After your search campaigns are performing acceptably, you can turn your attention to the content network.

Wednesday: Are Your CTRs High Enough?

What are "good" CTRs and conversion rates? That's a tough question to answer generally, because PPC results can vary quite a bit from industry to industry, from site to site, and even within ad groups in a single campaign.

But here are some safe generalizations:

- CTR will always be higher for products or services already in strong demand, and lower for those that are relatively unknown, new, multifaceted, and/or difficult to describe. For example, lots of people search for recipes online, so an ad that's triggered by the keyword *guacamole recipe* will result in high CTRs if the text promises to provide the ultimate recipe for guacamole.

- Conversion rates will always be higher for "soft" offers than for "hard" offers. So an ad that offers free downloadable MP3 songs will result in a higher conversion rate than an ad that leads to a site selling high-priced products or services.

If you use the techniques described in previous chapters (especially creating small, tight ad groups), you should be dissatisfied with CTRs that are lower than 2 percent. For low-demand products or services (the latter case in the first bulleted item in the preceding list), the best CTRs may never rise above 3–4 percent.

But for higher-demand products or services, you should shoot for 5 percent and above, and though double-digit CTRs are tougher to achieve, they should be your ultimate goal. It's not unusual for even nonbranded free offers to result in conversion rates of 20–30 percent or even higher.

Conversion rate ranges are similar. A good conversion rate for a hard offer would be a minimum of 2 percent. For business-to-consumer (B2C) e-commerce sales, it shouldn't be difficult to achieve above 5 percent. For softer offers, including low-priced products or free trial software downloads, 10–20 percent or higher conversion rates are definitely achievable.

Of course, every campaign is going to be different. What you should focus on is this: What is my CTR or conversion rate now, and how can I make it better? Regardless of whether your CTR is 2 percent or 20 percent, you should always be thinking of ways to improve your campaigns' performance. So the answer to the question "Are my CTRs high enough?" is no, because they can always be better.

Thursday and Friday: Are You Reaching Your Target Conversion Rates and Costs?

Surprisingly, the question of whether you are hitting your target conversion rates, CPA numbers, and ROI might not be a yes/no proposition.

You may launch your campaign, immediately achieve five-to-one returns, scale up to spending $1,000 per day (then $10,000), and look like a rock star to your company's chief marketing officer (CMO). This could happen, but it's rare.

The process of optimizing an ad group and reaching your target conversion rates and costs is going to look something like this:

1. Your *ad group is producing conversions*, but your average CPA is high by about 20 percent.

2. You look over the ads you are running, and realize that one of your ads is achieving a two-to-one ROI while all the other ads are bleeding the budget.

3. You write better ads and start to break even.

4. You then model future ads based on that first, acceptably performing one—creating better and better variations.

Repeat this process many times, and eventually you'll find yourself with a pretty great money-making machine.

Whether or not you are reaching your targets is going to be based on the expectations put on your time by you and/or your managers. Optimization is an iterative process of determining what is working—whether it is an ad, a keyword (or type of keyword), or a particular landing page (or model for landing page)—and building and testing progressively better variations.

Week 20: Perform Early Course-Correction

One of the advantages of activating a new account gradually is that you can minimize risk and mitigate mistakes as much as possible. This week, you're going to build on the things that you've done right initially, making sure that you have your PPC boat pointed in the right direction that it continues in that direction.

Monday: Activating Additional Ad Groups

Last Monday, you began by activating your best ad groups first. After you have those humming along, it's time to get going with the rest of your efforts. Consider today a reiteration of last week's exercises, applied to a broader range of keywords and ad groups. The process corresponds to Figure 8.8 of last week, but in greater detail.

Is your daily ad spend meeting or exceeding budget caps? We assume that you've done a good-enough job with your initial high-CTR keywords to justify flipping the switch on the rest of your campaigns. Just remember that your daily ad spending for any individual campaign could exceed your daily budget cap by as much as 20 percent.

How are your CTRs looking? As we said previously, you should aspire to and work to achieve double-digit CTRs and correspondingly high quality scores. Review the ad copywriting tips from Chapter 5, "Month 2—Create Great PPC Ads," experiment with the ad tests and alternatives we discussed in Chapter 5 (creating headlines, alternating the lines of your body copy, and adding bells and whistles to your display URLs), and make sure that your keywords are arranged into well-organized ad groups. One caveat: Consider improving CTRs with phrase- and exact-match keywords before adding broad-match keywords.

How are your conversion rates looking? Have your general, competitor, and branded keywords helped to increase conversion volume without exceeding your CPA targets? Are you breaking even at the keyword, ad group, or campaign level? If the answer is yes, you can draw upon your data to expand your general keyword list.

Even though we've structured these lessons on a week-to-week model, that doesn't necessarily mean that you turn on your branded keywords one Monday, and then you turn on your general terms the next Monday. It's entirely possible that you will activate your next set of ad groups as soon as the very next day, and maybe more likely that you will make a few rounds of revisions on your content network campaigns (which can take a couple of weeks) before activating ad groups containing general keywords.

Tuesday: Adjusting Ad Group and Keyword Bids

Today's lesson is relatively straightforward when you have sufficient click and conversion data. After you see how much you are spending as compared to how much it costs to drive a conversion, you can make better-informed bid decisions.

The model for profitable PPC results is quite simple. You want to maximize PPC *profit margin*, as shown in the following equation:

PPC profit margin = number of clicks ÷ (revenue per click − cost per click)

You can affect each of the components of PPC profit margin with these actions:

Number of clicks: Increase the CTR for existing keywords and increase the number of keywords.

Revenue per click: Refine keywords by removing low-converting keywords that cost more than they are worth, improve landing-page conversion rates, or write more-compelling ads.

Cost per click: Increase CTR (to earn quality score–based discounts) or reduce bid prices.

One way to increase the number of clicks is to increase your bid prices. Let's say your revenue per click is $1. This means that, theoretically, you can spend up to $1 per click without losing money. Let's also assume that the average CPC is only $0.25. So it's safe for you to increase the number of clicks by increasing the bid price, and you should be able to continue making per-click profit if your clicks cost anything under $1.

Another example: Imagine you are bidding and being charged $1 per click, and that your ads are appearing in position 1. Your revenue per click comes out to only $0.25. The action you should take is simple: *Reduce your bid to a maximum of $0.25.* You will certainly see a decrease in the volume of clicks, but the lower average CPC will ensure that all conversions yield profit.

Wednesday: Adding Keyword Variations to Winning Ad Groups

After parts of your newly activated campaigns are producing acceptable results, you should start optimizing keyword lists by using the Search Query Performance report. This is especially true for any ad groups that include broad-match keywords, and to a lesser extent, phrase-match keywords. You can find this report under the Reports tab of your AdWords account.

Review the Search Query Performance Report

The Search Query Performance report shows you the exact search queries that Google has chosen to match with your keywords. As you review this report, you will find search queries that will be highly relevant for your campaigns—so you should add them to the appropriate ad groups. You will also see many queries that are not at all relevant to your products and services—often, as mentioned earlier, occurring as a result of Google's aggressive matching of broad-match keywords to a too-wide variety of synonyms.

Here is a way to quickly get to the information you're looking for in the report:

1. Export the report in CSV format and open it in Excel. Enable the Filter function within the Data section.

2. Sort the spreadsheet data by the Clicks column. This way, the search queries with the most clicks will be at the top.

3. Using the Filter function, filter out any keywords that have fewer than five clicks. This will shorten your list of search queries, because many of the terms in this report will have generated only a few impressions or only a few clicks. We suggest filtering out the search queries with fewer than five clicks, because there could be numerous terms that generated very few clicks, and you should give those search queries time to gain more data. You want to focus your attention on the actions that will generate the biggest results at the fastest pace, and adding hundreds of keywords that received only one or two clicks each is going to waste your time.

   After you've completed these steps, the search queries with the largest number of clicks should be at the top of the report. Now you will focus your attention to the Conversions column of your report.

4. Using the Filter function, filter out any search queries that have not converted. Because the overall goal is to generate conversions and revenue, you don't want to create keywords based on search queries that are not converting well. Your report should now contain the search queries that received a substantial number of clicks and conversions. By now, your report should be looking much more manageable!

5. Review the list of search queries and compare them against the keywords that are currently in your account. Add the terms that are relevant (they're getting clicks and generating conversions) to the appropriate existing ad groups, or create new ad groups for them.

Review the Opportunities Tab

You may have noticed a tab labeled Opportunities in your AdWords account. As your newly activated account accrues traffic, AdWords will collect keyword suggestions that may be relevant for your campaigns. As illustrated in Figure 8.9, the Opportunities tab is located in the main navigation section of your AdWords account.

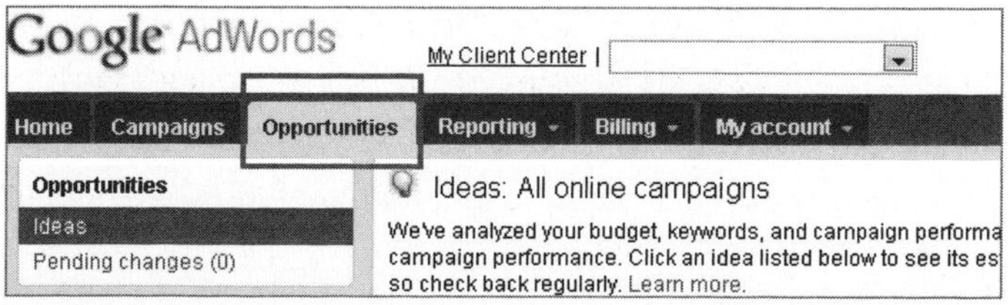

Figure 8.9 You can find additional keyword suggestions on the Opportunities tab within your AdWords account.

The AdWords system regularly reviews how you could increase impressions and clicks by adding new, relevant keywords. Similar to the ones you find in the Search Query Performance report, these new keyword suggestions are mostly derived from search queries that were matched to your existing keywords.

As shown in Figure 8.10, keyword suggestions are provided at the ad group level. You can preview the suggestions by clicking Preview. You can also see the estimated monthly searches for all of the suggested terms in each ad group.

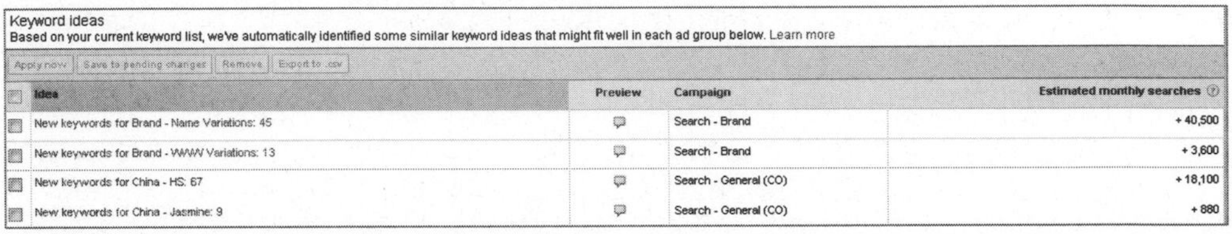

Keyword ideas Based on your current keyword list, we've automatically identified some similar keyword ideas that might fit well in each ad group below. Learn more			
Apply now Save to pending changes Remove Export to .csv			
Ideas	Preview	Campaign	Estimated monthly searches ⓘ
New keywords for Brand - Name Variations: 45	🗩	Search - Brand	+ 40,500
New keywords for Brand - WWW Variations: 13	🗩	Search - Brand	+ 3,600
New keywords for China - HS: 67	🗩	Search - General (CO)	+ 18,100
New keywords for China - Jasmine: 9	🗩	Search - General (CO)	+ 880

Figure 8.10 Keyword suggestions in the Opportunities tab are provided at the ad group level.

As with any automated keyword suggestion tool, not all of the keywords you find here will be right for your campaign. You need to review the suggested terms closely to make sure that you're choosing the keywords that bolster your volume and enhance your performance. You should also be wary of the suggestions AdWords makes regarding which ad groups the keywords should be added to the suggestions that keep your ad groups small and tightly themed. And create new ad groups if AdWords suggests keywords that don't fit well in your existing ad groups.

Thursday and Friday: Adjusting Campaign Budget Limits

Hopefully, the only word that you will have to think about today is *up*. A great PPC campaign is one in which you make more money for every click than you spend on each click. Under these circumstances, in order to scale up your efforts, your goal is to buy as many clicks as you possibly can.

If you feel like everything is going great in your campaigns, and you want to know whether there is room to increase your daily budget, you can run an Impression Share report to see if any daily budgets are restricting your volume potential. Impression share data tells you the number of impressions your ads received out of all of the available impressions on the Google Search Network. This report displays the percentage of impressions your ads received compared to the number you may have missed.

To view your impression share data, you'll need to run a Campaign Performance report, and then add in the impression share data by clicking the Add or Remove Columns link and adding these columns to your Campaign Performance report:

Impression Share: This displays the impression share data for each campaign.

Impression Share Lost (Budget): This tells you how much impression share you may have lost because of insufficient daily budgets.

Impression Share Lost (Rank): This tells you how much impression share you may have lost because of low-ranking keywords within your campaign.

Exact Match Impression Share: This tells you the impression share for only the exact-match keywords within your campaign.

You can't get impression share data at the ad group or keyword level. Also, impression share applies only to the search network, and not the content network.

With this information, you may see that you are losing impression share because of budget restrictions. So you can increase your campaigns' daily budgets in order to increase volume. However, you should increase budgets only for campaigns that are generating a great ROI.

In the next chapter, you'll explore account analysis and optimization in greater depth.

Month 6—Optimize Your Campaign

9

Now that your campaign is active, your next objective is to monitor and improve your campaign's performance. Google provides excellent tools and reporting functions that help you pinpoint the challenges and opportunities within your account.

In this chapter, you will learn how to generate and interpret campaign performance reports. You will also learn how to turn your analyses into action plans that will help you reach the ultimate goal of the professional PPC campaign manager: steady improvement in sales volume and profit.

Chapter Contents

Week 21: Review Your Top-Level Reports

With separate campaigns for each distribution channel, ad groups for each product or service, comprehensive keyword lists, and multiple ads in each ad group, your PPC account contains an enormous amount of information. Digging into all this data can be intimidating. Where do you start? How do you know what to look for in order to make changes? Don't stress too much. Just start at the top.

To properly monitor and optimize a PPC campaign, you need to start at the highest levels of your account and work your way down to the more granular details. Think of it as peeling an onion. You need to peel back each layer of data in order to find exactly what you're looking for. Another, more technical, term for this review process is *root cause analysis* (RCA).

RCA is a problem-solving method that focuses on finding and eliminating the cause of the issue at hand, rather than just fixing a particular symptom. By addressing the root cause of a problem, your chances are increased that the issue will be resolved properly the first time, and you'll gain a stronger understanding of what caused the problem in the first place. By approaching your PPC performance issues in this manner, you're not just looking for problems; you're looking for effective solutions to these problems.

The process of implementing an RCA approach to PPC analysis and optimization looks like this:

1. Define the problem.

2. Run reports to gather your data.

3. Review the reports for performance trends and relationships.

4. Identify possible causes.

5. Identify possible solutions.

6. Implement the solutions that you think will be effective.

7. Observe the results of your solutions.

This is why you need to start at the top levels of your account when reviewing the performance of your PPC campaign. If you dive straight into the more granular levels of your account, you may be looking in the wrong place and fixing only a symptom of your problem.

Keep root cause analysis in mind as you walk through these AdWords reports. As we mentioned earlier, you're going to be looking for root causes of issues (or opportunities) as if you were peeling back layers of an onion. Figure 9.1 shows the layers of your PPC account.

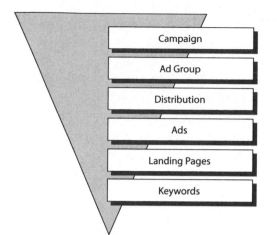

Figure 9.1 To optimize your PPC account, first look at your campaigns and then work your way down to keywords.

We wish there were a template method to analyze and optimize your PPC campaign. We wish we could say, "Complete steps 1, 2, and 3, and you'll have all the actionable analysis you need to enhance your performance." But every PPC account has a unique structure with unique goals, challenges, and opportunities. Over the next four weeks, we'll walk you through how to utilize each report in AdWords. By the end of this chapter, you should be able to use these reports to optimize your own accounts.

Monday: Campaign and Ad Group Reports

All of the reports we discuss in this chapter can be found on the Reporting tab of your AdWords account. As shown in Figure 9.2, when you click the Reporting tab, a few options are presented. To access your account reports, click Reports (the first option).

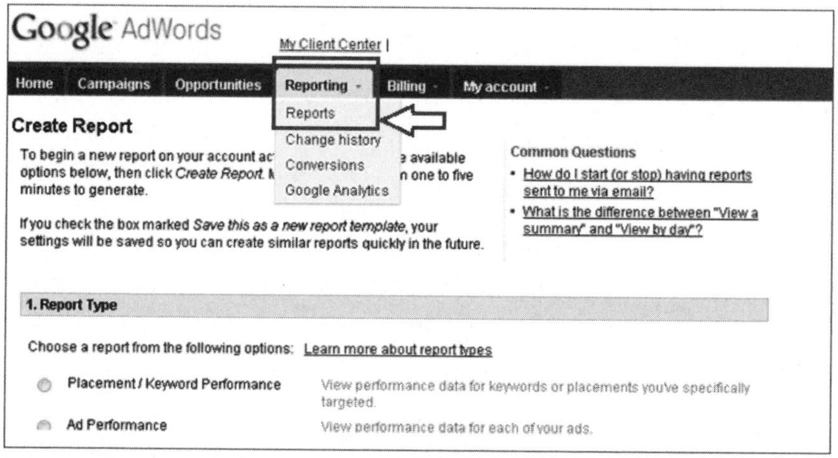

Figure 9.2 The Reports tab contains all your AdWords reports.

The reporting section in AdWords is rather intuitive and easy to follow. As shown in Figure 9.3, creating a report is a four-step process:

1. Select a report type.

2. Choose the settings, for unit of time, date range, and which campaigns or ad groups you would like to view in the report.

3. Select any additional advanced settings.

4. Create a report template, schedule it to run automatically, or elect to have it e-mailed to you.

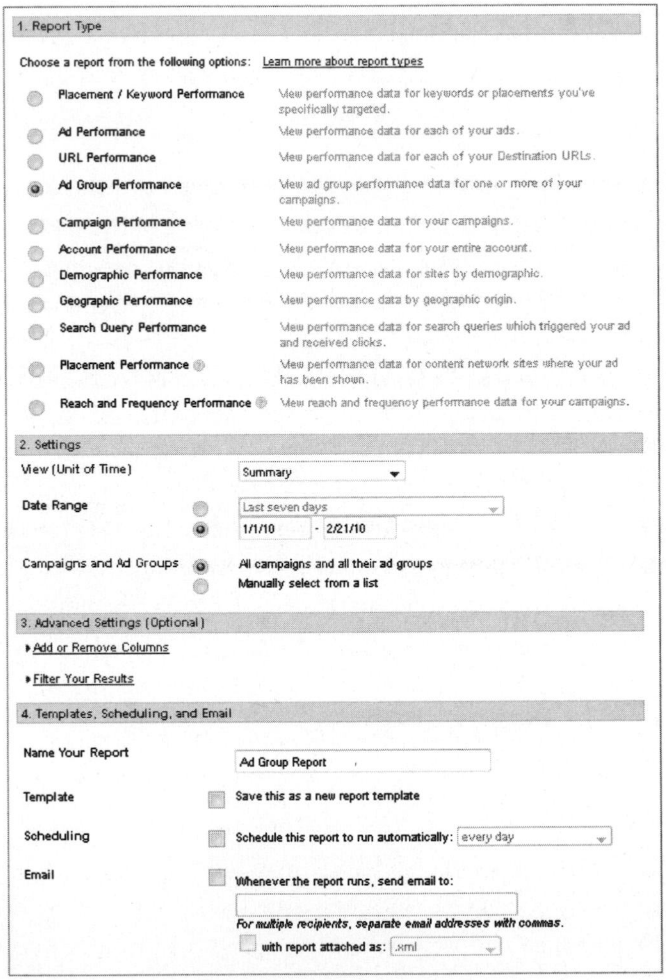

Figure 9.3 The four steps to creating a report in AdWords

After you run a report within AdWords, you can easily export the data to Microsoft Excel. We suggest that you take this step for the following reasons:

- You can format the report so that it's easier to read.

- You can sort and filter data in order to find the information you need quickly.

- You can keep a copy of the report for your files.

We recommend starting with campaign-level reports to determine where issues may be lurking. Within a Campaign Performance report, you can review the impressions, clicks, click-through rate (CTR), cost per click (CPC), conversions, conversion rate, and cost per acquisition (CPA).

The examples throughout this chapter center on locating problem areas within your account that are underperforming. You will also want to use the root cause analysis methodology to identify what's performing well and to generate more volume from those positively performing areas of your account.

While analyzing your campaign report, you need to identify which campaigns are performing acceptably and which are not. After you have singled out which campaigns are not meeting your performance criteria, you need to peel back the onion and move down a level to ad group–level reporting. The objective of the Ad Group Performance report is similar to the Campaign Performance report—you are looking for ad groups that are underperforming. By *underperforming*, we mean ad groups that are not meeting your preset goals. These goals shouldn't be measured by CPC or CTR alone, but also by your conversion metrics such as number of conversions, conversion rate, and CPA.

An ad group's performance could be suffering for a few reasons. Here are some common issues that cause ad groups to perform below par:

- Poorly grouped keywords, so there are too many unrelated terms in one ad group

- Unregulated match types, where broad match is hurting your performance

- Poorly written ads

- Neglected ad split tests, where weak ad text is bringing down the ad group

- Underperforming distribution channel

As you review your ad groups, single out which ones need additional attention. Focus your optimization efforts on these ad groups. Tomorrow we are going to discuss one of the advanced settings that can be used on your campaign and ad group reports.

Have You Gathered Enough Data?

Creating an optimization plan based on incorrect data or small sample sizes can be a major impediment to the success of your PPC campaign. At every level of an account, you need to have a statistically significant number of clicks and conversions to determine what is working. How big a sample size do you need in order to make decisions?

We would love to be able to say that you need *x* number of clicks and *y* number of conversions before conducting your analysis. Unfortunately, the answer is not that easy. Remember, every PPC account is different. So, the amount of traffic that each campaign, ad group, or keyword needs to accumulate enough data will vary greatly. Some large-scale, high-volume campaigns can generate enough data in a shorter amount of time, whereas smaller campaigns will need time to mature and gather clicks.

This means that PPC campaigns that drive a great deal of traffic need more-frequent attention and optimization than lower-traffic campaigns. This may go without saying, but the last thing we want any PPC advertiser to do is *set it and forget it*, which means launching your PPC campaign and believing that the hard work is over. The truth is, after you launch your campaign, the work is just beginning.

So, what is the answer to the question "Have you gathered enough data?" The answer is unique to your own PPC campaign. You may need 100 clicks to make a decision, or you may need 500 to determine whether an ad is performing well or whether a keyword doesn't belong in your campaign. We just want to emphasize the importance of click volume and statistical significance when analyzing your campaign.

We'll provide advice on minimum sample sizes and provide tools for comparing ad performance in upcoming chapters on ad testing and landing page testing.

Tuesday: Network Distribution Reports

We emphasize starting at the top when analyzing your account. One way to start at a 1,000-foot view, so to speak, is to review your network distribution before diving into the minutiae of your campaigns. By this we mean reviewing your Google Search Network, Search Partner Network, and Content Network distribution.

Before looking at ads, keywords, match types, placements, or any other detailed level of your account, you should gain an understanding of how your campaign is performing as a whole on the various Google networks. Network distribution can be analyzed at a few levels of your account, but for this example, we're going to focus on campaigns and ad groups.

To display your campaign's network distribution on your report, click the Add or Remove Columns link under Advanced Settings, and then click the Ad Distribution and Ad Distribution: With Search Partners check boxes, as shown in Figure 9.4.

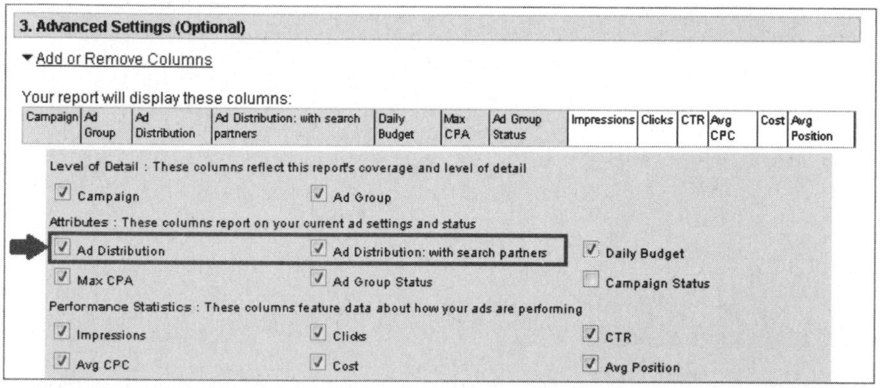

Figure 9.4 Your network distribution can be reviewed at the campaign, ad group, ad text, and URL levels of your campaign.

If you select only the Ad Distribution column to be displayed on your report, you will see the performance of your search and content networks, with the Google search and search partners data combined. If your search network and content network distributions are separated into different campaigns as we have been recommending, this selection won't do you much good. When reviewing your search campaigns, you should also select Ad Distribution: With Search Partners. This way, you can review your Google search distribution as well as your search partner distribution.

For example, let's say you want to know how your campaign is performing on the Google Search Network and the Google Search Partner Network. You would choose Ad Distribution: With Search Partners. When you export the report into Excel, it will look similar to Table 9.1.

▶ **Table 9.1** Google Search and Search Partners in Your Excel Report

Distribution	Impressions	Clicks	CTR	Cost	Conv.	Conv. Rate	Cost/Conv.
Google Search	19,659	981	4.99%	$1,976.27	122	12.44%	$16.20
Search Partners	8,659	423	4.89%	$876.27	32	7.57%	$27.38
Totals/Averages	**28,318**	**1,404**	**4.96%**	**$2,852.54**		**5.40%**	**$18.52**

From this report, you can see whether a search network is hindering your performance. Unfortunately, if you find that to be the case, you can't do anything to remedy the situation. Any changes you make in Google search campaigns affect your search partner performance; however, you can't make adjustments solely to your search partner distribution. The only optimization option for the search partner network is to turn it off or on. This option is adjusted at the campaign level, as shown in Figure 9.5

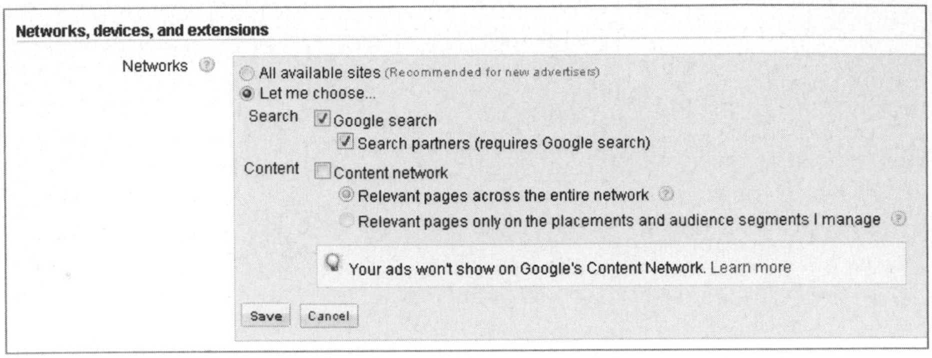

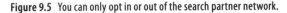

Figure 9.5 You can only opt in or out of the search partner network.

Wednesday: Ad Performance Reports

At this point, you've already peeled back a few layers of your account, including campaign, network distribution, and ad group. Now you need to review your ad performance. As we've mentioned in several places throughout this book, you should always be split testing your PPC ad copy in each ad group. Continuously testing and improving your ad performance is one of the most powerful ways to optimize PPC campaign performance.

When analyzing an Ad Performance report, you should look for ad test pairs with enough conversion data to show a statistically significant difference in their performance. In Chapter 10, "Month 7—Test Ads by Using Advanced Techniques," we go into more detail about how to determine the winners and losers of advanced ad split testing.

Weekends Are the Low Tide

When gathering data within your account in order to analyze your performance, you need to understand that search traffic is cyclical. You will probably find that the highest search volume occurs Monday through Thursday, while Friday through Sunday are slower days for clicks and conversions.

You need to consider which days are the peaks and valleys for click volume and conversion rates for your account. One of the best methods to mitigate these fluctuations is to include a wide range of days in your reporting. This is especially important when you're comparing data before and after you make a change to your account.

For example, let's say you make a change to your account on Wednesday. When the following Monday rolls around, you may want to see how this change has affected your performance. A logical way to find out whether you've made a smart change is to look at the data since the change (four days ago) and the four days prior to the change. However, this means you would be comparing a block of time that includes Sunday through Wednesday to a block of time that includes Thursday through Sunday.

In this example, we can almost guarantee that it will look as if the change you made was a failure. Weekends usually have lower search volume, lower CTRs, and lower conversion rates. When reviewing these reports, make sure to include at least seven days within your reports in order to mitigate the weekend effect.

This is another reason why you need to gather enough data to discern the signal from the noise. If you don't gather enough data and you use the preceding example to analyze your account, you're going to make the wrong decisions.

Thursday: URL Performance Reports

A URL Performance report shows you the performance based on ad destination URLs (not to be confused with display URLs). You will be able to see the performance of specific destination URLs, or pages, even if the URL is the destination of several different ads across several ad groups.

However, because the performance of a landing page is so dependent on an ad group's keywords and the search query matched to them, and also the ad text paired with the keywords and landing pages, there are usually few valid inferences one can make about URLs spread across several ad groups. For this reason, we believe the URL report is less meaningful and less useful than other performance reports.

Friday: Placement/Keyword Performance Reports

At this point, you've run a Campaign Performance report and an Ad Performance report, determined which campaigns need attention, and narrowed your analysis to a few particular ad groups (or perhaps even just one ad group). Now you need to analyze the keyword performance of those ad groups by using the more detailed Placement/Keyword Performance reports.

If you neglect to follow our step-by-step, root-cause analysis process, then you may end up with "analysis paralysis." This means that you have a huge set of data points at your fingertips, but you don't know where to start looking. In other words, you're paralyzed. You can run Placement/Keyword Performance reports for all of your campaigns and ad groups at once, but that is a lot of data to look at closely. Keep focused by looking in specific areas of your account that need attention, and you'll develop a reliable method of actionable analysis.

Because keywords are the bedrock of your PPC campaign, the Placement/ Keyword Performance report is one of your most valuable reports. With this report, you are looking for keywords that are underperforming. These are the terms that are generating a high CPA or a low CTR. You are also looking for keywords that are doing well. These are the terms that are generating conversions that are below your CPA goal.

As with any report you run in AdWords, you need to run your Placement/ Keyword Performance report for a time frame that will provide enough data for you to make confident decisions. Depending on the impression volume of your campaign, you may be able to look at the last seven days of data in order to see performance trends. However, we suggest that you look at keyword performance through a wider lens, by including at least fourteen days of the following data in your report:

Underperforming keywords: These are keywords that are generating conversions with a CPA that's unacceptably higher than your target CPA. Here are just a few of the many reasons a keyword may be underperforming:

- Your keyword bid is too high.
- The ad text is not relevant to this keyword.
- The landing page is not highly targeted to this keyword.

High-performing keywords: As you review your Placement/Keyword Performance report, you will find keywords that are resulting in relatively low-cost conversions; that is, significantly below the target CPA. When you find these terms, you can take the following actions:

- Increase the maximum CPC to improve the position of the corresponding ad—which usually results in a higher volume of clicks.
- Conduct keyword research using this keyword as the seed term to find additional variations.
- Move this keyword, along with close variations, into a separate ad group so that you can write ad copy that's closely related to the keyword.

Viewing Performance Data in the Web Interface

Throughout this chapter, we are focusing on running reports within the Reporting section of AdWords. However, you can gain insight into your account's performance directly within the AdWords web interface.

The Segment button opens a drop-down menu (shown in the following screenshot) that enables you to view data across different traffic segments.

You can segment data by network: Google Search, Search Partners, and Content Network. You can also view data segmented by Day, Week, Month, Quarter, Year, and Day of the Week time frames, and compare performance from period to period. You can also segment by Device to see how mobile devices perform, and by Click Type when you are using the AdWords click-to-call ad type. You also have the option to filter data by specific metrics. As shown in the following screen-shot, you can see how to filter campaigns, ad groups, keywords, or ads by specific metrics such as cost, CTR, impressions, conversation rate, and quality score.

Data segmentation and filters can help save time when you're reviewing performance data. However, when you are just getting started with PPC management, we suggest that you run reports within the Report Center. This way, you will build up the analytical skills to know what you're looking for within an account, how to find this information, and where to make appropriate adjustments. You can also export and save spreadsheet reports for later reference.

Week 22: Review Your Deep-Level Reports

Last week, you looked at performance data of the high levels of your account in order to discover the root causes of performance fluctuations. This week, we are going to explore the deeper levels of AdWords accounts. These reports will show you how to focus your view at a more finely grained level.

Monday: Search Query Reports

The Search Query report shows performance statistics for the search queries that resulted in your ads being triggered. This report is available for only the search network. This data can be used to gain a deeper understanding of how users are searching for your product or service.

The difference between a Search Query report (SQR) and a Placement/Keyword Performance report is that the SQR displays the actual search query that triggered your ad. The Placement/Keyword Performance report reports on only the keywords currently in your account.

As you review an SQR, you'll find search queries that triggered your ads on keywords that are not currently in your account but that may be doing well. You can add these terms to your account. Reviewing your SQR on a regular basis is a great way to continually grow your keyword list. This is a great keyword research tactic, because the terms you pull from your SQR are already driving relevant traffic to your site.

Within your SQR, you may also find search queries that are irrelevant and garnering poor results (generating impressions but no clicks, or clicks but no conversions). If the search queries are completely irrelevant, you should add them to your negative keyword list. If they are relevant, or somewhat relevant, you may consider creating a separate ad group for them, with better-targeted ads and lower bids to see whether you turn these "so-so" keywords into reasonable performers.

Let's take a look at how to use the SQR more specifically to expand and refine your ad groups. Within a specific ad group, let's say you have a variety of *gourmet coffee*–themed keywords such as these:

- *Gourmet coffee*
- *Best gourmet coffee*
- *International gourmet coffee*

Within the SQR, you see the following relevant search queries that aren't included in the keyword list:

- *Gourmet coffee gifts*
- *Gourmet coffee website*
- *Dark roasted gourmet coffee*

These are good and relevant keywords, and you should add these to your account. You could add them to the Gourmet Coffee ad group, or create separate new ad groups for these terms. For example, now that you know that visitors found your website by using gift-related search terms, you could build a new ad group whose root keywords are *gourmet coffee gifts*.

The SQR can also help you find variations or synonyms of your existing keywords. Let's face it: It's impossible to target every single variation or synonym of each keyword. It would take days or weeks to try to predict every possible search query. If you did this, you would waste an enormous amount of time, and your keyword list would be unmanageable. However, the SQR can provide insight into which variations are actually receiving traffic.

Within the SQR, you may also find search queries that are not relevant for your product. Here are examples of search queries made by users looking for information, not to buy, or looking for a product you don't offer:

- *How to make gourmet coffee*
- *Gourmet coffee cake*
- *Roast my own gourmet coffee beans*

Armed with this SQR data, you can add negative keywords to your campaign or ad group to prevent your ads from being shown to someone using such irrelevant queries while conducting a search. To do this, you add negative keywords that are made up of the roots of the irrelevant queries, like this:

- *How to make*
- *Coffee cake*
- *Roast my own*

These negative keywords will prevent your ad from showing for any search query that includes the phrases *coffee cake*, *how to make*, or *roast my own*.

The SQR is a powerful report that can help expand and refine your campaigns and ad groups. Use it frequently.

Microsoft Excel Is a PPC Manager's Best Friend

When you run an SQR, you will be provided with thousands of search queries, and you may feel inundated with information. The same feeling can occur when running large-scale Placement/Keyword Performance reports or Placement Performance reports. When you open the Excel document, don't panic. There are a few Excel features that can make your life easier by enabling you to see the data you need quickly.

The two features we use the most frequently are Sort and Filter. Both of these helpful functions are located on the Data tab within Excel, as shown in the following screenshot taken in Excel 2010.

continues

The Sort function enables you to sort information in ascending or descending order. For example, the following keyword report options will sort keywords by cost in descending order.

With the Filter function, you can filter your data by any column within your report. You can choose to look at only active keywords that have generated more than 10 clicks and that are in position 4 or higher. When you select the Filter function, a series of drop-down menus will be added to the header columns. These drop-down menus let you filter the data. For example, you can filter the report to show only active keywords, as shown here.

You can then filter this keyword report by cost per conversion in order to find keywords with a CPA of less than $20, for example. When these two filters have been applied, you will be looking only at keywords that are active with a cost per conversion of less than $20, as shown here.

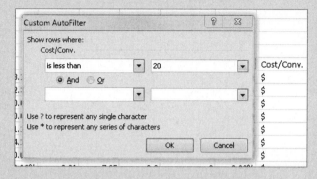

Microsoft Excel is a PPC campaign manager's best friend. You should get to know these two features very well, and use them frequently in order to analyze your data more quickly and in more-digestible chunks.

Tuesday: Impression Share Reports

Based on "share of voice" metrics used in traditional advertising, *impression share* (*IS*) provides you with a tool to gauge how effectively you are targeting your potential market. Impression share is a metric that represents the percentage of impressions that your ads were shown out of the total number of available impressions for your target market. Impression share is calculated at the account and campaign levels. The following elements of your account factor into impression share:

- Campaign budgets
- Keyword bids
- Keyword match types
- Ad rank
- Dayparting

When you include IS data in a report by selecting one or more of the check boxes shown in Figure 9.6, you are seeking to gauge the share of voice for a campaign. The report will display the campaign or ad group's IS, and you can find why you may be losing IS by adding the metrics Lost IS (Budget) and Lost IS (Rank).

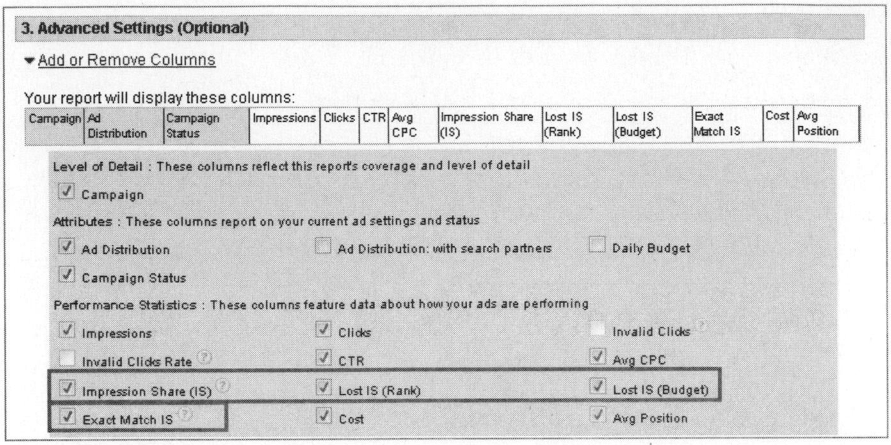

Figure 9.6 IS stats are found in the Advanced Settings for AdWords reports.

You can include the following IS metrics in an AdWords report, each providing a different insight into your campaign's or ad group's performance:

Impression share (IS): This metric tells you how often your ads are being displayed as compared to the total number of available impressions.

Lost IS (Rank): This metric indicates the percent of total impressions you lost because your ads did not show on the first page of search results. Because most searchers don't click through to the second page of search results, Google considers an impression "lost" if the ads are not displayed on the first page, or when ads are not shown at all because of low quality scores or low bids.

Lost IS (Budget): If your daily budget is set too low, your ads will not show at all times of the day. This metric shows the percent of total impressions lost because the budget is set too low.

Exact Match IS: The core IS percentage is calculated based on the performance of all of your keywords, regardless of match type. However, Exact Match IS will show you the number of times Google matched a user's search query *exactly* with one of the keywords you are actively bidding on.

What is a good IS? This differs for each campaign, because various strategies and settings can affect IS. You should view an IS of 70 percent or more as acceptable. Anything less than 70 percent should raise a red flag. An acceptable Exact Match IS, on the other hand, should be 80–85 percent. IS percentages under 100 percent are perfectly OK, because when IS approaches 100 percent, it becomes more likely that your ads are being displayed for a variety of irrelevant search terms.

Here are some reasons that IS can be unacceptably low:

Low ad rank: Your bids are low, or the keyword-and-ad combination earns a low quality score.

Low daily budgets: Your daily budgets are set too low, and therefore your ads are not showing at all times of the day.

Not targeting broad match: Broad-match keywords accumulate a large number of impressions, because using them tells Google to display your ad even when the search query is only tangentially related to the keywords. Using only phrase and exact-match keywords tells Google to display ads only in reaction to search terms that contain the literal versions of the keywords. So using only phrase and exact match will likely result in low impression share.

A frequently asked question is whether geo-targeting plays a role in IS percentage. The short answer is no. Google calculates the IS within the scope of your account and/ or campaign's settings, including geo-targeting.

How can you improve your IS percentages and ultimately improve PPC performance? Here are two useful tactics:

- If either your account-wide IS or Exact Match IS is low, your first action should be to segment the data by campaign so that you can make more-targeted, accurate changes. Looking at account-wide data will give you the big-picture view of your overall IS performance, but it won't provide you with a road map to begin making campaign-specific changes.

- At the campaign level, determine whether you are losing IS because of your budgets. Depending on the situation, this could be remedied by simply increasing your daily budget. But what if you are already hitting your daily campaign budgets and don't have the additional money to put toward PPC? Try lowering your bids incrementally to drive more clicks through your budget (think of your budget as a bottleneck). However, this may also result in lower IS, because lower bids will cause lower ad positions. In this case, you'd see the Lost IS (Budget) improve and Lost IS (Rank) get worse.

What if you're losing IS because of ad rank? In other words, what if despite your best intentions, your ads are consistently ranked poorly and/or not displaying on page 1 of the search results? As with most things related to quality score, this is slightly more complicated. One tactic that could give you a boost is to increase bids, though this might get you back into trouble with budget concerns! The more intelligent tactic is to focus on improving your quality score through improved campaign optimization and writing highly relevant ads.

Wednesday: Geographic Performance Reports

Geographic performance can be viewed at the account, campaign, and ad group levels of your account. However, you can adjust your geo-targeting settings only at the campaign level, so this is where we suggest you focus your efforts. When you select the Geographic Performance report on the Reports tab of AdWords, you can select the advanced settings, as shown in Figure 9.7.

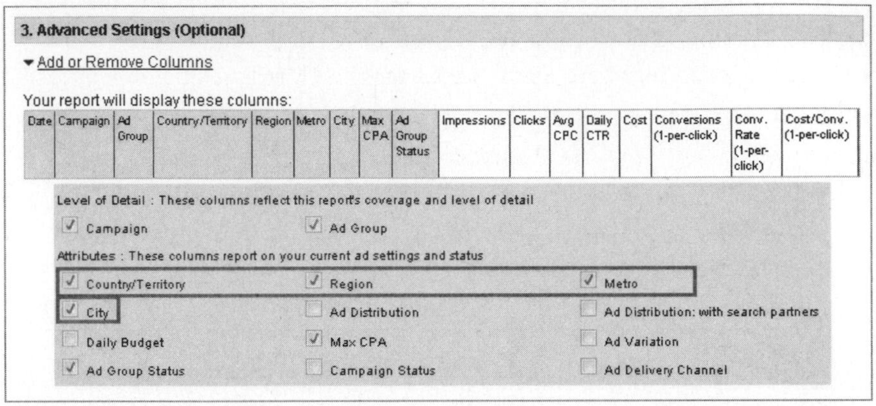

Figure 9.7 Advanced geographic attributes that can be added to your report

You can view your geographic performance at different levels within this report: Country/Territory, Region, Metro, or City. You can view the different states or cities where your ads get the most clicks and generate the most conversions.

This is a helpful report, but it does have one drawback: You can view your performance data only in daily increments. For example, if you want to see how different cities have performed over the past 60 days, the report will provide this data, but it will give you every state and its performance broken down into daily figures. This isn't an insurmountable problem, but it's annoying when you're trying to quickly analyze this report. You will need to tally the performance of each location (whether it is a city, region, or metro area). Just keep this in mind when running this report.

As you review this report, you may find that a specific state or city is doing very well or very poorly. For the geographic areas that are doing well, you may want to target them specifically. Conversely, you may want to remove from your distribution any cities or areas of the country that aren't performing well for your account.

Targeting a Specific Location

Geo-targeting can help make your ads more relevant to users in specific areas, which can improve your PPC ads' relevancy as well as enhance your CTR and your overall performance. Let's say that the Chicago area converts well for your campaign. You may want to create a new campaign targeted specifically to this area. This way, you can write ad copy that mentions Chicago specifically, and makes your ads more relevant to these users. (We covered targeting specific geographic locations in Chapter 4, "Month 1—Research Keywords and Establish Campaign Structure.")

Removing Your Ads from a Specific Location

If a location doesn't perform well, you may want to remove it from a campaign. For example, let's say that many people in the Chicago area click on your ads, but they don't convert. Follow these steps to make this adjustment:

1. Click the Settings tab in the AdWords web interface view of your campaign.

2. In the Locations and Languages section, click the Select One or More Other Locations link under Locations. A map dialog box appears.

3. Click the Exclude Areas within Selected Locations link in the lower-left corner of the screen, as shown in Figure 9.8.

4. Select the geographic locations that you would like to exclude from your campaign.

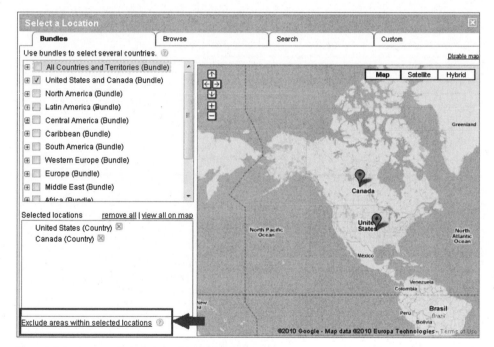

Figure 9.8 Locations can be excluded within your campaign settings.

Thursday: Placement Performance Reports

As an advertiser, you're always looking for perfect insight into how well your Google content ad campaigns are performing. With the Placement Performance report (PPR), you can further fine-tune your content campaigns to make sure you're getting the most out of your ads. With this report, you'll see where Google has chosen to display your content ads. That alone is a gold mine of information, but the report also includes almost all of the performance data that you get in Placement/Keyword Performance reports.

You can choose whether to run a PPR that shows campaign-level or ad group–level performance data. You can also choose to view just the domain names of the sites displaying your ads, or the exact URLs of each page displaying ads. We suggest you choose just the domain names, which makes interpreting performance data easier. You can choose any time interval—but keep in mind that Google started accumulating placement data June 1, 2008, so you won't be able to generate reports for any dates prior to that. Underneath the Date Range setting, you'll see an option to report on all campaigns and ad groups, or to select specific ones. You can choose any campaign, even though only data from content campaigns will be reported.

Focus on the valuable performance data for each domain: number of impressions, number of clicks, average CPC, total cost for the time period specified, total number of conversions, conversion rate, and cost per conversion.

The first thing to check is the length of the domain list. The optimal number of sites will vary depending on the specificity of your ad, product, or offer. Here's a rule of thumb: If the number of sites is small (for example, fewer than 10), your content campaign is probably targeted too narrowly. Try using fewer negative keywords, or increase your ad group's bid price to merit appearing on more sites.

More commonly, the list of domains will be very long—from dozens of sites to hundreds. This often means your ads are appearing on many inappropriate sites—ones with subject matter that bears no relation to your ad, product, or service.

This is bad news. The main reason that content campaigns perform so poorly in terms of CTRs and conversion rates is that ads are displayed on inappropriate sites—that is, sites whose frequent visitors don't include people interested in the advertiser's products or services. Most often, this occurs because advertisers use the same keyword lists for their content ad groups as they do for their search ad groups—a definite "worst practice." If your PPR list is still too long, there's a way you can weed out poorly performing sites: the Google Site Exclusion tool.

All Google AdWords content campaigns have dead wood. Google Content Network sites that display your ads but deliver few clicks or conversions rob you of profits. However, Google Site Exclusion data can help you increase ROI. You can use this data in your PPR to your benefit in many ways, especially for weeding out poorly performing sites. Most obvious are sites that garner a significant number of clicks without delivering conversions. Less obvious are sites that deliver few or no clicks and no conversions, but many impressions.

To exclude poorly performing sites, click the Networks tab in your AdWords account. Toward the bottom of this tab, you can add exclusions at the ad group and campaign levels, as shown in Figure 9.9.

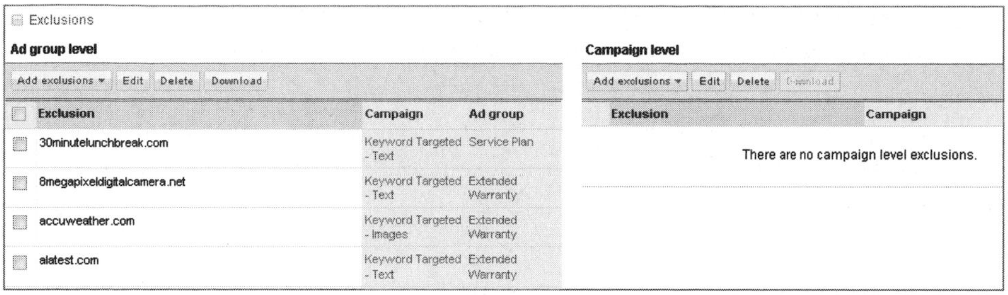

Figure 9.9 Websites can be excluded at the ad group and campaign levels.

Here are some tips for using the PPR and evaluating your content network performance:

Voracious sites: Several sites carrying Google ads, including MySpace and YouTube, attract huge volumes of traffic that, in aggregate, perform well only for companies or products that have mass consumer appeal. Many advertisers will want to avoid these sites.

Microsurgery: You can generate PPRs that show specific subdirectories and even pages where your ads have appeared. You can then use the Site Exclusion tool to exclude only subdirectories and pages. This may be overkill, though, unless you're dealing with sites with huge volumes of traffic.

Vote early, vote often: The persistent PPC advertiser will want to run PPRs frequently. New publisher sites join the Google AdSense program every day. (Recently, the roster of new publisher sites included media monster magazines *Glamour, Teen Vogue, Allure, Self,* and even the venerable *The New Yorker.*)

Filtering Your Report Data

We have mentioned a few times that some of the reports in AdWords can provide an almost over-whelming amount of information. To get to the most important data more quickly, you can add filters to your reports with the Report Center's advanced settings.

For example, the following Advanced Settings screen illustrates how we set up a series of filters for our PPR to show results only from placement within ad groups that are active, have generated more than five conversions, and have a cost per conversion of less than $20.

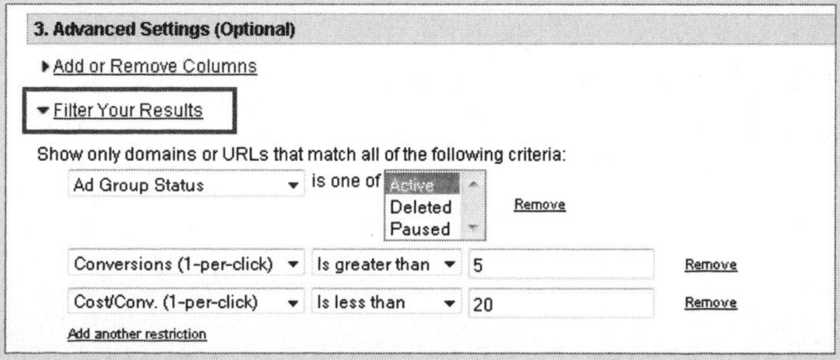

Friday: Reach and Frequency Performance Reports

The Reach and Frequency Performance report shows you how many users saw your site-targeted ad and how frequently they viewed it over a period of time. This report data is available at the site, ad group, and campaign levels for CPM (cost per thousand impressions) placement-targeted campaigns only.

We suggest that you create CPC- or CPA-targeted campaigns. Therefore, you won't run this frequently. However, if you decide to create a CPM placement-targeted campaign, this report will enable you to gauge the effectiveness of your brand-related efforts on the content network.

Week 23: Create Additional Useful Reports

In the first two weeks outlined in this chapter, you explored the reports that provide the core performance metrics of your account, as well as reports that provide additional insight that may not be apparent by just looking at keywords or ads. This week, you'll learn about the additional advanced reports that are available in AdWords.

Monday: Quality Score Reports

Quality score is very important to your PPC performance. To improve your quality score, you need to monitor it and continually optimize your campaign. We'll dive deeper into quality score enhancement strategies next week, but today we'll discuss how to find your keywords' quality score.

To learn your keyword quality scores, run a Keyword Performance report with the Quality Score option selected in the advanced settings. This report will include quality score along with your other keyword performance metrics. Your keywords are given a quality score measurement between 1 and 10 (1 being the weakest score, and 10 being the strongest score). You can then sort your keywords by quality score in order to find the terms that have low scores. Because quality scores are most heavily influenced by the CTR of the keyword and ad combination, the best tactics for improving quality scores are those that improve CTR—like ad testing and ad group segmentation.

Tuesday: Demographic Performance Reports

The Demographic Performance report provides demographic information about users who saw your ads on the Google Content Network. The information provided in this report is supplied by publisher sites that have chosen to share this information with Google. You can run this report at the campaign and ad group levels of your account.

With the information provided in this report, you may decide to target specific demographic groups (such as female users over the age of 35) on the Google Content

Network. To do this, click Campaign Settings for one particular content campaign, click the Demographic Bidding link at the bottom of the screen (under Advanced Settings), and click the check boxes for the gender and/or age groups you want to *exclude* because they don't convert well for your campaign, as shown in Figure 9.10.

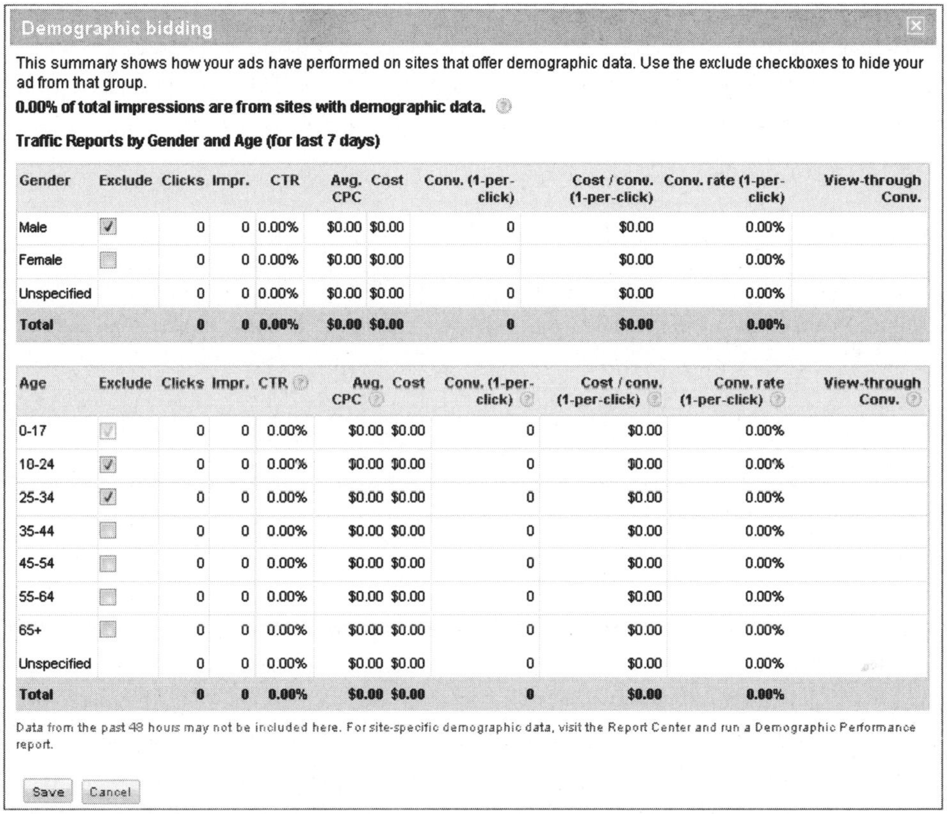

Demographic bidding

This summary shows how your ads have performed on sites that offer demographic data. Use the exclude checkboxes to hide your ad from that group.

0.00% of total impressions are from sites with demographic data.

Traffic Reports by Gender and Age (for last 7 days)

Gender	Exclude	Clicks	Impr.	CTR	Avg. CPC	Cost	Conv. (1-per-click)	Cost / conv. (1-per-click)	Conv. rate (1-per-click)	View-through Conv.
Male	☑	0	0	0.00%	$0.00	$0.00	0	$0.00	0.00%	
Female	☐	0	0	0.00%	$0.00	$0.00	0	$0.00	0.00%	
Unspecified		0	0	0.00%	$0.00	$0.00	0	$0.00	0.00%	
Total		**0**	**0**	**0.00%**	**$0.00**	**$0.00**	**0**	**$0.00**	**0.00%**	

Age	Exclude	Clicks	Impr.	CTR	Avg. CPC	Cost	Conv. (1-per-click)	Cost / conv. (1-per-click)	Conv. rate (1-per-click)	View-through Conv.
0-17	☑	0	0	0.00%	$0.00	$0.00	0	$0.00	0.00%	
10-24	☑	0	0	0.00%	$0.00	$0.00	0	$0.00	0.00%	
25-34	☑	0	0	0.00%	$0.00	$0.00	0	$0.00	0.00%	
35-44	☐	0	0	0.00%	$0.00	$0.00	0	$0.00	0.00%	
45-54	☐	0	0	0.00%	$0.00	$0.00	0	$0.00	0.00%	
55-64	☐	0	0	0.00%	$0.00	$0.00	0	$0.00	0.00%	
65+	☐	0	0	0.00%	$0.00	$0.00	0	$0.00	0.00%	
Unspecified		0	0	0.00%	$0.00	$0.00	0	$0.00	0.00%	
Total		**0**	**0**	**0.00%**	**$0.00**	**$0.00**	**0**	**$0.00**	**0.00%**	

Data from the past 48 hours may not be included here. For site-specific demographic data, visit the Report Center and run a Demographic Performance report.

Save Cancel

Figure 9.10 Exclude gender and/or age groups.

Wednesday and Thursday: Google Analytics Reports

Google Analytics is a powerful tool that enables you to gain deeper insight into how your users are interacting with your website. You can set up goal funnels to see where users abandon your shopping cart. You can review your bounce rate to see how many don't even make it past one page on your website. There is a wealth of knowledge that Google Analytics can reveal to you, and it's free!

We could write an entire book on using Google Analytics to its fullest extent, but luckily, we don't have to. Avinash Kaushik has already written an excellent book titled *Web Analytics: An Hour a Day* (Sybex, 2007), which will teach you everything you need to know about setting up analytics on your site.

Within Google Analytics, we suggest that you review the following advanced reports:

Goal funnel reports: The reports that focus on your conversion funnel are extremely important. They can tell you where you can make improvements to your conversion process.

Organic traffic reports: There may be terms that are generating traffic to your site via organic listings, but you're not targeting them via your PPC. You can then add these terms to your account to get a boost.

Referring sites reports: These reports show which sites are referring traffic to your website. If there is a website that consistently drives quality traffic to your website, you may be able to target that site via the Google Content Network. This tactic will help you acquire more real estate on that site.

Friday: The My Change History Report

My Change History enables you to review all account changes in a quick, orderly fashion. If multiple people are managing a single PPC account, this report is indispensable for creating an instant audit trail showing who did what, and when. Not only can you choose a specific time period, but you can also slice and dice the records by account manager and the type of change that was made (for example, was it a bid increase or an ad text change?).

With the option to see your change history in a performance-related timeline, you can see how these alterations affected your performance. In other words, it's an extremely valuable resource for managing AdWords.

Within each campaign and ad group, you can click View Change History to see a My Change History report with the data presegmented by the date range and campaign or ad group you were already viewing, as shown in Figure 9.11.

The My Change History report can help you detect when an alteration to your account caused a fluctuation in your performance. If you see a downward trend in conversion rate, you can view the My Change History report to help pinpoint when changes were made that correlate to the performance decline.

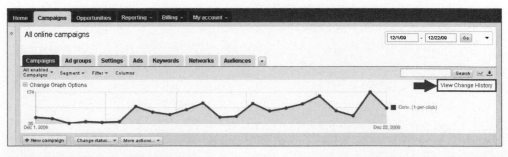

Figure 9.11 View your account's change history.

Save Yourself Time and Set up Automated Reports

Google AdWords has a helpful reporting feature that enables you to generate automated reports. Any report that you create within AdWords can be generated automatically on a regular schedule.

As shown in the following example, you can set up a report to be sent to your e-mail inbox on a daily basis. Just give your report a name, save it as a template, select your scheduling preference, and enter the e-mail address where you want the report to be sent.

4. Templates, Scheduling, and Email

Name Your Report
Daily Keyword Report

Template ☑ Save this as a new report template

Scheduling ☑ Schedule this report to run automatically: every day ▾

Email ☑ Whenever the report runs, send email to:
joe@clixmarketing.com
For multiple recipients, separate email addresses with commas.
☑ with report attached as: .csv ▾

Week 24: Act on Your Data and Optimize Your Account

We have covered the majority of the available reports within AdWords. By now, you are familiar with the performance metrics that you need to monitor, but what are some best practices for optimizing your performance? This week, we are going to cover core strategies to help you optimize your campaign's performance.

Of course, as we've said numerous times previously, each PPC account is different. Therefore the methods for overcoming challenges and seizing opportunities within your account will be unique to your results and goals. However, some tried-and-true optimization techniques can be applied to almost any PPC campaign. Each day this week, we'll review a different core metric of PPC campaigns as well as some proven strategies to help improve your performance and results.

Monday and Tuesday: Improving Your CTR

Click-through rate (CTR) is one of the mission-critical statistics of your account. If you can't get users to click on your ads, you have a fundamental problem. If you feel that your CTRs are lower than they should be (and any good PPC account manager should almost always feel this way, because you should always be striving for a better performance), you can use a few fundamental tactics to improve your CTR.

There are many more tactics to enhance your CTR than what are provided here. We could write another entire book for improving CTR, conversion rate, quality score, and content network distribution. However, the tactics provided here are good starting points for optimizing your performance.

Restructure Your Ad Groups

When it comes to ad group structure, our mantra is that almost every keyword in your ad group should appear in your text ads. Your CTR may suffer if your ads are not highly relevant to a user's query. The best way to ensure that your ads have a high level of relevancy is to make sure all of your text ads highlight the keywords in the corresponding ad group.

Why is this important? Here are a few reasons:

- When the keywords appear in the ad text, the search engines show them in boldface to attract the searchers' eyes.
- When a searcher sees their search term boldfaced in the ad, there's a greater likelihood they'll choose that ad over competing ads that don't include the term.
- Such ads get the best CTRs, which the search engines reward with higher quality scores, which in turn gets you better ad positions at lower prices.

If upon reviewing your campaign structure you find that your ad groups contain too many keywords, you should break them down even further into more-granular themes. For example, an ad group with 40 keywords could probably be separated into two to four different, tighter ad groups. Even an ad group with 15 keywords can probably be broken down into smaller groups.

Test New Ad Copy

Your ad copy is one of the most important factors in your CTR. Testing new PPC ad copy is a continuous process that you will do throughout the life of your account.

However, if over a specific amount of time, you notice that your CTR is declining or not improving as quickly as planned, you should review your ad split testing by running Ad Performance reports. There are probably ads that are hindering your progress by having a low CTR and conversion rate. In Chapter 10, we go into greater detail about split testing your ads properly in order to determine outcomes in which you can be confident.

Expand Your Negative Keyword List

Removing your ads from irrelevant search queries is just as important as targeting highly relevant search queries. The most common reason your ads may be appearing for untargeted search queries is that your keywords or keyword match types are too broad. Casting a wide net is important for generating traffic to your website, but if your net is too wide, you'll pull in a great deal of trash along with the prize catches.

Here are some reasons your keyword focus may be too general:

Targeting broad-match keywords: Broad match can help increase your visibility on the search engines and increase your overall volume. However, if you choose to use broad match, you need to also build out an extensive negative keyword list. It is highly likely that your broad-match keywords are being displayed for search queries that Google has deemed relevant, but that you know are not relevant. Because you know your audience best, you can gain greater control over your distribution by implementing negative keywords to exclude irrelevant broad-match traffic.

Targeting general, single-word keywords: Single-word keywords such as *coffee, guitars,* and *tea* are great for ensuring a large volume of impressions and clicks, but that can be dangerous. We suggest that you don't include single-word keywords within your ad groups unless they are very targeted to your core audience and are words for which there are few synonyms. For example, a keyword such as *fibromyalgia* is more targeted than *coffee,* because *fibromyalgia* is a very specific word with very few synonyms.

The fastest and easiest way to insert negative keywords into your campaigns and ad groups is via AdWords Editor. On the Negatives tab of your campaign in AdWords Editor (shown in Figure 9.12), you can add a single negative keyword by clicking the Add Negative button, or you can add a list of new negative keywords by clicking Make Multiple Changes.

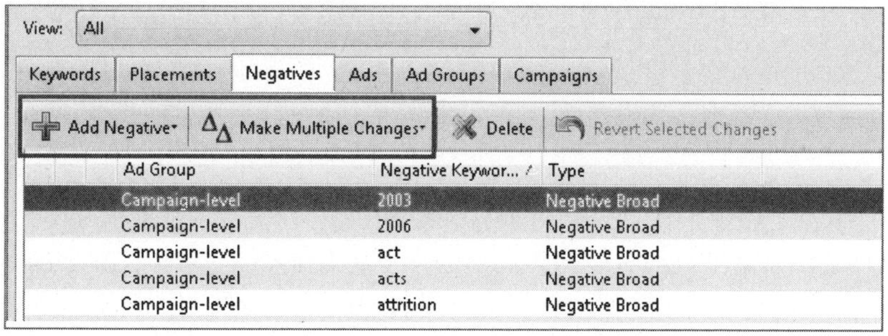

Figure 9.12 The most efficient way to add negative keywords is via AdWords Editor.

Wednesday: Improving Your Quality Score

As we mentioned in Chapter 2, "How the PPC Machine Works," having a good quality score is critical for your campaign. A quality score is considered good if it is 7 or higher. If you find that you have keywords with poor quality scores, you can use a few tactics to improve your performance.

Numerous factors affect quality score, but the most important is keyword CTR, which indicates to Google that your keyword and ad are relevant for a user's query.

One of the best ways to improve your quality score is to improve your CTR. The tactics you learned yesterday to boost your CTR will directly enhance your quality score as well. This way, you're killing two birds with one stone! These tactics include the following:

- Optimize your ad groups into smaller, tighter-themed segments.
- Write new ad copy that is more highly relevant to your keywords.
- Expand your negative keyword list.

There are other ways to boost your quality score that aren't ad- or keyword-centric.

Landing Page Contribution to Quality Score

The landing page component of quality score is a topic of debate in PPC circles, even though the reality is very simple: Poor-quality landing pages can affect quality score negatively, but there is no way to increase quality score by improving landing pages above an acceptable baseline. That acceptable baseline is determined mainly by two factors: whether the landing page loads quickly (fast is good; slow is bad), and whether the links from the landing page are connected to internal pages with relevant content or to external pages.

The bottom line is this: Design your landing pages to maximize conversions, and make sure that they load quickly. If you do these things, you will never need to worry about the landing page component of your quality score.

Thursday and Friday: Improving Your Conversion Rate

The most important factor affecting conversion rates is the effectiveness of the PPC landing page. Your PPC campaign will live or die as a result of its conversion rate. This section describes a few tactics that can improve your conversion rate, starting with one tactic that can improve both your CTR and your conversion rate. We'll go into greater detail regarding landing page design and optimization in Chapter 11, "Month 8—Test and Optimize Landing Pages."

Make Sure Your Ad Copy Primes the Pump

Your PPC ad copy should "prime the pump" when it comes to the desired conversion action on your landing page. In yesterday's lesson we discussed writing new ad copy, and in Chapter 10 we'll discuss advanced ad testing techniques. For now, we want to focus on calls to action in your ads.

Before users hit your landing page, they should already know what action you want them to take. How is this done? Include a clear call to action in your PPC ad.

Whatever the conversion action is on your landing page, make sure to mention this in your ad. Here is a short list of calls to action that you may want to use:

- *Buy now!*
- *Sign up now!*
- *Enroll today!*
- *Reserve now!*
- *Book now!*
- *Order now!*
- *Join today!*
- *Apply now!*
- *Start today!*

You should always include a call to action within your PPC ad copy. Of course, you don't have to use these exact phrases, but your ad copy should motivate a user to click on your ad, and the user should have the proper expectation of what to do on the landing page. Tying your ad copy and landing page closer together will help increase your conversion rate.

Review Your Contact Form or Shopping Cart

Lead-generation advertisers should never take their contact form for granted. Your lead form is extremely important to your PPC success. You may think that the headline, the copy of the page, and the graphic elements are more important than your contact form—but you would be wrong. The contact form is just as important as the rest of the elements on your landing page.

The contact form for lead-generation advertisers is where users make their leap of faith. They've probably never heard of your company, but when they saw your PPC ad, they were intrigued, so they clicked. This means your landing page has done a good job on following through and inspiring the user to action. Don't let your contact form drop the ball when you've carried it this far! You need to help the user make that leap of faith by ensuring that your contact form is appropriate for your target audience.

Keep your contact form short. Internalize the following statement that's been proven by many studies of offline and online form performance: *The more fields that are presented and the more information that is required, the lower the conversion rates.*

When designing a contact form, ask yourself the following questions:

- What information is critical for my sales team to thoroughly follow up with a lead?
- What is the least amount of information that we need to qualify a lead?

After you've answered these questions, take a look at your contact form. Remember, every piece of information you ask for is a reason for a user to stop filling out your form. Ask for only mission-critical information. If you ask for too much information too quickly, users won't trust you.

Similarly, e-commerce advertisers should also never take their shopping cart process for granted. If you want to increase your conversion rate, you should take a step back and look at your purchase process carefully. Better yet, ask someone else to make a purchase from your site. This person doesn't need to be a usability expert—just ask a friend or relative to go to your website, make a purchase, and give you honest feedback on the process.

When you ask someone to review your shopping cart process, you may hear some harsh criticism, but it's what you need to hear. Your shopping cart process can always be better. Your abandonment rate can always be reduced. After you've asked for feedback, take a step back and think about what would stop someone from making a purchase on your site. Is the process too long?

By setting up goals in Google Analytics, you can clearly see on which step of your shopping cart users tend to drop out the most. To enhance your shopping cart–abandonment rate, start with your weakest spot, where you lose the most sales.

Review Your Call-to-Action Buttons

This may seem like a small portion of your landing page, but the call to action is not to be ignored. Take a look at the button on the bottom of your contact form. What does it say? How does it look? Does it stand out on the page? Is it above the fold?

If the call-to-action button on your contact form is small, gray, and reads Submit, you're doing yourself a disservice. You shouldn't go in the opposite direction by using a flashing, annoying button either. It's difficult to say which type of button will work best for your landing page, so you should test different variations.

Find New Trust Symbols

Trust is a major factor in getting users to take action on your website. You have to offer what the users need, and they have to trust you with their information (whether it be a lead form or an actual purchase). Displaying your credentials is a great way to quickly tell users that you are a trustworthy business.

These credentials can relate to the security of your ordering process. Trust symbols can also be related to accreditations or certifications from your industry. Are you using these trust symbols to their fullest extent? Can you get them above the fold on your landing page? Look at your landing page and ask these questions—this can help enhance your conversion rate.

Check Your Privacy Policy and Returns Policy

Another way to convince users to trust you with their private information is to display a privacy policy and, for those advertisers who are e-commerce based, display a returns policy. You don't need to make these links bold or prominent elements on your landing page, but they should be present and easy to find.

Try Using Testimonials

Testimonials can be an effective way to give your conversion rate a boost. Do you have some very happy customers? Would they be willing to make a statement about your product or service? Would they perhaps even submit a picture for their testimonial?

Displaying a few testimonials that address your audience's core concerns is a way to kill two birds with one stone. For example, if reliability is an issue in your industry and this is where you competitors fall behind, try to find a testimonial that discusses your own reliability.

Month 7—Test Ads by Using Advanced Techniques

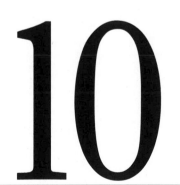

You learned ad copywriting basics in Chapter 5, "Month 2—Create Great PPC Ads," but now it's time to expand your horizons into more-advanced techniques and strategies for your pay-per-click (PPC) ads.

The techniques we discuss in this chapter can have a huge impact on your campaign's performance. We will show you how to automatically insert keywords into your ads, and we'll even show you how to list product images directly within the Google search results. Powerful stuff!

We'll also discuss how to properly split-test your various ad-text initiatives, as well as how to properly interpret the results of these tests.

Chapter Contents

Week 25: Implement Advanced Text Ad Design

Google AdWords includes a variety of options that can make your PPC ads more relevant and noticeable on the search engine results page, and if you implement these advanced options properly, you will increase your click-through rate (CTR) while maintaining an edge over your competitors. None of these advanced techniques will supersede the core strategies that we discussed in Chapter 5. These options should be implemented only after you've conducted a series of split tests. This way, you'll have a base knowledge of which benefits, messaging phrases, and calls to action perform best in your text ads.

This week, you'll explore each of these advanced AdWords ad options. Some of them are useful for product retailers, and one is more applicable to advertisers who want to appeal to a local audience, but you should read through each of these options to see whether any or all of them might work for you.

Monday: Google Dynamic Keyword Insertion

Relevancy is the name of the game for PPC advertising. Relevant ads will generate a higher CTR, which improves your quality score, and they can result in a higher conversion rate. Dynamic keyword insertion (DKI) is a feature that can help make your text ads more keyword-focused and relevant to a user's search query. To use this tool, you just need to insert a short token into your text ad. Then each time your text is shown, Google AdWords will automatically insert the closest matching keyword from your ad group into your ad copy.

As discussed in Chapter 5, the keywords directly related to a user's search query are in bold within a PPC advertisement. For example, in Figure 10.1, you can see that our search query is *gourmet coffee*, and there are a number of smart advertisers who are specifically highlighting this term.

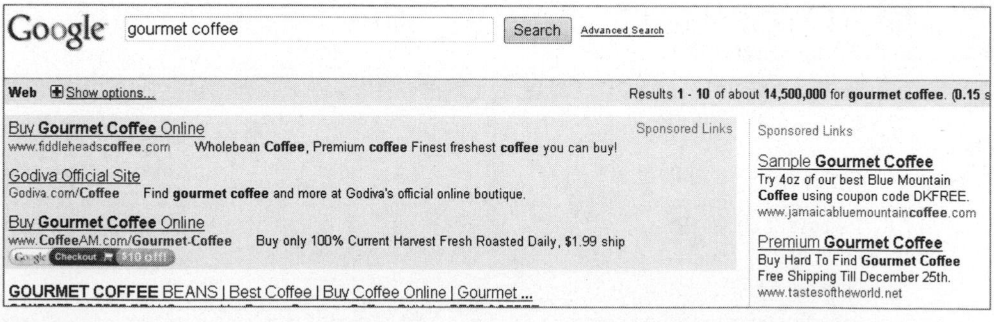

Figure 10.1 Smart advertisers make sure that their ads are relevant and display a user's search term within their PPC ad text.

The dynamic keyword insertion feature makes your text ads more relevant by inserting directly into the ad the keyword from your ad group that most closely matches the user's search query. In many cases, that means your ad will have the exact text of the user query. To use dynamic keyword insertion, all you need to do is insert the following code into your text ad:

```
{keyword:default text}
```

You can interpret this token almost as a placeholder. The `keyword` instruction before the colon tells Google AdWords to display the keyword from your ad group within the PPC advertisement. The `default text` parameter is what Google AdWords will display in case the keyword is too long to fit into the ad.

Dynamic keyword insertion can be used in each line of a text ad. You can automatically insert keywords into the headline, body copy, display URL, and destination URL. Let's look at dynamic keyword insertion in action. Because we searched for *gourmet coffee* in the preceding example, let's go ahead and continue with that theme. The following text ad uses dynamic keyword insertion within the headline as seen within the Google AdWords interface.

<u>Purchase</u> {KeyWord:Gourmet Coffee}_
Wide Selection of International
Coffees. Free Shipping. Buy Now!
www.TastyCoffeeShop.com

How will this text actually appear within the Google search engine results? Let's say that our ad group contains these three keywords: *Italian coffee*, *French coffee*, and *Guatemalan coffee*. Here is how the ad may appear, depending on the keyword:

Keyword: Italian coffee

<u>Purchase Italian Coffee</u>
Wide Selection of International
Coffees. Free Shipping. Buy Now!
www.TastyCoffeeShop.com

Keyword: French coffee

<u>Purchase French Coffee</u>
Wide Selection of International
Coffees. Free Shipping. Buy Now!
www.TastyCoffeeShop.com

Keyword: Guatemalan coffee

<u>Purchase Gourmet Coffee</u>
Wide Selection of International
Coffees. Free Shipping. Buy Now!
www.TastyCoffeeShop.com

In the first two examples, you can see that the dynamic keyword insertion worked successfully. In the third example, the term *Guatemalan coffee* has too many characters to display within the headline, so the default text of *Gourmet Coffee* was utilized instead. Keep in mind that if a broad or phrase-match keyword triggers your ad, the keyword that was matched to this query will be displayed within your text ad. For example, you may have the keyword *French coffee*, but the user query is *best French coffee*—the keyword in the ad text will display as *French coffee*.

From the preceding examples, you can see that dynamic keyword insertion can help make your ads more relevant to a user's query. However, if the function is not implemented correctly, your ads may appear incoherent and irrelevant. The following sections describe some mistakes to avoid.

The One-Word Headline

Be aware: When utilizing dynamic keyword insertion, you relinquish a little bit of control over how your ads appear to users. Within all of the previous examples, you'll notice that we use an active verb, *Purchase*, to complement our keyword. We do this in order to make the headline read naturally and smoothly. If you don't construct your ad groups or text ads properly, your performance could suffer.

You need to take into account the keywords within your ad group before using dynamic keyword insertion. For this example, let's say you have the single-word keyword *Coffee* in your ad group. If you don't pay close attention to your dynamic keyword insertion function, you could end up with a text ad like this:

> <u>Coffee</u>
> Wide Selection of International
> Coffees. Free Shipping. Buy Now!
> www.TastyCoffeeShop.com

Sure, the headline in this text ad displays the single-word keyword, but it will look weak in comparison to your competitors who are not using dynamic keyword insertion, or those who are using it better than you. As with any automated function, it can work improperly if not implemented and managed closely.

Incorrect Code Insertion

The small snippet of simple code for dynamic keyword insertion is actually quite delicate. Because advertisements can make or break your PPC performance, this advanced feature needs to be handled with care. A small error can be detrimental to how your ads appear.

The errors that can creep into the insertion code are as minute as an extra space. For example, if you misspell *keyword* within the insertion code, like this:

```
{KyWord :default text}
```

your ad will appear like this:

> <u>Purchase {KyWord:Coffee}</u>
> Wide Selection of International
> Coffees. Free Shipping. Buy Now!
> www.TastyCoffeeShop.com

So be careful when implementing your code.

Misspelled Keywords

Many PPC advertisers bid on misspelled versions of their core keywords and brand terms. This is a good strategy, because many search queries are misspelled. If you use dynamic keyword insertion within an ad group that contains misspellings, however, your ads are going to appear with misspelled keywords. This can make your ads look spammy and poorly written.

To avoid this mishap, you should quarantine all of your misspelled keywords to their own ad groups and refrain from using dynamic keyword insertion in these ads.

Using the Google AdWords Ad Preview Tool

If you insert a series of text ads into your ad groups and you want to see exactly how they'll appear on Google, you can use the Google AdWords Ad Preview tool (`https://adwords.google.com/select/AdTargetingPreviewTool`). In Figure 10.2, we used this tool to see how our ad may appear for the keyword *gourmet coffee*. The Ad Preview tool provides a sample of how ads may appear on an actual Google search results page. When using this tool, you're not actually entering live queries into Google—so you're not generating false impressions for your competitors, or more important, for your ads.

Figure 10.2 The Google AdWords Ad Preview tool shows ads within an actual Google search results page.

Quality Score and Dynamic Keyword Insertion

Dynamic keyword insertion (DKI) is not the golden ticket to a higher Quality Score within AdWords. Text ads that are keyword-focused and highly relevant to the terms within an ad group are preferred by Google. Using dynamic keyword insertion doesn't automatically indicate to Google that your ads are more relevant than ads that are not using this feature.

Now we're going to toss out a contradiction and say that dynamic keyword insertion could improve your Quality Score. Google evaluates ad copy and keywords in real time. This means that each keyword's Quality Score is determined after the keyword is triggered by a search query and inserted into the ad text. In these terms, dynamic keyword insertion can help improve your Quality Score by making sure your keyword-to-ad-text relationship is as close as possible.

The most notable way dynamic keyword insertion could improve your Quality Score is by increasing your CTR. Regardless of whether you implement this advanced option, if you have a great CTR and it's been improving over time, you will improve your Quality Score.

Yes, we contradicted ourselves, but we wanted to make the point that dynamic keyword insertion is not the easy way to higher Quality Scores. When implemented correctly, and not used as a crutch for poor account structure (more on that later!), it can be helpful.

You can also alter the capitalization of dynamically inserted keywords, as shown in Table 10.1 for the example keyword *French Coffee*. Keep in mind that default text is not affected by any of the capitalization settings you see here. The default text will display as it is typed within the actual advertisement.

▶ **Table 10.1** How Capitalization Can Affect Dynamic Keyword Insertion

Ad Title	How the Ad Will Appear
Purchase {keyword:Gourmet Coffee}	Purchase french coffee
Purchase {Keyword:Gourmet Coffee}	Purchase French coffee
Purchase {KeyWord: Gourmet Coffee}	Purchase French Coffee
Purchase {KEYWord:Gourmet Coffee}	Purchase FRENCH Coffee
Purchase {KeyWORD:Gourmet Coffee}	Purchase French COFFEE
Purchase {KEYWORD:Gourmet Coffee}	Purchase FRENCH COFFEE

Yes, this means that you may use all capitalization, but this shouldn't be abused. Your ads still need to undergo the approval process, and if the Google AdWords system indicates that your ad will stray from standard editorial guidelines, it will be rejected. We suggest that you stick with the *Keyword* or *KeyWord* capitalization.

To get a better grasp on how your ad text will appear within Google search engine results pages (SERPs) when you use DKI, you can check out Deke. Deke is a DKI ad simulator, provided by Find Me Faster. You can find this tool at the following site:

www.findmefaster.com/deke.htm

Don't Use Dynamic Keyword Insertion as a Crutch

Dynamic keyword insertion can be a great way to tweak your ads and give them that little relevance boost. However, too many advertisers use this tool as a workaround for poor account structure. We advise you not to use dynamic keyword insertion as a crutch.

Many advertisers think that they can create ad groups with hundreds of unrelated keywords and use dynamic keyword insertion in order to make their text ads relevant for this wide array of keywords. This is not a good idea, and we suggest you not do this. If you are currently employing this strategy, please stop reading and go restructure your ad groups right now.

In fact, your dynamic keyword insertion strategy should be the polar opposite. Ad groups should always contain a small list of tightly themed keywords. If your ad groups are too large, with a disparate list of keywords, your ads might not make any sense. If you can't fit your core keywords into your ad text without using dynamic keyword insertion, that is a sure sign that you have some account restructuring in your future.

Outside of the account-structure factor, you shouldn't use dynamic keyword insertion to make your ads unique. If all of your competitors are using dynamic keyword insertion, then the playing field Is leveled and you need other strategies to make your ads stand out from the pack.

Don't just assume that if the keyword is present in the ad, your ad-writing work is done. You need to have clearer language, better benefits, more-motivating calls to action, and more-targeted messaging than your competitors—fitting your keyword into the ad is just one piece of this complex puzzle.

Tuesday: Ad Sitelinks

The Ad Sitelinks option within Google AdWords allows advertisers to display up to four additional links under their usual text ad. According to Google's AdWords Help pages, their goal is to "extend the value of your existing AdWords ads by providing additional links to content deep within your sites." Google has said that early testers of this feature found that Ad Sitelinks made it easier to direct users to relevant information and drive them deeper into the sales funnel.

Currently this option is in a beta test, and Google is including advertisers based on a *quality threshold*. So, how do you know if you qualify for Ad Sitelinks? Within your Campaign Settings tab, you will see a notification that you can use Ad Sitelinks, as shown in Figure 10.3.

When you click the Edit link to show additional links to your site, you'll see the option to insert text links and destination URLs, similar to the example shown in Figure 10.4. Remember, because you are making this change at the campaign level, all of the ads within this campaign are eligible for Ad Sitelinks. You need to determine which links are appropriate for all of the ads within a given campaign.

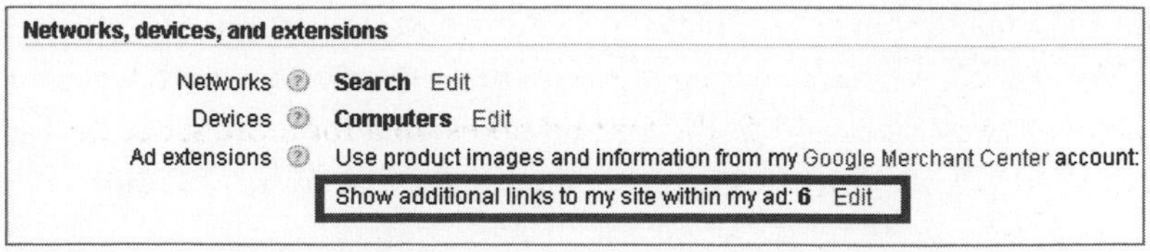

Figure 10.3 If you qualify for the Sitelinks option in AdWords, you'll see this notice within the Networks, Devices, and Extensions section.

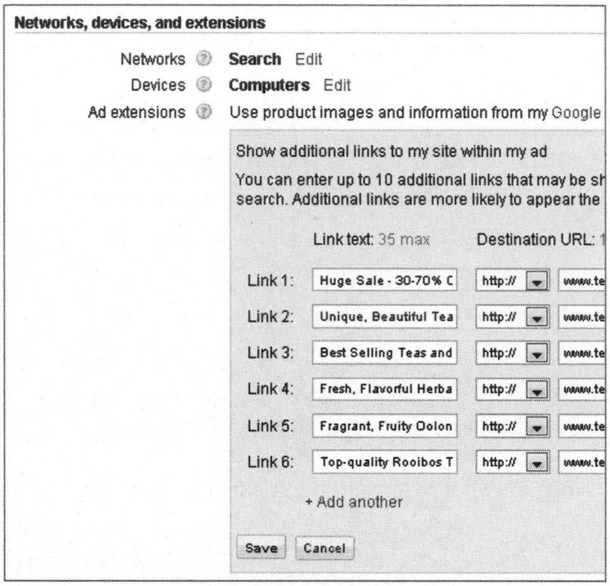

Figure 10.4 You can insert additional link text and destination URLs to content located deeper within your website.

When you are given access to Ad Sitelinks in your campaign settings, you will be asked to preload up to 10 destination URLs from your website (as shown in Figure 10.4). On a search-by-search basis, Google will choose from this list to display four additional links under your text ad. You have no control over which four links are selected by Google. To maintain a modicum of control over your site links, you can simply insert the most important four links. This way, you know which four links will be displayed. Figure 10.5 shows an example of how ads appear when you use Ad Sitelinks.

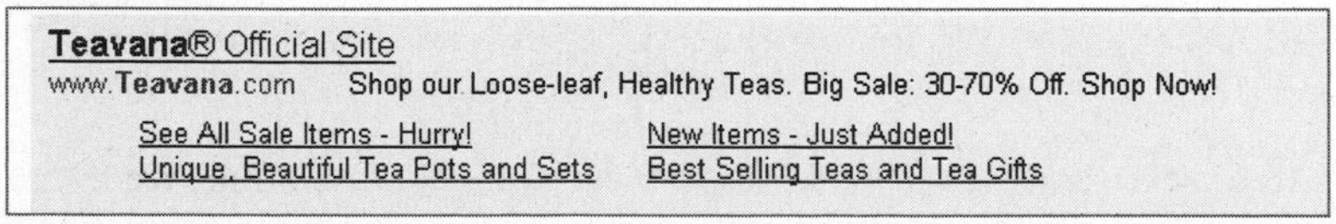

Figure 10.5 Ads that use Ad Sitelinks will appear with four additional text links.

Site links not only make it easier for users to locate other important information on your site; they also allow you to gain additional real estate on the search engine results page. As you can see in Figure 10.5, the text ad takes up a lot more space at the top of the page than an ad without site links. This means your ad is more difficult to ignore and could help increase your CTR.

When inserting link text and destination URLs, you should use our standard ad-writing techniques. We know our target audience well, and we know what is most important to them. For the ad within Figure 10.5, we included links to our sale items (with a call to action), recently added items, popular items (tea pots and sets), and our best-selling core products (teas). You'll want to implement a similar strategy for your site links.

Ad Sitelinks enables you to build trust with users. Also, you can get users to your conversion actions more quickly. You'll need to decide what is most important to your core audience. Here is a list of areas within your website to which you could link your text site links:

- Additional products within your website
- The contact form of your website
- A standard PPC landing page with promotional copy and a contact form
- Unique benefits of your service/product; each corresponding site link can lead users to additional information on a specific benefit
- A page within your website that describes your expertise and/or credibility, such as certifications, previous speaking engagements, and the like
- A page that highlights customer testimonials

You are charged the same price when a user clicks any of the links within your ad. If a user clicks more than one link within your ad in one session, Google will treat these additional clicks as duplicates, and you won't be charged. So, this means a user could click all four of your site links, but you'll be charged only once.

After this option is activated and you have inserted your additional text links, they will not always appear within your text ads. Site links will be displayed when an ad offers the "best answer" to a user's query. How Google determines which ad is the "best answer" is not clearly defined. Also, site links are most likely to be displayed as a result of unique branded-term queries. Here is a quick list of tips to maximize the chances of displaying your Site links:

Your ad should be ranked in the first position. Site links appear most frequently for branded terms because it is less difficult for those terms to consistently attain top rankings.

Your ad should have a very high Quality Score. Throughout this book, we focus on improving your Quality Score in order to attain higher rankings and lower your cost per click (CPC). The ability to display your site links more frequently is another result of your optimization efforts.

Your additional text links must direct users to pages that are part of your main website. All of the text links in your ad, including the main headline link, should point to the same website.

Your Sitelinks will appear only on Google.com search results pages. This feature does not apply to the content network or the search network.

Wednesday: Product Extensions

The Product Extensions feature in AdWords was originally called AdWords Product Plusbox. At its core, this feature allows advertisers to highlight pictures and additional information about their products directly within their ads on Google.com. Similar to Ad Sitelinks, this feature is available only on Google.com because product extensions don't appear on the search network or content network.

As we mentioned for Ad Sitelinks, these advanced options in AdWords are very helpful for numerous reasons, but one of the best is that they allow you to occupy so much more real estate at the top of the search engine results page. You'll agree that the ad in Figure 10.6 occupies a great deal of space. It features the Ad Sitelinks option but also displays actual product images, product names, and prices.

Figure 10.6 Product Extensions ads display images of products.

You can activate the Product Extensions feature at the campaign level. Just go into your Campaign Settings tab, and within the Networks, Devices, and Extensions section, as indicated in Figure 10.7, you'll see where you can link your Google Merchant Center account to your AdWords account. This will activate the Product Extensions feature for this campaign (and you'll need to do this for every campaign in which you would like to utilize this feature).

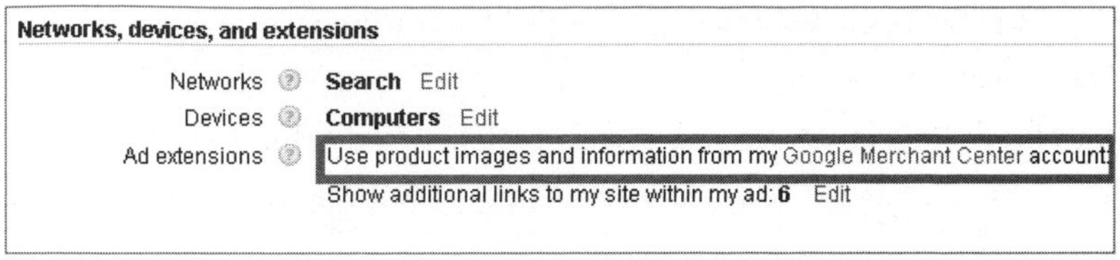

Networks, devices, and extensions		
Networks ⑦	**Search** Edit	
Devices ⑦	**Computers** Edit	
Ad extensions ⑦	Use product images and information from my Google Merchant Center account	
	Show additional links to my site within my ad: **6** Edit	

Figure 10.7 You'll need to link your Google Merchant Center account in order to use the Product Extensions feature.

With this feature, you don't get to specify which keywords will trigger Product Extensions displays. Google will match items from your product feed to user search queries when relevant. Want to make sure you're covered? Link your product feed to all campaigns that are currently bidding for product-related keywords on Google.com.

Similar to Ad Sitelinks, all clicks within your ad are charged at the same rate. If a user clicks more than one link or product image within your ad in one session, Google will treat these additional clicks as duplicates, and you won't be charged. Therefore, a user could click on all of the products in your ad, but you'll be charged only once.

To take advantage of this feature, you will need to link your Google Merchant Center account (formerly Google Base) to your AdWords account. If you don't have a Google Merchant account, you can go to http://google.com/merchants and create one. After your product feed is uploaded and active, you simply need to enter your account ID into AdWords in order to link the two together.

When creating your Google Merchant account, keep in mind that in order to display your products within Google search engine results pages, you must include the following information for each product in your product feed:

- Link
- Price
- Product image
- Description
- Title

Thursday: Product Listings

The Product Listings and Product Extensions features are set up similarly. The core difference between these two features is that product listings aren't displayed along with your core text ad. Instead, these are product images that appear in the Sponsored Links section of the search engine results page in place of your text ad, without a headline, ad copy, or display URL.

Another difference between the features is that product extensions can be associated with CPC or cost-per-acquisition (CPA) bids. The Product Listings feature works solely on a CPA basis. Therefore, you pay only when a user clicks on the listing *and* makes a purchase. In other words, product listings are analogous to an affiliate program you conduct via the search results pages. Figure 10.8 shows how the Product Listings feature appears on the search results page on Google.com (our search query was *baby bedding*).

Figure 10.8 Product listings contain a product name, price, and advertiser name.

To utilize the Product Listings feature, you will need to link your Google Merchant Center account to your AdWords account. The steps to accomplish this task were detailed within the "Wednesday: Product Extensions" section. After you link your two accounts together, it may take up to 12 hours for your product listings and product extensions to appear within the search engine results pages.

Both of the product-based features in Google AdWords are geared toward retail-focused advertisers who have multiple products they would like to display directly on Google.com. The Ad Sitelinks feature can be used by advertisers who focus on sales or lead generation.

Reporting for Product Listings and Product Extensions Features

Let's say that by now you've created your Google Merchant Center account and you've linked it to all of the campaigns in your AdWords account, so how do you know how your various advanced text ad features are performing? Within the Google AdWords reporting interface, you can gain quite a bit of insight.

The reports for the product-related features are still called Plusbox, which is the old name of these options—so don't be confused when looking for the necessary reports. As you can see in the following image, there are quite a few options available.

Product Extension Columns : Information about user interaction with your ads enhanced with Product Extensions ⓘ

☐ Plusbox Impressions   ☐ Plusbox Expansions   ☐ Offer Clicks

☐ Headline Clicks when ad showed a Plusbox   ☐ Headline Clicks after Plusbox Expansion   ☐ Plusbox Show Rate

☐ Plusbox Expansion Rate   ☐ Normalized Plusbox Expansion Rate   ☐ Headline CTR when ad showed a Plusbox

☐ CTR when Plusbox was expanded

With these reports, you can see how the product-related features are performing. You can report the number of impressions, the number of times users click the Show More Products link on the search engine results page, and the number of times users click the ad text headline after viewing additional products. You can then review your performance and optimize accordingly.

Friday: Local Extensions

This advanced Google AdWords feature allows you to dynamically append your business's physical location to your text ads. The Local Extensions feature is most useful for advertising businesses with physical locations. Utilizing this feature can draw attention to your ad and increase your CTR because a user can see your address. This feature can also help prevent untargeted clicks, because a user may determine that you're too far away or not easily accessible and therefore won't click on your ad.

Advertisers with local extensions display the street, city, state, and zip code within their text ads. We conducted a search for *self-storage Chicago* because the storage industry is driven by proximity to the user (users probably want a storage facility close to their home). In Figure 10.9, you can see that self-storage advertisers use local extensions to display their addresses.

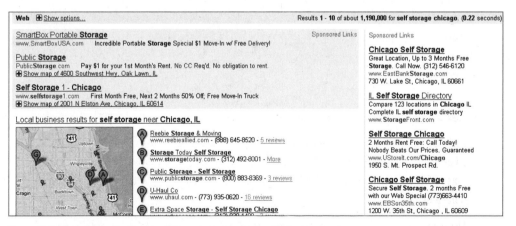

Figure 10.9 Most of the advertisers on this page are using the Local Extensions feature.

You may also notice that for the top three positions, there is a link under the ad text that states, "Show map of..." for the advertiser's location. Advertisers that qualify for the top positions will be given a boost to their ad with this link. When you click the link, you can see a map of the advertiser's location as well as expanded contact information, as shown in Figure 10.10.

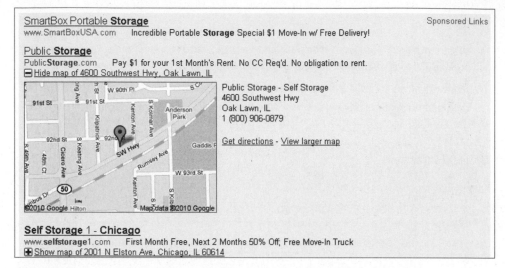

Figure 10.10 Top-ranked advertisers will be given additional advantage within Google search results.

The Local Extensions feature is activated at the campaign level of your AdWords account. Within the Locations, Languages, and Demographics section of your settings, you can choose to show relevant addresses with your ads. As you can see in Figure 10.11, you have two options for adding local extensions: You can use addresses from a Local Business Center (LBC) account or use manually entered addresses. If you don't have an LBC account, you can manually enter your address.

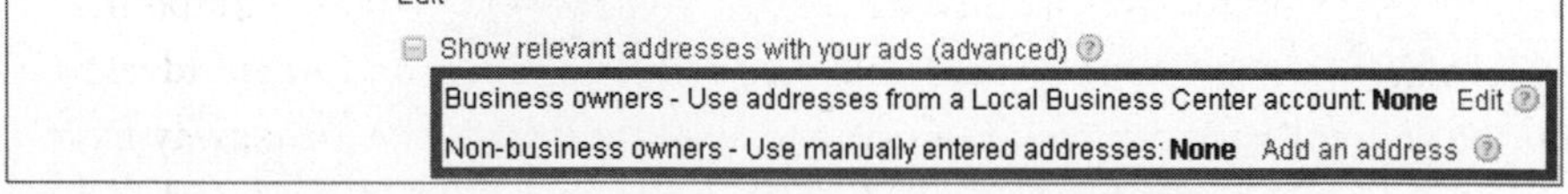

Figure 10.11 Options for linking a Local Business Center account to your Google AdWords account

It is recommended that you link your Local Business Center account to your Google AdWords account in order to activate this feature. If you don't have an LBC account, you can create one at www.Google.com/LocalBusinessCenter.

After local extensions are activated, Google will match a user's location or search query to your business information and show your address where applicable. Local extension information will appear only on Google.com and Google Maps. Your ads will appear as regular text ads on the Google Search Network and Google Content Network.

Getting Your Text Ads on Google Maps

A study conducted by MarketingCharts (www.marketingcharts.com) reports that 80 percent of consumer spending occurs within 50 miles of their home. Another report from this same source states that 63 percent of consumers use search engines first in order to locate a local business. If your business is driven by local searches, it is mission-critical to get your text ads on Google Maps. So, how can you make this happen? Here are a few options:

Local Business Center: By opening an LBC account, you can add your business information as a listing directly to Google Maps. These listings appear within the organic listings and are displayed at no charge to the advertiser.

Google Search Network: You can target Google Maps in your AdWords account by making sure that you've activated the Google Search Network within your campaign settings.

Mobile devices: Within the Networks, Devices, and Extensions section of your AdWords account, you can target the Google Search Network as well as Desktop and Laptop Computers and/or iPhones and Other Mobile Devices with Full Internet Browsers. If you select the All Available Devices option, your ads will appear not only within Google Maps for searchers using desktops or laptops, but also on mobile devices for searchers who are conducting local searches.

Week 26: Insert Ad Text Symbols

As you may have noticed, we want to make sure your PPC ads are as relevant and targeted as possible. By now, you've surely picked up on this theme, but we want to drive this point home because it's the key to PPC success. Aside from creating highly relevant text ads (there, we said it again!), you also want to create ads that are unique and capture the user's attention. On a search engine results page, you are competing against organic listings, real-time Tweets, videos, product listings, and other advertisers. Within the content network, you are vying to steal the user's attention away from the content they've already chosen to read. This is a tall order for a PPC ad with only 95 characters.

This week, we are going to review some tactics that aren't geared toward relevancy but more toward making your text ads unique. Every day this week, you're going to explore symbols that you can insert into your PPC ad text in order to draw the user's attention to your ad. The core objective of these symbols is to make the user think for a split second, "What's that?" You can view these symbols as a shot across the bow, but this should inspire you to make your ads even more engaging because you have only a split second to deliver a highly effective message.

We have spoken to PPC managers who have seen a 25–100 percent increase in their CTR by inserting text symbols into their PPC ads.

Monday: Bullets and Squares

You can use bullets and squares to not only call attention to your ad, but also to offset specific benefits. In Figure 10.12, you can see how we have created ads that use bullets to highlight benefits that may be exceedingly important to our customers. Sure, we sacrificed a few characters to get these bullets in here, but they may pay off.

Figure 10.12 Using bullets to highlight potentially important information

Squares can be used for the same effect. You can highlight special offers or unique selling points specific to your business, as shown in Figure 10.13.

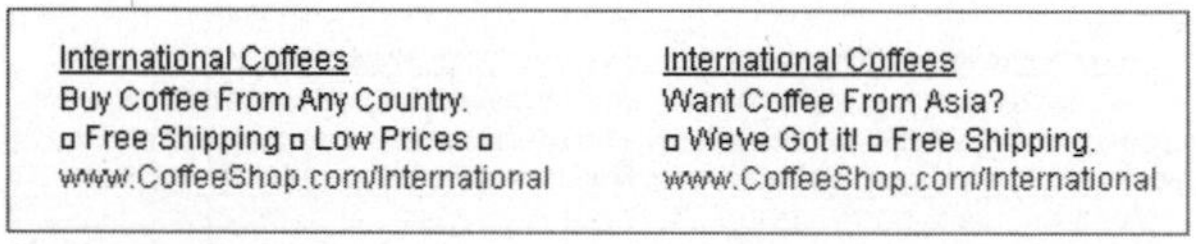

Figure 10.13 You can use squares to call attention to unique selling points within your PPC ad text.

Note that Google editorial policy specifically prohibits the use of unnecessary punctuation to call attention to an ad. So ads like these might be disqualified.

Tuesday and Wednesday: Multiple Characters in One

Squeezing as much information as possible into your PPC ads is a constant struggle. Every character counts. You may be able to save space by using some symbols that include multiple letters but are recognized as one character in Google AdWords. Figure 10.14 provides a sample (there are additional multiple-character symbols not shown). Although some of these characters will be used in very few situations and in highly specific ad texts, you can test them in ads to see whether they have a positive effect on ad performance.

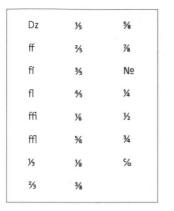

Dz	⅕	⅝
ﬀ	⅖	⅞
ﬁ	⅗	№
ﬂ	⅘	¼
ﬃ	⅙	½
ﬄ	⅚	¾
⅓	⅛	℅
⅔	⅜	

Figure 10.14 Characters you can use to save space in your PPC ads

Thursday and Friday: Non-English Punctuation and Random Characters

If you are targeting an international audience, you can achieve a higher level of relevancy in your PPC ads by using non-English characters and punctuation. You can use the Insert > Symbol function in Microsoft Word to find non-English punctuation as well as a wide range of characters that may apply to your offering. Figure 10.15 displays characters that should be accepted by Google AdWords.

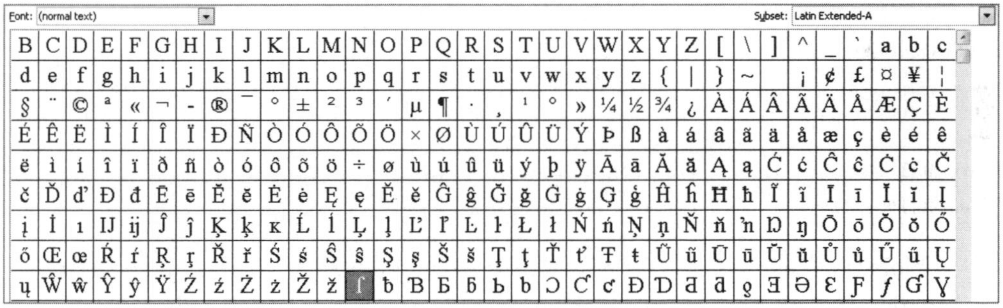

Figure 10.15 Latin-related characters that you can test in your PPC text ads

Week 27: Use Google Content Nontext Ads

The available impression volume on the Google Content Network is vast and continually growing. Within this distribution channel, there are websites that accept only text ads, some that accept only banner ads, and some that display a mixture of ad formats (text ads, banner ads, and video ads). By using standard text ads, you can cover a lot of ground on the Google Content Network, but there are additional opportunities to expand your reach by creating banner and video ads.

This week, we'll discuss best practices for creating static and animated banner advertisements, as well as video advertisements. We'll cover how to create banner ads for mobile devices. And we'll discuss *banner fatigue* and how this can affect your campaign's performance.

Monday and Tuesday: Static and Animated Banner Ads

Remember, the prospect on the content network is not in the mindset of actively searching for a product or service. This user, in all likelihood, is already consuming the content they're interested in, and they aren't looking for you. So just like traditional print advertising, your banner ads need to distract the reader's attention away from the "articles" and toward your ads. Generally speaking, you have to show them something even better than what they are already doing.

The strategies that we discussed for content network text ads in Chapter 7, "Month 4—Advertise on the Google Content Network," will also apply to banner ads. Here they are again:

- Scream
- Bribe
- Stand apart
- Get imperative
- Be Malthusian

If you don't recall what these mean, you can refer to Chapter 7 for further details. These strategies also apply to the design of your static and animated banner ads.

Here are some additional tips for creating awesome banner ads:

Create quick-loading advertisements. Google allows files up to 50KB to be uploaded. For quick load times, you should consider keeping your banner file size under 25KB. This can be difficult when you're designing awesome-looking images, but you want the ads to load extremely quickly. To keep your file size as small as possible, include only one or two movements within your animated banner ads.

Give users a reason to click. You need to draw a user's attention away from the content they are already reading. To do this, you need to give them a reason to click on your ad. What would motivate someone in your target audience to click on your ad? The promise of a free white paper? A special discount? The chance to win a prize? Highlight whatever appeals most highly to your target audience in your banner ad.

Use a strong call to action. You need to have compelling calls to action at every step of your paid search marketing: within the ad, on the landing page, in the shopping cart, and so on. Phrases such as *Buy now*, *Shop now*, and *Sign up now* can significantly improve your CTR.

Try blue underlined text. Internet users are used to links appearing in blue underlined text. Familiarity can help encourage users to click on your ad.

Include your logo and domain. Building trust with users is crucial. You may not want to devote a large amount of space in your banner ad to your logo or domain address, but displaying this information in your ad (usually at the bottom) can help increase CTR.

Use cohesive design. Your banner ads should be an extension of your website or landing page. These ads should be part of your overall branding and advertising strategy. Hundreds of thousands of people may see these ads, so make sure that you maintain your brand messaging continuity.

Animate what's important. You're trying to get the user's attention, but you're also trying to draw their eye to the most important information.

Mirror targeted website content. When targeting specific websites within the Google Content Network, you should design your banner ads with consideration for the content of the site and how this information is presented. If you specify a news website, you could make your image ad look like a news story, perhaps with a striking, unique headline or image. This way, your image ad looks less like an advertisement, but you're still drawing attention to your ad (and away from the content of the page).

Change your banners frequently. Studies have shown that a banner ad starts losing effectiveness after the third time a person has seen it. If they haven't clicked on it by then, they probably won't.

Let's review the standard sizes and formats available for banner ads (static and animated). The following measurements refer to pixel size:

- Banner (468×60)
- Leaderboard (728×90)
- Square (250×250)
- Small square (200×200)
- Large rectangle (336×280)
- Medium rectangle (300×250)
- Skyscraper (120×600)
- Wide skyscraper (160×600)

We suggest developing the following ad sizes for as many products and services as you can. The reason we suggest these ad sizes is that they are simply the most common ad units on the Internet.

- Leaderboard: 728×90
- Medium rectangle: 300×225
- Wide skyscraper: 160×600

Wednesday: Video Ads

Video ads can deepen initial user engagement without being intrusive. Videos can have a higher recall rate, which is great for branding. There are a number of options for running video ads within the Google Content Network. Some video ads have been tested within the SERPs on Google.com, but the majority of ads in this format are distributed on the content network. There are three main video ad formats: click-to-play, in-stream, and InVideo. The most popular video format is the click-to-play ad, so we'll discuss it first.

You may have seen click-to-play ad formats numerous times, but you may not have even noticed. That's the point, to some extent. They are not intrusive, but if they catch a user's attention, video ads can convey information quickly and efficiently.

Unfortunately, we can't show moving video ads in the static pages of this book, but we can still describe what goes into a successful click-to-play video ad. There are five main components of a click-to-play video, and each one is critical to your ad's response rate. These five components are as follows:

Starting image Every click-to-play video displays a static image until a user clicks the Play symbol to start the video. This is the first level of engagement for video ads: convincing a user to click and play your video ad. Because this is your first impression (pun intended), the starting image has to entice the user away from the content they're currently reading, and toward your advertisement.

Elements of a successful starting image with a high click-to-play rate are similar to those of a successful standard text ad or banner ad. You should include an eye-catching image of your product. The illustration within the starting image should be vibrant and hard to miss.

Because you're focusing on the image, you won't have much room for actual text, but you can try to highlight some core messages. Include the core benefit that appeals to your target audience. Also, you can include a call to action. Because this is a video ad, the initial user intent is to gain additional information. Your call to action could be *Learn More, See How*, or even the straightforward *Click to Play*.

Video The starting image is only the first step in the engagement process. The most important element of a video ad is the actual video itself.

If a user has taken the initiative to at least give your ad a sliver of their attention, you have to take full advantage of this small window. You have a small time frame to deliver an informative, unique, and inspiring message. The purpose of your video ad is to get the user to click on the actual ad and arrive at your landing page and the desired action. Studies have shown that an average user's attention span drops off a cliff after about 45 seconds. For optimal response, you should keep your video ads under 30 seconds, and you should deliver your most compelling information within the first 15 seconds of the video.

The content of your video needs to be entertaining and informational. You drew the user's attention away from content that they already found interesting, so your video ad needs to maintain their interest. Users are more likely to view an entire video ad if it doesn't have an "advertisement feel." Highlighting a narrative, a "special report," or an unforgettable character that delivers information about your product or service can enhance your CTR.

If there is any way that you can make the user feel like they've made a small discovery, then you're on to something special. Who doesn't like to find something cool, funny, or unique that they can share with their friends? Can you present your information in such a manner that the user doesn't feel like they were served an ad, but instead that they unearthed some new, hip product? That's pretty inspiring.

This point boils down to peaked interest and inspiration. After you've snagged a user's attention and kept it, then you have to inspire them to abandon the content they're enjoying to learn more about your product.

Ending image So, you pulled in the user with your starting image, and they actually watched all 30 seconds of your video ad—what do you do now? Tell them what you want them to do! The ending image should have your final compelling argument for a user to click through to your website to make a purchase or request additional information. If the user has watched the entirety of your video ad, you've obviously captured their imagination. So the ending image should redeliver the core benefit of your product or service and how it will make this user's life better—and tell them what to do (*Click now!*).

Display URL Google requires that you enter your display URL, and it will appear at the bottom of your video ad. Unfortunately, there isn't a great deal of optimization to do with this line because it's so small. However, we do have a tip (of course!). If your URL consists of a couple of words, they should be capitalized. For example, www.TheCoffeeStore .com is recognized and read more quickly than www.thecoffeestore.com.

Destination URL Regardless of the medium (text, banner, or video), the advertisement is simply the vehicle to get the user to your website or landing page. The look, feel, and delivery of your video ad should form a cohesive message with your landing page. Your video ad has created a certain expectation of what the user plans to see on your website or landing page. If the ad is lighthearted in nature but your landing page is not, there will be a disconnect.

Google has created a page with lots of examples of video ads that advertisers have used in the

www.google.com/intl/en_us/adwords/select/afc/ads/videoadsdemo.html

We'll walk through the steps for how to upload a click-to-play ad into your Google AdWords account. The process for inserting a video ad within the new Google AdWords interface isn't highly intuitive. You have to know where to look, because it's kind of buried. Here is the step-by-step process to upload the required files for your video ads:

1. Go into the Ads tab within any ad group of your campaign. Remember, you must have the content network on in this campaign.

2. Click the New Ad button just below your performance stats.

3. Choose Display Ad Builder from the drop-down menu.

4. Choose Video from the list of categories.

5. Choose Click-to-Play from the video format options.

6. Provide your ad name, starting image, ending image, video file, display URL, and destination URL on the screen shown in Figure 10.16. On the right, you can preview how your ad will appear on the Google Content Network.

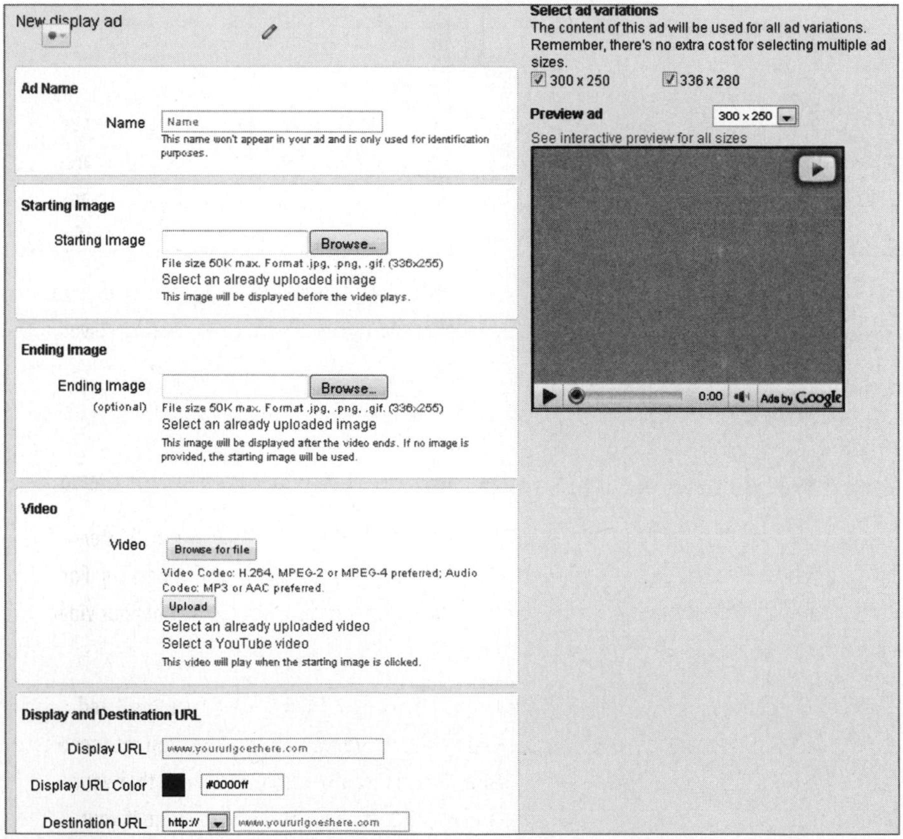

Figure 10.16 You'll need a starting and ending image to upload your video, as well as your actual video file and destination URL.

7. Click Save Ad and you're done.

There are two available video ad sizes:

- 300×250 (medium rectangle)
- 336×280 (large rectangle)

Aside from click-to-play, Google offers a couple of other video ad formats: InVideo ads and in-stream video ads. We won't focus on InVideo ads, because they need to be purchased directly through YouTube (not Google AdWords). The other new video format is in-stream videos.

An in-stream video plays during, before, or after an original online video within a content publisher's website. Your ad can play for up to 60 seconds at the beginning, in the middle, or at the end of a video; however, publishers can limit your ad content to 15 seconds or less. If a user clicks on your ad while it's playing, you'll be charged for the click.

Honestly, we haven't tested these video ad formats yet, but as online video becomes more prevalent, these ad formats could gain more traction.

Video Ad Metrics to Measure

Google provides a stable of helpful reports in order to gauge the effectiveness of your video ads. You can measure the rate and depth of user interaction with your video ads as well as the core conversion metrics (number of conversions, conversion rate, and cost per conversion). Here are the report columns that are specific to video ad reports and are critical to evaluating your video ad performance:

Interactions: This column presents the core number of interactions each video ad has received.

Interaction rate: This column reports the percentage of users who actually clicked to view your video ad.

Avg. cost per interaction: Here you will find how much each view of your video costs on average.

Playbacks: There are different percentages of playback stats (25 percent, 50 percent, 75 percent, and 100 percent). This stat tells you what percentage of your video users are viewing. For example, the 75 percent playback stat tells you how many users viewed 75 percent of your video before pausing, clicking away, or clicking on your URL.

With these reports, you can gauge the success of your video ads. The first two columns listed here can give you an idea of how your starter image is performing. If your interaction rate seems low, you may want to upload a new starter image. If your CTR is low, this may mean that your video isn't appealing highly to your audience, and you should consider a revision. And if your conversion rate seems low and your cost per conversion is too high, there may be a disconnect between your video and your landing page. With a low conversion rate, you may want to consider optimizing your landing page.

Continues

Video Ad Metrics to Measure *(Continued)*

Within these content network campaigns, you should also remember to run your placement performance report frequently. There may be poorly performing websites that are bringing down the average response of your video ads. By preventing your ads from appearing on these sites, you can improve your overall performance.

Thursday: Mobile Banners

Mobile advertising is gaining steam every year. According to Millennial Media forecasts, the mobile web audience in the United States will reach 100 million unique users in 2010. This is half of the web audience, which means that mobile marketing can't (and shouldn't) be ignored.

You can specifically target mobile devices within your Google AdWords campaign settings. Within the Networks, Devices, and Extensions section of your campaign settings, you can select the devices on which you would like to display your ads. As shown in Figure 10.17, your options include All Available Devices, Desktop and Laptop Computers, and iPhones and Other Mobile Devices with Full Internet Browsers.

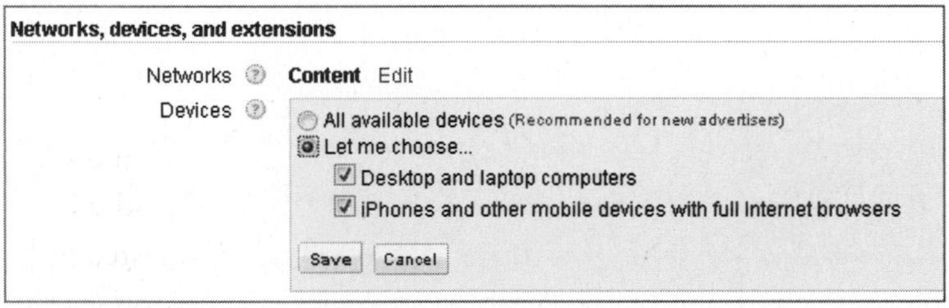

Figure 10.17 Create separate campaigns for your mobile ads by targeting the appropriate devices within your campaign settings.

Uploading your mobile banner ads is relatively painless. Within your mobile device–targeted ad group, you just need to click the New Ad button under your Ads tab and then select Mobile Ad (WAP Only).

Though not required by Google, you'll get the best results if your mobile ad is linked to a site page that is specifically designed to display well on mobile devices. If you don't have a mobile site, and your business is driven by phone calls, you can link your mobile ad directly to your phone number so users can call you. The click-to-call option is available only for text ads, not for banner ads.

When creating your mobile banner ad, remember that this tiny piece of media needs to work really hard despite its diminutive size. Like its beefier counterpart on a standard HTML site, the mobile ad needs to quickly accomplish the following:

- Persuade the potential site visitor to concentrate their attention on the ad, rather than the screen or page content that's the main attraction
- Create a connection between the user and the site or page's subject matter
- Highlight features and benefits
- Make sure the wrong people aren't persuaded to click
- Describe the action you want the user to take on the landing page
- Include a call to action

That's a pretty tall order for an ad of any size, much less one that measures just a cell-phone-screen wide and a few pixels tall. Ideally, you want any ad you create to include everything in the preceding bulleted list. However, successful mobile ads can focus on just one strong benefit, feature, or call to action and be very successful. You should create a series of mobile ads with different benefits or calls to action, and then test to see which ad generates the best results.

Let's look at a few examples. First, Figure 10.18 shows a mobile ad from Pepsi.

Figure 10.18 A pretty good mobile banner ad from Pepsi

This one works pretty well. The word *Free* always helps attract the eye, and the images are simple and motivating. It's easy to understand that clicking on the ad will lead to the opportunity to win a free car—but even if the ad viewer isn't interested in that, they'll probably at least be impressed by the Pepsi logo and the exhortation to *Enjoy Pepsi*.

Let's look at a less-effective example. Figure 10.19 shows a mobile ad from Land Rover:

Figure 10.19 A mobile banner ad from Range Rover

Though the message is pretty clear—there's a Range Rover for sale—there's nothing that tells the ad viewer what to do. The advertiser clearly wants the viewer to click on the ad, but they don't tell the viewer that, and there's no indication of how the ad viewer will benefit from the click. If the objective of the ad campaign is to persuade people to test-drive a Range Rover, the ad might perform better with the simple addition of a line such as *Find Your Local Dealer*.

We love the simplicity of the ad in Figure 10.20. Unmistakably targeted at Superman fans, the call to action is clear and compelling: If you click on the ad, you'll to be taken to a clip of an upcoming movie.

Figure 10.20 A simple, unique mobile banner ad that is closely tied to the call to action

Get the picture? Keep it simple—make the benefit and action clear, and you'll be enjoying those double-digit CTRs every time.

Turn Off Mobile Devices for Non-mobile Campaigns

When a new campaign is created in Google AdWords, it is set by default to display ads on all computer devices, including smart phones like the iPhone and Android devices. So you may be running a mobile marketing campaign without even realizing it!

As we've pointed out in this section, however, successful mobile ad campaigns require specific ad design and text-ad-writing techniques. For this reason, we strongly recommend that you create separate AdWords campaigns targeting mobile devices. You can do so by deselecting the Desktop and Laptop Computers check box in the campaign Device settings for mobile campaigns.

Likewise, if your campaign's ads will not display well on mobile devices (and this is true for the majority of campaigns), you'll save some money by deselecting the iPhones and Other Mobile Devices with Full Internet Browsers device type in your campaign settings.

Friday: Banner Fatigue and Ad Rotation

Let's face it: Everyone is bombarded with advertising messages all day, every day. You've surely seen the studies that try to pin down how many marketing messages the average American sees every day. The actual number varies widely between reports, but a similar conclusion can be extracted: We see way too many advertisements all day, every day.

The constant barrage of ads leads to *banner fatigue*. This means that you can take our advice and design the most relevant, engaging banner ad ever—but members of your target audience may never see it, even when it's right in front of their eyes! There are two kinds of banner fatigue. Users may become blind to your ads because you've been running the same ad for too long, and now it's just static. Or users who visit the same website every day have trained their eyes to focus only on the content of the site and not the ads. For example, if someone reads a blog every day, they know exactly where the articles are posted and exactly where the ads are posted, and they eventually just block out the ads.

To keep your messaging fresh and minimize banner fatigue, you should frequently rotate the display of a variety of ads. There is no predetermined interval at which you should upload new ads, but let's just say you should do it frequently.

Next week, we'll discuss split-testing your advertisement. You should always be testing your ads, learning what works and what doesn't work, and optimizing your campaign accordingly. This will keep your ads fresh, and over time your overall performance will improve.

Week 28: Perform Advanced Ad Testing

We hate to tell you this, but you will never write the perfect PPC ad. You will spot flawless PPC ad text as often as you see the Loch Ness monster skimming the surface of Loch Ness. Maybe you're thinking, "That's why I bought this book…so you can teach me how to write the perfect PPC ad!" We can't tell you what is going to work best for your audience, but we can help you lay the groundwork so that you can test and refine your ad text to something close to perfect.

This is one of the core principles of paid search marketing success: refinement and optimization. Throughout the testing process, you will try ad variations that seem like clear winners, but once launched, their performance stinks. And there will be ad texts that should tank but instead resonate with your audience. The key to testing anything (ad text, landing pages, and so on) is to not get emotionally attached. If an ad doesn't generate a great response, it's got to go.

You won't know what works and what doesn't work unless you continuously conduct split tests. This week, you'll learn how to prepare your account settings in order to conduct tests properly, learn what elements of text ads you should test, see how to set up A/B testing, and discover how to interpret the test results.

Monday: Set Up Split Tests

Before you insert your first test PPC ad, you need to ensure that your campaigns are set up properly in order to generate accurate results. If you miss this step of the process, your ad testing will never get off the ground and you will not be refining your way to perfect ad texts. You want to make sure that all of your ad texts are rotating evenly in order to give each ad equal exposure. The process to set up split testing is slightly different for each search engine. Split testing is a testing method that involves splitting PPC traffic evenly between one ad and another.

Google AdWords

To make sure your split tests are being conducted properly, you have to make sure that each ad is getting an equal amount of face time with your target audience. Trying to be helpful, the default setting in Google AdWords is to set your ads to Optimize, but this is not the optimal setting for split testing. You will find the ad rotation settings under Advanced Settings on your Campaign Settings tab.

By selecting the Optimize setting, you are not conducting a true split test. In effect, you are allowing Google to determine the outcome of your test by eventually favoring the ad with the highest CTR. If you are optimizing solely toward CTR, this could be a helpful feature. However, you should opt for the Rotate setting, as shown in Figure 10.21.

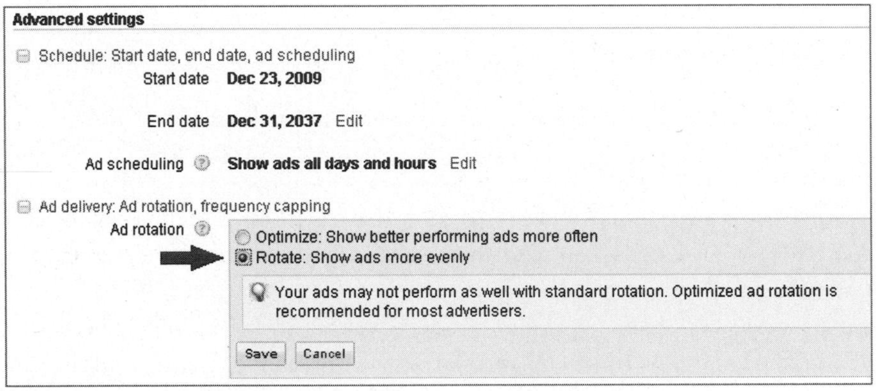

Figure 10.21 To conduct effective split tests, select Rotate: Show Ads More Evenly.

Yahoo! Search Marketing

The ad rotation setting within the Yahoo! Search Marketing interface is a bit trickier to find and adjust. Similar to Google AdWords, Yahoo!'s default setting is to optimize your ad delivery so that over time, the ad with highest CTR receives the highest percentage of the available impressions.

Within each group, there is a set of buttons above the names of your ads. This is where you can adjust your ad rotation. Click the Optimize Ads button, shown in Figure 10.22, and then click No when Yahoo! asks whether you want the ad with the highest performance to automatically display more often.

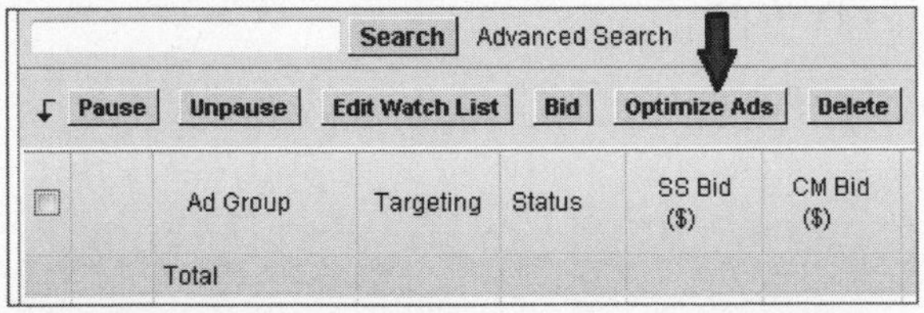

Figure 10.22 To adjust your ad rotation in the Yahoo! Search Marketing interface, click the Optimize Ads button to turn off this default setting.

Microsoft adCenter

The Microsoft adCenter is quite a bit easier to use than the Yahoo! Search Marketing interface (although it's still lagging behind Google AdWords, as we'll discuss in Chapter 12, "Migrate Your Campaign to Microsoft and Yahoo!"). However, adCenter is really missing the boat when it comes to ad text testing. adCenter automatically optimizes your text ads in order to favor the variation that receives the highest CTR. Because adCenter is lacking here, you should conduct your split testing in Google and Yahoo!, and then implement your best-performing ads in this search engine.

Tuesday: Know What to Split Test

The elements to test in your ad text and the combinations of these elements are almost endless! In Chapter 5, we discussed the elements of successful text-ad writing, but now we'll go through the elements that you may want to test in your text ads in order to increase user engagement.

Keyword Density

Relevance is the key to a successful ad. You can achieve a high level of relevance by displaying the keywords in your ad group within your text ad. But how many times does your keyword need to appear in the ad in order to obtain the maximum CTR?

You test putting your keyword into every line of your ad: the headline, ad copy lines 1 and 2, and the display URL. It should go without saying that your keyword should appear at least once in your text ad. But how do users respond if your keyword is only in your headline? What happens when your keyword is in your headline and the body copy? If you add your keyword to your display URL, does this increase your CTR? For example, here are different levels of keyword density for the search term *gourmet coffee*:

> **Low Keyword Density**
>
> Handpicked **Gourmet Coffee**
> Wide selection of international
> coffees. Great price. Ships free!
> www.CoffeeStore.com

> **Medium Keyword Density**
>
> Handpicked **Gourmet Coffee**
> Wide selection of **gourmet**
> **coffees**. Great price. Ships free!
> www.CoffeeStore.com

> **High Keyword Density**
>
> Handpicked **Gourmet Coffee**
> Wide selection of **gourmet**
> **coffees**. Great price. Ships free!
> www.CoffeeStore.com/**Gourmet-Coffee**

There is no magic number for how many times your keyword should appear in your ad in order to generate the best results. This is the point of testing. You may find having your keyword only in your display URL is enough, or perhaps it needs to appear more often.

Calls to Action

Testing has shown that people will more often take an action if it's explicitly spelled out for them. Try to be more creative than *Visit our site* or *Click to see*. For example, here's an ad with no call to action:

> <u>Get Government Grants</u>
> Many are eligible for money
> from the feds. Up to $15,000.
> www.washingtondough.com

And here's the same ad with an explicit call to action:

> <u>Get Government Grants</u>
> See if you can get up to $15,000.
> Take our 5-minute test!
> www.washingtondough.com

You need to test a wide array of calls to action in order to determine what appeals best to your target audience. Your call to action is also determined by the desired conversion action on your landing page. If you are advertising an e-commerce website with numerous products, you may test calls to action such as *Buy Now*, *Purchase Now*, *Shop Now*, and so on.

Different Benefits

You should test emphasizing different benefits of your product or service, not just the features. Features describe the product or service that you're selling, whereas benefits describe the positive emotions your customers will experience.

While working your way through Chapter 5, you wrote out a list of benefits that your product or service has to offer. Now is the time to break out that list. You should test highlighting different benefits in your ad text. Let your audience tell you which benefits are most important to them.

Offers or Specials

Never underestimate the power of a good deal. Who doesn't want a great deal? Try highlighting different offers in your PPC ad to see what draws the most attention. You can test anything from free shipping to *buy 1, get 1 free* deals.

Price Points

There is a number of different ways to display price in your PPC ad text. For some users, seeing a dollar sign will resonate most. For other users, a percentage discount means more. You should test various pricing terminology in your ad. Also, you should test where you put the price. It could be in your headline, copy line 1, or copy line 2.

For example, let's say a pound of your gourmet coffee is $10 and that's a 10 percent discount off the normal price. You can test different ways of stating your price in your PPC ad.

Here is an example of an ad that states the price of the product:

> **Handpicked Gourmet Coffee**
> Exotic coffees. 1lb only $10.
> Wide selection. Buy now!
> www.CoffeeStore.com

This example highlights the percentage off the normal price:

> **Handpicked Gourmet Coffee**
> Exotic coffees. Wide selection.
> Buy now for a 10% discount!
> www.CoffeeStore.com

This example highlights both the price and the discount:

> **Handpicked Gourmet Coffee**
> Exotic coffees. 1lb only $10.
> Buy now for a 10% discount!
> www.CoffeeStore.com

Free Offers

Our testing has shown that offering something for free boosts clicks and conversions. Some clients worry that too many clicks will come from tire-kickers who don't intend to buy, but we've found that the increased return on investment (ROI) usually more than covers any additional cost. Use free offers when your product or service is high priced or technically complex, and/or the sales cycle is long.

Almost any advertiser can create something of value that can be given away. Here are some examples:

- Downloadable free-trial software
- Downloadable or physical white papers
- E-newsletter subscriptions
- Downloadable audio or video information or entertainment

Display URL

This element of ad text can seem minute and unimportant. However, PPC ads have little space to convey messages, so you need to take full advantage of every character. The display URL is 35 characters that shouldn't be squandered.

Test inserting the ad group's core keyword into the display URL. This may seem unimportant, but it's one more way to highlight the keyword and make your ad relevant and help it stand out. Remember, keywords even in the display URL are in bold within Google search results.

You could test capitalizing your URL in different ways. For example, you could test the following:

www.coffeestore.com/gourmet-coffee

www.Coffeestore.com/Gourmet-coffee

www.CoffeeStore.com/Gourmet-Coffee

Punctuation

Try using periods, exclamation points, and question marks in your ads. For example, ads with exclamation points can convey a sense of urgency and excitement. Test different punctuation to see what works best!

Dynamic Keyword Insertion

We won't get into great detail on dynamic keyword insertion here, because we already explored this topic at the beginning of this chapter. However, this is another element of ad copy that you should test.

Wednesday and Thursday: Conduct Initial A/B Split Testing

Testing and improving ad copy is essential to optimizing overall PPC campaign performance. Improving ad text leads to a better CTR and quality score, which can help drive your CPC down and/or let you buy more clicks per dollar. In other words, this has a direct impact on your campaign's ability to increase the number of profitable sales.

Today you are setting up a simple A/B split test within your ad group. The goal of a simple A/B split test is to directly compare two distinct, separate text ads in order to determine which one appeals best to your target audience. Aside from uploading ads into your ad group and seeing which one beats out the other, there is a methodology that needs to be followed in order to conduct a successful split test.

Test One Variable at a Time

When conducting ad-text split testing, you want to get a clear picture of what messaging or benefits work best. To get started with ad testing, you may want to test only one variable at once. This will make interpreting your results easier. Writing and launching ad text isn't too difficult, so there is a temptation to upload a ton of ads at once and see what works. However, if you don't have a lot of experience in split testing, you should start with less-complicated tests.

Launch with No More Than Three Ads

If you launch numerous ads at one time, it's going to be difficult to monitor their performance and extrapolate any useful data from the test. You should launch with no more than three ad variations in each ad group, highlighting one variable per test.

Gain Enough Data to Make a Confident Decision

We often get asked the question, "How many clicks should each ad have before determining a winner in my split test?" The answer usually goes something like, "How long is a piece of string?" We don't mean to be facetious, but the point is that it varies greatly. The outcome of your ad-text split tests is determined when you have a high level of confidence that one ad variation is generating the best results. To gain this confidence, you need to have enough data to make a statistically valid decision.

The crux of successful ad-text split testing is being able to determine a clear-cut winner. You may be able to declare a winner after each of your ad variations has generated 100 clicks, or it may take 500 clicks to gain enough data to make a decision, or even more! So how do you know if you've allotted enough time and gathered enough performance data?

Various free websites and tools can help you determine the outcome of your split tests. However, your friendly authors of this book have created a spreadsheet to help you know when you've gained enough data for your split test, as well as determine the winning ad variations. You can download this spreadsheet at our book website:

    http://ppchour.com

We'll walk you through how this spreadsheet works, and how it helps you decide whether you've gained enough data to assert the outcome of your ad testing.

First, you need to enter the data from your split test, which includes impressions, clicks, cost, and conversion rate, as illustrated in Table 10.2.

▶ **Table 10.2** Enter the Initial Data from Your Split Test

Ad Variation	Impressions	Clicks	Cost	Conversions
1	9,205	488	$503.00	92
2	10,010	604	$564.00	78

In Table 10.2 both ad variations have generated over 9,000 impressions, over 400 clicks, and over 75 conversions. We want to learn two things: Have we gathered enough clicks and conversions to make a decision, and if we have enough data, which ad is our winner? The spreadsheet automatically determines your click-through rate, conversion rate, cost per click, and cost per conversion.

Next, the spreadsheet calculates a projection that shows you what would have happened if either of these ad variations had received all of the impressions accrued during the test. Table 10.3 displays how many clicks and conversions an ad variation would have generated if it had received all of the available impressions.

The projections in Table 10.3 are derived by adding together the impressions received by ad variations 1 and 2, and then applying each ad's preexisting click-through rate, cost per click, and conversion rate.

▶ **Table 10.3** If Either Ad Variation Had Received All of the Impressions in This Test, This Is What Would Have Happened

Ad Variation	Impressions	Clicks	Cost	Conversions
1	19,215	1,019	$1,049.99	193
2	19,215	1,159	$1,082.64	150

In Table 10.2, the difference in the number of conversions generated from the two ad variations wasn't very great (a difference of only 14 conversions). However, when you project what would have happened if either ad had received all the available impressions, the difference becomes more apparent. In Table 10.3, ad variation 1, if it had received all of the impressions, would have generated 193 conversions, which is 43 more conversions than variation 2. Here we get an indicator that ad variation 1 would have generated more conversions.

Ultimately, you want to know which ad variation has the best performance and will generate the most revenue. The spreadsheet helps you understand which ad variation has the greater revenue potential. All you need to do is enter an Average Order Value into the indicated field within the spreadsheet. For this example, we entered an Average Order Value of $150.

In Table 10.4, you can see how much revenue each ad variation would have generated if it had received all of the impressions during the test. The Order Value column is determined by multiplying your Average Order Value by the number of projected conversions. The Revenue column is determined by subtracting the total projected Cost of each ad variation from its Order Value.

▶ **Table 10.4** Revenue Potential for Each Ad Variation

Ad Variation	Order Value	Revenue	Result
1	$29,950.00	$27,900.00	Pick Me
2	$22,500.00	$21,417.00	

In Table 10.4, ad variation 1 has a greater revenue potential. The spreadsheet calculates the variation in results, evaluates the confidence level that there is a winning ad variation, and automatically displays *Pick Me* next to the stronger ad.

The spreadsheet also displays your Conversion Rate Confidence and Click-Through Confidence. To be certain that you've chosen the right ad variation, you want to make sure that you're at least 95 percent confident that your winning ad will actually perform better.

Table 10.5 shows that your confidence level is 95 percent or higher. When you see that your confidence level is 95 percent or higher, you have a winner for your ad-text split test! This means that each ad variation has accrued enough performance data to determine a winner.

▶ **Table 10.5** Confidence Level in Your Ad Test Results

Conv. Rate Confidence	CTR Confidence
95% or higher	95% or higher

However, what happens when you see the information in Table 10.6 within your Conversion Rate Confidence?

▶ **Table 10.6** Ad Test Results That Don't Have a High Level of Confidence

Conv. Rate Confidence	CTR Confidence
Not confident	95% or higher

This means that you don't have a clear winner for your split test. You can receive a Not Confident rating if you haven't generated enough performance data, or if the performances of your ad variations are very similar. For example, we would receive a Not Confident rating if our initial data looked similar to Table 10.7.

▶ **Table 10.7** Ad Variations with Similar Performance

Ad Variation	Impressions	Clicks	Cost	Conversions
1	9,205	488	$503.00	92
2	10,010	604	$564.00	89

Sure, both of the ads have generated more than 450 clicks, but there is a difference of only three conversions between the two ad variations. This means that the ads are performing similarly and there is no clear winner. You need to gain more data to make a decision.

Also, you may receive a Not Confident rating if you have a small sample size. In Table 10.8, our ad variations have each received fewer than 100 clicks.

▶ **Table 10.8** Ad Variations That Have Not Received Enough Clicks

Ad Variation	Impressions	Clicks	Cost	Conversions
1	4,205	98	$123.00	13
2	5,010	91	$121.00	11

In the instance of Table 10.8, you need to allow more time for the ad variations to gain additional impressions, clicks, and conversions, because you don't have enough data to make a confident decision.

Don't Base the Outcome on CTR Alone

Of course, we all want to increase our CTR, but this shouldn't be the only statistic you measure during your split tests. You need to measure CTR, conversion rate, cost per conversion, and any other key performance indicators.

Going Beyond the Initial A/B Split Test

The goal of this initial test process is to establish your control ad. This ad is your champion—the one that has outperformed all of the other variations. After you have conducted a few initial A/B split tests, you should refine your testing methodology.

As you test different variations of PPC ad copy, you will have some winners, and you will have a lot of losers. Think about it: If you're constantly testing, and your test ads often fail to beat your control ad, then you're devoting a large amount of traffic to underperforming ads and only a portion of your traffic to your best ads. This means that you're hindering the performance of your campaign, even as you're trying to make it better.

Don't worry—there is strategy to mitigate this problem with split testing. The goal of this strategy is to help you devote less traffic to poorly performing ads while continuing to test as much as possible. We'll walk through this process for one ad group in which a few initial A/B split tests have already been conducted.

After you've determined your winning control ad, create three copies of this proven ad within your ad group (so you end up with the original ad and three copies). Next, insert one copy of your new test ad into your ad group, which we call the *challenger ad*. Now you have a total of five ads in your ad group (four ads that represent the control ad, and one new challenger ad).

This way, you are devoting only 20 percent of your traffic to this new ad, so if it tanks, you have mitigated the risk.

If your challenger ad performs worse than your control ads, you should pause it along with the rest of your copied control ads. Then move on to your next test and start over at step 1! However, if your challenger ad is generating a better result than your copied controls ads, you should begin to eliminate your copied ads.

Let's say that after one week, the challenger ad is doing better than your copied control ads. In this case, you should kill one of these copied ads in order to devote more traffic to your challenger ad. Let's say a few days later, the challenger ad is still doing better than your copied ads. Now you can remove another copied ad. You can continue this way until you're eventually testing your challenger ad against your original control ad. This is when the real test begins! If your challenger ad outperforms the original control ad, you have a winner on your hands! If the control ad wins again, it's back to the drawing board.

Friday: Reflect on the Outcome of the Test

This seems obvious, but we just want to make sure that you build in a step for analysis after your split test. You should reflect on implications of the test you just completed. What does it mean? What have you learned? Are you surprised at the outcome? If so, why? How will this affect your future testing?

After you've completed this cycle, start over again! Your testing process should be structured and frequent. Ideally, you will launch a split test, determine a winner, launch another split test, and so on. You will constantly test against your best-performing control ad. Never think that you've hit the ceiling—you can always improve your ad text. So keep testing your way to perfection—or at least as close to perfection as possible!

Other Tools for Evaluating Split-Test Results

As you can see, determining winners from A/B splits can be difficult. However, some tools can help you determine whether your test has generated enough results to declare a statistically valid winner. They won't interpret the results for you—they'll just indicate whether you have a winner.

Each of the following tools works a little bit differently, so you may like one more than the rest, but their core functions are similar. You can use these tools for some quick analysis; however, you should not rely solely on these websites to determine the outcome of your split tests. Having a basic understanding of how these tests are determined will help you make the right decision for your campaign.

- Split Tester (www.splittester.com)
- Teasley Statistical Calculator (www.teasley.net/free_stuff.htm)
- Split Test A/B Calculator (www.splittestcalculator.com)
- PPC Ad Split Testing Tool (www.websharedesign.com/tools/ppc-ad-split-testing-tool)

Month 8—Test and Optimize Landing Pages

In Chapter 10, "Month 7—Test Ads by Using Advanced Techniques," we discussed designing and testing your landing page to maximize conversion rates. In this chapter, you're going to learn how to optimize your landing page by conducting more-rigorous testing. You'll learn which elements of your page you should test, how A/B and multivariate tests differ, and how to interpret test results.

Chapter Contents

Week 29: Plan Your Tests

This week, you're going to learn how to plan your landing page testing. The foundation of a successful landing page optimization requires knowing which elements of your landing page can significantly increase your conversion rate, and which method to use to properly and thoroughly conduct experiments on your landing page.

Monday: Prioritizing Test Elements

The whole point of testing your landing page is to enhance your conversion rate, increase your sales, and improve your ROI. You want to prioritize your testing so that you are optimizing the elements of your landing page that will have the biggest impact on your conversion rate. This means you shouldn't start your testing process with the minute details of your landing page that will not have a major impact on your performance.

Do this now: Review your landing page and make a list of what the user sees when first hitting your landing page, and the components of your page that can influence a user to take the desired conversion action (whether it be completing a contact form, making a purchase, downloading a piece of exclusive information, or any other action that has value to your business). When reviewing your list, ask yourself the following questions about each possible factor for testing:

- Does this element of my landing page directly influence users to take action?
- Why is this component of my landing page important?
- How can I improve this piece of my landing page?
- What do I expect to happen if I make a change?

Now, take this list and prioritize it so that the most important factors on your landing page are at the top. This is where you should start your testing.

Tuesday: Testing Headlines

When it comes to testing and optimizing your landing pages, it's a good idea to start at the top. Never underestimate the power of your landing page headline. A landing page headline that is relevant to a user's search query and delivers a clear and engaging message can significantly enhance your bounce rate, time on site, and, most important, conversion rate.

Numerous usability studies have stated that you have 5–10 seconds to convince a user that they've arrived in the right place. Perhaps your headline alone can't convince a user that they've arrived at their final destination, but the headline can inspire them to check out the rest of your landing page to see whether you have what they're looking for.

Today we'll describe some tactics that you can test in your headlines. There are many other tactics you can employ, but the following sections should get you started in your headline testing.

Emotional Messages

It's easy to forget that you don't want to just sell a product or service to your visitors—you want to make a connection. Highlighting unique benefits that present your products in the most appealing light is a good strategy. However, you need to brainstorm and find out how your product or service appeals to your target audience on an emotional level.

How will your offering improve your customers' lives? Will it make their lives easier? Will they complete a task faster because of your product? You should think long and hard about what you have to offer users who arrive at your landing page, write a series of emotionally driven headlines, and then test to see whether this type of messaging appeals to your audience.

Call-to-Action Messages

Your headline exists to inspire the visitor to explore the rest of your landing page on the way to becoming a customer. A good headline not only is relevant to a user's query and unique enough to grab a user's attention, but it should also aid in the conversion process. By clearly stating within the headline what you want the user to do on your landing page, you're moving the user along in the conversion process.

A technique you should test is use of the *call-to-action* headline. Here are some examples of call-to-action headlines:

- *Sign Up For Our Free Newsletter Today*
- *Download Our Revolutionary White Paper Now*
- *Open A Free Account Now And Start Saving Time*

This approach is more direct and perhaps a bit more sales-focused, but it may appeal to your target audience, so it's worth testing.

Time-Based Messages

There is nothing wrong with giving users a little push. We all have trouble making a decision at one time or another, and sometimes a deadline can motivate us to take action. If your product or service can be presented in a time-sensitive manner, you should test the time-based headline technique.

Here are some examples of headlines that utilize this technique:

- *Save $100 When You Register By April 15*
- *Get Free Shipping When You Order In The Next 48 Hours*
- *Our White Paper Is Free Only Until November 1*

We mentioned previously that individuals enter queries into a search engine because they are looking to answer a question or meet a need. Can you predict the core question that your audience wants to answer when arriving at your landing page? Asking this question in your headline can show users that you understand the problem they are trying to solve.

You can conduct an A/B split test to determine whether displaying statements or questions in your headlines is most effective for your audience. Here are a couple of examples that show the contrast between a question-driven headline and a statement-driven headline:

Statement: *Publish Your Book Now*

Question: *Looking to Publish Your Book?*

Statement: *Save Time and Money with Our Software*

Question: *Want to Save Time and Money? Try Our Software*

Remember that if you ask a question in your headline, you need to answer your own question with the body copy of the landing page.

Other Things to Test in Your Headlines

There are many other ways to test the landing page headline. For example, you might want to try one or more of the following in your headlines:

- Exclamation points
- Larger and smaller font sizes
- Different font types
- Different colors
- Numbers
- Shorter and longer copy

Wednesday: Testing Body Copy

After your headline has done its job to grab the visitor's attention and inspired that person to read on, it is the job of your descriptive body copy to do the heavy lifting of convincing the visitor to take the desired conversion action.

The copy on your landing page should provide a clear picture of what you have to offer (whether you're offering a service or product) and how your offering will benefit the visitor. After reading the copy on your landing page, the visitor should have a solid idea of how your product or service is going to make their life better. If your body copy is successful, it will inspire confidence in your product and trust in your company, and naturally lead to more conversions.

What is the best way to write body copy that is succinct, interesting, and benefit focused, and makes an emotional connection with your target audience? The techniques we described in Chapters 1, 2, and 5 are good sources of information about writing persuasively. However, the benefits that appeal to your specific target audience and the level of emotional appeal will be unique to your product. The following subsections describe a few body copywriting techniques that you should test in order to see what appeals best to your audience and provides the best conversion rates.

Short vs. Long Text

We have had success using both very short and very long body copy. You need to ask yourself: What is the least amount of information a user needs to be convinced to take action? Can you whittle down your messaging to a few sentences but still provide enough information? The amount of information needed for each audience is going to differ greatly.

The shortest text that we've used to generate leads successfully was four sentences. The longest was an entire mini-site, packed with statistical information, charts, and graphs. Keep in mind, these landing pages were not for the same client. These clients were targeting very different users with very different products.

There is no magic number of sentences that should be included in your body copy. You should test short copy against longer copy to determine which works better.

Bullet Point List vs. Block Text

If users can scan your landing page and quickly understand what you have to offer and why they should buy from you, then your landing page is doing what you need it do. Often, bulleted lists will work better for quick scanning than paragraphs and full sentences. If you can break your copy into bullet points, you should certainly test this technique. Here are some benefits of using bullet points:

- They are easy to comprehend quickly.
- They stand out on a page.
- They don't waste space; they get straight to the point.
- Users' eyes are drawn to them.

You may find that having a mixture of block text and bullet points generates the best conversion rate. The bullet points used on your landing page should highlight the core benefits of your product or service.

Testimonials

Sometimes people need to be convinced by other people. This persuasion often comes in the form of customer testimonials. Including customer testimonials in your body copy and other areas of your landing page can boost your trustworthiness to users. The Internet can be a scary place filled with companies that are less than reputable. You need to establish trust with your visitors before they will provide their contact information. Testimonials from happy, satisfied customers can build confidence and assure the visitor that your company does good work.

Well-written testimonials can also speak directly to your target audience's core concern. If reliability is a major concern in your industry, your testimonials should be geared toward the quality of your product. If speed is what separates your company from your competitors, provide testimonials that speak to your ability to deliver quickly.

Thursday: Testing Offers

One of the most crucial elements of your landing page is the offer. A clear, enticing offer will certainly gain a visitor's attention. Your offer needs to be relevant and timely, and have a sense of exclusivity. Users who see the offer should feel as if it were crafted especially for them.

A good location to test your offer is in the headline of your landing page. As we discussed on Tuesday, the headline's core objective is to inspire the user to explore the rest of the landing page. A visitor who sees an attractive offer in the headline will be much more likely to take the time to read your awesome body copy. As with any type of direct marketing, you need to continuously test your offer to see what appeals best to your audience. Your offer doesn't always need to include a "free" element, but the following list will give you an idea of the types of offers you can try:

- *Free additional information*
- *Free shipping or faster shipping*
- *Free upgrade*
- *Free installation*
- *Free consultation*
- *Free sample*

Think about what your audience values most dearly, and put that into your offer. What kind of offer gives you an edge over your competition? Remember, your offer shouldn't be unrealistic or negatively affect your ROI, such as a "buy one, get one free" offer. You want customers, but not at the cost of severely damaging your overall profit.

Friday: Testing Other Elements of Your Landing Page

The number of elements that you can test on your landing page is almost limitless. As a rule, anything that can influence a visitor is worth testing. When it comes to gaining your audience's attention quickly, deepening visitor engagement, and increasing conversion rate, there is always room for improvement.

This week, we have covered the text-based elements of your landing page that you can test rather easily. From these tests, you can quickly see improved performance. Today, we're reviewing the other elements of your landing page that you should consider testing.

Contact Form

The contact form on your landing page is a critical piece of the conversion process. You can have an amazing headline that grabs users' attention, body copy that convinces them to take action, and an undeniable offer, but if your contact form is poorly constructed, it can destroy the performance of your entire landing page.

The most appropriate and successful contact form is going to look different for every audience and industry. For some industries, asking several questions to qualify and categorize the leads works best. Other industries need customers to fill out just a few basic fields, such as name and e-mail address.

Think about when you get to a website or landing page with a product or service that you want to learn more about. If the contact form takes up the screen from top to bottom, and it looks like an IRS form that requests your name, address, e-mail, phone number, and more, what is your initial reaction? You probably think, "Do I really want to give out this much information? Is this worth it?" Your audience shouldn't have similar feelings when seeing your contact form.

To test your contact form, you should ask yourself the following questions:

- What is the least amount of information I or my sales staff needs to follow up with a lead?
- Do I really need the lead's address now, or can I get that when I follow up with them via telephone?
- Do I really need to know the size or revenue of their company to qualify them as a lead, or can I start the conversation, gauge their needs, and see if they're a good fit my product?

Try testing the shortest contact form that will enable you to follow up with leads properly.

For your particular industry, you may need to get a lot of up-front information before a lead ever hits your database. If this is the case, you should test the format and layout of your contact form. Remember that every required field on your contact form is another reason for a user to bail and not complete the form.

The end result of your testing should be a contact form that can be completed quickly and easily, regardless of the length. The shorter, the better.

Hero Shot

The *hero shot* is the main image that is displayed on your landing page. You don't want to clutter up your landing pages with tons of images, because that could be distracting, so you need to test and choose an image that supports your main product benefits and the claims on your landing page.

For example, if you're selling extended service plans for a line of televisions, your hero shot may include a happy family watching a pristine television. Visitors arriving on this landing page are probably already looking to protect their television in case something goes wrong and they need to repair or replace it. The happy family image paints a portrait of the end result that the user wants to achieve: uninterrupted television enjoyment.

Trust Symbols

If there is one thing you should take away from all of the landing page design and testing in this book, it's that you need to forge a sense of relevancy and trust with your audience and every individual user. Without this foundation, your PPC performance will suffer.

With regard to creating trust with users quickly, we'll defer to a well-known cliché: A picture is worth a thousand words. Within seconds, you need to convince visitors that they've arrived in the right place. Then you have a small window to persuade them that you are better than your competitors. After your visitors decide you have what they want, then they must decide whether they can trust you with their personal information when they fill out your contact form or go through your shopping cart.

Just stating, "You can trust us!" is not going to give the user a warm and fuzzy feeling about your website. In fact, that kind of statement may have the opposite effect. How well do you trust someone who says things like, "Sure, you can trust me." If you have to say it in such bold terms, something is off. Using trust symbols relieves you from having to make such a statement, and symbols can be interpreted quickly and easily. Here is a list of trust symbol types that you should test on your website:

Verified website symbols: Try displaying symbols that tell the user that your website is secure and safe, as shown in Figure 11.1.

Client logos: Visitors can get a sense of your company's credibility if you display logos of your marquee clients, as shown in Figure 11.2. You should test this technique to see whether it enhances your conversion rate.

Industry certifications: If possible, you should acquire certifications within your industry that will be meaningful to your audience. Try adding these to your landing page to see whether they enhance your conversion rate.

Figure 11.1 There are many types of symbols that can instill a sense of trust with users.

Figure 11.2 Client logos can quickly show visitors that your company can be trusted.

Product Images

Web users are very visual in nature. If they can't see, feel, or hold your actual product, they at least want to see a picture of it. You should test using different pictures of your product on your landing page. Do you have the kind of product that can be pictured with people, in different settings, from different angles?

Call-to-Action Button

The button on your contact form or shopping cart may not seem very important, but trust us: it's extremely important. You need to seize every available opportunity to keep prospects moving through the conversion funnel. The call-to-action button on your landing page can give users that little extra push to complete the conversion action. Here is a list of elements you should test for your call-to-action button:

Color: Numerous published studies have proven that the color of a call-to-action button affects conversion rates. You should do your own testing to see what color appeals best to your audience.

Text: You can take various approaches with the text on your call-to-action button. Your button can contain descriptive text that tells users what to do, such as *Buy Now* or *Get Your Free Quote*. You can also try using arrows that guide the users' eyes toward the contact form.

Size and shape: The call-to-action button should stand out on your page so that users know what they are expected to do. Test larger buttons as well as smaller buttons. You might think that larger buttons would be better because they're easier to spot, but that's not always the case. You need to conduct your own tests to see what works best for you.

Week 30: Use Google Website Optimizer

Last week, you learned the various elements that you can test on your landing pages. Now you need a convenient, easy-to-implement method for creating multiple tests on your landing pages in order to improve your conversion rate. We highly recommend that you use Google Website Optimizer for your landing page testing. This week, you'll be introduced to how Website Optimizer works, how you can implement this platform on your landing pages, and why it can make your landing page testing fast and easy.

Monday and Tuesday: Introducing Google Website Optimizer

Google Website Optimizer is an essential tool that enables you to easily launch A/B and multivariate testing on your website in order to increase your conversion rates. The platform is robust, easy to use, and best of all, it's free! There are other, and sometimes very costly, conversion testing applications that require you to create custom URLs for testing and implementation. However, with Website Optimizer, you can use an existing web page URL to conduct your tests, and the reporting dashboard is very intuitive and helpful.

Here is an overview of setting up Website Optimizer:

1. Identify the page or pages you want to test. For the purpose of this week's topic, you should choose a high-traffic landing page.

2. Define which element you want to test. In A/B testing, you test one element at a time by rotating two or more nearly identical variations of your landing page, also known in Website Optimizer as your *original page*. (With A/B testing, you can also test entirely different versions of your landing pages; we'll talk more about that on Wednesday and Thursday of this week.)

3. Identify your conversion confirmation page. Website Optimizer requires that you have an end point that the user must reach. This way, Website Optimizer will be able to report response rates of your tests. Because you're setting up testing on your landing page, the confirmation page you use for Website Optimizer should probably be the same page that you use to track conversions within Google AdWords.

4. Tag your landing pages. Website Optimizer will provide small snippets of code known as *tags*. You need to add these tags to the original page, the variation page(s), and the conversion page to allow tracking. On your original page, you need to insert the control script tag at the top of your landing page code and the tracker script tag at the bottom of the page (before the </body> tag). On your variation page(s), you need to install the tracker script tag. You also need to tag the conversion page with the conversion script tag. Website Optimizer will rotate your original and variation page(s) for every visitor to your landing page URL. Your test elements will rotate evenly among all of the visitors to your landing page. You can access the results and reports of various statistics within Website Optimizer to see which variant is the most effective.

In this chapter, we're providing an introduction to Google Website Optimizer. Our goal is to get you started and inspire you to use this extremely helpful tool! After you've read this chapter and accessed your Website Optimizer account (and perhaps even launched your initial A/B split), then we suggest you get to know this tool extremely well. We highly recommend that you pick up *Always Be Testing: The Complete Guide to Google Website Optimizer* by Bryan Eisenberg and John Quarto-vonTivadar (Sybex, 2008) so that you can gain an expert level of knowledge about this tool.

Accessing Google Website Optimizer

You can access Google Website Optimizer from within your Google AdWords account. As shown in the following example, just open the drop-down menu from the Reporting tab of the Google AdWords interface. Within this drop-down menu, you can click Website Optimizer to access your account.

You will arrive at a page that looks similar to the following example. (In this example, no tests have been created yet.)

Wednesday and Thursday: Tagging Pages for Google Website Optimizer

To utilize Google Website Optimizer, you need to insert the proper tags. Inserting these tags is not overly complicated, and you (or your web development team) should be able to complete this process in a short amount of time. Three tags need to be implemented on your test landing page: the control script tag, section script tag, and tracker script tag.

Control Script Tag

The *control script tag* drives your experiment and tells Google where your content variations are located. You should place your control script code at the beginning of your original page's source code, immediately after the opening <head> tag.

Section Script Tag

The *section script tag* should be placed at the beginning and end of a page section that contains a test element. Each test page will have at least one (and probably more) sections to be tagged. For example, let's say that you want to test the headline of your landing page. You would place the section script tag right before and after the HTML code for your headline.

Tracking Script

The *tracking script* needs to be placed on the test landing page as well as the conversion confirmation page. This snippet of code indicates to Website Optimizer when an action has been taken after a particular testing element was displayed. The tracking script should be placed at the bottom of your test landing page and conversion page.

Wrapping Up

To set up an initial A/B test, you need to name your experiment, identify the test pages that you want to include in your test, and identify the conversion page for the test. Setting up an experiment can be completed in one screen, as shown in Figure 11.3.

Website Optimizer makes it easy to find these three codes for placement on your landing page. After you have configured your test, the next screen within the setup process provides all the tags you'll need, as shown in Figure 11.4. Google provides each snippet of code and tells you where to place that code.

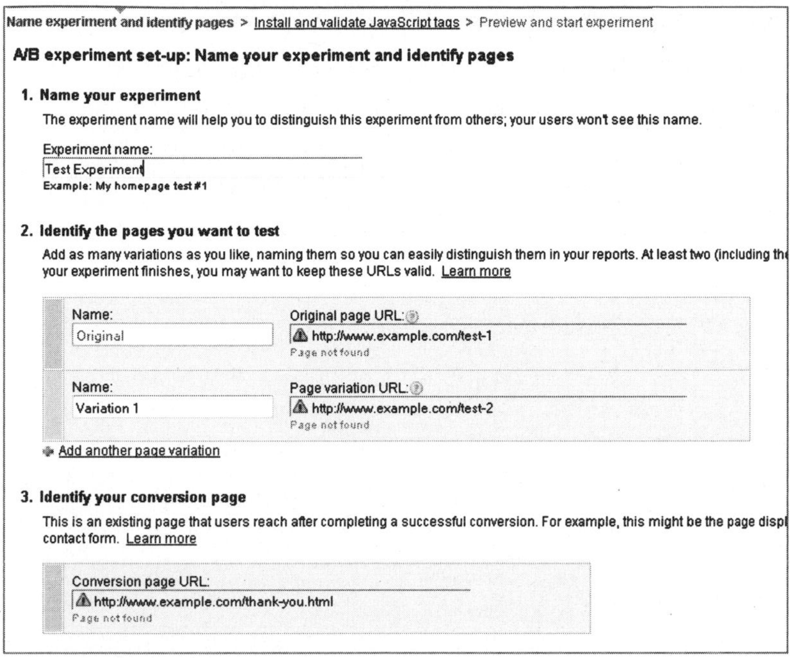

Name experiment and identify pages > Install and validate JavaScript tags > Preview and start experiment

A/B experiment set-up: Name your experiment and identify pages

1. Name your experiment

The experiment name will help you to distinguish this experiment from others; your users won't see this name.

Experiment name:

Test Experiment

Example: My homepage test #1

2. Identify the pages you want to test

Add as many variations as you like, naming them so you can easily distinguish them in your reports. At least two (including the your experiment finishes, you may want to keep these URLs valid. Learn more

Name:

Original

Original page URL: ⓘ

⚠ http://www.example.com/test-1

Page not found

Name:

Variation 1

Page variation URL: ⓘ

⚠ http://www.example.com/test-2

Page not found

✚ Add another page variation

3. Identify your conversion page

This is an existing page that users reach after completing a successful conversion. For example, this might be the page displ contact form. Learn more

Conversion page URL:

⚠ http://www.example.com/thank-you.html

Page not found

Figure 11.3 Naming and identifying your test elements is quick and easy.

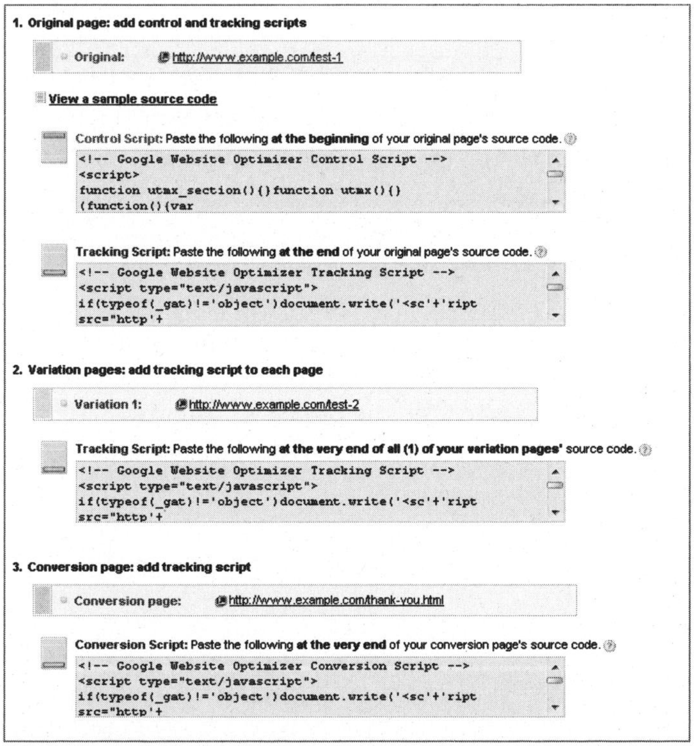

---

1. Original page: add control and tracking scripts

Original: 🔗 http://www.example.com/test-1

📄 View a sample source code

Control Script: Paste the following **at the beginning** of your original page's source code. ⓘ

```
<!-- Google Website Optimizer Control Script -->
<script>
function utmx_section(){}function utmx(){}
(function(){var
```

Tracking Script: Paste the following **at the end** of your original page's source code. ⓘ

```
<!-- Google Website Optimizer Tracking Script -->
<script type="text/javascript">
if(typeof(_gat)!='object')document.write('<sc'+'ript
src="http'+
```

2. Variation pages: add tracking script to each page

Variation 1: 🔗 http://www.example.com/test-2

Tracking Script: Paste the following **at the very end of all (1) of your variation pages'** source code. ⓘ

```
<!-- Google Website Optimizer Tracking Script -->
<script type="text/javascript">
if(typeof(_gat)!='object')document.write('<sc'+'ript
src="http'+
```

3. Conversion page: add tracking script

Conversion page: 🔗 http://www.example.com/thank-you.html

Conversion Script: Paste the following **at the very end** of your conversion page's source code. ⓘ

```
<!-- Google Website Optimizer Conversion Script -->
<script type="text/javascript">
if(typeof(_gat)!='object')document.write('<sc'+'ript
src="http'+
```

Figure 11.4 Google Website Optimizer codes are easy to find and install.

Friday: Validating Your Pages

After the three Website Optimizer tags have been implemented on your landing page, you'll need to validate the code. Website Optimizer will visit your pages and check for correct installation of your code. If there are problems with the code, you'll be notified of the error and told on which page the error occurred. To validate the code, just click Validate Pages at the bottom of the page that contains your three landing page tags, as shown in Figure 11.5.

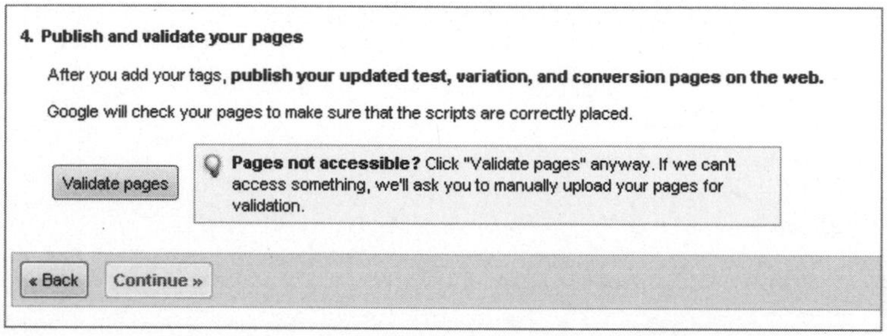

4. Publish and validate your pages

After you add your tags, **publish your updated test, variation, and conversion pages on the web.**

Google will check your pages to make sure that the scripts are correctly placed.

Validate pages   ○ **Pages not accessible?** Click "Validate pages" anyway. If we can't access something, we'll ask you to manually upload your pages for validation.

« Back   Continue »

Figure 11.5 Validate the code on your landing page to finalize the test implementation.

Week 31: Conduct A/B and Multivariate Tests

This week, you'll learn the two core testing methods that are available in Website Optimizer: A/B split tests and multivariate tests. Each method presents unique benefits as well as challenges. By the end of this week, you'll understand the two types of testing and which one may be right for you.

Monday and Tuesday: Using A/B Split Testing

A/B split testing enables you to test entirely different landing pages against each other. We recommend starting with A/B testing, because it's simpler to set up than multivariate testing, and A/B test results can be easier to interpret.

For example, Figure 11.6 shows our original landing page, and Figure 11.7 shows our new landing page. We could split-test these two versions. After we install the proper tags and launch our A/B split test, Website Optimizer will rotate these landing pages evenly between users.

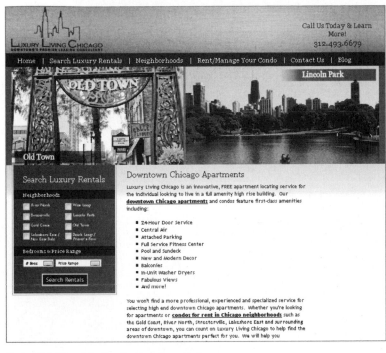

Figure 11.6 The original landing page in our test

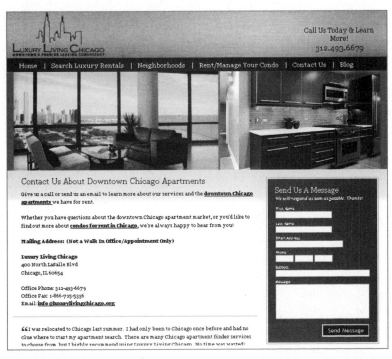

Figure 11.7 The new version of our landing page in the test

Testing without Google Website Optimizer

We suggest that you take full advantage of Google Website Optimizer. However, every organization is different, and you may run into some snags when trying to implement the Website Optimizer tags. Don't worry—if this happens to you, it doesn't mean that you can't conduct landing page testing; it just means that you'll have to utilize another method for testing.

You can still conduct A/B split tests on your landing pages by splitting the traffic in an ad group in Google AdWords. Here is a step-by-step process for launching A/B tests by splitting the traffic in your AdWords ad group:

1. Create two versions of your landing page. You should either test one element of your landing page (headline, body copy, or product image) or entirely different versions of your page with major layout divergences.

2. Create two copies of the same text ad within your AdWords ad group. Send each of these ads to your different landing pages. This way, the only variation in your test is the landing page.

3. Make sure that you set your ad rotation options to Rotate rather than Optimize. The AdWords default setting is Optimize, which means Google will monitor your ad performance and eventually send more traffic to the ad with the higher click-through. If this happens, traffic will not be separated evenly between your test landing pages. When you choose the Rotate setting, your ads will rotate evenly.

4. Monitor the performance of your ads to see which variation generates the best conversion rate.

This method is not perfect. Ad rotation assures only that over time, ads A and B will be seen the same number of times, while other factors such as time of day can affect how often either ad is displayed within a certain range of time. But for most advertisers, this method is sufficient and easier to implement than other methods that require programming and the use of non-Google software tools.

Wednesday and Thursday: Using Multivariate Testing

Multivariate testing enables you to test multiple elements of your landing page simultaneously. With this type of testing, you identify one or more sections of your web page, such as a headline, product image, block of descriptive text, or call-to-action button, and then design some variations for each section. During the experiment, viewers will see a combination of page section variations. Website Optimizer collects data on the effectiveness of each combination and helps you analyze the outcome of your experiment.

For example, Figure 11.8 shows the sections of a website that could be tested using the multivariate technique. For this website, you could test section 1 (the introduction image of the website), section 2 (the headline), section 3 (the product images), and section 4 (the description body copy). With multivariate testing, you can experiment with all of these elements at the same time in order to see which section and which combination garners the best results.

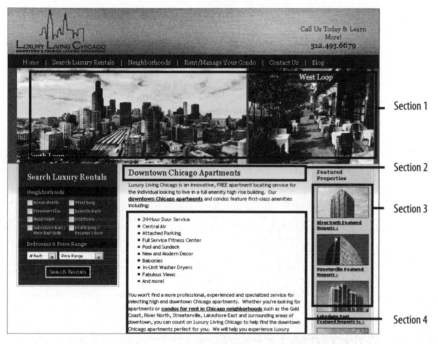

Figure 11.8 Testing multiple elements of your landing page at the same time

Common Landing Page–Testing Mistakes

Here are some common mistakes that should be avoided when testing landing pages:

Don't make the conversion confirmation page more than one click away: Keep your conversion process simple in order to launch, review, and analyze tests quickly.

Don't make your tests too complicated: Multivariate testing is great, but don't launch too many variables at once. This will make determining the outcome of your tests more difficult.

Don't test insignificant page elements: You want to test the elements of your landing page that will have the biggest impact on your conversion rate. Remember, the objective of split testing on your landing page is to increase your conversion rate.

Don't stop your test too early: Determining the results of your landing page tests too soon can yield faulty outcomes. Resist the temptation to draw conclusions before you see Website Optimizer reports that indicate enough data has been accumulated. You'll see during the course of the test that the data will shift, supporting a winning element one day that becomes a loser two days hence. Make sure that you gather enough data to make a statistically confident decision.

Friday: Choosing the Right Test Method

Choosing the right test method is crucial for properly optimizing your landing page and increasing your conversion rate. You don't want your tests to take too long, or on the other hand, not garner enough traffic for each variation to make a statistically confident decision. The major factors that can help you determine which testing method is right for your campaign are as follows:

Amount of traffic: The more traffic your landing page receives, the quicker you should be able to determine the outcome of your test. If you are in an industry that doesn't generate a huge amount of traffic, you will need more time for the test to run. If you fall into the category of a lower-traffic site, you may want to choose an A/B split test; or if you get a good deal of traffic, multivariate testing might a good alternative for you.

Current conversion rate: The lower your average conversion rate, the longer your test will take to determine a winner. So, you may not want to include too many variables in your test. In this case, A/B testing may be the right choice for you. Of course, hopefully, you'll increase your conversion rate through your testing! If your website gets a high volume of traffic with a higher conversion rate to start, multivariate testing is a good option.

Number of combinations: The more combinations you include in your test, the longer you'll need to determine an outcome. This ties in closely with the amount of traffic to your website and your conversion rate. The higher the volume and conversion of your website, the more combinations you can include while expecting a statistically significant outcome within a reasonable amount of time.

Experience with Google Website Optimizer: If you are just getting started with Website Optimizer, you may want to start off with a basic A/B split test. After you get acclimated to using the platform, you may want to move on to multivariate testing.

You should consider these and other factors when deciding which type of landing page test is right for you. Overall, if your website generates a low amount of traffic with a low average conversion rate, then you should initiate your optimization process with A/B split tests.

Week 32: Report and Interpret Results

At this point, you have determined which type of landing page test is best for your campaign, created the elements that you would like to test, implemented the proper Website Optimizer tags, and gotten your test up and running. Now it's time to review the reporting features provided by Website Optimizer that will help you determine the results of your tests.

Monday and Tuesday: Reporting in Google Website Optimizer

The reporting features within Website Optimizer are insightful, helpful, and easy to use. Website Optimizer uses two types of reports—combination reports and page-section reports—to display the progress of your tests and to provide suggestions on which test variation or combination is your winner.

Combination Report

A *combination report* shows the results for all combination variations that you are currently testing on your landing page. This report enables you to compare how each variation is performing with regard to other combinations as well as the original version of your landing page.

Figure 11.9 shows a combination report in Website Optimizer.

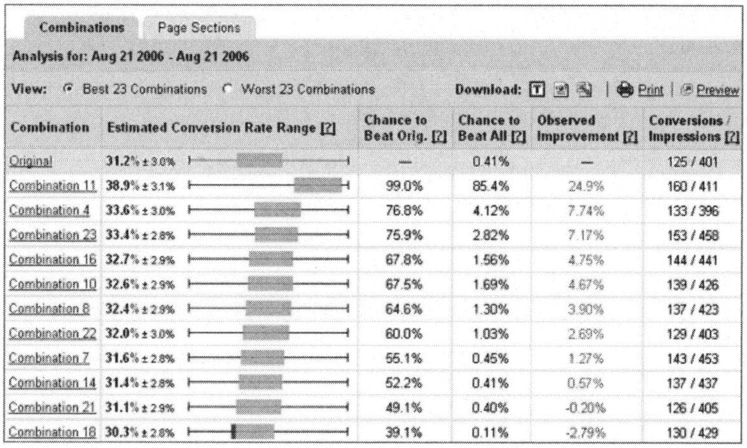

Combination	Estimated Conversion Rate Range [?]	Chance to Beat Orig. [?]	Chance to Beat All [?]	Observed Improvement [?]	Conversions / Impressions [?]
Original	31.2% ± 3.0%	—	0.41%	—	125 / 401
Combination 11	38.9% ± 3.1%	99.0%	85.4%	24.9%	160 / 411
Combination 4	33.6% ± 3.0%	76.8%	4.12%	7.74%	133 / 396
Combination 23	33.4% ± 2.8%	75.9%	2.82%	7.17%	153 / 458
Combination 16	32.7% ± 2.9%	67.8%	1.56%	4.75%	144 / 441
Combination 10	32.6% ± 2.9%	67.5%	1.69%	4.67%	139 / 426
Combination 8	32.4% ± 2.9%	64.6%	1.30%	3.90%	137 / 423
Combination 22	32.0% ± 3.0%	60.0%	1.03%	2.69%	129 / 403
Combination 7	31.6% ± 2.8%	55.1%	0.45%	1.27%	143 / 453
Combination 14	31.4% ± 2.8%	52.2%	0.41%	0.57%	137 / 437
Combination 21	31.1% ± 2.9%	49.1%	0.40%	-0.20%	126 / 405
Combination 18	30.3% ± 2.8%	39.1%	0.11%	-2.79%	130 / 429

Figure 11.9 Example of a combination report in Website Optimizer

As you can see in the figure, a combination report contains the following information:

Estimated Conversion Rate Range: This is the most important information within your report. Within this column, you can see how well each combination of your test is performing relative to your original versions. The results are displayed as statistics as well as in a visual representation of a color-coded bar that indicates how each combination is doing. When you see a combination marked in green, this means it's doing better than your original. If a combination is doing worse than the original, it will be marked in red.

Chance to Beat Original: This statistic shows the likelihood that a certain combination will eventually generate a higher conversion rate than your original. When this number goes above 95 percent or below 5 percent, the corresponding bar will be all green or all red, respectively.

Chance to Beat All: This statistic displays the likelihood that a specific combination will generate a better result than all of the other combinations in the experiment. When the statistics in this column are positive, above 95 percent, this means that a specific experiment combination is a likely candidate to beat the other test combinations and replace your original combination, therefore becoming the new control variation. Poor statistics in this column mean that a specific experiment combination will not out-perform the original combination.

Observed Improvement: This column tells you how much of an improvement each combination makes over the original, measured as a percentage.

Conversions/Impressions: This statistic is straightforward. It's just the raw data of how many conversions and page views a particular combination generated.

Page Section Report

The *page section report* tells you which variations within each page section generated the best response. In this report, you can see each section of your landing page, and each section is broken into your different variations. Figure 11.10 is an example of a page section report.

Combinations	Page Sections						
Analysis for: Aug 21 2006 - Aug 21 2006							
Sort By: ● Relevance Rating ○ Order Created					Download: T ⬚ ⬚ | 🖶 Print | 👁 Preview		
Relevance Rating [?]	**Variation**	**Estimated Conversion Rate Range [?]**		**Chance to Beat Orig. [?]**	**Chance to Beat All [?]**	**Observed Improvement [?]**	**Conversions / Impressions [?]**
Section 2	Original	29.1% ± 1.0%		—	0.11%	—	951 / 3273
4 / 5	Variation 2	32.5% ± 1.0%		99.9%	99.8%	11.9%	1099 / 3380
	Variation 1	29.1% ± 1.0%		52.8%	0.13%	0.26%	975 / 3347
Section 3	Original	28.3% ± 1.2%		—	0.02%	—	684 / 2417
4 / 5	Variation 1	32.6% ± 1.2%		100%	89.7%	15.2%	833 / 2555
	Variation 3	30.9% ± 1.2%		97.9%	10.1%	9.33%	758 / 2450
	Variation 2	29.1% ± 1.1%		73.2%	0.18%	2.80%	750 / 2578
Section 1	Original	30.8% ± 0.8%		—	89.4%	—	1529 / 4960
1 / 5	Variation 1	29.7% ± 0.8%		10.6%	10.6%	-3.71%	1496 / 5040

Figure 11.10 Example of a page section report in Website Optimizer

This report contains much of the same information as the combination report. The core difference is the Relevance Rating, which displays how much impact a certain page section has on your experiment. For example, in Figure 11.10, section 1 has a rating of 1, which means this section didn't have a significant impact on the experiment. Let's say that this section was the call-to-action button. The low rating would tell you that the call-to-action button didn't carry a lot of weight. Conversely, section 2 and section 3 have a rating of 4, which means that they have the most impact on your landing page performance and this experiment.

Wednesday and Thursday: Interpreting Test Results

Interpreting reports within Website Optimizer is just about the easiest part of implementing, launching, and reviewing your landing page testing. As you saw in yesterday's lesson, Website Optimizer monitors each combination or page section and helps you determine when a statistically valid winner has been reached in each experiment. To determine a winner of an experiment, Google makes sure that each combination has received a large-enough traffic and conversion sample. Also, before suggesting a winner, Google wants to make sure that the performance between the variations is significantly different.

Website Optimizer can tell you which combination or variation generates the best response. However, it's up to you determine *why* a variation appeals best to your audience. After you have determined the winner of your test, here are a few questions that you should ask yourself before launching the next test:

- Why did this combination or variation win the experiment?
- Why does this combination or variation generate the best response?
- How is this combination or variation better than the other variations in this experiment?
- How can I improve on my winning combination or variation?

Write out the answers to these questions. Think about the outcome of your experiment and start planning your next test.

Friday: Reaching the End of Your Landing Page Testing

When do you reach the end of your landing page testing and optimization? The simple answer is, "Never!" Your landing pages can always perform better and they can always be optimized. Even if you launch a test and the experiment improves your conversion rate significantly, there is still room for improvement.

Think about the list of test elements we presented in this chapter. You should continue to optimize your landing pages until you've tested each of these elements. If you feel like you've run out of ideas or need inspiration, here is a reminder of the landing page elements you should test:

- Headlines
- Body copy
- Call-to-action buttons
- Contact form
- Shopping cart process
- Color scheme
- Product images
- Hero images

- Layout
- Trust symbols
- Adding or removing navigation
- Different conversion actions

If you ever reach a point when you think you have finished testing your landing page, just remember this: Your competitors are probably still testing—and improving their conversion rate and ROI as a result.

Month 9—Migrate Your Campaign to Microsoft and Yahoo!

In the first 11 chapters we focused on Google AdWords because Google possesses the lion's share of search volume, and many capabilities and features that aren't available from Yahoo! and Bing. This approach also reflects our counsel that you build and optimize your campaigns on Google, and then replicate your campaigns on Yahoo! and Bing.

This chapter compares the advertising interfaces for Google AdWords, Yahoo! Search Marketing (YSM), and Microsoft adCenter. The objectives of this chapter are to help you transfer your AdWords campaigns into YSM and adCenter, and to optimize campaign performance by taking advantage of the strengths of each advertising platform.

Chapter Contents

Why Yahoo! Search Marketing and Microsoft adCenter Matter

With regard to search volume, Yahoo! comes in second to Google—a very distant second. Figure 12.1 shows data from a comScore report for each search engine.

As you can see, Google has a 65 percent share of searches conducted during this time frame. And this is why the majority of your PPC strategy will be devoted to this search engine. However, if you completely neglect Yahoo! and Microsoft, you'll be neglecting to display ads for almost 30 percent of the total search queries each month. The report in Figure 12.2 tells the tale.

comScore Core Search Report* October 2009 vs. September 2009 Total U.S. – Home/Work/University Locations Source: comScore qSearch			
Core Search Entity	Share of Searches (%)		
	Sep-09	Oct-09	Point Change Oct-09 vs. Sep-09
Total Core Search	100.0%	100.0%	N/A
Google Sites	64.9%	65.4%	0.5
Yahoo! Sites	18.8%	18.0%	-0.8
Microsoft Sites	9.4%	9.9%	0.5
Ask Network	3.9%	3.9%	0.0
AOL LLC Network	3.0%	2.9%	-0.1

Figure 12.1 2009 comScore data showing relative Google, Yahoo!, and Microsoft reach

comScore Core Search Report* October 2009 vs. September 2009 Total U.S. – Home/Work/University Locations Source: comScore qSearch			
Core Search Entity	Search Queries (MM)		
	Sep-09	Oct-09	Percent Change Oct-09 vs. Sep-09
Total Core Search	13,836	14,309	3%
Google Sites	8,975	9,362	4%
Yahoo! Sites	2,600	2,571	-1%
Microsoft Sites	1,305	1,412	8%
Ask Network	541	552	2%
AOL LLC	416	412	-1%

*Based on the five major search engines including partner searches and cross-channel searches. Searches for mapping, local directory, and user-generated video sites that are not on the core domain of the five search engines are not included in the core search numbers.

Figure 12.2 comScore data that shows the relative number of search queries per search engine

In just a single month, Yahoo! sites generate 2.6 billion queries and Microsoft sites generate 1.4 billion. That's a lot of potential ad impressions to leave on the table for your competitors.

Different Look, Same Strategy

On the surface, Yahoo! Search Marketing and Microsoft adCenter PPC user interfaces are quite different from Google AdWords. Each interface provides different reporting features, and each displays campaign contents differently. Regardless of these variations, the core strategies are the same.

Each search engine wants to provide the best user experience possible. As a PPC advertiser, you want to help the search engines provide a great user experience by supplying highly qualified and relevant advertisements. To do this, you need to mirror the strategy that you implemented in Google. Creating tightly focused ad groups, writing compelling ad texts and utilizing landing pages with the highest conversion rates will result in a relevant, positive user experience and set you up for success.

The objective of this chapter is to give you a quick overview of the Yahoo! Search Marketing and Microsoft adCenter interfaces and how they differ from Google AdWords. But remember, the fundamental PPC strategies still apply.

Week 33: Understand YSM Differences and Advantages

Overall, you'll probably find that the Yahoo! Search Marketing user interface is not as user-friendly as Google AdWords. Although your account is structured into campaigns and ad groups just as it is on AdWords, the user interface is more cumbersome, and the reporting capabilities fall far short of AdWords. But as we said earlier, this doesn't mean you should neglect Yahoo!.

Monday: Standard and Advanced Match Types

Now that you know Google AdWords like the back of your hand (at least you should if you've read the previous chapters closely), we'll use AdWords as a basis for comparison when discussing differences between the two search engine interfaces. The first major difference is the keyword match type strategy.

You are now familiar with these three AdWords match types: broad, phrase, and negative. Within the YSM interface, you are not given as many options. It's sort of an all-or-nothing situation. The available match types are advanced, negative, and standard.

Advanced Match Type

The *advanced match type* is the default match type for each level of your account. The advanced match type is similar, but not quite equivalent, to the AdWords broad match.

With Yahoo!'s advanced match, your ads are eligible to appear for a wide range of search queries. This means that your keywords may be matched to queries that are not in your campaign but that have been deemed relevant to your keyword's user intent by Yahoo!. The relevancy of these additional search queries is questionable, and this is why you should tread carefully when using this match type.

Google's broad match allows your ad to show on similar phrases and relevant variations of your keywords. For example, if you have the broad-match keyword *tennis shoes*, your ads may show for related queries such as *tennis*, *shoes*, *buy tennis shoes*, *running shoes*, and *tennis sneakers*. Advanced-match keywords in Yahoo! can be matched to an even wider range of terms.

If you have the advanced-match keyword *gourmet coffee*, you could match a wide range of search queries such as these:

- *Gourmet coffee* (core keyword)
- *Gourmet coffees* (plural version)
- *Learn about gourmet coffee* (phrasal usage)
- *Coffee by gourmets* (different order)
- *Gourmat cofee* (misspellings)
- *Coffee* (singular version)
- *Italian Gourmet coffee* (specific search term)
- *Gourmet tea* (related search)

However, your ad may be triggered by either *gourmet* or *coffee*, and this can lead to wildly irrelevant search queries. The list of search queries for either of the root terms is extensive.

If the scope of a targeted keyword expands beyond its original intention, your click-through rates and conversion rates can suffer, and this can lead to a lower Quality Index and higher costs per click.

There are benefits to using advanced-match keywords. You can expand the reach of your campaign with less up-front effort. You can upload your core set of keywords, and Yahoo! will display your ads on queries that have not yet been targeted in your campaign. This can save time with regard to keyword research. Advanced match is not for the faint of heart or advertisers that are willing to take the risk of opening the search query floodgates.

Advanced match in Yahoo! can threaten your ROI more than Google's broad match. This is because Yahoo! offers fewer tools to help refine the wide net you're casting with an advanced match. In AdWords, you can run a Search Query Performance report to see the raw search queries that are triggering your advertisements. Yahoo! does not currently offer a search query report. This means that you're flying blind, in a sense. With this match type, you are relying on Yahoo! to match your keywords to search queries that are relevant to your services and/or products. Sure, with broad match in Google you are doing the same thing, but you can gain insight into what they deem as relevant. With Yahoo!, once your advanced-match keyword is launched, you can't refine your negative keyword list from direct search queries within Yahoo!

Negative Match Type

We highly recommend that you copy your negative keyword list from Google AdWords into Yahoo! If a term isn't relevant and doesn't convert in Google, it's a pretty sure bet that it will perform poorly in Yahoo! as well, so you should go ahead and exclude it. You can exclude up to 500 keywords at the account level, up to 1,250 keywords within each campaign, and up to 500 keywords in each ad group.

Standard Match Type

The other end of the match type spectrum in Yahoo! is their *standard match type.* This match type works a lot like Google's exact match, except that with standard match, Yahoo! may also show your standard-match keywords for common misspellings and closely related variations.

With this match type, you are casting a much smaller net, but it is much more focused. This means that your traffic should be more relevant, leading to a higher CTR and conversion rate. But your traffic volume will be significantly lower, and you'll have far less visibility.

Setting Match Types at Different Levels of Your Account

Within AdWords, you set your match types keyword by keyword. Within your Yahoo! account, match type settings can be established at the account, campaign, ad group, and keyword levels. However, if you aren't careful, you could incorrectly set up your match type targeting.

The higher-level match type settings override the lower-level settings. This means that if you choose the standard match type at the account level, you'll be able to choose only the standard match type for your campaigns, ad groups, and keywords. If you want to have keyword-level control of your match types, you need to set your match type to Advanced at the account, campaign, and ad group levels.

We recommend selecting advanced match at the higher levels of your account, because it gives you more flexibility to change between the standard and advanced match types at the keyword level.

Tuesday: Geo-targeting

You can choose where your ads will be displayed, similar to Google AdWords (the comparisons continue!). We'll start from the highest point: the account level. At the account level, you can specify which continents you want to target. By default, Yahoo! Search Marketing in the United States is set to present ads to the United States and Canada. Other continents are blocked by default.

Unless you sell to customers on other continents, we advise keeping the default setting to block all other continents. If you remove the block from these countries, international users who search from their country on Yahoo! may see your ads.

CHAPTER 12: MONTH 9—MIGRATE YOUR CAMPAIGN TO MICROSOFT AND YAHOO!

312
■

Creating a successful PPC campaign is all about measurements, refinements, and optimization. Running yours ads on all continents will certainly expand your reach, but you'll have no control and your performance will suffer greatly if you can't actually sell to the clients in all these places.

One big difference between Google and Yahoo! is their approach to international campaigns. In Google AdWords, you can target any or all countries at the campaign level in your account, and your ads will be displayed in those countries on Google's local search engine. Yahoo! is a completely different beast. If you specifically want to target international customers, Yahoo! requires you to set up a different account in each country where you want to do business. To do this, you need to contact Yahoo!'s customer service to create these accounts for you.

At the campaign level, you can begin to get more specific with your targeting. You can target states, cities, zip codes, and designated marketing areas (DMAs). A DMA is a region determined by Nielsen Media Research that has been used by offline marketers and ad agencies for many years for targeting their advertising.

Figure 12.3 shows how you can target an ad by state. In this case, the targeted states are Indiana and Illinois.

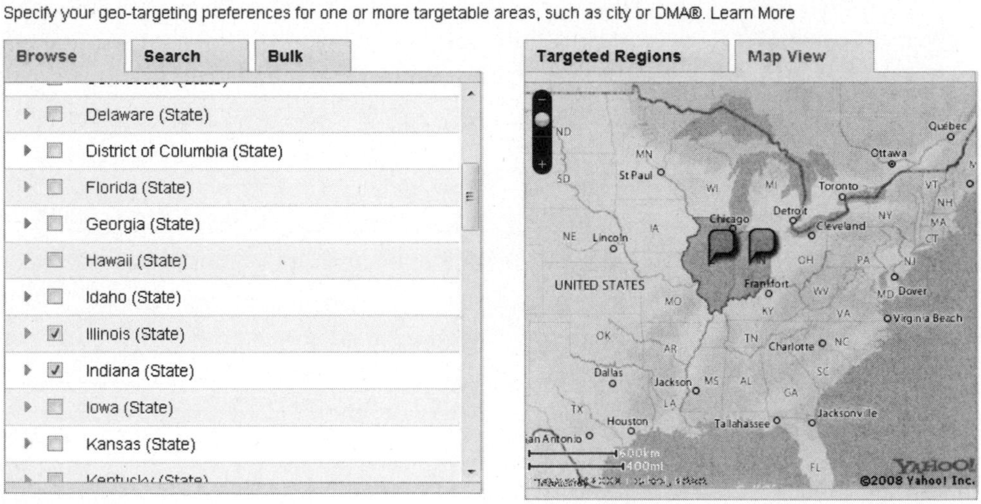

Figure 12.3 Geo-targeting Indiana and Illinois

If you want to get more specific with your targeting, you can choose a certain city or DMA. In Figure 12.4, the target is the Chicago area.

As you can see, you can also select the surrounding cities within the Chicagoland area. So, you can get rather specific with your geo-targeting. This is extremely helpful for businesses that want display ads only in smaller markets. These settings can be altered at either the campaign or ad group level.

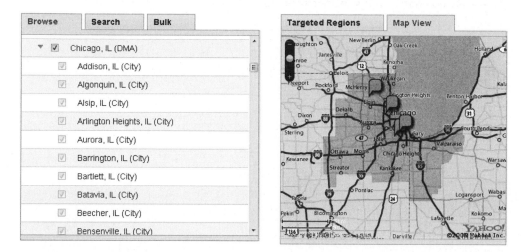

Figure 12.4 Geo-targeting Chicago

You can also choose to target your ads by zip code. Just enter the zip code that you'd like to target, and Yahoo! will provide additional information on this level of targeting, as shown in Figure 12.5.

Whether you choose to target by city or zip code, you will get the same result: geo-targeting at a more granular level.

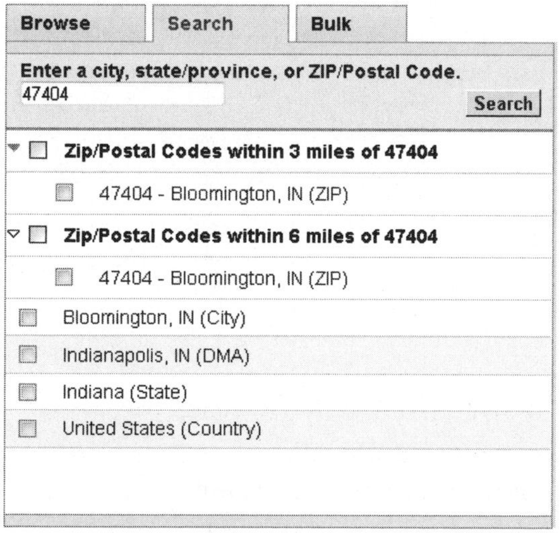

Browse   Search   Bulk

Enter a city, state/province, or ZIP/Postal Code.
47404   Search

▾ ☐ **Zip/Postal Codes within 3 miles of 47404**
   ☐   47404 - Bloomington, IN (ZIP)
▿ ☐ **Zip/Postal Codes within 6 miles of 47404**
   ☐   47404 - Bloomington, IN (ZIP)
☐ Bloomington, IN (City)
☐ Indianapolis, IN (DMA)
☐ Indiana (State)
☐ United States (Country)

Figure 12.5 Geo-targeting by zip code

Wednesday: Ad Types and Lengths

Within the Yahoo! interface, you can display only one type of advertisement: text ads. Unlike Google AdWords, you cannot upload image, mobile, TV, or any other types of ads. You could say that Yahoo! is sticking with the basics.

The format of text ads doesn't vary greatly between search engines, but there are some nuances that are worth noting. And within the actual search engine results pages, ads are displayed in a parallel fashion.

The basics are still present: headline, ad copy, display URL, and destination URL. You are allotted 70 characters within the short description of your ad, and your display URL can be 35 characters long. This is similar to a Google ad.

However, in Yahoo! your headline can be 40 characters long (in Google AdWords you have only 25 characters). Your ad copy isn't broken into two lines of 35 characters each; instead, you have 70 characters without line breaks. Yahoo! decides where the line break will occur when the ads are displayed. And the most distinct difference is the presence of the Long Description option, as shown in Figure 12.6.

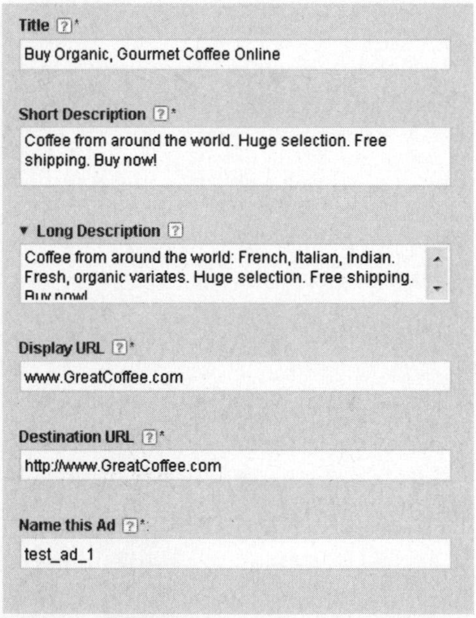

Figure 12.6 Long description in Yahoo! ads

The long ad text version is utilized primarily on Yahoo!'s content network. The majority of websites display the short version, but some websites display the long ad texts. A long description is optional, but a short description is required.

Your ad-writing strategy in Yahoo! should be parallel to your Google AdWords strategy. Everything we discussed in Chapter 5, "Month 2—Create Great PPC Ads," is valid here. You want to write ads that are keyword focused, benefit driven, and highly geared toward your target audience.

Actually, writing ads in Yahoo! is slightly easier, because you don't have the character limitation for each ad copy line as you do in AdWords. In Yahoo!, you have just one block of 70 characters. You also have a little more breathing room in the headline—you can use up to 40 characters. Because you have this additional space in the headline, you should be sure to use it! If you are copying ads from AdWords into Yahoo!, you may be able to squeeze in an additional descriptive word or even a short call to action such as *Buy Now!*

Dynamic Keyword Insertion in Yahoo!

In Yahoo!, you have a dynamic keyword insertion option when writing ad copy. It's pretty easy to use. If you click the Insert Keyword Automatically link just below your headline or short description, you'll see the following screen.

You will need to insert your default text. This means that if the keyword that triggered your ad is too long to be displayed in the given space, your default text will appear. The following example shows how the headline looks with keyword insertion.

If used properly, dynamic keyword insertion can be helpful, but if you structure your campaigns and ad groups properly, you shouldn't even need to use this option. Remember, each ad group should contain only a few tightly themed keywords. This will make writing relevant ad text easy. Too many search marketers use dynamic keyword insertion as a crutch. They think that they can throw a large number of keywords into an ad group and then rely on dynamic keyword insertion to make their ads relevant. This is not a good strategy, and we suggest that you don't do it.

Thursday: Ad Scheduling

You may find that your target audience is more likely to convert at certain times of the day. If so, you may want to take advantage of the ad scheduling feature. With this tool, you can increase your bids during certain times of the day to gain additional visibility. You can also choose not to run your ads at all on certain days that have been proven to have lower conversion rates.

Ad scheduling can be set at either the campaign or ad group level. To alter your ad scheduling, open your campaign settings screen. As shown in Figure 12.7, Ad Scheduling is in the Targeting section of your account settings.

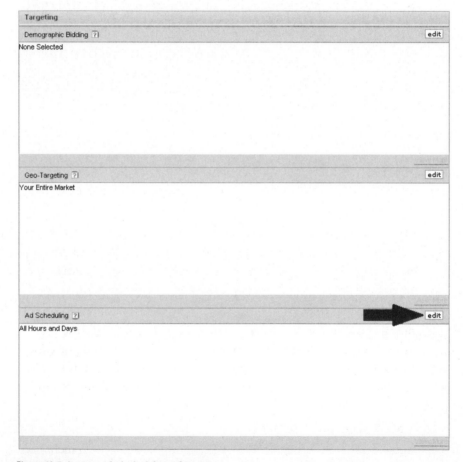

Figure 12.7 Location of ad scheduling information

When you click Edit, a new screen that looks like Figure 12.8 pops up within your browser. Here you can you adjust when your ads will display and you can also create settings to adjust keyword bids automatically for certain days or times of the day.

316

CHAPTER 12: MONTH 9—MIGRATE YOUR CAMPAIGN TO MICROSOFT AND YAHOO!

Specify a schedule to run your ads, or allow them to run anytime. Learn More

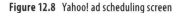 = Scheduled Days and Times   **Display ads based on:** The audience's time zone (default) Edit

	SUNDAY ☑ All Day	MONDAY ☑ All Day	TUESDAY ☑ All Day	WEDNESDAY ☑ All Day	THURSDAY ☑ All Day	FRIDAY ☑ All Day	SATURDAY ☑ All Day
Midnight							
1:00 a.m.							
2:00 a.m.							
3:00 a.m.							
4:00 a.m.							
5:00 a.m.							
6:00 a.m.							
7:00 a.m.							
8:00 a.m.							
9:00 a.m.							
10:00 a.m.							
11:00 a.m.	Bid + 0%	Bid + 0%	Bid + 0%	Bid + 0%	Bid + 0%	Bid + 0%	Bid + 0%
Noon							
1:00 p.m.							
2:00 p.m.							
3:00 p.m.							
4:00 p.m.							
5:00 p.m.							
6:00 p.m.							
7:00 p.m.							
8:00 p.m.							
9:00 p.m.							
10:00 p.m.							
11:00 p.m.							

Note: Ad scheduling accuracy is not guaranteed and may vary depending on the accuracy of user information, as well as other factors.

Figure 12.8 Yahoo! ad scheduling screen

By deselecting the All Day check box under a certain day, you can completely stop your ads from displaying on that day. If you want to automatically increase your keyword bids, follow these steps:

1. Click on any day of the week, and a screen similar to Figure 12.9 appears.

2. On this screen, you can select the hours for which the automated bid adjustments will start and end. In the Start field, put the time when bids should increase. In the End field, put the time at which your bids should lower back down.

3. Set the amount by which your bid will increase. You have two options to automatically increase your keyword bids: Bids can be increased by a specific percentage of your original bid (for example, increase bids by 10 percent), or bids can be increased by a specific dollar amount (for example, increase bids by $1). In Figure 12.9, we have chosen to increase our bids by 20 percent from 8 a.m. to 1 p.m.

4. Click Apply to set your automated bids.

You're not finished yet. You'll notice in Figure 12.10 our bids have been increased by 20 percent during the appropriate time. However, because of a poorly crafted default setting in Yahoo!, you may accidentally pause your ads for the other times of the day. The white space on this screen indicates the times that your ads are *not* showing.

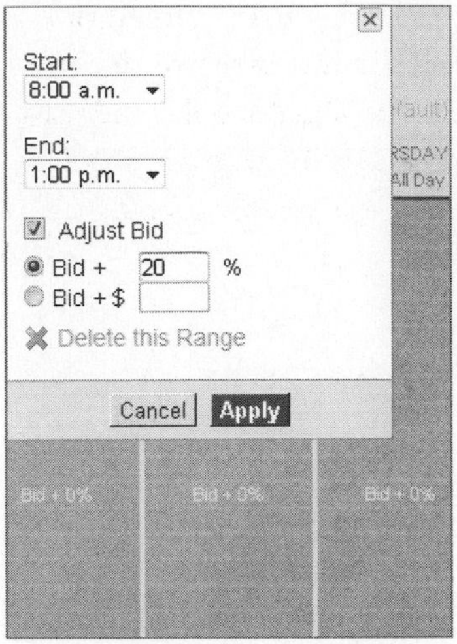

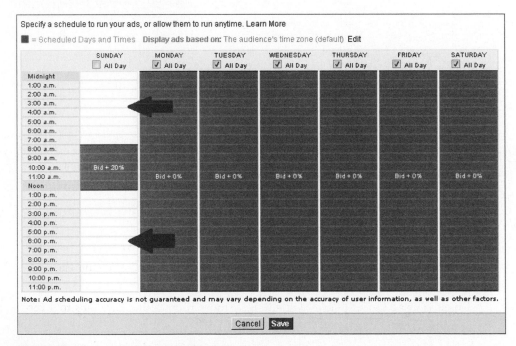

Figure 12.9 Bid adjustments for time of day

Figure 12.10 Ads are not displaying during these times.

5. Click on the times of the day when your bids should not be affected by the auto-mated bid increase. For the example in Figure 12.10, you need to click on the specific day and choose to run your ads from midnight to 8 a.m. with no bid

changes. You then need to select the other times for which you ads should run without bid changes, which is from 1 p.m. to midnight in this example. When you are finished, the bid adjustments for this specific day should look similar to Figure 12.11. In this example, we've adjusted only one day. To adjust bids for any other day, you'll have to complete each of these steps again for each day.

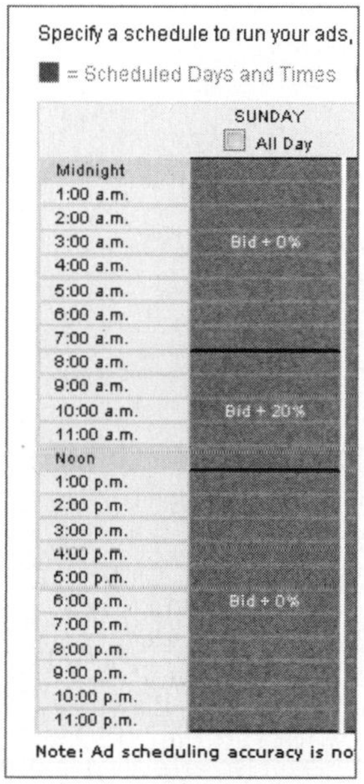

Figure 12.11 Bid increases based on time of day

You can only automatically increase bids—you can't automatically decrease them. So, if you want to only increase bids, you're finished. However, if you want to decrease them as well, you can use the following workaround procedure:

1. Determine how high and low you want to adjust your bids.

2. Determine when these bid changes should automatically occur.

3. Within your ad groups, set your bids to the lowest price that you want them to be throughout the day.

4. Adjust your ad scheduling so that you have more room to increase bids to a certain degree.

With this process, your actual keyword bids are set to the lowest price you want pay, and you can use the ad scheduling tool to increase bids. This way, you are increasing and decreasing bids in order to enhance your conversion rate.

How Time Zones Affect Ad Scheduling

There is one major difference between the Yahoo! and Google AdWords ad scheduling tools: time zones. Ad scheduling within your AdWords campaigns is based on the time zone you have chosen for your account. Your ad will appear during the hours in your account rather than the time zone of the area you are targeting.

For example, let's say your account time zone is set to U.S. Pacific standard time (PST), but your ads are targeting New York, which is three hours ahead. So if you schedule your ads to run from 12 p.m. to 4 p.m., they will run from 12 p.m. to 4 p.m. in areas within the PST zone, but they will appear from 3 p.m. to 7 p.m. in New York.

Within the Yahoo! ad scheduling tool, you can use one of the following two options in order to target different times of the day:

Your account time zone: If you select this option, your ad schedules and bid adjustments will be based on the time zone you specified for your account. This means that prospective customers outside of your account time zone may see your ads earlier or later than your scheduled period (depending on the difference between their time zone and your account time zone).

Audience time zone: With this option selected, your ad schedules and bid adjustments will be based on the time zone of the prospective customers to whom your ad is displayed.

We suggest that you choose the audience time zone. This will make your life easier because you won't have to do the time zone adjustments in your head—Yahoo! will do it for you.

Friday: Demographic Targeting

Google AdWords offers demographic bidding, but it's available only for the content network. Yahoo!'s demographic bidding is available for both sponsored searches and the content network. You can target by age and gender. You can adjust these settings at the campaign level within your account. Within the settings screen of any campaign, you will find the Demographic Bidding option in the Targeting section, as shown in Figure 12.12.

Similar to ad scheduling, you can only increase bids for select demographics. Also, you can block only one age group (0–17). Figure 12.13 shows an example of a campaign that increases bids for women who are between 40 and 59 years old.

However, before you begin adjusting your demographic targeting, you need to make sure that you're making the right changes. You need to have the data that supports your changes. To acquire this data, you should first activate demographic reporting within each campaign by selecting the Turn On Demographic Reporting for This Campaign check box, as shown in Figure 12.13. When you enable this check box, the system starts tracking your marketing data for each of the demographic groups available on the Demographic Bidding page. If you do not select this check box, the system will not track the information, the performance report for demographics will have no information, and you'll need to wait in order to gain enough data to make a statistically valid decision.

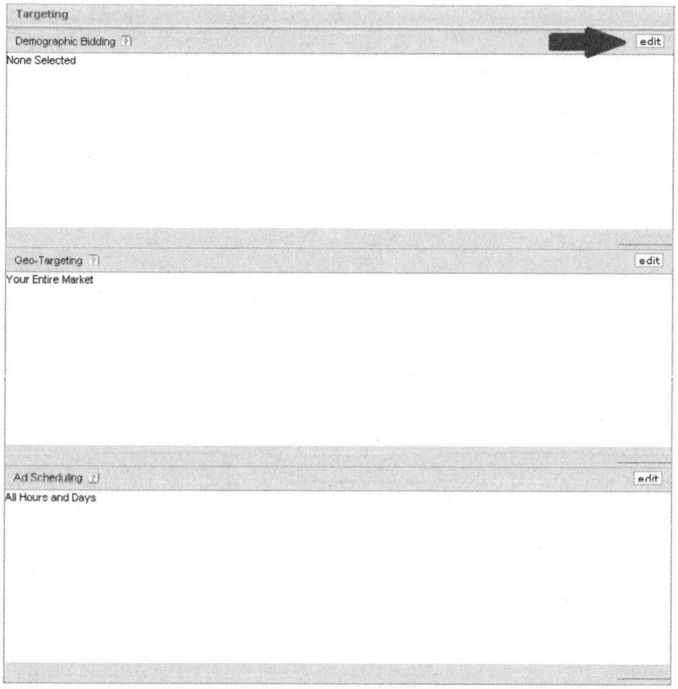

Figure 12.12 Click Edit to adjust your demographic bidding.

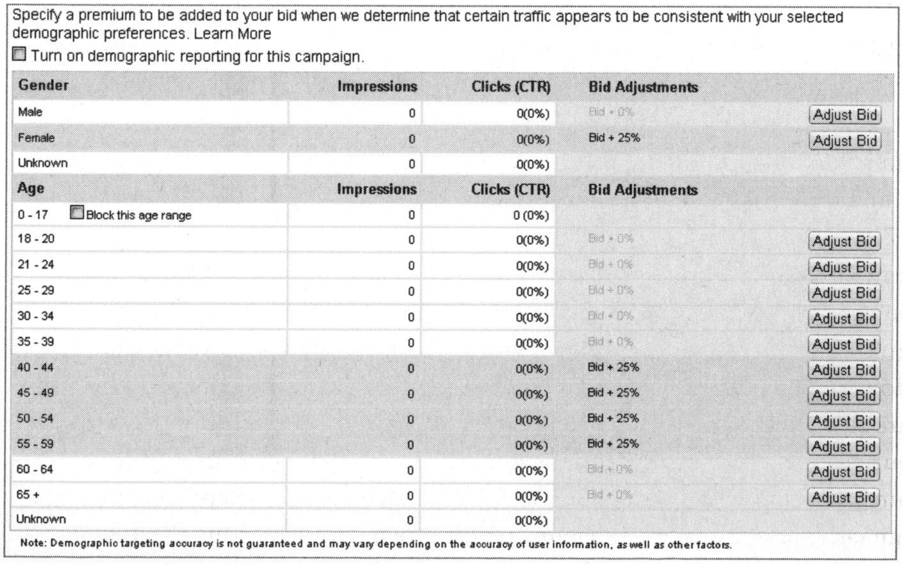

Specify a premium to be added to your bid when we determine that certain traffic appears to be consistent with your selected demographic preferences. Learn More

☑ Turn on demographic reporting for this campaign.

Gender	Impressions	Clicks (CTR)	Bid Adjustments	
Male	0	0(0%)	Bid + 0%	Adjust Bid
Female	0	0(0%)	Bid + 25%	Adjust Bid
Unknown	0	0(0%)		

Age	Impressions	Clicks (CTR)	Bid Adjustments	
0 - 17 ☐ Block this age range	0	0 (0%)		
18 - 20	0	0(0%)	Bid + 0%	Adjust Bid
21 - 24	0	0(0%)	Bid + 0%	Adjust Bid
25 - 29	0	0(0%)	Bid + 0%	Adjust Bid
30 - 34	0	0(0%)	Bid + 0%	Adjust Bid
35 - 39	0	0(0%)	Bid + 0%	Adjust Bid
40 - 44	0	0(0%)	Bid + 25%	Adjust Bid
45 - 49	0	0(0%)	Bid + 25%	Adjust Bid
50 - 54	0	0(0%)	Bid + 25%	Adjust Bid
55 - 59	0	0(0%)	Bid + 25%	Adjust Bid
60 - 64	0	0(0%)	Bid + 0%	Adjust Bid
65 +	0	0(0%)	Bid + 0%	Adjust Bid
Unknown	0	0(0%)		

Note: Demographic targeting accuracy is not guaranteed and may vary depending on the accuracy of user information, as well as other factors.

Figure 12.13 Bid changes based on demographics

Reporting Differences in Yahoo!

We're not going to sugarcoat this: The Yahoo! interface is severely lacking in reporting capabilities. We don't want this section to turn into a list of gripes, so we'll do our best to stay constructive. You may be a little spoiled by the breadth of reporting within Google AdWords, so Yahoo!'s reporting is going to seem pretty slim in comparison.

The first major drawback to Yahoo!'s reporting is their lack of time-frame adjustments. By this we mean that you can't break down a specific time frame into different measurements such as weeks or months. For example, if you want to see how your campaigns performed each month over the last 12 months, you would have to run a separate report for each month. You can't tell Yahoo! to run the report for the past 12 months and show you the data for each month. This makes running thorough reports very cumbersome.

The following performance reports are available in the Yahoo! interface:

- Ad Performance
- Daily Performance
- Keyword Performance
- Performance by Geographic Location
- Performance by Gender Demographic
- Performance by Age Demographic
- Scheduling Performance
- Daily Spending Performance
- URL Performance

The other drawback to Yahoo!'s reporting is that you can't select specific campaigns or ad groups that you'd like to review. For example, if you want to run a report for a certain ad group in order to see how your ad text testing is going, you will need to run an Ad Performance report for the entire account. You have to export this report into Excel and sort it accordingly. To drill down on a specific ad group or keyword, you have to complete this process for every report you run.

Basically, you can extrapolate enough data out of Yahoo!'s reporting tools to manage and optimize your account, but they don't make it easy. So, how can you get around a lot of these shortcomings? Use Google Analytics!

We highly recommend that you tag your ad text destination URLs so that you can track your Yahoo! PPC performance in Google Analytics. You may be thinking, "I don't need to tag my URLs, because I can already see Yahoo! traffic in my Analytics reporting." You would be thinking correctly, but you're seeing only organic traffic from Yahoo!. If you don't tag your paid search URLs, Google Analytics will aggregate all of your Yahoo! traffic, and you won't be able to parse out your paid search performance. This is why tagging your destination URLs is so important.

Tagging your URLs properly for Google Analytics isn't difficult. In fact, Google has a tool to help with this specific task: the Google Analytics URL Builder. The tool is pretty straightforward, as you can see in the following screenshot.

Step 1: Enter the URL of your website.

Website URL: *

(e.g. *http://www.urchin.com/download.html*)

Step 2: Fill in the fields below. **Campaign Source**, **Campaign Medium** and **Campaign Name** should always be used.

Campaign Source: *   (referrer: google, citysearch, newsletter4)

Campaign Medium: *   (marketing medium: cpc, banner, email)

Campaign Term: (identify the paid keywords)

Campaign Content: (use to differentiate ads)

Campaign Name*:   (product, promo code, or slogan)

Step 3

[Generate URL] [Clear]

You can follow these steps to build a tracking URL for your PPC campaign:

1. Type your landing page URL into the Website URL field.

2. Type your campaign source into the Campaign Source field. In this example, our campaign source is Yahoo!.

3. Type **CPC** into the Campaign Medium field (because we are tagging a cost-per-click campaign).

4. Type a keyword into the Campaign Term field if you want to track individual keywords.

5. Type a name for the ad version into the Campaign Content field if you want to track your ad performance.

6. Type the name of the campaign into the Campaign Name field.

This tool is easy to use, but if you need to tag a lot of URLs within your account, it can be time-consuming. You may need a much faster way to get your paid Yahoo! account to appear in Google Analytics. Under the Administration tab in your YSM account, click the Tracking URLs link. Here you can turn on the tracking URL feature. Now, Yahoo! will append your destination URLs with a snippet of tracking code.

Week 34: Understand Microsoft adCenter Differences and Advantages

Microsoft has been putting a lot of time into enhancing the look and usability of the adCenter interface, and it shows. adCenter used to be sluggish, clunky, and somewhat difficult to navigate. However, the interface has received a few facelifts, and Microsoft has done a good job of making adCenter relatively user-friendly. With the launch of Bing, the reworking of adCenter, and the partnership with Yahoo!, Microsoft is finally attempting to dramatically increase Bing search volume.

Monday: Keyword Match Types

The keyword match type options that are available for Microsoft adCenter are identical to those for Google AdWords. The four match types are broad, phrase, exact match, and negative match. With the exception of negative match, AdCenter designed their match types to be functionally equivalent to Google's implementation. Here's a quick rundown of how each match type works:

Broad match: This match type casts the widest net. With broad match, your keywords can trigger ads for search queries that match your keyword exactly, or queries that contain just a portion of your keyword.

Phrase match: With phrase match, the search queries need to contain your entire keyword in order to display your advertisement. Users can tack on anything before or after the keyword, but as long as the keyword is present, your ad will display.

Exact match: This match type performs just as you think it would, given its name. The search query has to match your keyword exactly in order to trigger an advertisement.

Negative match: Of all three major search engines, adCenter has the most complicated negative keyword system. We'll give it to you in simplified terms. There are three tiers at which negative keywords can be added to your account:

Campaign: Campaign-level keywords apply to all keywords in a specific campaign.

Ad group: If you load keywords at the ad group level, they supersede the campaign-level keywords.

Keyword: You can associate negative keywords with specific keywords. The keywords added at this level of your account will supersede the ad group–level and campaign-level negative keywords.

Tuesday: Geo-targeting

Similarly to Google AdWords and Yahoo!, you can target specific geographic locations. Before you launch any PPC campaign, you need to seriously consider where you want your ads to appear. You should take full advantage of the geo-targeting tools in each PPC interface in order to generate the most qualified traffic possible.

Unlike Google, which allows only campaign-level geo-targeting, within adCenter you can alter your geographic settings at the campaign or ad group level. Being able to geo-target at the ad group level can help you get very granular with your targeting, and *granularity* is one of the core drivers for a successful PPC campaign. You want to be as specific and targeted as possible.

To access your geo-targeting information, click the Change Settings link next to the campaign name. Establishing your geographic targeting settings is fairly logical. As you can see in Figure 12.14, you can select any country in the world to target.

As you make your selections for where you'd like to target your ads, you'll see a green box displayed within the map on the screen. Figure 12.15 shows what the screen looks like after Indiana and Illinois are selected.

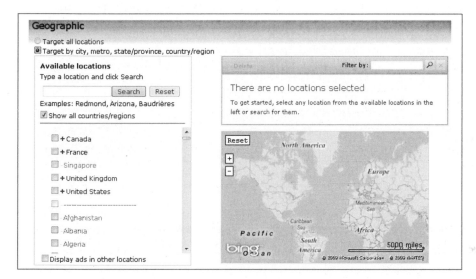

Figure 12.14 adCenter geo-targeting

Figure 12.15 Geo-targeted states

Be careful when you are altering your geo-targeting at the campaign and ad group levels. The campaign-level targeting overrides the ad group–level targeting. For example, if you choose to target Indiana and Illinois at the campaign level, but you target Alabama at the group level, your ad group–level targeting will not be valid. If you want to start specific locations at the ad group level, you should select the Target All Locations option at the campaign level.

Wednesday: Ad Types and Lengths

The ad type options in adCenter are similar to those in Yahoo!—adCenter also sticks with the basics. The only options available within the interface are text ads and mobile ads. Figure 12.16 shows adCenter's Create Text Ad screen and its options.

Figure 12.16 adCenter Create Text Ad options

adCenter text ads can contain 25 characters in the headline, 70 characters in the body copy, and 35 characters in the display URL. The headline length is the same as in Google AdWords, but the body copy parameter is similar to the one in Yahoo!. You are provided with a 70-character block, and you don't have to worry about creating two lines of copy with 35 characters each. Working with just a 70-character block makes writing PPC ads so much easier. (Google could learn a thing or two from Yahoo! and Microsoft on this particular topic. Are you listening, Google? Hello?)

Mobile ads are also available in adCenter. Writing great mobile ads can be a challenge, mainly because the character count is so limited. As you can see in Figure 12.17, advertisers are allowed 18 characters for the headline and 18 characters for the ad text. How are you supposed to make a meaningful connection with your target audience in such a small space?

Figure 12.17 adCenter mobile ads

To write relevant, action-orientated mobile ads, there are a few tactics you can employ. Here is a quick strategy list:

Keyword-rich: As with any PPC ad, you have to make sure that your ad is highly relevant to a user's query. Making sure that your mobile ad is keyword focused will boost your relevancy to the user. With such limited space, you're likely to get only one keyword in your ad, so make sure it's the most important, root keyword that is in the ad group.

Desired result: As you saw in Figure 12.17, the word *buy* is used in the example ad title, because that's ultimately what we want the user to do (buy our coffee). So, we are already setting up our conversion action.

Call to action: You have the option to display your phone, website, or both within your mobile advertisement. Whichever path will lead to a higher conversion rate is where you should direct your mobile user. If users are more likely to convert on the phone, display only your phone number. If they are more likely to convert on your website, you should display your website. Or you can cover all your bases and display both.

When you choose to include your website within your mobile ad, you'll notice that adCenter gives you the option to also include the contact information from your free business page. An adCenter business page is a web page that is specifically formatted for display on a mobile phone or other mobile device. If you don't have your own mobile-enabled website to link to from your mobile ads, you can create and link to a business page instead. You can see the mobile ad options in Figure 12.18—a very helpful resource!

CHAPTER 12: MONTH 9—MIGRATE YOUR CAMPAIGN TO MICROSOFT AND YAHOO!

328
■

Create mobile ad ?

ⓘ Mobile ads are displayed on the search network only.

Ad title: Buy Gourmet Coffee
18 characters maximum   Insert dynamic text

Ad text: Call For Coffee Deals.
18 characters maximum   Insert dynamic text

Include this contact information in the ad:
○ My phone number ?
○ My website ?
⦿ My phone number and website

Use the contact information from my **free business page** ?
Create a business page

Business name: Great Coffee Company
20 characters maximum

Phone number: (555) 555-5555
10 characters maximum

Display URL: www.GreatCoffee.com
The URL shown in your ad.   20 characters maximum   Insert dynamic text

Destination URL: ⦿ http:// ○ https:// ○ Keyword destination URL
The webpage that customers go to when they click your ad.   www.GreatCoffee.com

Mobile ad preview:

Ad: Buy Gourmet Coffee
Call For Coffee Deals.
Call(555) 555-5555
www.GreatCoffee.com

The mobile ad preview shows you approximately how your ad will appear on a mobile device. Line breaks and ad size will vary depending on the ad's position on the webpage and the user's mobile device.

Learn how to customize your ad using dynamic text.

Figure 12.18 adCenter mobile ad options

Depending on the nature of your business, product, or service, you'll have to decide which call-to-action tactic you should employ. This also depends on what you want to achieve with your mobile ads.

Dynamic Keyword Insertion in adCenter

adCenter has the most sophisticated dynamic keyword insertion features. Here you have the ability to automatically insert into your ad text a keyword that matches the user's query, which is similar to how the Google AdWords and Yahoo! systems function. adCenter also offers a dynamic parameter feature that is solely unique to this system.

First, we'll review the keyword insertion tool. For the following example, we dynamically inserted a keyword from our ad group into the headline of our advertisement. You will want to include default text in case the search query is too long and will not fit into the allotted space. The default text comes after the colon in the expression {keyword: }. In the example, the default text is *Coffee*.

Create text ad ✕

Ad title: Great Prices on {keyword:Coffee}
25 characters maximum   Insert dynamic text

Ad text: Coffee from around the world. Free shipping. Bu
70 characters maximum   Insert dynamic text

Display URL: www.GreatCoffee.com
The URL shown in your ad.   35 characters maximum   Insert dynamic text

Destination URL: ⦿ http:// ○ https:// ○ Keyword destination URL
The webpage that customers go to when they click your ad.   www.GreatCoffee.com

1017 characters maximum   Insert dynamic text

Text ad preview:

Great Prices on {keyword:Coffee}
Coffee from around the world. Free shipping. Buy now!
www.GreatCoffee.com

Line breaks and ad size will vary depending upon the ad's position on the webpage and the viewer's browser settings.

Learn how to customize your ad using dynamic text.

Default text within an advertisement should be at least a portion of the root keyword for each ad group. In the preceding example, our ad group is Gourmet Coffee, so the default text is *Coffee* in order to make sure that our ads are relevant for the user's search query if their keyword cannot be dynamically inserted.

The other dynamic insertion feature is the placeholder or parameter function: the {param} setting. This option can be used in conjunction with the dynamic keyword insertion tool. You can make your ads even more targeted and relevant using this feature.

To use the {param} tool, you first need to insert the variables into your keywords. This tells adCenter how you want to populate your ads with the dynamic text. In the following example, we entered the variables that we'd like to display within our ads—which in this case is a price of $9 for our gourmet coffee keywords.

| Keyword (100 characters max.) | Negative keywords (1024 characters max.) | Search match types | | | Displays on content network | Destination URL {param1} (1022 characters max.) | Placeholder {param2} (70 characters max.) | Placeholder {param3} (70 characters max.) |
		Exact	Phrase	Broad				
buy gourmet coffee online		☐	☐	☐	Yes		$9	
gourmet coffee		☐	☑	☐	Yes		$9	
roasted gourmet coffee		☐	☑	☐	Yes		$9	

< Back   Continue >

For example, you could create an ad that looks similar to this:

> Buy {keyword:Gourmet Coffee}
> {keyword:Gourmet Coffee} from around
> the world. Starting at {param 2}. Buy now!
> www.GreatCoffee.com

And when a user searches on the phrase *roasted gourmet coffee*, this is how our ad will appear on Bing:

> Roasted Gourmet Coffee
> Organic gourmet coffee from around
> the world. Wide variety. Buy now!
> www.GreatCoffee.com

Just remember, even though each {param} variable can each contain 70 characters the ad title cannot exceed 25 characters and the ad text cannot exceed 70 characters. So, when you're using placeholders in the ad title or ad text, be careful not to exceed these limits.

Aside from displaying the parameter variables within your ad texts, you can also dynamically generate destination URLs by using this feature. Within the Keyword tab (shown in the previous example), you can insert destination URLs for keyword-level destination URL tracking.

Also, you can dynamically insert your keywords into the destination of your ad. The purpose of this tool is to track which keywords generated the click, and you can track the user interaction of that particular term. We don't use the parameter feature in the destination URL, because there are other ways to get this information. If you're using an analytics package, you won't need to use this tool.

Thursday: Ad Scheduling

Microsoft adCenter offers an ad scheduling feature like the other paid search interfaces. The implementation of this feature looks slightly different from the others, but the end result is the same: It enables you to schedule when your ads will appear on Bing.

You can set up this feature at either the campaign or ad group level. We suggest that you set up ad scheduling at the campaign level. If you have ad groups that perform better at different times of the day, it may be an indication that you need to rethink your account structure in order to be as targeted as possible with your ad groups and campaigns. Also, managing a campaign that has 20 ad groups that are all running at different times, for example, is an optimization nightmare.

So, now that you're convinced that setting up ad scheduling at the campaign level will work best, let's discuss how to adjust these settings. On the Campaign screen, click the Change Settings link. Within your campaign settings screen, you'll notice that there are Additional Settings options, as shown in Figure 12.19.

330
■

CHAPTER 12: MONTH 9—MIGRATE YOUR CAMPAIGN TO MICROSOFT AND YAHOO!

Figure 12.19 adCenter additional settings for scheduling

This is where you can adjust your ad scheduling settings. You will need to adjust your settings first by the day of the week and then by the time of day. When you select the Target by Day of Week option, you'll get a screen that looks similar to Figure 12.20.

Figure 12.20 adCenter day-of-the-week targeting

In this figure, you can see that we've chosen to display our ads during the work week. Here you can automatically increase your bids for certain days of the week. If you find that one day of the week converts better than the others, you may just want to increase all of the bids in your campaign on that given day and be finished. However, in most cases you'll find that certain times on specific days convert best. So, you'll want to adjust your hourly settings as well.

There is less control when adjusting hourly targeting in adCenter than there is with the Google AdWords or Yahoo! interface. As shown in Figure 12.21, your hourly bids can be adjusted in blocks of early morning, morning, midday, afternoon, evening, and late night. For example, as you can see in the figure, we are going to increase all bids within this ad group by 20 percent between the hours of 7 a.m. and 2 p.m.

Figure 12.21 adCenter hourly ad scheduling options

As a result of these settings, our ads will run Monday through Friday, but not on the weekends. On the weekdays, our bids will increase automatically between 7 a.m. and 2 p.m. By default, Microsoft adCenter ad scheduling is based on the time zone of the user, so you don't have to worry about adjusting time zones as you have to do in Google AdWords.

After you make your ad scheduling changes, you will be sent back to the campaign settings page. Click Save to implement your changes.

Friday: Demographic Targeting

Within the campaign settings section, you can adjust your demographic targeting to target your ads to specific age groups and genders. You can set your demographic targeting at either the campaign level or the ad group level.

The data used for demographic targeting comes from information reported by MSN customers. The information that MSN uses to determine the demographic profile of a user is determined by the information that individual provided when registering the Microsoft Windows product. This information is also pulled from a user's Windows Live/Bing account. Unfortunately, this can create a layer of complexity when targeting by demographics—for example, if a wife fits into the targeted demographic, but the Windows software is registered to the husband.

In Figure 12.22, we are targeting both genders and all age groups. We are automatically increasing bids on females who are ages 25–49. These selections are our target market, but that doesn't mean we want to completely remove males or other age groups from our distribution. Within this screen, you first need to choose to whom you want to display ads, and then adjust that bid. In this example, we want to target both genders, but we want to bid higher on women.

Figure 12.22 adCenter demographic targeting options

Reporting Differences in adCenter

The reporting features in adCenter aren't as robust as in Google AdWords, but they are much better than in Yahoo!. Here is a quick list of the available performance-based reports in adCenter and a short description of each:

Account Performance: Statistics at the account level

Campaign Performance: Statistics at the campaign level

Ad Group Performance: Statistics at the ad group level

Keyword Performance: Statistics for individual keywords

Destination URL Performance: Statistics for your landing pages

Ad Performance: Statistics for your ad texts

Ad Dynamic Text Performance: Statistics to track your dynamic insertion performance

Website Performance: Statistics about ad groups that contain bids on website placements in the content network

332

CHAPTER 12: MONTH 9—MIGRATE YOUR CAMPAIGN TO MICROSOFT AND YAHOO!

Publisher Performance: Statistics about the websites where your ads appear, which is useful for determining whether certain websites should be excluded from your campaign

Search Query: Statistics about specific search query strings

Age Group and Gender Targeting: Statistics by ad group, campaign, age group, and gender

Geographical Location Targeting: Statistics by ad group, country/region, state, and metro area

The reporting in adCenter is similar to that in Google AdWords in the sense that after you select the report you want to run, you can then select the proper campaigns or ad groups. Within these reports, you can alter your columns and layout so that your report contains only the data that you select (a very nice feature). You can also set up template reports that can run automatically and be sent directly to your inbox (another nice feature).

One major shortcoming of reporting within adCenter is that you can pull data for only the previous 92 days. This severely limits the ability to monitor and optimize PPC accounts properly. Hopefully, adCenter will address this issue so that PPC managers will be able to gather as much data as they need to make the right decisions about their account.

Week 35: Create Google AdWord Exports

Every activity that takes time away from campaign optimization and strategy can hinder your ability to improve your PPC performance. Migrating your account structure between search engines used to take up a considerable amount of time, with an equal portion of frustration. Each of the "big three" search engines have made exporting and importing campaigns less painful.

Monday and Tuesday: Creating the Root CSV from AdWords Editor

Exporting out of Google AdWords is now relatively easy. The release of AdWords Editor was met with much rejoicing from PPC managers around the world, and it's what we use to export an AdWords campaign.

AdWords has numerous ways in which you can export your account. The root menu in Figure 12.23 shows that you can export your account into a few different formats: a Comma-Separated Values (CSV) file, which is compatible with Microsoft Excel; a ZIP file, which is typically used for archiving purposes; or an AEA file, which is an AdWords Editor Archive file that's great for sharing AdWords campaigns among individuals who don't have access to the same AdWords account. AEA files can also be helpful when mirroring AdWords accounts, because these files are for exclusive use within AdWords Editor.

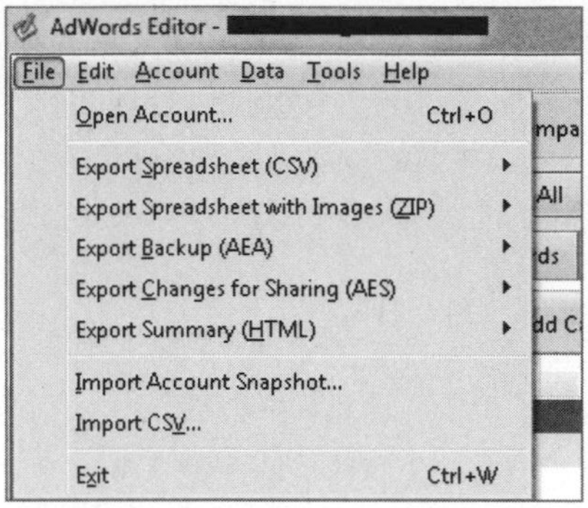

Figure 12.23 AdWords Editor export options

If you plan to move elements of one AdWords campaign into another, exporting an AEA file is your best bet. If you plan to export your AdWords account and upload it into Yahoo! or MSN, you'll want to use a CSV file.

Because the objective of this section is to discuss the exporting of AdWords accounts and uploading them into adCenter and Yahoo!, we'll focus on creating CSV files. As you can see in Figure 12.24, you have a few options to export a CSV file: You can export the whole account, selected campaigns and ad groups, the current campaign, the current ad group, or the current view.

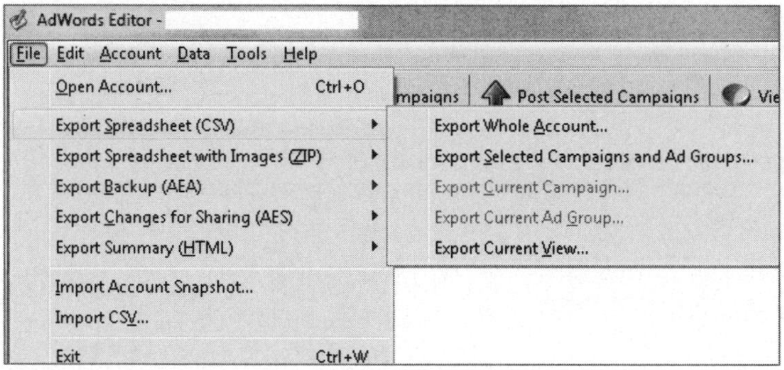

Figure 12.24 AdWords Editor Export Spreadsheet (CSV) options

If you want to upload the entire account into another search engine, the Export Whole Account option is your best bet. However, if you want to export only certain campaigns or ad groups, the second option should be your choice. The options for exporting the current campaign, ad group, and view mean that you will export the data that is currently displayed on the AdWords screen.

The great thing about AdWords Editor is that exporting your campaign is basically a one-step process. Just make your selection from the export options, and the result will be a file on your computer that contains all of the data within your Google AdWords account.

334

CHAPTER 12: MONTH 9—MIGRATE YOUR CAMPAIGN TO MICROSOFT AND YAHOO!

Wednesday and Thursday: Creating the Root CSV from Yahoo!

Yahoo! has made exporting campaigns rather user-friendly as well. You have two easy-to-use options for exporting the data from your account: You can create an export directly from the Yahoo! Search Marketing interface or from the Yahoo! Search Marketing Desktop application.

To create an export directly from the Yahoo! Search Marketing interface, click the Download Campaigns button within the Campaign tab of your account. When you click this button, you're given the option to include keywords, include ads, and/or exclude deleted components, as shown in Figure 12.25.

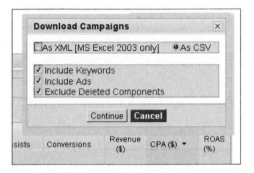

Figure 12.25 Yahoo! Download Campaigns export options

You can also export your Yahoo! campaign from the Yahoo! Search Marketing Desktop application. This is Yahoo!'s version of AdWords Editor. On the front page of the application, just click the More Actions link and select the Export to Bulksheet (CSV) option from the drop-down menu, as shown in Figure 12.26.

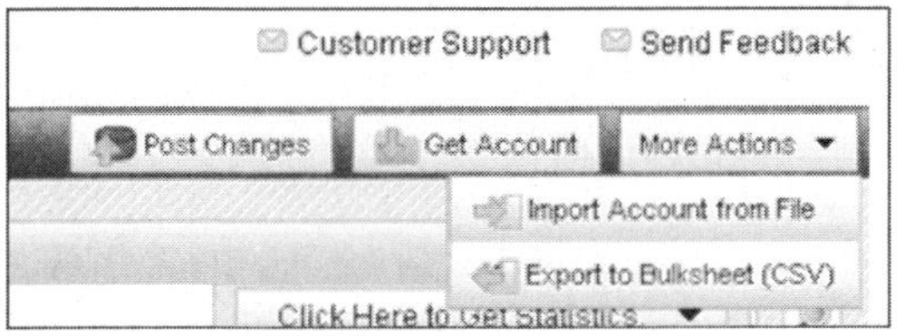

Figure 12.26 YSM Desktop exporting

Friday: Creating the Root CSV from adCenter

We would like to take a moment to say that the adCenter team has taken very positive strides in making their interface and various tools much more user-friendly and effective. One of the recent feathers in their proverbial cap is Microsoft adCenter Desktop. With this program, campaign creation and optimization have been streamlined, and exporting and importing are very logical processes.

To export your campaign within adCenter Desktop, you just need to click the Export button within the main navigation toolbar, as shown in Figure 12.27. Clicking this button will automatically download a CSV file that contains all of the information within your account.

Figure 12.27 adCenter Desktop exporting

Week 36: Upload and Fine-Tune

In week 35 we walked you through the process of exporting your campaign from each of the big three search engines. Now we'll walk you through the process of uploading your AdWords account into Yahoo! and Microsoft adCenter. But first, here are some reasons you would want to do this:

Uniformity of reporting: Mirroring your campaigns so that their campaign structure and name conventions are parallel will save you a lot of time and headaches when trying to sift through data.

Ease of management: If your campaigns are mirrored, you'll have a better understanding of how your ad groups are structured in each search engine, and you'll be able to access data within your campaigns faster and easier.

Time saved during account creation: This one is pretty obvious. You don't want to build an AdWords account from scratch and then turn around and do the same exact thing in adCenter and Yahoo!.

Monday: Uploading into Yahoo!

We'll give Yahoo! credit where it's due. They realized that the majority of PPC managers wanted to create and optimize their Google AdWords account and then upload their campaigns into the Yahoo! PPC interface. So, Yahoo! has made importing your AdWords account relatively painless. Building on last week's lesson, you should already have an exported CSV file of your AdWords account (via AdWords Editor). Follow these steps to upload your CSV file to Yahoo!:

1. On the main overview page of your Yahoo! Search Marketing account, click the Import Campaigns button, as shown in Figure 12.28.

2. On the following page, click the Import a Yahoo! or Third-Party File button.

3. On the next page, you can search for the file that needs to be uploaded. Just click Browse to search for your file, as shown in Figure 12.29.

CHAPTER 12: MONTH 9—MIGRATE YOUR CAMPAIGN TO MICROSOFT AND YAHOO!

336
■

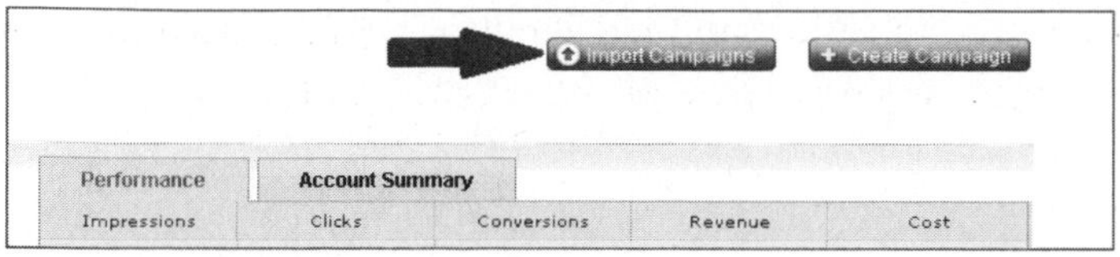

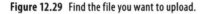

Figure 12.28 Click to upload files into Yahoo!.

Import Campaigns

Account:

Select the account from above for importing

Select Yahoo! or Third-party File to Import

Browse your computer for your Yahoo! or third-party file (such as Google Adwords).

Note:Quality scores and targeting settings will not be imported.

Browse for file:

[ ] [Browse...]

[Import File]

Figure 12.29 Find the file you want to upload.

4. Decide how to handle duplicate campaigns. The drop-down menu provides these options: Create a New Campaign, Merge Campaign Data, Overwrite an Existing Campaign, and Ignore Duplicate Campaign. When you're uploading new campaigns into a new account, you can select Create New Campaign, because there will be no duplicated campaigns due to the import.

5. Select the Advanced Options that you want displayed on the screen, as shown in Figure 12.30. We suggest you select Include Excluded Words (Negative Keywords) and Include Campaign Budget. If you have keywords with destination URLs, you'll want to select Include Keyword Destination URLs.

6. Click the Import File button, and your file uploads. A status bar appears on the page to let you know the progress of your upload.

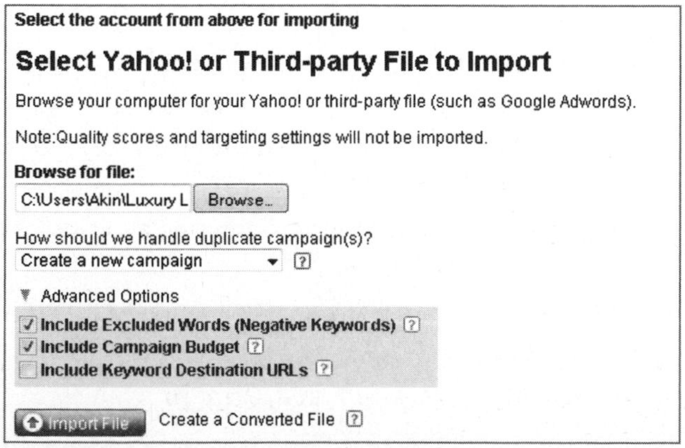

Select the account from above for importing

Select Yahoo! or Third-party File to Import

Browse your computer for your Yahoo! or third-party file (such as Google Adwords).

Note:Quality scores and targeting settings will not be imported.

Browse for file:

C:\Users\Akin\Luxury L [Browse...]

How should we handle duplicate campaign(s)?

[Create a new campaign ▼] [?]

▼ Advanced Options

[✓] **Include Excluded Words (Negative Keywords)** [?]
[✓] **Include Campaign Budget** [?]
[ ] **Include Keyword Destination URLs** [?]

[Import File] Create a Converted File [?]

Figure 12.30 Advanced options for Yahoo! file uploads

CHAPTER 12: MONTH 9—MIGRATE YOUR CAMPAIGN TO MICROSOFT AND YAHOO!

338
■

This completes the upload process of the Yahoo! Search Marketing interface. You can upload your AdWords into Yahoo! via the Yahoo! Search Marketing Desktop as well. To use the YSM Desktop tool to upload your file, just follow these steps:

1. On the upper-right side of the YSM Desktop tool, click the More Actions button. A drop-down menu is displayed. Select the Import Account from File option, as shown in Figure 12.31.

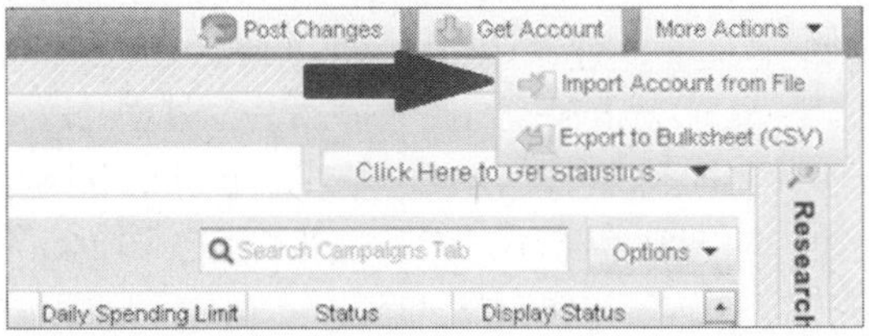

Figure 12.31 Location of the import tool in YSM Desktop

2. You will be prompted to choose a file for upload. Select your AdWords Editor CSV file.

3. After you've selected the proper file, your upload will begin. A screen similar to Figure 12.32 appears, and this is where you can spot-check your data for any possible errors. In this screen, you can also select the type of file that you are uploading, such as Google, MSN, or Other.

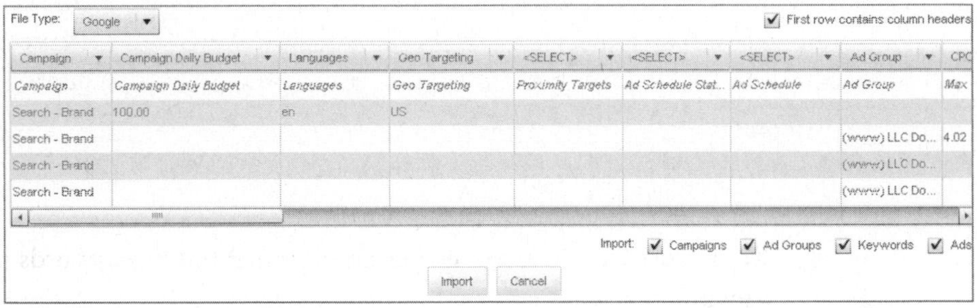

Figure 12.32 Spot-check your upload for errors.

4. Click the Import button to begin your file upload. If there are errors in the upload, a screen displays to notify you of this.

Tuesday: Troubleshooting Yahoo! Import Problems

We have been discussing the differences between Yahoo! Search Marketing and Google AdWords throughout this chapter, and these differences will be apparent when you upload your AdWords account into Yahoo! Here is a list of issues to look for when uploading into Yahoo!:

Singular/plural keywords: Your AdWords keyword list is going to be truncated significantly when uploaded into Yahoo!. This is because keywords are managed differently in Yahoo!. In AdWords, you should have the singular and plural versions of your keywords. Because of Yahoo!'s advanced match, a keyword can match for both the singular and plural variations. Either the singular or plural variation of your keywords will be removed when uploaded into Yahoo!. There doesn't appear to be a standard method of removing these variations. Sometimes the singular is removed from the upload, and sometimes the plural version is removed. As long as both versions aren't removed during the upload, you'll cover both the singular and plural version with one keyword.

Match types: As we discussed earlier in this chapter, Yahoo! has three match types: standard, negative, and advanced. However, AdWords has four (broad, phrase negative, and exact). If you have all three AdWords match types within an ad group, two variations will be removed upon uploading. There is no getting around this because match type is set at the ad group level. In Yahoo!, you can't have multiple match types in one ad group. Be prepared. Only one version of your keyword will be uploaded, and it will be targeted to the ad group–level match type.

Content limitations: There are varying limits between Yahoo! and AdWords as to how many campaigns, ad groups, and keywords you can have in an account. You will receive errors during your upload if your AdWords account exceeds the Yahoo! account limits. Here are the content thresholds for each account:

Yahoo!:
- Campaigns: 20 campaigns per account
- Ad groups: 1,000 ad groups per campaign
- Keywords: 1,000 keywords per ad group; 100,000 keywords per account

Google AdWords:
- Campaigns: 25 campaigns per account
- Ad groups: 2,000 ad groups per campaign
- Keywords: 2,000 keywords per ad group; 50,000 keywords per account

Geo-targeting: Geo-targeting settings will not be carried over between accounts. The default setting for Yahoo! is to target their entire network, which includes the United States and Canada. If you need to target a specific area, these settings will need to be adjusted.

Ad scheduling: Ad scheduling settings will transfer between accounts. Yahoo!'s default setting is to show ads at all times of the day. If you want to target specific days or specific times of the day, these settings will need to be adjusted.

Wednesday: Uploading into adCenter

Again, we applaud the adCenter team for making the uploading of a Google AdWords campaign a pretty clean process. As you saw in the example in the previous section, the Yahoo! upload feature can be slightly "buggy." In comparison, the adCenter Desktop tool is pretty bug free. There is nothing better than when an application works with no (or very few) complications.

As you can see in Figure 12.33, you can click the Import button contained within the main navigation of the Desktop tool. Just select the file you want to upload, and you're finished. On the screen that follows, you can check all of the elements of your upload for errors, which we highly suggest you review just to make sure everything uploaded properly.

Figure 12.33 adCenter Desktop tool Import link

Thursday and Friday: Reviewing Campaign Uploads

After you've completed your Google AdWords import into Yahoo! or adCenter, you should go through and double-check everything within your account. Yes, these tools work well for the most part, but that doesn't mean they're completely void of errors.

Here is a quick checklist of account elements that you should review after you've completed your uploads:

Campaign structure: Review all of your campaigns and ad groups to make sure everything is in the right place. This may seem elementary, but we've seen ad groups end up in the wrong campaign, keywords end up in the wrong ad groups, and ads end up in the wrong ad groups.

Destination URLs: You should have changed all of your destination URLs before you uploaded your CSV file. However, now is a good time to review all of your tracking URLs to make sure that they are correct. Tracking parameters within URLs are extremely sensitive—if one character is incorrect, your analytics program may not track your performance accurately.

Keyword bids: Always check your bids after an upload. Not too many errors occur with bid prices, but this is another delicate element of your campaign. It's easy for a $0.28 bid to get switched to a $2.80 bid (or even $28.00!). Just to be safe, review your bids.

Account settings: Account settings can be silent killers. It's relatively easy to spot an out-of-place keyword or ad text, but an incorrect account setting may not be so apparent. Here are the campaign and ad group settings that you should check after an account upload:

Daily budgets: Make sure all of your daily budgets are correct at the campaign level.

Ad rotation: Yahoo!'s default setting is to optimize your ad delivery. This means they take the ad with the highest CTR and display it more often than the others in your ad group, which makes conducting ad text testing nearly impossible. So, you need to go into your campaigns and switch this setting.

adCenter doesn't allow you to change the ad rotation option. It automatically begins to show ads with a higher CTR. This is a shortcoming of the adCenter system.

Distribution channels: Make sure all of your search-network and content-network settings are correct. Removing your ads from a distribution channel by accident can cause many missed impressions, but activating a distribution you didn't mean to activate can negatively affect your cost per lead and ROI.

Ad scheduling: Your file uploads will not contain any ad scheduling data, so you'll need to update these settings manually.

Appendix A: Advanced AdWords Editor

The early days of pay-per-click (PPC) advertising provided few opportunities for efficiency or portability in account management. For a time, you were limited to adding keywords, writing ad copy, and adjusting bids within each account's web interface. Then came the spreadsheet, which opened up opportunities for bulk changes and offline editing. PPC management through bulk spreadsheets was a huge step forward, but it was time-consuming and error prone. It wasn't until Google released the AdWords Editor desktop application that PPC advertisers experienced true efficiency and portability.

What Is AdWords Editor?

AdWords Editor is an easy-to-use desktop application that directly connects advertisers with their Google AdWords PPC campaigns. Enter your login and password, and all of your campaigns, ad groups, keywords, ads, and bids are downloaded to your computer. After your PPC campaigns have been downloaded, you have the freedom to edit or add to any element offline and then upload those changes to your Google AdWords account at your convenience. Figure A.1 displays how your account appears when you open AdWords Editor.

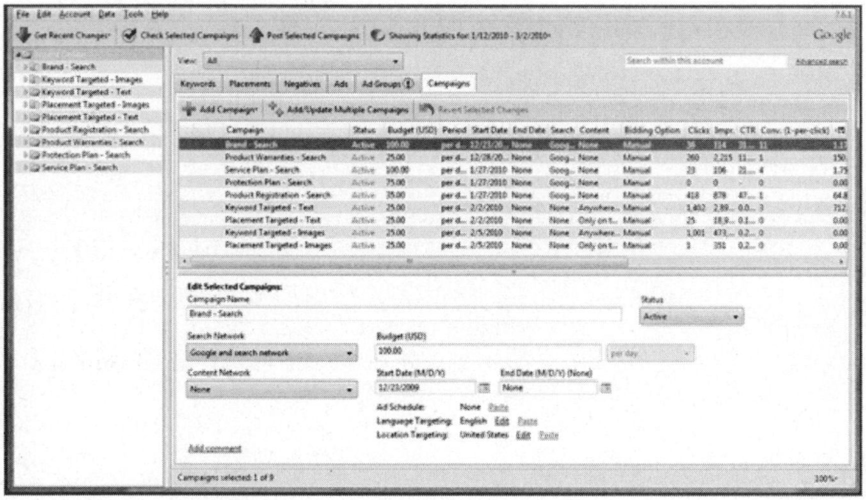

Figure A.1 The opening screen of AdWords Editor

We think AdWords Editor is extremely beneficial to PPC managers. Here is a short list of things it allows you to do:

- Work offline to make important PPC account changes anytime, anywhere.
- Manage multiple Google AdWords accounts from your desktop.
- Save time on crucial PPC management tasks through mass offline editing and keyboard shortcuts.
- Clean up your accounts and expand them with helpful, built-in duplication and research tools.
- Export your campaigns for backup, sharing, or uploading into other PPC platforms.

Getting Started

Before you can get started, you need to download AdWords Editor. Google provides this software for free at www.google.com/intl/en/adwordseditor/index.html, as shown in Figure A.2. The software is available in Windows and Macintosh versions.

Figure A.2 You can download Google AdWords from here.

Opening and Downloading Your Account

After you have downloaded and installed AdWords Editor, the next step is to download your AdWords account into the application. Choose File from the main menu and then click Open Account. Click the Add Account button and follow Google's instructions for entering your AdWords e-mail and password, as shown in Figure A.3. The first time you open an AdWords account within AdWords Editor, all of your campaigns are automatically downloaded into the application.

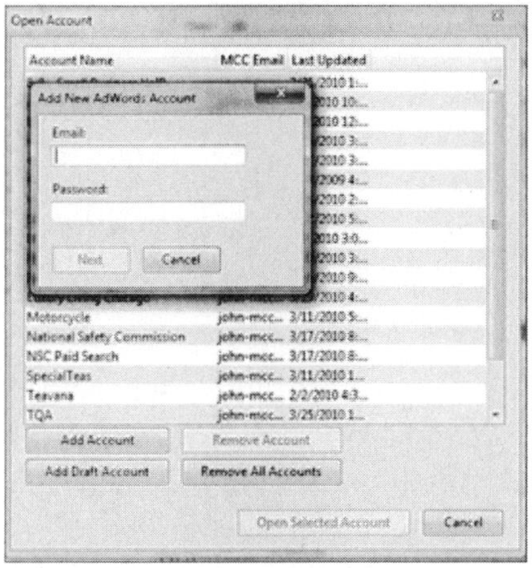

Figure A.3 Opening your AdWords account

Other than the very first time you use AdWords Editor, it is important that you use the Get Recent Changes function before beginning each subsequent editing session. This ensures that you are working with the latest campaign information. This is especially important if more than one person has been working on the account, thereby increasing the likelihood that changes have been made to the account since the most recent AdWords Editor session.

For similar reasons, it's important to avoid having two or more people using AdWords Editor at the same time. If a set of changes is uploaded immediately before another, the second set may overwrite the first. Close communication among PPC campaign managers can help avoid this.

Downloading Campaign Statistics

To ensure that you are making the best changes for your PPC campaigns, it is always a good idea to view account performance statistics. AdWords Editor enables you to download your campaigns' performance data to do just that. In the main menu of AdWords Editor, find the View Statistics button and click it. You can choose from preset date ranges or set a custom date range for which statistics will be downloaded, as shown in Figure A.4.

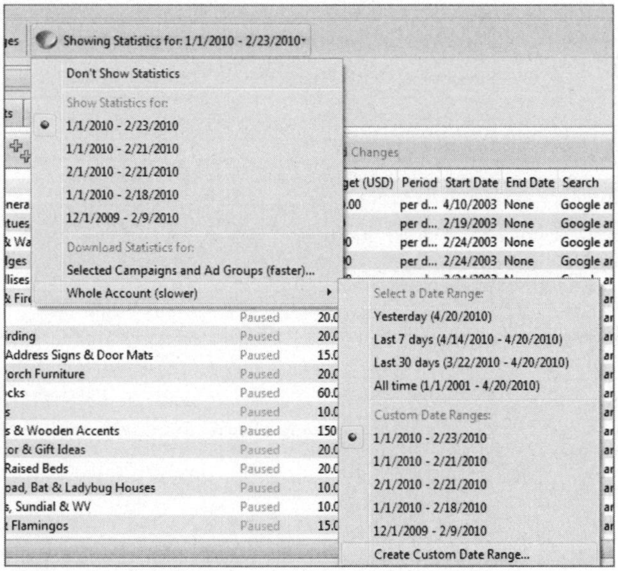

Figure A.4 Set a time range for downloading statistics.

Uploading Your Changes

The changes you make within AdWords Editor remain on your computer until you upload them into AdWords. Therefore, it is important to post your changes every time you've finished making them to ensure that your work is going into your live account!

To ensure a smooth process, uploading your changes has two stages:

Stage 1—check changes: Clicking the Check Changes button in the main menu forces AdWords Editor to review the changes you've made for errors and to be sure they follow AdWords' rules and guidelines. The Check Changes with AdWords dialog box, shown in Figure A.5, informs you of anything that will not be uploaded to your account so you can fix it.

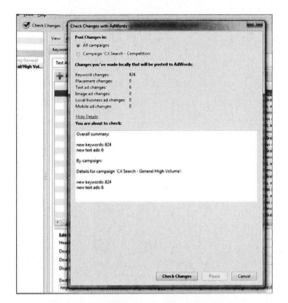

Figure A.5 Check changes before posting to AdWords.

Stage 2—post changes: Clicking Post Changes in the main menu starts the process of uploading your changes to AdWords, as shown in Figure A.6. Depending on the volume of changes made, this process can be either really fast or really slow. Either way, AdWords Editor displays its progress and notifies you of any changes that did not post correctly to your account.

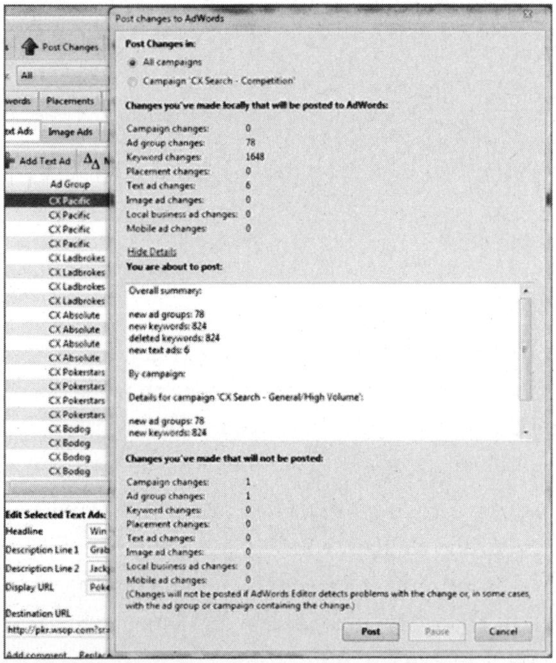

Figure A.6 Posting changes live to your AdWords account

Navigating, Editing, and Expanding Your Campaigns

On the left side of the AdWords Editor application you'll see a browser-style list of your account's campaigns and ad groups. Initially, you will see your campaigns listed alphabetically—both active and paused campaigns. Each campaign name is preceded by a triangle indicating that it can be expanded to show the ad groups it contains. As shown in Figure A.7, clicking the triangle opens that campaign to display all of the ad groups (once again, both active and paused).

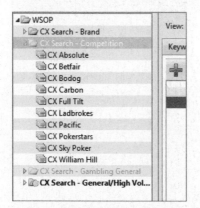

Figure A.7 AdWords Editor uses a browser-style navigation system.

Although the left-hand campaign navigation goes to only the ad group level, rest assured that you can access every level of your AdWords account. Directly under the main menus, there are six tabs that enable you to access each layer of data from campaigns to keywords to ads, as shown in Figure A.8.

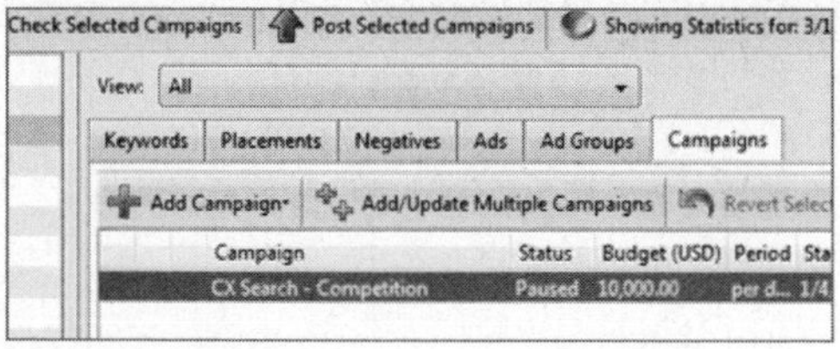

Figure A.8 Use tabs to navigate within campaigns.

Campaigns

Under the Campaigns tab, you can edit existing campaigns and their settings as well as create new campaigns from scratch.

Editing Campaign Settings

Editing a campaign within AdWords Editor means you can manipulate the network, budget, status, language, and location targeting, as shown in Figure A.9. Other

settings, such as Ad Rotation, cannot be managed within AdWords Editor—you'll
need to set these from within the AdWords web interface.

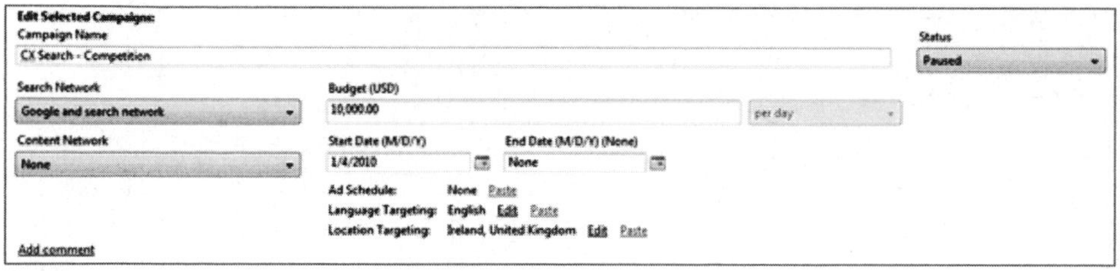

Figure A.9 Edit existing campaign settings directly from AdWords Editor.

Creating Campaigns

To create a new campaign, click the Add Campaign button. You can choose either cost-
per-click (CPC) or cost-per-thousand-impressions (CPM) bidding strategies, depending on your needs, as shown in Figure A.10. It is even possible to create the campaign
in *Draft* status, meaning the campaign remains within AdWords Editor until you are
ready to upload it.

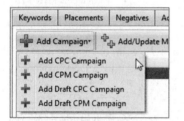

Figure A.10 Options for creating new campaigns

After choosing CPC or CPM, you are presented with a screen to begin building
your campaign, shown in Figure A.11. This screen is identical to the one used for editing campaigns, except you are also given the option to create the first ad group.

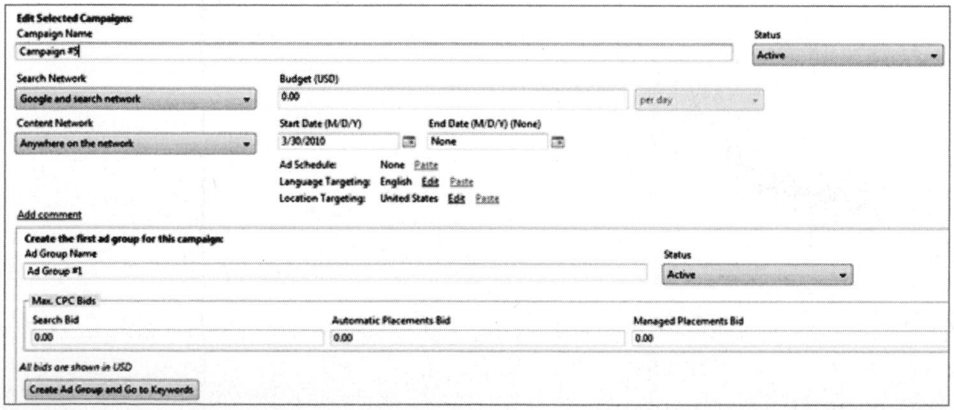

Figure A.11 The screen for creating a new AdWords campaign

Ad Groups

The process for editing and creating ad groups works almost the same way as the process for campaigns. The only real difference is the options available.

Editing Ad Group Settings

In AdWords Editor, you can quickly change the settings of existing ad groups by clicking on the ad group name. This opens the interface where you can change the name, status, or ad-group-level bids, as shown in Figure A.12.

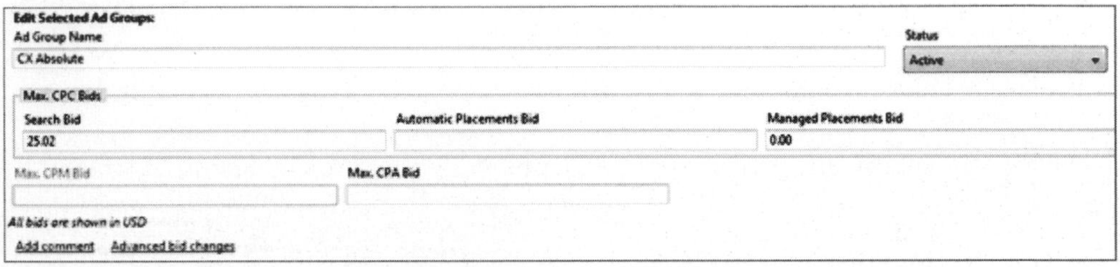

Figure A.12 Edit existing ad groups in AdWords Editor.

Creating Ad Groups

Creating new ad groups is as easy as finding and clicking the Add Ad Group button, shown in Figure A.13. This opens the ad group editing interface, where you can create the name, set the active status, and set ad-group-level bids, as shown in Figure A.14.

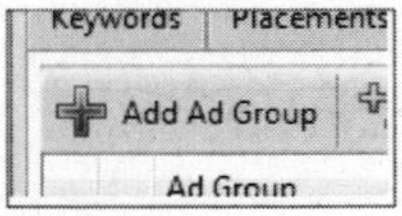

Figure A.13 Create a new ad group.

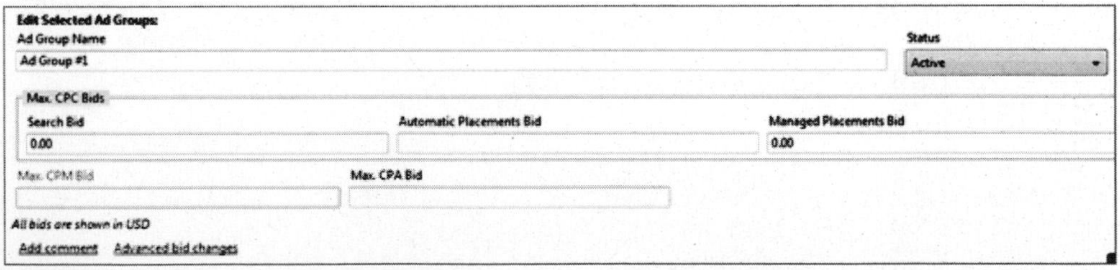

Figure A.14 Manage the settings for a new ad group.

Keywords

Manipulating keyword lists is one of the most time-consuming PPC management tasks. AdWords Editor is a real time-saver in that regard, whether you are adding a single keyword or thousands of keywords.

Editing Keyword Settings

In AdWords Editor, you can edit the settings of an existing keyword by simply clicking on the keyword. As shown in Figure A.15, you can edit the keyword itself, change match type or status, and update its bid and destination URL. If you need to edit multiple keywords, simply highlight all of the keywords—and when you make a change in the settings, it will be applied to all highlighted keywords.

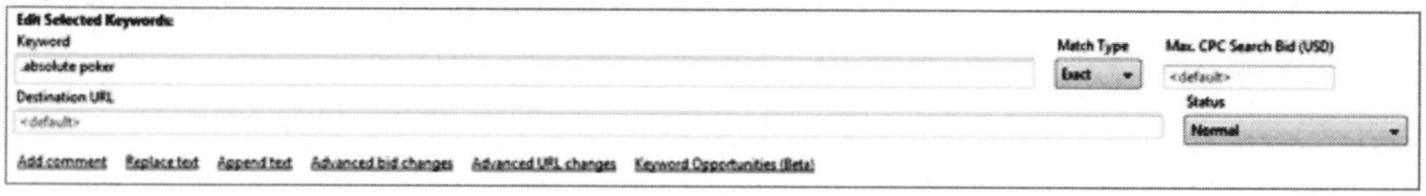

Figure A.15 Edit a keyword and its bid, match type, URL, and active status.

Adding Keywords

You can add new keywords one at a time by clicking Add Keyword, shown in Figure A.16. A more efficient method is to choose Make Multiple Changes, as shown in Figure A.17, and add as many keywords as you'd like. If you don't specify a match type, bid, or destination URL, AdWords Editor will set the Match Type to Broad Match, use the default ad group settings for Bid, and use the Destination URL from your ads, as shown in Figure A.18.

Figure A.16 Add a single new keyword.

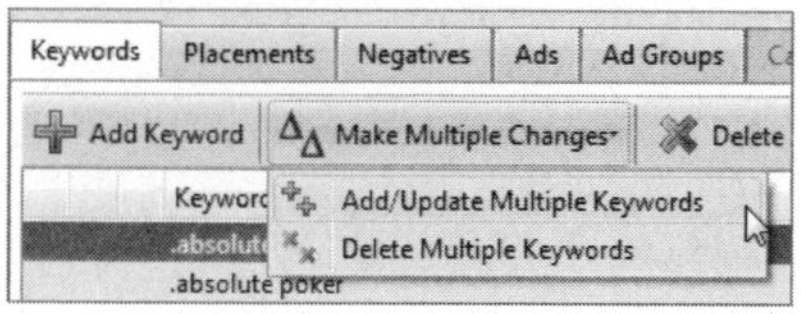

Figure A.17 Add multiple new keywords.

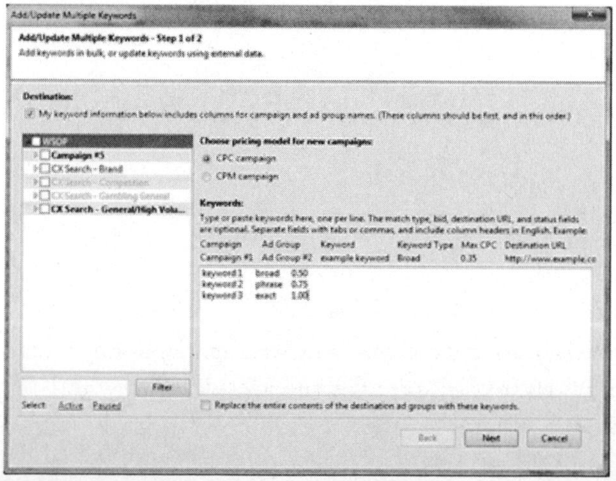

Figure A.18 Include match type and bid details with new keywords.

Keyword Research

Keyword research is an activity that often requires you to work in a separate application or web browser and then copy and paste keywords into a PPC account or a spreadsheet. AdWords Editor brings the power of the Google Keyword tool to you *within* the AdWords Editor application via the Keyword Opportunities feature, shown in Figure A.19.

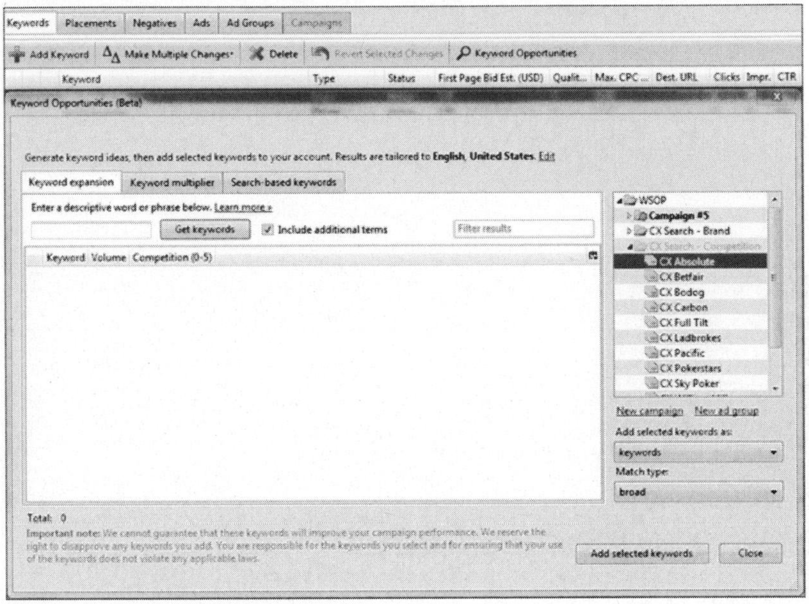

Figure A.19 The Keyword Opportunities tool

The options are as follows:

Keyword Expansion: Enter a term, and the Google Keyword tool returns a list of related keywords.

Keyword Multiplier: Use this tool to combine two or three lists of keywords into compound keyword phrases.

Search-Based Keywords: Insert a website URL, and this tool returns a list of keywords related to that website.

Placements

AdWords Editor enables you to manipulate your managed placements in campaigns targeted to Google's content network. Within AdWords Editor, you can edit, add, or remove placements just as you can with keywords. When adding a placement, remember that it can be a domain (such as example.com) or full URL (such as www.example.com/fun-stuff), which determines the granularity of your targeting. You can edit the placement itself, as well as the bid, the status, and the destination URL, as shown in Figure A.20 and Figure A.21.

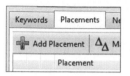

Figure A.20   Add new placements for the content network.

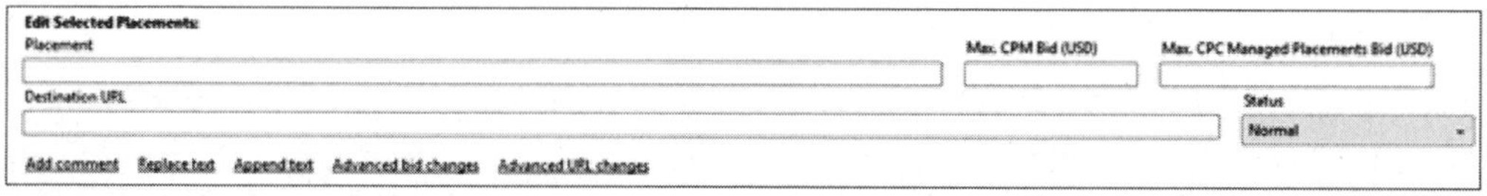

Edit Selected Placements:
Placement   Max. CPM Bid (USD)   Max. CPC Managed Placements Bid (USD)

Destination URL   Status
                                                                                                                             Normal

Add comment   Replace text   Append text   Advanced bid changes   Advanced URL changes

Figure A.21   Edit a placement's settings.

Negatives

The use of negative keywords and placements is one of the key skills necessary for expert PPC management. Fortunately, AdWords Editor includes features that make changing negative keyword and placement lists fast and easy.

When you click the Negatives tab, AdWords Editor displays an interface nearly identical to that for managing keywords. Clicking the Add Negative button opens a drop-down menu, shown in Figure A.22, from which you can choose to add a negative keyword or negative placement at the ad group level or the campaign level.

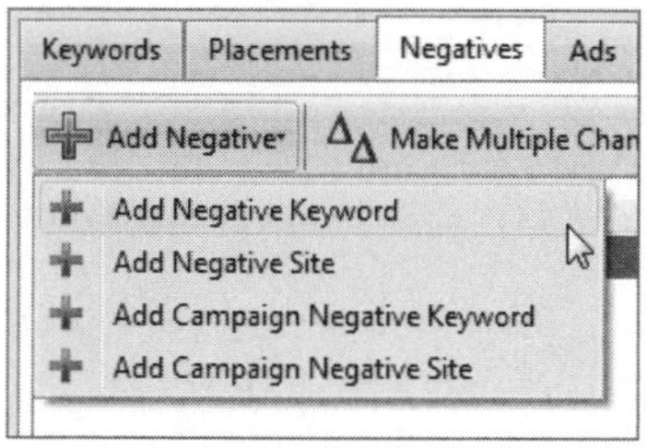

Keywords   Placements   Negatives   Ads

Add Negative▾   Make Multiple Chan

+ Add Negative Keyword
+ Add Negative Site
+ Add Campaign Negative Keyword
+ Add Campaign Negative Site

Figure A.22   Add negative keywords and placements to your campaigns.

After you have chosen to add a negative keyword or placement, you are presented with a dialog box like the one shown in Figure A.23, where you can manually enter the keyword or placement (and for keywords, a match type).

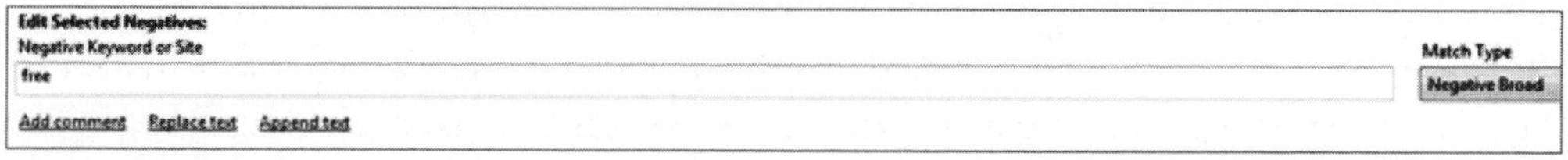

Edit Selected Negatives:
Negative Keyword or Site   Match Type
free   Negative Broad

Add comment   Replace text   Append text

Figure A.23   Edit a negative keyword and its match type.

Ads

Managing ads in bulk or adding or revising tracking parameters can be a tedious task when using the AdWords web interface, even with a spreadsheet. AdWords Editor greatly simplifies ad creation and editing. It provides a fast, intuitive interface for managing text ads, image ads, local business ads, and mobile ads.

Text Ads

Within the Ads section of AdWords Editor, the Text Ads tab is on your left, as shown in Figure A.24. Text ads are displayed as the default, because they are the most widely used ad format. Your ads will be displayed in rows, with each element in a separate column. This approach enables you to quickly sort your ads to compare performance data or make bulk changes. As you edit or create a new text ad, AdWords Editor displays an ad preview in real time as you type, as shown in Figure A.25.

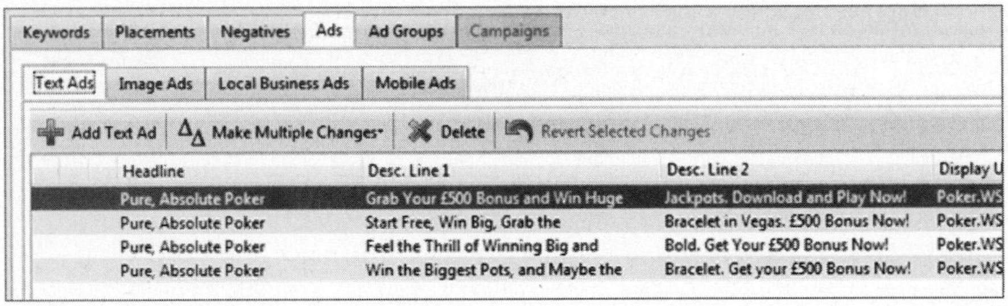

Figure A.24 This is where you review and manage text ads.

Figure A.25 Edit text ads with a preview as you type.

Image Ads

As shown in Figure A.26 and Figure A.27, you can upload and manage image ads directly from AdWords Editor. With static images, you are even shown an ad preview. (Figure A.26 depicts an animated ad and a Play button for previewing.)

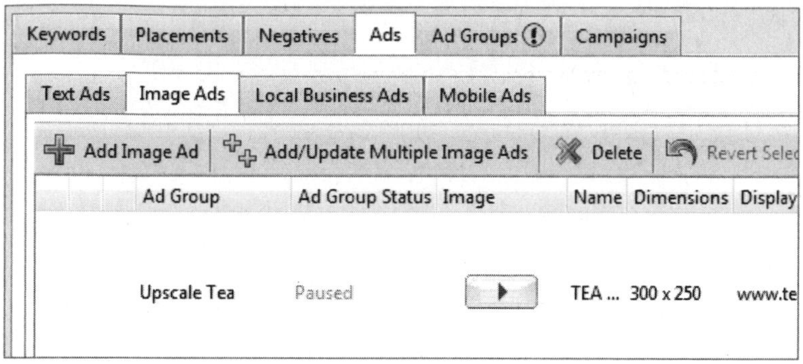

Figure A.26 Managing image ads in AdWords Editor

Figure A.27 Edit an image ad's display, destination URL, and active status.

Local Business Ads

A *local business ad* is an ad format that is tied directly to a business owner's Google Local Business Center account. This directs Google to display ads within Google Maps in reaction to searches for, or related to, your business. As shown in Figure A.28 and Figure A.29, local business ads include much more information than a standard text ad, including address, phone number, and business name. As with all ad types, AdWords Editor displays an ad preview as you create your ad.

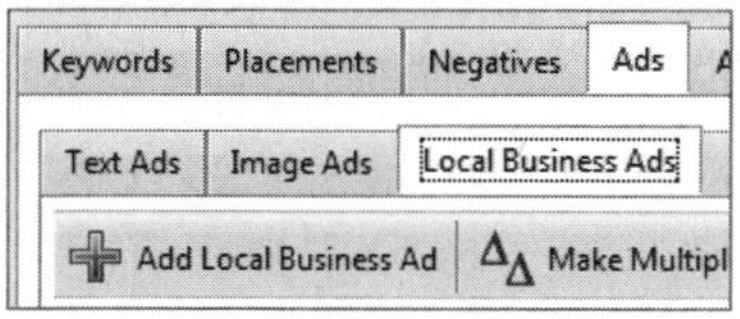

Figure A.28 Manage local business ads.

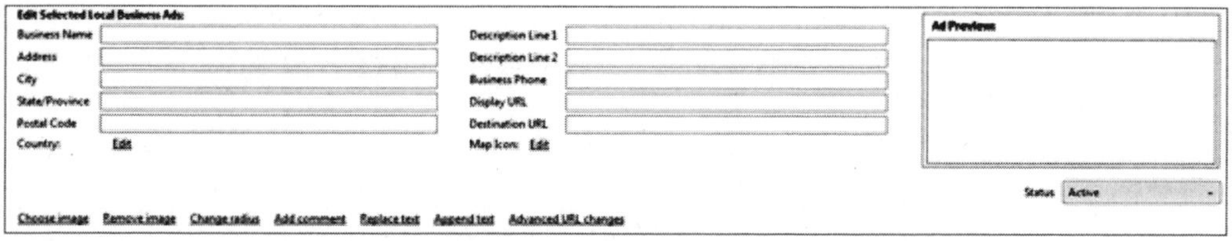

Figure A.29 Edit a local business ad's details with a preview as you type.

Mobile Ads

As shown in Figure A.30, mobile ads can be created and launched directly from AdWords Editor. AdWords Editor makes it simple to create mobile ads, and shows you a semi-realistic preview of the ad, shown in Figure A.31, while you type.

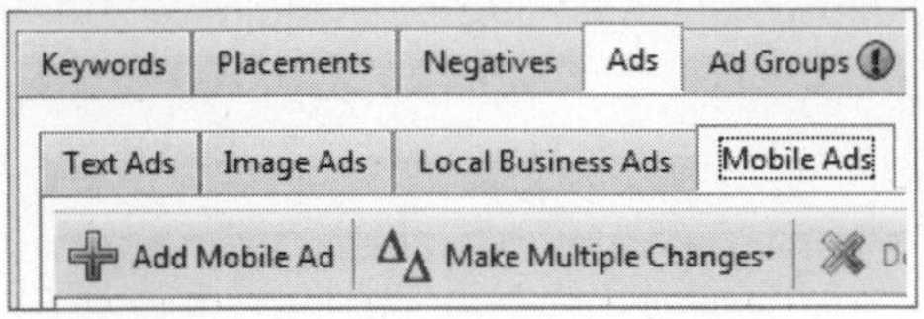

Figure A.30 Managing mobile ads in AdWords Editor

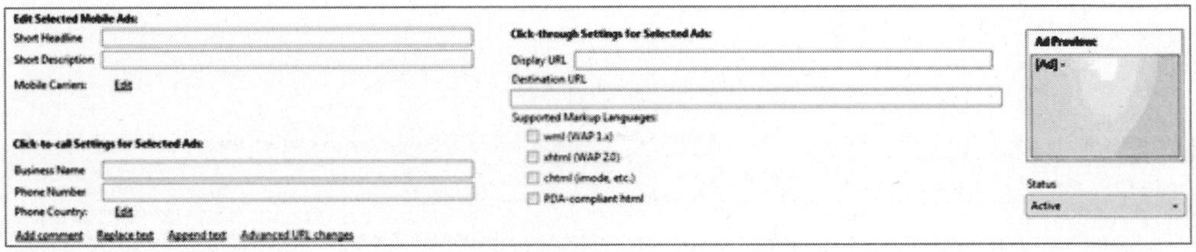

Figure A.31 Edit a mobile ad's details with a preview as you type.

Saving Time with AdWords Editor

One of the best features of AdWords Editor is the ability to use keyboard shortcuts, and more specifically, the standard Cut, Copy, and Paste keyboard shortcuts. These fundamental editing actions can be applied to any structural element of your account, keywords, ads, and even entire ad groups and campaigns.

Cut, Copy, and Paste can be applied by using these keyboard shortcuts:

Cut: Ctrl+X

Copy: Ctrl+C

Paste: Ctrl+V

If you have trouble remembering keyboard shortcuts, Google has included these functions in the menu system, shown in Figure A.32.

Here are some ways you can save time with Cut, Copy, and Paste when managing your AdWords PPC campaigns:

- Create exact copies of campaigns and ad groups, including ads and keywords, in seconds. This can be done within a single account or between multiple accounts that you are editing within AdWords Editor.

- Copy large groups of keywords to expand into new match types. For example, you can copy all of the broad-match keywords from an ad group, immediately paste them into the same ad group, and change the pasted keywords' match type to Exact by using the Match Type drop-down menu.

- Copy language and location settings at the campaign level and paste them into another campaign.

- Copy destination URLs and apply them to large groups of ads simultaneously.

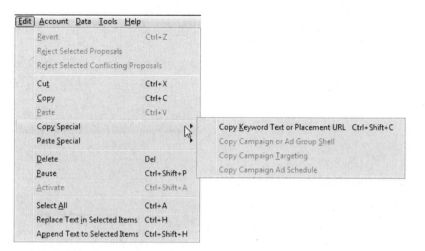

Figure A.32 Save time with Cut, Copy, and Paste.

Find and Replace

Another tremendous time-saver in AdWords Editor is the ability to find and replace text. This feature really becomes a time-saver when you need to make changes to large groups of keywords or ads. AdWords Editor lets you select all of your affected keywords and ads and then change a single word or phrase in all of them simultaneously.

There are two ways to use Find and Replace in AdWords Editor:

Keyboard Shortcut: Ctrl+H

Contextually: Depending on what component of your account you are editing, you will see a Replace Text link at the bottom of the screen whenever Find and Replace is available. Simply click the link and make your change.

Detailed Ad Text Changes

AdWords Editor has simplified the process of making ad text changes with powerful functions such as Append Text and Advanced URL Changes. Both can be accessed via links that appear at the bottom of the screen when ads are being displayed.

Append Text: This function enables you to add a word, phrase, or parameter to the beginning or end of any line in your ad, and to as many ads as needed simultaneously. Using the dialog box shown in Figure A.33, simply choose the section of your ad to be changed.

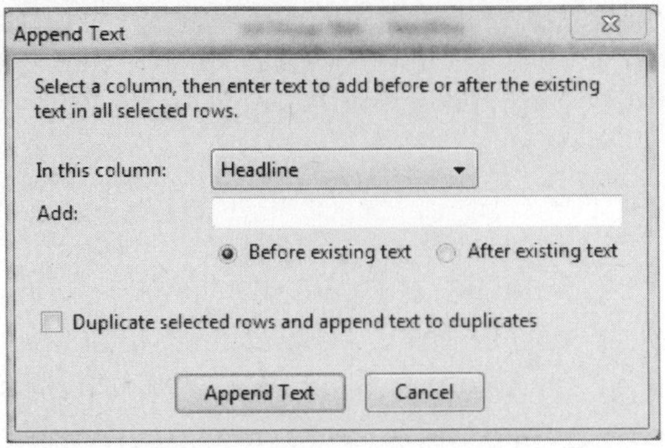

Figure A.33 Append text to any line of your text ads.

Advanced URL Changes: The options in Figure A.34 enable you to change (via links that appear at the bottom of the screen when ads are being displayed) all destination URLs simultaneously by replacing the entire URL, appending text to the end of the URL, or removing a parameter from within the URL. For example, if your site moves to a new domain, you can use this function to change all of your ad's URLs to point to the new domain.

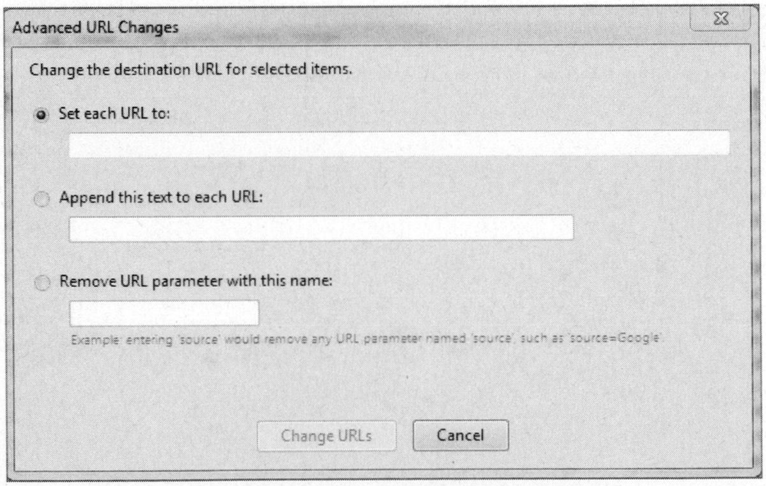

Figure A.34 Manage complex URL parameters with Advanced URL Changes.

Spreadsheets Are Still Important

In addition to its built-in functions, AdWords Editor has the capability to import and export files. Backing up precious data is easy. And you can export campaign elements to CSV, make changes by using powerful spreadsheet software such as Excel, and then import the data back into AdWords Editor—making complicated bulk campaign changes fast and simple.

Backup Files (AEA)

Although the chances of you losing your AdWords account information are slim, it's always a possibility. Fortunately, AdWords Editor allows you to create a backup copy of an entire AdWords account, which can be restored at any time. It's also a good idea to create a backup file before doing a major overhaul of your campaigns, running a short-term test, or making seasonal ad changes. We recommend saving backup files before starting any significant campaign editing.

Whatever the scenario, AdWords Editor makes it easy to do backups. Choose Export Backup (AEA) from the File menu. Save this file to your hard disk and rest assured that you can import this file and restore your account at any time.

Export Changes (AES)

If several people are working on the same AdWords account, you'll appreciate the feature that lets you export changes to share. The file that is generated can be imported by a team member running AdWords Editor. Choose Export Changes for Sharing (AES) from the File menu and share the file as needed. The recipient of the file has the opportunity to import it, examine the changes, and choose to accept (and upload) the changes or reject them.

Export Spreadsheet (CSV)

CSV is an all-purpose file format that enables you to export account data for many purposes. Among the most important are making global edits or porting your AdWords account structure to another PPC platform. Choose Export Spreadsheet (CSV) from the File menu to export in this format.

Global Edits

There could be many reasons for wanting to make global edits. For example, many PPC managers find it easier to make ad changes and create test variations by using spreadsheet software. Others prefer to examine and manipulate performance data (such as sorting it) by using a spreadsheet.

Upload to Yahoo! or MSN

Porting your AdWords accounts to Yahoo! Search Marketing or Microsoft adCenter is one tedious chore that can be sped up and simplified by using AdWords Editor. Yahoo! and Microsoft have recently made changes to the systems they use to import such spreadsheets.

Import Changes

When you are ready to apply changes from a spreadsheet or from a backed-up or shared file, you must import the file into AdWords Editor. For Backup (AEA) and Sharing (AES) files, choose Import Account Snapshot from the File menu. For CSV spreadsheets, choose Import CSV from the File menu. In both instances, AdWords Editor will prompt you with a dialog box to browse for your file to import.

Working with General Tools

AdWords Editor includes several useful utilities that let you find and edit duplicate keywords, segment your keywords into new ad groups, and expand keyword lists by performing keyword research.

Find Duplicate Keywords Tool

The bigger your PPC campaigns become, the higher the likelihood that you will accidentally place keywords into multiple ad groups or campaigns. Sometimes it is necessary to do this based on search instead of content campaigns, when creating uniquely geo-targeted campaigns or when targeting all three match types (broad, phrase, and exact). However, when you have the same keyword of the same match type competing against itself in multiple search ad groups, the wrong ad may appear when the keyword is matched with a search query. The Find Duplicate Keywords tool in AdWords Editor can help you avoid this.

To access this tool, choose Tools from the main menu and click Find Duplicate Keywords. You are presented with options for word order, match type, and the location of duplicates, as shown in Figure A.35. Although you can manipulate these options for your own needs, the most common settings are as follows:

Word Order: Strict word order

Match Types: Duplicates must have the same match type

Location of Duplicates: In the whole account

This tool enables you to see search keywords that are competing with each other. If you have more than one geo-targeted campaign, you should change the Location of Duplicates setting to In the Same Campaign (across Ad Groups)."

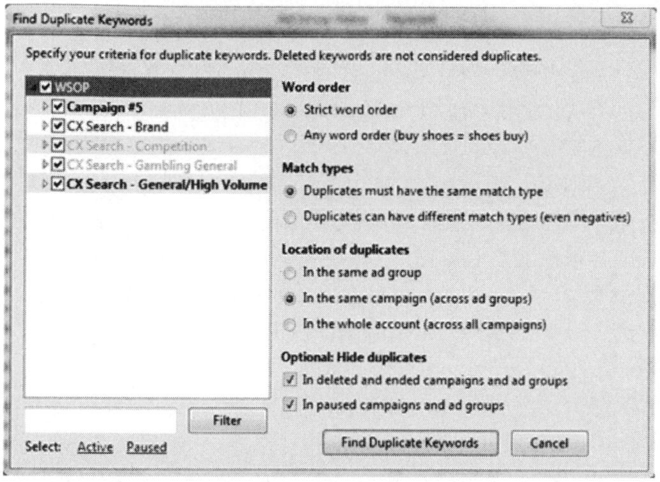

Figure A.35 The Find Duplicate Keywords tool

Keyword Grouper

The Keyword Grouper is a powerful tool that can provide a huge benefit by breaking down your keyword lists into smaller, more tightly themed ad groups. To use this tool, choose Tools from the main menu and click Keyword Grouper.

The only input required from you on the Keyword Grouper, shown in Figure A.36, is to choose a campaign and an ad group. Keyword Grouper then reviews all of the keywords in an ad group and generates a list of common terms that it suggests should be separated into distinct ad groups. When you click Next, you are shown all of the new suggested ad groups and the keywords that will be moved if you agree with the suggestions. When you click Finish, those ad groups are created.

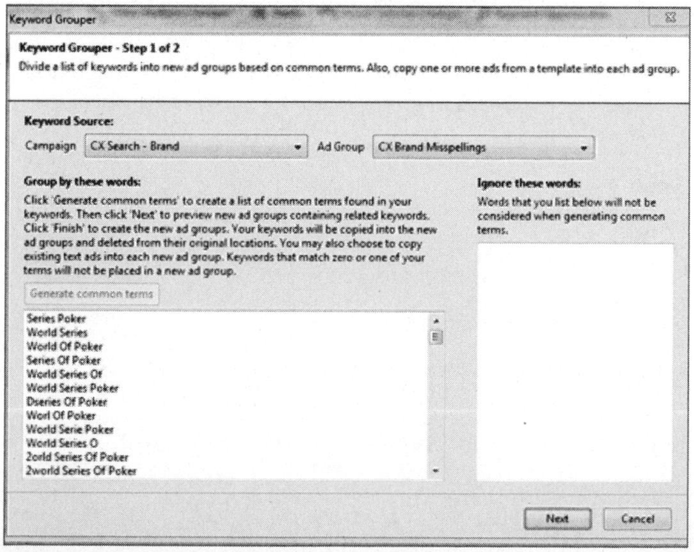

Figure A.36 The Keyword Grouper tool

Keyword Opportunities

The Keyword Opportunities tool is an extension of the online Google Keyword tool and can be found both in the AdWords Editor menu system and inline when managing keywords.

The Keyword Expansion, Keyword Multiplier, and Search-Based Keywords tabs of this tool enable you to generate lists of new keywords and then immediately add them to existing campaigns and ad groups. As you research new keywords, a drop-down menu of your campaigns and ad groups can be found on the right-hand side of the tool, as shown in Figure A.37.

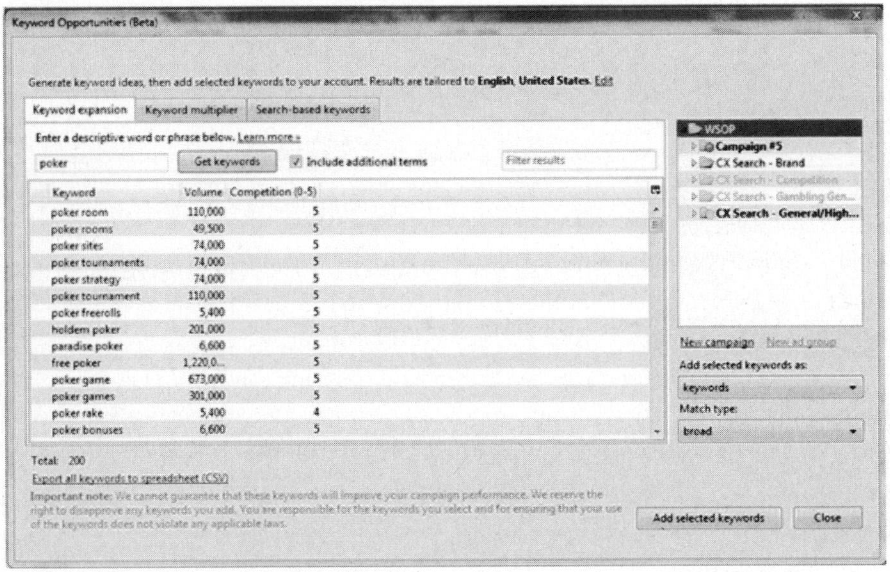

Figure A.37 The Keyword Opportunities tool

Appendix B:
Facebook PPC

By now, you've certainly heard of the Internet phenomenon called Facebook, the world's leading social networking site. Facebook PPC advertising enables advertisers to reach a huge number of people—an estimated 400 million worldwide. And you're in luck, because Facebook PPC advertising has so much in common with search engine content network advertising, which you learned to master in Chapter 7, "Month 4—Advertise on the Google Content Network." This appendix provides an overview of the techniques and skills you need to turn Facebook into a source of profitable conversions. Facebook PPC advertising operates under a similar bid model as the search engines. Advertisers specify the maximum cost per click (CPC) that they are willing to pay, and ads are displayed more or less frequently based on the maximum CPC bids entered by competing advertisers. Like Google, Facebook also offers a CPM bidding and pricing model, but we suggest that you stick to CPC bidding.

Facebook ads appear on pages throughout the site, adjacent to page content. But there's a crucial difference between the content networks and Facebook: In a content network, ads are placed in relation to advertiser input regarding the nature of website pages on which they want ads to appear, whereas on Facebook, they are placed in relation to the types of *people* that the advertiser wants to reach. Each Facebook visitor sees ads that are relevant to *that visitor*—in other words, each visitor sees a different version of each page, with the collection of ads customized for that person.

It's this hyper-targeting capability, along with Facebook's status as a relatively new advertising medium that still has a relatively low level of competition (and average CPCs), that makes Facebook PPC advertising so attractive.

Getting Started

Starting your first Facebook ad campaign is simple and straightforward. The steps are unusual compared to those required to get started with search engine PPC advertising, so we'll walk through each one with ample illustration.

First, go to www.facebook.com/advertising. If you already have a Facebook account for your personal profile, don't log into it. We suggest that you keep your advertising and personal accounts separate by creating an account that is different from your Facebook profile.

Next, click the Create an Ad button. You'll see a screen like the one shown in Figure B.1, enabling you to create your first ad.

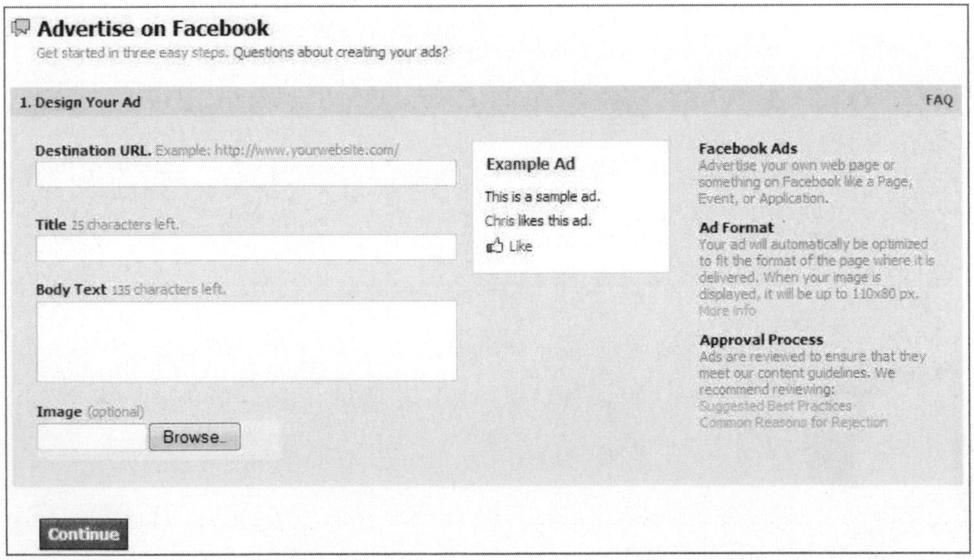

Figure B.1 The Facebook ad design screen

This ad template should look familiar to PPC advertisers. Facebook enables you to enter a destination URL for the ad, a title of 25 characters, and body text that can be 110 characters long. Including an image is optional, but we *strongly* advise you to do so. Remember what we said in Chapter 4, "Month 1—Research Keywords and Establish Campaign Structure": A display ad needs to work hard to attract attention to itself and away from the rest of the page content—and an image can do that much more efficiently than mere text.

Your ad will appear in various sizes, depending on the format of the page where the ad is displayed. Don't worry—Facebook will optimize the size and appearance of the ad to fit the page.

For the purposes of the discussion in this appendix, we'll focus on one ad type: the one that appears on any kind of Facebook page (except the home page). Although you can create ads that advertise a particular Facebook page, event, or application, we'll leave it to you to explore those options.

You'll find that the Facebook rules for ad text are more stringent than the rules for search engines. For example, letters in a sentence must be capitalized in a standard way—no initial caps like those we've shown you in Google ads. The Facebook Help pages are clear regarding the restrictions—read them carefully.

After you've entered ad text and uploaded the ad image, your screen will look like Figure B.2. Click the Continue button to proceed.

Figure B.2 A completed Facebook ad

Targeting Facebook Ads

On the next screen (shown in Figure B.3), you'll see the most important strength of Facebook advertising: the ability to tightly define the Facebook users to whom your ad should be displayed.

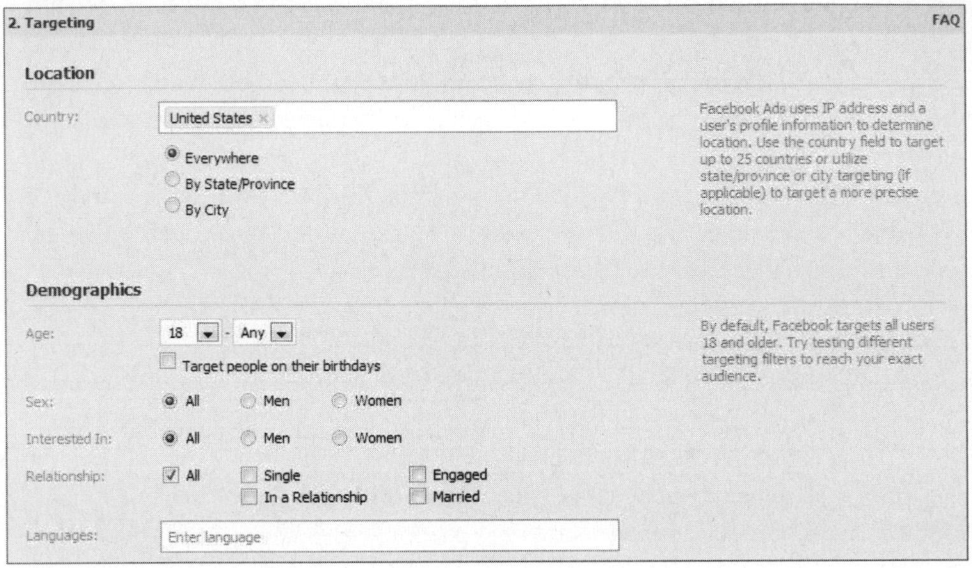

Figure B.3 The first targeting screen

First you can define the location. Here's where you'll encounter for the first time the Facebook text entry field that also functions as a pop-down menu. You can specify which country or countries you'd like to target. If you select just one country, you will get a second targeting option that lets you narrow your target audience to states and/or provinces, or to the city level. To narrow your selection, simply click the By State/Province radio button or the By City radio button and then type the first few letters of the state or city you'd like to target. A list of state or city names that start with the first letter you type will drop down, and that list will change as you type each subsequent letter, as you can see in Figure B.4.

As you type or select a new entity (for example, a particular city), the number of people shown in the Estimated Reach box will change, as shown in Figure B.5. Keep an eye on this as you add more targeting specifications.

Next, you have the option to specify demographic characteristics of your target audience, as shown in Figure B.6. You can choose specific age segments, their gender, whether they're interested in men or women, what kind of relationship they're in, and what languages they speak. You can even display ads to a target audience consisting only of people celebrating birthdays the day of the ad display! This kind of targeting is available because people have specified these attributes on their Facebook profile pages.

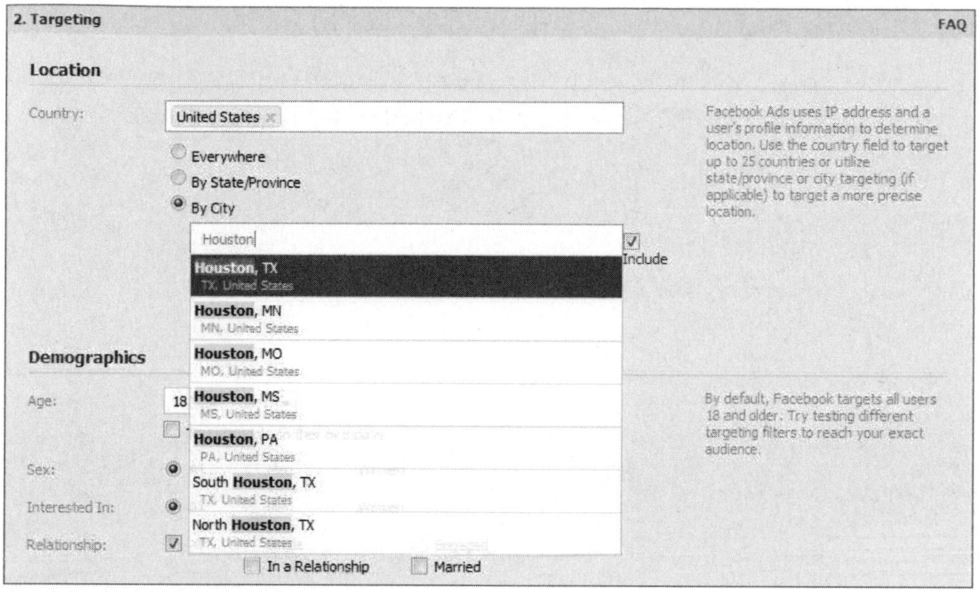

Figure B.4 The City drop-down menu

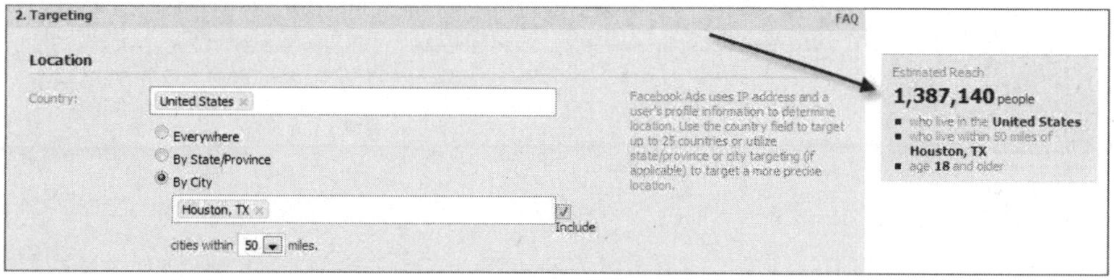

Figure B.5 The Estimated Reach box

Figure B.6 The Demographics section

After you click the Continue button, you'll see a new section with a powerful function: the Likes & Interests section, shown in Figure B.7 (which also shows the Education & Work section that we'll describe later). Here you can zero in to target *exclusively* people with very particular interests, hobbies, and proclivities.

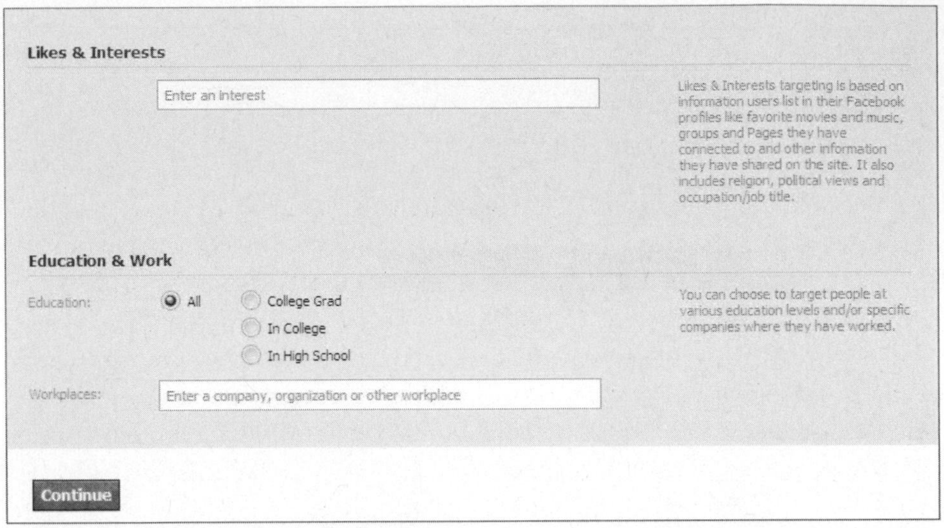

Figure B.7 The Likes & Interests and Education & Work sections

Although there is no published list of all the likes and interests that are available for targeting, it's certain that the number runs into the tens of thousands. So you'll need to use your imagination and all of the customer research you've done to decide which interests to target. The persona definition exercise you conducted in Chapter 4 will be really helpful here!

In Figure B.8, you can see the results of typing the acronym *ppc* into the Likes & Interests field. The list that drops down constitutes the interest groups that Facebook can target.

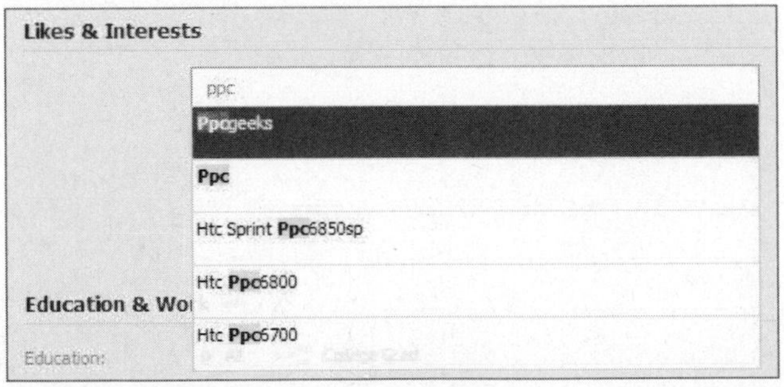

Figure B.8 Typing *ppc* into the Likes & Interests field

Assuming we're targeting people interested in PPC advertising, there are at least three groups that probably don't match, because they seem to be composed of people interested in a particular phone model. A Facebook search on the word **ppcgeeks** reveals that it might pertain to a fan page related to the aforementioned phone, or to a profile page that relates to PPC advertising. As you can see in Figure B.9, we decided to take our chances and include it regardless of that ambiguity.

Figure B.9 List of PPC-related likes and interests

It's important to note that listing several likes and interests does not narrow the target audience to people whose interests encompass *all* of the ones included. In other words, Facebook treats the likes and interests as being separated by a logical OR. So in Figure B.9, we're telling Facebook, "Show my ad to people interested in ppc OR ppc-geeks OR Google AdWords." Note also that the other attributes we've chosen (gender, age, location, and so on) are cumulative—in other words, Facebook treats them as separated by a logical AND. It's possible that Facebook will someday allow advertisers the option of combining all likes and interests with a logical AND, but for now, the hyper-targeting capabilities are sufficient and powerful.

After setting up the Likes & Interests field for your first campaign, you can specify the Education & Work attributes of the target audience (shown at the bottom of Figure B.7). You can choose only college graduates, or people who are attending high school or college. Then you can choose to include people from specific companies or organizations. The associated field works the same as previous ones: Start typing to see a list of companies and organizations that can be targeted.

The next account creation step is to set campaign budgets and bid prices, which you can see in Figure B.10. Here you choose the billing currency, name your first campaign, and set the daily budget—which, similarly to the search engines, lets you specify the maximum amount that you're willing to pay per day.

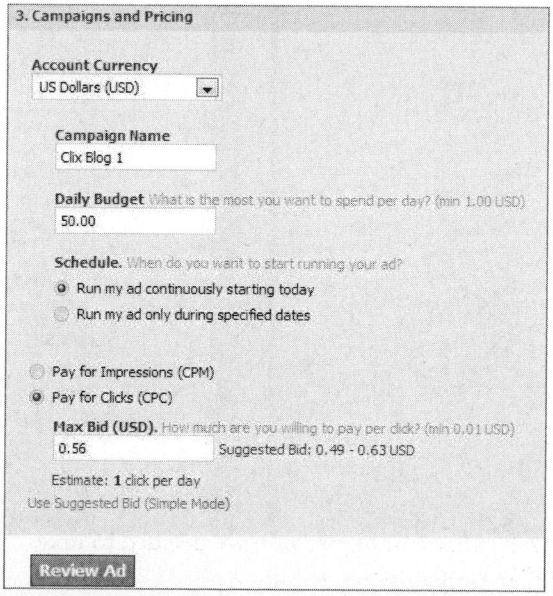

Figure B.10 The Campaigns and Pricing screen

You can also choose to start the campaign immediately, or run the campaign only during a time interval you specify. Next, choose the bidding option (typically CPC) and specify the bid price. Facebook helpfully suggests a maximum bid, which tends to be in the middle of the suggested bid spread that it also displays.

Inexplicably, clicking the Review Ad button takes you to a screen where you can't review the ad (yet); instead, you're asked to specify whether you have a Facebook account. As mentioned, it's a good idea to create a new account that you'll use only for advertising purposes. To do this, click the I Do Not Have a Facebook Account button; enter an e-mail address, a password, and your birth date; and type the Security Check words in the text box (see Figure B.11). Then click the Sign Up Now! button.

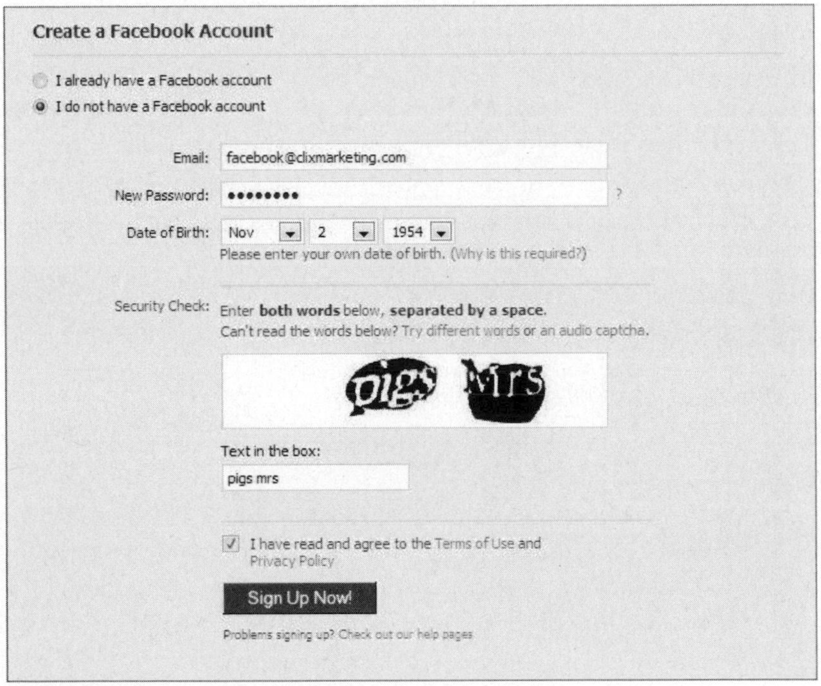

Figure B.11 Creating a new Facebook account for advertising

You'll then be able to review the ad you created, and enter credit card information, as you can see in Figure B.12. Click the Place Order button, and you'll be finished with setup!

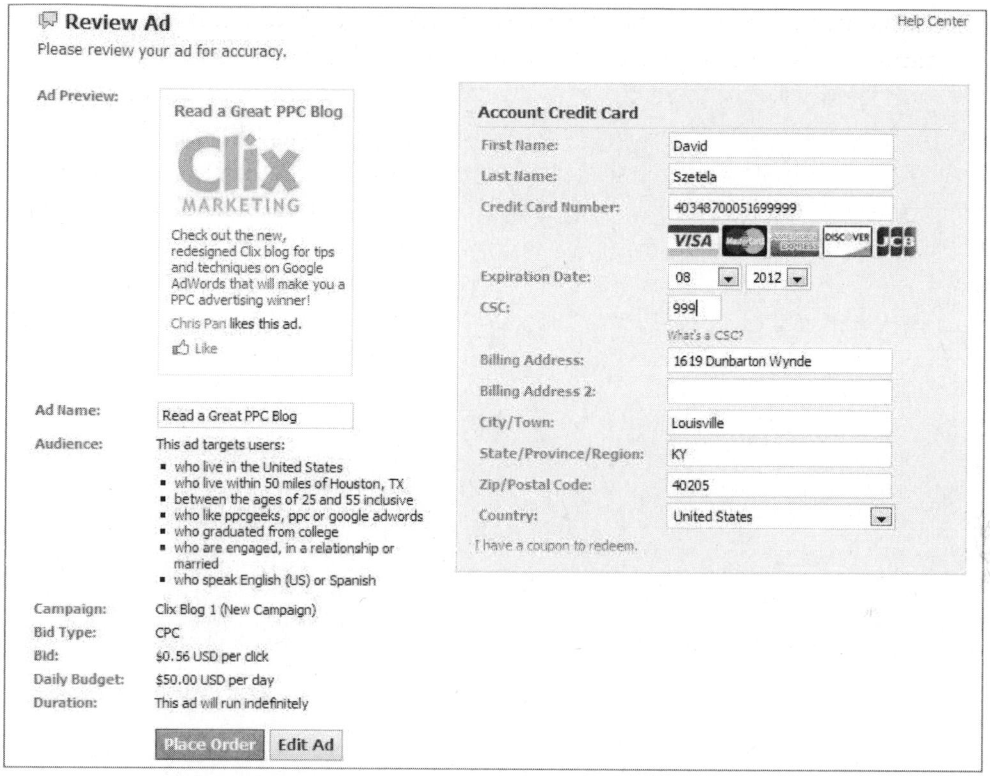

Figure B.12 Final account setup screen

Managing and Reporting

The next screen is the one you'll see whenever you subsequently log in to your account. As shown in Figure B.13, the page is arranged in a browser-like structure, with functions on the left side and the action area occupying the majority of the screen.

You'll refer to this screen often—it's equivalent to the screen you see when you click the Campaigns tab in the Google AdWords web interface. It shows performance data for all campaigns within the account for the time period you specify: the number of impressions and clicks; the average click-through rate (CTR), CPC, and cost per thousand-impressions (CPM); and the total amount spent.

One of the first things you should do is set up conversion tracking by clicking the Tracking link in the upper-left navigation bar. Implementing Facebook conversion tracking will seem simple and familiar if you've set up conversion tracking for AdWords or another PPC platform. Just select a conversion type (Lead, Purchase/Sale, and so on), as shown in Figure B.14. Facebook will then provide a segment of JavaScript code, as shown in Figure B.15, which you should copy and paste on the conversion completion page.

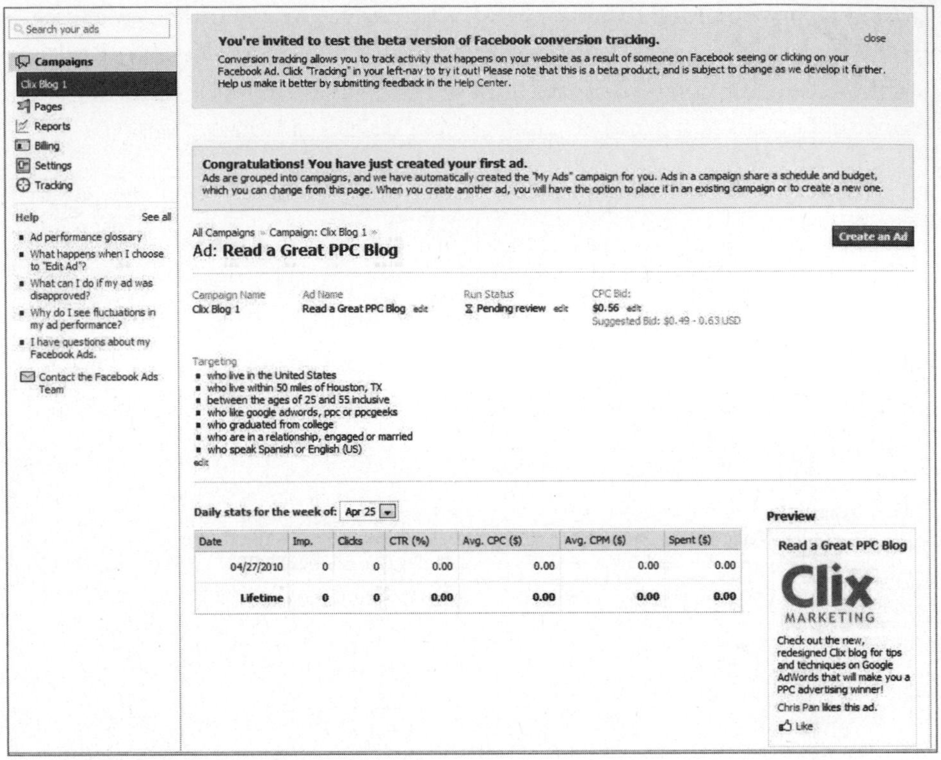

You're invited to test the beta version of Facebook conversion tracking. close

Conversion tracking allows you to track activity that happens on your website as a result of someone on Facebook seeing or clicking on your Facebook Ad. Click "Tracking" in your left-nav to try it out! Please note that this is a beta product, and is subject to change as we develop it further. Help us make it better by submitting feedback in the Help Center.

Congratulations! You have just created your first ad.
Ads are grouped into campaigns, and we have automatically created the "My Ads" campaign for you. Ads in a campaign share a schedule and budget, which you can change from this page. When you create another ad, you will have the option to place it in an existing campaign or to create a new one.

Search your ads

Campaigns
Clix Blog 1
Pages
Reports
Billing
Settings
Tracking

Help   See all

- Ad performance glossary
- What happens when I choose to 'Edit Ad'?
- What can I do if my ad was disapproved?
- Why do I see fluctuations in my ad performance?
- I have questions about my Facebook Ads.

Contact the Facebook Ads Team

All Campaigns » Campaign: Clix Blog 1 »
Ad: Read a Great PPC Blog   Create an Ad

Campaign Name	Ad Name	Run Status	CPC Bid:
Clix Blog 1	Read a Great PPC Blog edit	⏳ Pending review edit	$0.56 edit

Suggested Bid: $0.49 - 0.63 USD

Targeting
- who live in the United States
- who live within 50 miles of Houston, TX
- between the ages of 25 and 55 inclusive
- who like google adwords, ppc or ppcgeeks
- who graduated from college
- who are in a relationship, engaged or married
- who speak Spanish or English (US)
edit

Daily stats for the week of: Apr 25 ▾

Date	Imp.	Clicks	CTR (%)	Avg. CPC ($)	Avg. CPM ($)	Spent ($)
04/27/2010	0	0	0.00	0.00	0.00	0.00
Lifetime	**0**	**0**	**0.00**	**0.00**	**0.00**	**0.00**

Preview

Read a Great PPC Blog

Clix
MARKETING

Check out the new, redesigned Clix blog for tips and techniques on Google AdWords that will make you a PPC advertising winner!

Chris Pan likes this ad.
👍 Like

Figure B.13 Main account management screen

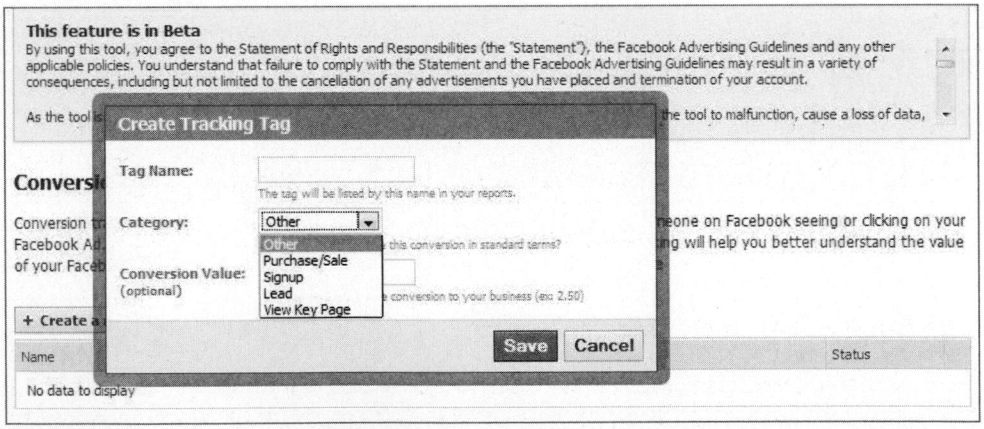

This feature is in Beta
By using this tool, you agree to the Statement of Rights and Responsibilities (the "Statement"), the Facebook Advertising Guidelines and any other applicable policies. You understand that failure to comply with the Statement and the Facebook Advertising Guidelines may result in a variety of consequences, including but not limited to the cancellation of any advertisements you have placed and termination of your account.

As the tool is   the tool to malfunction, cause a loss of data,

Conversi

Conversion tr   eone on Facebook seeing or clicking on your
Facebook Ad   ng will help you better understand the value
of your Faceb

Create Tracking Tag

Tag Name: [   ]
The tag will be listed by this name in your reports.

Category: [Other   ▾]
                Other
                Purchase/Sale   this conversion in standard terms?
                Signup
Conversion Value: Lead
(optional)   View Key Page   e conversion to your business (ex. 2.50)

Save   Cancel

+ Create a

Name				Status
No data to display				

Figure B.14 Choosing the type of conversion event to be tracked

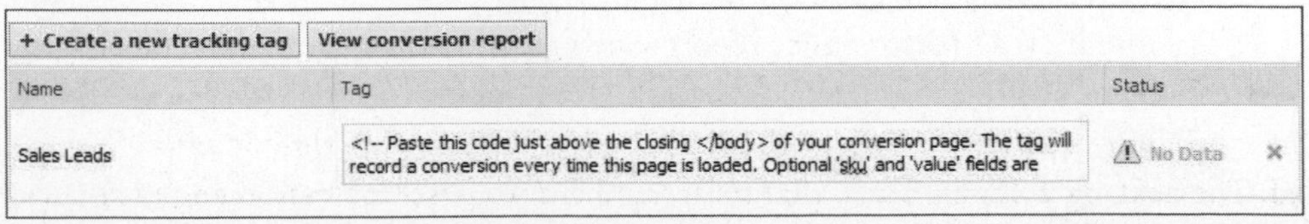

+ Create a new tracking tag   View conversion report

Name	Tag	Status
Sales Leads	<!-- Paste this code just above the closing </body> of your conversion page. The tag will record a conversion every time this page is loaded. Optional 'sku' and 'value' fields are	⚠ No Data ✕

Figure B.15 Facebook displays JavaScript code for the conversion completion page.

After you've completed the conversion tracking code generation step, you'll see the screen shown in Figure B.16. The newly created ad will remain in Pending Review status until the ad is approved—a process that can take up to 24 hours. You'll also see performance data that will start to accumulate after the new ad begins running.

Figure B.16 Ads remain in Pending Review status until approved by Facebook.

Using Facebook Ad Performance Reports

While the web interface displays valuable performance data such as CTR and average CPC, Facebook lets you create detailed reports for any time interval. We won't describe all possible reports in this appendix; instead, we'll explain the metrics you'll see in a few of the reports that you'll run most frequently.

The first is an ad performance report showing conversion data—like the one you see in Figure B.17. This report contains seven columns of conversion-related data. The first column shows the total number of conversions for the time interval specified. The next six columns break that total number into post-impression and post-click conversions.

Data for this report is not available after 04/25/2010.							

View Advertising Report   Permalink   Export Report (.csv)   Generate Another Report

Report Type: Conversions by Conversion Time   Summarize By: Account   Time Summary: Daily   Date Range: 04/01/2010 - 04/27/2010

Date	Tag Name	Conversions	Post-Imp (0 to 24 hours)	Post-Imp (1 to 7 days)	Post-Imp (8 to 28 days)	Post-Click (0 to 24 hours)	Post-Click (1 to 7 days)	Post-Click (8 to 28 days)
04/01/2010	Contact Form Submission	403	96	10	29	265	1	2
04/02/2010	Contact Form Submission	745	187	7	9	539	2	1
04/03/2010	Contact Form Submission	464	85	15	2	350	11	1
04/04/2010	Contact Form Submission	242	34	4	1	187	16	0
04/05/2010	Contact Form Submission	5	0	0	0	5	0	0
04/06/2010	Contact Form							

Figure B.17 Conversion report showing post-impression and post-click conversions

Post-impression conversions are ones that result from people seeing the ad but not necessarily clicking on it. This is similar to Google's tally of view-through conversions, and lets the advertiser see how effective ads have been at influencing conversions even if the site visitor doesn't click on the ad the first time they see it.

Post-click conversions are equivalent to the ones Google calls one-per-click conversions. These are conversions that have happened after the site visitor has viewed *and* clicked on an ad.

In both cases, Facebook helpfully breaks down the number of post-impression and post-click conversions that happen within the first day of viewing or clicking the ad—and within the first week and the first four weeks. This helps you see that frequently people see an ad or click on an ad and then come back later to take the conversion action. This is information that's crucial in order for you to calculate the true return on investment (ROI) of your Facebook advertising expense.

The report shown in Figure B.18 is likely to be unfamiliar to you. It's the Responder Profiles report, which shows data regarding some of the likes and interests of people who have clicked on your ad. This is a gold mine of information that you can use to even more finely hyper-target your Facebook ad campaigns—and even your content network advertising on Google and elsewhere.

For example, let's say that the ad campaign is intended to draw visitors to a site that sells gourmet popcorn. Armed with the data shown in Figure B.18, the advertiser could create a separate ad campaign that targets viewers of the TV series *NCIS*, which is the favorite show of many of the people who clicked on ads within the initial campaign.

Campaign Name	Interest	# Clickers (Interests)	Rank by Estimated CTR (Interests)	Book	# Clickers (Books)	Rank by Estimated CTR (Books)	Movie	# Clickers (Movies)	Rank by Estimated CTR (Movies)	Music	# Clickers (Music)	Rank by Estimated CTR (Music)	TV Show	# Clickers (TV Shows)	Rank by Estimated CTR (TV Shows)
Clix Ads															
	travel	165	1	bible	469	1	titanic	123	1	country music	182	1	closer	140	1
	scrapbooking	119	2	twilight series	94	2	green mile	104	2	classic rock	260	2	big bang theory	154	2
	family	212	3	stephen king	72	3	gone with wind	275	3	gospel	279	3	amazing race	130	3
	shopping	143	4	nora roberts	71	4	fried green tomatoes	90	4	country	880	4	private practice	161	4
	movies	214	5	harry potter	67	5	wizard oz	126	5	contemporary christian	79	5	medium	173	5
	art	105	6	shack	63	6	twilight	88	6	pop	157	6	ncis	662	6
	gardening	300	7	dean koontz	60	7	color purple	100	7	christian	137	7	csi	568	7
	music	344	8	mysteries	67	8	steel magnolias	113	8	hip hop	72	8	hgtv	176	8
	dancing	90	9	gone with wind	55	9	star wars	76	9	jazz	349	9	csi miami	234	9
	camping	140	10	holy bible	55	10	forrest gump	74	10	blues	165	10	ghost whisperer	187	10

Figure B.18 Responder Profiles report showing Likes & Interest data regarding people who have clicked on an ad

The ad in the *NCIS* campaign could feature the headline *Solved: The Best NCIS Snack*. It could feature an image of one of the most recognizable stars of the show (for extra points, the advertiser could find a photo of the star eating popcorn!), and include in the ad's body copy, *NCIS commercial time is the best time for Acme Gourmet Popcorn. See all the yummy flavors!*

This kind of hyper-targeting can be even more powerful when paired with landing pages that echo the messages and promises of the ads. We'll explain this by referring to a fictitious campaign that is intended to attract players in England to an online casino site. Figure B.19 shows an example of hyper-targeting by geographic location *and* interest. In this case, we're targeting roulette players who live in the charming seaside town of Swanage.

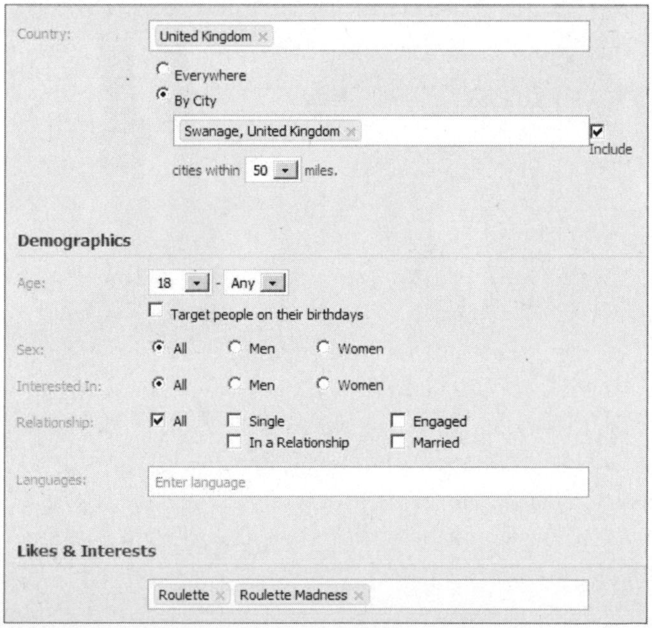

Figure B.19 Hyper-targeting by geographic location and interest

Figure B.20 shows the ad associated with this hyper-targeting—intended to attract the attention of roulette players in Swanage by featuring the town name in the headline and an image of a roulette wheel.

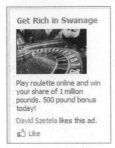

Figure B.20 Ad targeting roulette players in Swanage

It's likely the ad will enjoy a high conversion rate relative to a less-targeted ad that simply offered a variety of casino games to a geographically dispersed audience. But there's icing on the cake: When the ad is paired with a similarly targeted landing page, conversion rates can be at their highest possible.

Figure B.21 shows the landing page paired with the Swanage roulette ad. The headline and subheadline are designed to grab the visitor's attention by reflecting their interests and location, matching those in the ad on which they've just clicked.

Figure B.21 Landing page for Swanage roulette players

The headline and subheadline deliver the following messages:

1. We know you just came from Facebook.
2. We know you like roulette.
3. We encourage you to try to become the biggest winner in your town.

It's likely this page will result in a higher conversion rate than a page that tries to appeal to a broad audience with a generic message such as *Play lots of different games in our casino.*

Figure B.22 shows the landing page that would be associated with an ad campaign targeted to blackjack players in Bournemouth.

Figure B.22 Landing page for Bournemouth blackjack players

Hopefully, this appendix has convinced you that the combined power of Facebook's hyper-targeting capabilities and its massive audience can help you create very successful ad campaigns. And thinking in terms of tailoring ads and landing pages to appeal to small, targeted groups will help improve your success with display ad campaigns on the Google Content Network and elsewhere.

Index

Improve your online marketing with AN HOUR A DAY!

Written by industry-leading professionals, these books break down online marketing topics into bite-sized pieces that can be easily digested over your lunch hour. Just pick a topic and get started today.

For more information visit www.sybex.com/go/houraday

Wiley, the Wiley logo, and Sybex are registered trademarks of John Wiley & Sons, Inc.

SYBEX
An Imprint of WILEY
Now you know.